How To Do Things with Dance

How To Do Things with Dance

Performing Change in Postwar America

Rebekah J. Kowal

Wesleyan University Press

MIDDLETOWN, CONNECTICUT

Wesleyan University Press
Middletown CT 06459
www.wesleyan.edu/wespress
© 2010 by Rebekah J. Kowal
All rights reserved
First paperback edition 2012
Manufactured in the United States of America
ISBN for the paperback edition: 978-0-8195-6898-4

Wesleyan University Press is a member of the Green Press Initiative.
The paper used in this book meets their minimum
requirement for recycled paper.

Library of Congress Cataloging-in-Publication Data
Kowal, Rebekah J.
How to do things with dance : performing change in postwar
America / Rebekah J. Kowal.
p.   cm.
Includes bibliographical references and index.
ISBN 978-0-8195-6897-7 (cloth : alk. paper)
1. Modern dance—Social aspects.   2. Postmodernism.
[1. United States—History—1945–]   I. Title.
GV1783.K68 2010
792.8—dc22
2009049292

5 4 3 2 1

In memory of Cynthia Jean Cohen Bull, my professor at
Barnard College, who first showed me how dance could do things and
who gave me the gift of her final musings months before she died.
May this book continue her scholarly legacy.

In tribute to the historians in my family, my parents, Sheila and Ira
Kowal, and my grandparents, Jennie and Leon Kowal and
Ethel and Archie Slawsby, all of whom ignited and fanned my
fascination with the past.

For David, Noah and Isaac Bullwinkle.

CONTENTS

ACKNOWLEDGMENTS

This book would not exist without the help of numerous people. This project would never have begun if it had not been for my undergraduate work in Dance at Barnard College. Special acknowledgment goes to Cynthia Jean Cohen Bull, who embodied in her example how a dancer could wear many hats and who first taught me how to think about dance in political terms.

Although I did not expect to study dance in graduate school, what began as a Master's thesis thankfully led to a dissertation. For this I have many at New York University to thank. I am grateful for the wisdom of Jean-Christophe Agnew, who taught my first year graduate seminar on American postwar culture, for urging me to write about something I felt passionately about: dance. I am also deeply grateful to George Yúdice for believing in me and in this project and for his wonder as it unfolded; Randy Martin, whose counsel and guidance have served me in innumerable and profound ways; and Andrew Ross, Toby Miller, and Daniel Walkowitz, who nudged me to situate this study in a broad historical and political context. Conversations and courses with other scholars including Lizbeth Cohen, Lisa Duggan, Pat Hoy III, Carol Krinsky, Fred Moten, José Muñoz, Tricia Rose, Richard Sennett, Marcia Siegel, Kenneth Silver, and Richard Turner proved instrumental to my early thought process. This project also benefited greatly from the knowledge and impetus of friends and colleagues in graduate school. Among these, David Serlin stands out for his help in my hatching plans to tackle this subject and for his generous and sustained investment in my work. I am also indebted to my dissertation group writing partners, Sheila Boland and Julia Ritter, and Bridget Brown, Sandie Friedman, and Leslie Paris, for their insight, criticism, and companionship along the way. I also want to thank my good friends Andrea Brunholzl and Joan Punyet Miró for their encouragement.

The process of transforming my dissertation into this book has been long, and I have many to thank for its becoming. First among these would be Susan Foster and Randy Martin. From the beginning Susan challenged me to take on the racial dimensions of this subject matter, asked me fundamental questions, and graciously gave of her time. Randy provided a sense of the bigger picture of my arguments with his trenchant syntheses of the issues at stake. Others include Mark Franko, for his rigorous attention to detail and helping me formulate my methodology; Linda Kerber, for her provocative comments on early iterations of this project; and Rachel Fensham and Kimerer LaMothe, for their sage wisdom, example of scholarly rigor, and comments on my introduction. I am also grateful to Anthea Kraut, Jacqueline Shea Murphy, Harilaos Stecopoulos, and Priya Srinivasan for their comments on drafts and their sustained engagement with my work. Special thanks go to Anthea for her collegiality and friendship. This book would not be what it is without the involvement of the three readers commissioned by Wesleyan University Press, all of whose insights pushed me into new interpretive territory and helped me summon the courage I needed to hone my main idea. I also want to acknowledge the contribution of other scholars whose ideas I have factored in along the way. Thanks especially to Ananya Chatterjea, Tommy DeFrantz, Jane Desmond, Ann Dils, Nadine George-Graves, Maris Gillette, Claudia Gitelman, Brenda Dixon Gottschild, Ellen Graff, Kathy Lavezzo, Julie Malnig, David Roman, Richard Schechner, Theresa Tensuan, and Linda Tomko.

My scholarly work has been sustained by the financial support and efforts of colleagues at many institutions. The New York University Graduate School of Arts and Sciences helped fund the research and writing of my dissertation through a Dean's Dissertation Fellowship. Thanks go to Nikhil Singh for helping me secure this award. The Andrew W. Mellon Foundation and Haverford College, through a postdoctoral fellowship in Performance Studies, provided the means by and environment in which I made the crucial transition from graduate school to a lively scholarly community. I am especially indebted to Kimberly Benston for his investment in me and my work and his kindness, continued mentoring, and commitment to imbricating the performing arts and humanities. Thanks also to Elaine Hansen, J. David Dawson, and Carol Henry for their nurturance, as well as to the members of the Haverford Humanities Center seminar on performance, especially Aryeh Kosman and Deborah Roberts. At the same time, an appointment as a regional scholar at the University of Pennsylvania's Humanities Forum gave me access to another interdisciplinary scholarly community through participation in a seminar on "style." Engagement with diverse groups of scholars and audience members has heightened my sense of the cultural, historical, and political stakes of this book. I am grateful to Jonathan Katz at Yale University for inviting me to present my work at the conference Queerness in the Americas, 1946–1956, and to Ananya Chatterjea at the University of Minnesota for including me in events surrounding the restaging of Anna Sokolow's *Rooms* in 2006, funded by the Sage Cowles Land Grant Chair.

Financial support from the University of Iowa has been substantial: from the College of Liberal Arts and Sciences, two Old Gold summer research awards and supplemental research and travel grants; from International Programs, several travel grants; from the Office of the Vice President for Research, an Arts and Humanities Initiative grant and book subvention award; from the Graduate College, several Research Assistants; from the Iowa Center for Research by Undergraduates, two scholar assistant awards.

In this breath, I would like to thank from the bottom of my heart my dedicated, diligent, and brilliant research assistants, Gretchen Alterowitz, Amanda Hamp, Amy Jacobus, and Eliana Trenam. In various ways your work has contributed to the breadth and depth of this book, and to the discussions in it. Amy deserves a special mention for seeing me through the final drafting, proofreading, and indexing processes and for her editorial acuity. Conversations with present and former colleagues in the University of Iowa Department of Dance have fortified me along the way. Special thanks go to Alan Sener, for his interest in my research and efforts to secure its viability; Jeffery Bullock and Jennifer Kayle, for their ideas and choreographic insights into this project; Eloy Barragan, for introducing me to Donald McKayle; and Charlotte Adams, Deanna Carter, Armando Duarte, and George de la Pena for their commitment to my work. I am also grateful to Kathleen Forbes for her friendship and willingness to give of herself to get this job done.

Many people have helped me to find and access primary materials including photographs and to secure copyright permissions. My gratitude extends to Tom Lisanti, Charles Perrier, Peter Riesett, and Alice Standin at the New York Public Library for the Performing Arts; Cory Greenberg at the Alvin Ailey Dance Foundation (whose images are included in the Alvin Ailey Dance Foundation Collection at the Library of Congress); Elizabeth Aldrich at the Library of Congress; Sue Goldman for the Estate of Arnold Eagle; Betsy Miller and Ann Vachon at the José Limón Dance

Foundation; Stephanie Earle and Anna Halprin at the Halprin Dance Foundation; Steven Macleod at the University of California, Irvine Special Collections and Archives; Dean Jeffery at the American Dance Festival Archives; Lorry May at the Sokolow Dance Foundation; Steve Bello at the Philippe Halsman Studio; Bruce Kellner for the Carl Van Vechten Estate; David Vaughan at the Cunningham Dance Foundation; Sylvia Kollar and John Tomlinson at the Paul Taylor Dance Foundation Archives; Mike Letourneau at Associated Press Images and Kimberley Tishler at the Visual Artists and Galleries Association; photographers Warner Jepson, Jack Mitchell, and Jack and Linda Vartoogian; and choreographer Donald McKayle. I am also most grateful to Victoria Phillips Geduld for sharing Pearl Primus' FBI file with me. Thanks to her patient and prescient efforts, new information can now come to light regarding Primus' artistic and political activities and investigation and penalization by the U.S. government. Deep appreciation goes to Donald McKayle, Paul Taylor, and David Vaughan for allowing me to interview them and whose words and histories I have sought to bring to life in these pages.

These acknowledgments would not be complete without recognizing the contributions of two editors: Ken Wissoker of Duke University Press, who commissioned readers of an early manuscript and expressed confidence that this project would be worthy of publication, and Suzanna Tamminen, who has nurtured its incarnation every step of the way and whose poetry has helped to shape this final form.

Profound thanks go to the members of my extended family, which includes my parents, Ira Kowal and Joellyn Duesberry and Sheila Kowal and Blake Chambliss, who have given me the gift of believing in what I am doing. Special recognition belongs to my mother, Sheila, who accompanied me on a research trip to Greensboro, North Carolina, and to her and my stepmother, Joly, for reading and commenting on final drafts of my manuscript. My thanks extend to my sister Jessica Kowal and my brother-in-law Blaine Harden, whose knowledge of the writing process and research acumen have been invaluable at various stages of this process and whose kindness I have greatly appreciated. I also want to thank Ashley Fuller for giving me peace of mind at home as I became engrossed in this journey.

Working on this book would not have been as compelling or fulfilling if it had not competed heartily for my time. For this I dedicate this book to my immediate family, David Bullwinkle, my partner, and my two sons, Noah and Isaac Bullwinkle. To Dave, may this project mark a chapter in our ongoing conversations about the overlap between epistemology and phenomenology. To Noah and Isaac, may this book illuminate how movement can change the world. To all of you, thanks for bringing me back to earth.

How To Do Things with Dance

INTRODUCTION

Modern Dance and the Cultural Turn to Action

T HIS is a book about the history of dance modernism in the United States after World War II. It is also a cultural history of the postwar period seen through the lens of modern dance. "Doing something" is at the heart of this relation. In the pages that follow, I hope to illuminate correlations between the gradual redefinition among choreographers of dance as a form of ordinary movement, and the growing sense among members of the general public (including dancers) of the power of movement to conduct progressive social change. Consider the following comparison in this context:

On Sunday, January 31, 1960, in New York City, choreographer Alvin Ailey premiered what would become his signature masterpiece, *Revelations*, at the 92nd Street YM-YWHA before a capacity audience. An aesthetic hybrid, the piece synthesized the movement languages of modern dance, ballet, jazz, and the African-American vernacular in compelling scenes staged to gospel music sung live.[1] For Ailey personally—the child of a single mother who moved constantly in search of work—the piece captured the emotional dependability of Sunday services. "As early as I can remember," he recalled, "I was enthralled by the music played and sung in the small black churches in every small Texas town my mother and I lived in. No matter where we were during those nomadic years, Sunday was always a churchgoing day. There we would absorb some of the most glorious singing to be heard anywhere in the world" (Ailey 1995, 97).

The first section, called "Pilgrim of Sorrow," "was about trying to get up out of the ground"—in the figures of abstract modern dance, it captured expressions of heartache and reverence to convey the historic oppression and resilience of African Americans; the second, "Wade in the Water," performed a baptismal or purification rite set on a river's edge; and the third, "Move, Members, Move," brought the gospel church to life, including "the holy rollers, and all that . . . church happiness" (Ailey 1995, 98–

FIG. 1.1 Alvin Ailey, Lucinda Ransom, and Loretta Abbott circa 1960 in "Wade in the Water" from *Revelations*. Photo is part of the "Alvin Ailey Dance Foundation Collection," which is housed at the Library of Congress. Used by permission of Alvin Ailey Dance Foundation.

99). In all, the work enacted the "fervor" that Ailey and other congregants felt in church on Sunday (97), transporting both dancers and audience members into a space, and state, of revelation. As Dorene Richardson, an original company member, recalled in the PBS series *Free to Dance*:

> The performance went very well, we thought. And we all seemed to know what we were doing . . . The end of the piece came, and the curtain came down. And we were standing behind the curtain, holding hands, ready to take our bow. And there was dead silence in the audience. They brought the curtain up. And as they brought the curtain up, the audience jumped to their feet. And you just heard this roar, this deafening roar of bravos, and applause and stamping, and banging on the seats. . . . And we just . . . looked around like "What's going on?

FIG. 1.2 Alvin Ailey circa 1960 in "Yellow" from *Revelations*. Photo is part of the "Alvin Ailey Dance Foundation Collection," which is housed at the Library of Congress. Used by permission of Alvin Ailey Dance Foundation.

Well just bow." And we bowed, and we bowed about ten curtain calls. (Vol. II, "Steps of the Gods")

On Monday, February 1, 1960, in Greensboro, North Carolina, less than twenty-four hours after the world premier of Ailey's *Revelations*, sit-ins began in downtown Greensboro. Ezell Blair, David Richmond, Franklin McCain, and Joseph McNeil, freshmen at the all-black North Carolina Agricultural and Technical College (A&T), bought sundries at the downtown F. W. Woolworth's five-and-dime store, then sat at the lunch counter and asked to be served.[2] Denied service by the waitress and then by the store's manager, the students remained at the counter until day's end, refusing to relent. Within a day, the sit-in led to more protests at Woolworth's and at other department stores along Elm Street, Greensboro's main shopping street. On February 2, "twenty-five men and four women students arrived at Woolworth's" (Chafe 1980, 84). Dressed in ROTC uniforms or their Sunday best, the students apparently passed the time at the counter reading schoolbooks and completing missed homework assignments. Throughout the day Wednesday, more students, coming in waves, filled most of the sixty-five lunch-counter seats. From Thursday to Saturday masses of students showed up to demonstrate against the segregated counters at Woolworth's and the nearby S. H. Kress store. On Thursday black and white students from surrounding schools participated, including three white women from Greensboro's Women's College. "By Friday more than 300 students were taking part in the protest." And on Saturday, "hundreds of students, including the A&T football team, descended on the downtown area" (Chafe 1980, 85). Tension mounted as black demonstrators and their white supporters converged upon the city's business district and were met by angry white crowds who called the protesters names, waved Confederate flags, and threatened violence. On Saturday night, both Woolworth's and the Kress store were forced to close due to bomb scares.

After nearly two weeks of protests, city officials agreed to negotiate and the protesters suspended their demonstrations. Tempers flared again in April, when it became apparent to Greensboro's blacks that the department store managers would not budge. Sit-ins began again, this time prompting city officials to arrest forty-five protesters. Incensed by the arrests, the black community organized a boycott of the variety stores. Fi-

FIG. 1.3 The Greensboro Four at the Woolworth's lunch counter, February 1960. Photo by John "Jack" Moebes. Reprinted courtesy of the *Greensboro News and Record*.

nally, facing a more than 30 percent drop in their profits, some of the managers gave in, opening the lunch counters at Woolworth's, S. H. Kress, and Meyer's department stores.

Occurring virtually on the same day, such events as Ailey's premier and the Greensboro sit-ins signify a moment in the historic struggle of African Americans against persistent forms of racism in the United States. At first glance, the juxtaposition of these events might appear to oversimplify their correlation by capitalizing on their synchronicity. Yet, in the terms set forth in this book, such a comparison exemplifies the role that movement—in both dance and social choreographies—played circa 1960 as a catalyst of social and cultural change.

In the performance of *Revelations* the portrayal of the African-American spiritual legacy transfixed dancers and audiences alike, forming a community through a shared experience. At the same time, the performance made good on Ailey's commitment to making the concert dance stage accessible to anyone regardless of race, class, or concert-going experience. As he put it, "I still dream that my folks down on the farm in Texas can come to an Ailey concert and know and appreciate what's happening onstage. That's my perception of what dance should be—a popular form, wrenched from the hands of the elite" (Ailey 1995, 101). In particular, African-American audiences, whose life experiences had largely been misrepresented by establishment modern dance or represented by proxy of white dancers, now found themselves and their stories at the heart of Ailey's prescient aesthetic fusion. In all of these ways, *Revelations* proved efficacious in its ability both to represent and bring about change.

In Greensboro, protesters' actions similarly galvanized community formation and social transformation. As I have argued elsewhere, the sit-ins were highly strategic forms of choreography, events extensively coordinated in advance but carried out as spontaneous (Kowal 2004). The action of sitting had wide-ranging consequences. Symbolizing the problem for blacks in the United States simply and effectively, the action of sitting at a segregated lunch counter sparked a movement by actors and onlookers united in their common drive for black civil rights. It achieved change on the ground, not only by defying the Jim Crow laws that forbade it in the first place but also by realizing the changes the protesters sought— the chance to exercise their prerogative to take a place at white society's table.

Through juxtapositions such as these, this book examines a sea change that occurred during the postwar years in the ways ordinary Americans used their bodies as agents of change. It focuses on the contributions of those in the modern dance community (dancers, dance makers, and viewers) whose work represents a theoretical convergence of viewing the body's movement in terms of action. Yet its vision is broader. For this, my methodology draws on historian Raymond Williams' notion of "structures of feeling." It holds that expressive practices, like dance, are often the first signs of cultural change, comprehensible but sometimes inchoate indications of a surfacing zeitgeist or mentalité. Guided by this principle, the book illuminates nodes of sociocultural "regularities" by juxtaposing artistic practices in modern dance against other cultural formations similarly invested in the politics of embodiment. These include U.S. foreign and domestic policies and administration of communist containment; housing construction and design in postwar New York City; the civil rights movement; and cultural constructions of gender, race, and sexuality mostly from mass media (e.g., books, magazines, television, movies). Reading dance practices in cultural terms, chapters build to reveal an emerging progressive body politic. Its characteristics include an increasing awareness among choreographers both of the efficacy of movement and of the stage as a penetrable space on which socially suspect, sanctioned, or marginalized modes of being and doing could be performed with relative impunity and exerted in the real world.

Support for this interpretation comes from scholarship on efficacy, drawn both from postwar sources, such as comparative linguist and cultural historian Johan Huizinga and ordinary-language philosopher J. L. Austin, and contemporary ones, like performance theorists Richard Schechner and Judith Butler. In *Homo Ludens* (originally published in 1938, translated into English and made available to American readers in 1950), for example, Huizinga underlines the correlation between the performative (exemplified here by play) and the real in their common root: ritual. To his mind, representation, or the doing of something with the intention of standing for something else, also suggested "representation" or the "actual reproduction" of one action by another (1950, 14).[3] Like Huizinga, Austin plumbed the constitutive potential of action in a lecture series entitled "How to Do Things with Words" presented at Harvard University in 1955 (and subsequently published). Outlining Austin's speech-act theory of "performative utterances," these lectures investigated a class of "statements" that did not fit into existing philosophical theories of meaning. "It was far too long the assumption of philosophers that the business of a 'statement' can only be to 'describe' some state of affairs, or to 'state some fact,'" he observed ([1962] 1972, 1).[4] But what about those statements, Austin wondered, that "masqueraded" as descriptions or declarations of fact but served other nonpropositional purposes (2)? What was their function in language, and for their users? Terming such statements "performative utterances," Austin gave several everyday examples, including the statement of "I do" in the context of a marriage ceremony.[5] Then he explained: "In these examples it seems clear that to utter the sentence (in, of course, the appropriate circumstances) is not to describe my doing of what I should be said in so uttering to be doing or to state that I am doing it: *it is to do it*" (6; emphasis mine). Saying both represented an action, and, at the same time, carried it out.

Contemporary scholarship goes further to suggest the social, political, and cultural stakes for performative efficacy. For his part, Schechner draws a continuum along events whose primary function is ritual and those serving as entertainment. He argues that regardless of function, efficacy is operative in all of these instances in signifying a transformation that is both symbolic and actual: "Not simply a doing but a showing of a doing" (2003, 114). Schechner's theoretical move has political significance in blurring the boundaries between typically fixed binaries like the sacred and the profane, or high and popular culture. Alternatively, Butler's work on the performativity of gender adapts notions of efficacy to the social sphere. In an essay entitled "Performative Acts and Gender Constitution," for example, she argues that gender is not a predetermined set of conventions that a person inhabits tacitly but a role that is "tenuously constituted in time—an identity instituted through a stylized repetition of acts" (1990b, 270). Herein lies the potential for the actualization of difference. In her words: "If the ground of gender identity is the stylized repetition of acts through time, and not a seemingly seamless identity, then the possibilities of gender transformation are to be found in the arbitrary relation between such acts, in the possibility of a different sort of repeating, in the breaking or subversive repetition of that style" (1990b, 271).

Given these precedents, what is novel about *How to Do Things with Dance* is not its recognition of the power of embodied action to bring about change, but rather its attempt to locate this power within the historical, sociopolitical, and cultural environment of postwar America. In the field of dance studies, the 1930s and the 1960s are commonly represented as exemplary historical moments, when artistic revitalization in modern dance resonated with, and even contributed to, broad-scale, popular, and organized political movements for social change.[6] Scholars tend to portray the postwar period in dance, when compared with these cultural watersheds, as artistically and politically stagnant, its choreographic oeuvre having limited sociopolitcal significance due to artistic insularity and apoliticism.[7] It is true that many postwar dance artists cultivated a distance between their artistic practices and the world. Yet it would be a mistake to assume that, for this reason, their work had little real import, or that it was any less revealing of postwar cultural dynamics and social relations than dance during any other period. By contrast, in this book I reveal the work of postwar dance artists as having social and political import. This book is also unique in its examination of the significance of the postwar reassessment in modern dance in broad cultural terms that do not rest primarily on artistic affiliation with the largely white, objectivist avant-garde.

The concept for this book began with my desire to position postwar modern dance as a particular window into postwar culture, as no such books existed when I started. My approach evolved over time, along with my decision to depart from standard interpretations. For those familiar with the period, the history of postwar modern dance presents a conundrum. Clearly, it saw a high point of disciplinary coalescence, bringing to fruition the first concerted efforts by dancers, dance critics, and audiences since the turn of the century to institutionalize modern dance practices in the United States. This occurred in various ways: through continued articulation (written and embodied) of an ideology of universalism; the founding of dance schools to provide first-rate training of increasingly codified modern dance techniques; and the establishment of patronage allegiances with colleges and universities, local theaters, and the nation-state. From one perspective, modern dance had come of age, having achieved the aims of its proponents; it was recognized as a culturally legitimate artistic discipline both within and outside of the field of dance.

As we will see in chapter 1, for example, the dominant aesthetic ideology of universalism, and its legitimization in the affiliation of modern dance artists with the international touring program under the auspices of President Dwight D. Eisenhower's Emergency Fund, provided a forum for the dance establishment's administration of a policy of containment all its own. It imposed normative artistic standards via decisions about funding on choreographers who wished to participate.[8] As Naima Prevots has shown, the process by which choreographers were considered for touring by members of the American National Theater and Academy (ANTA)-appointed Dance Panel in the mid-1950s crystallized aesthetic rifts that had been opening for years among factional constituencies (1998). Prevots brings fascinating and formerly classified documents into the light of day and situates them in a brief history of the cultural cold war. Yet she mainly concentrates on the politics within the dance community concerning aesthetic standards as they were exercised as stipulations for funding.

Chapter 1 moves beyond Prevots' illustration of artistic and political cooperation to illuminate a deeper and more fundamental ideological coordination between artistic and state apparatuses through a common grounding in universalism. In both postwar modern dance and the broader cultural arena, universalism signified the idea that all human beings shared essential characteristics regardless of the particularities of their lives or geographic location. In the field of modern dance, for example, universalism provided a basis for the operative assumption that dance, as an embodied experience, offered a "human language," or cultural "common denominator"[9] that could establish common ground for heterogeneous audiences. Likewise, as one of the dominant schools of U.S. foreign policy, universalism held that people across the globe, separated by geographical, religious, ethnic/racial, political, or cultural barriers could be unified through appeals to their shared human experiences.

Mobilizing an extensive array of primary texts, as well as secondary scholarship on the Popular Front, cold war foreign policies of containment, and postwar internationalism, chapter 1 examines how, in insidious and complex ways, the dominant aesthetic ideology of universalism in dance modernism synchronized with a universalist approach to foreign policy even as participants in the touring program asserted the necessity of artistic autonomy. As I will suggest here, the U.S. government's embrace of universal democracy and the dance establishment's valuation of the ideology of aesthetic universalism were both premised on the notion of the white Western subject as the norm.[10] In dance, as in the arenas of U.S. foreign and domestic relations, universalism, as it designated a hierarchy of values and system of privileges, was an "Achilles heel." It circumscribed the practices of modern dance to such an extent as to threaten their relevance to communities of artists and viewers. And it highlighted for all the world to see the contradictions inherent in the concepts "democracy," "liberty," and "freedom" as ideal rights applied to the world's people but bestowed inconsistently on all Americans.

The alignment of universalism in state and cultural apparatuses signaled both a concentration of power and its instability in serving as an impetus for change. In modern dance, for example, universalism promised and promoted a common rallying cry for diverse constituencies of dance artists, all of whom aspired to making work that revealed aspects of the human condition. In practice, however, it ended up serving as a point of artistic departure from aesthetic convention. Universalism, as it governed dance making and reception, was far from inclusive. Members of the artistic establishment applied it to justify their prescriptions for choreographic method, form, and content, all of which could be mapped onto various constituencies of the broader artistic community along racial, sexual, or ethnic lines. Although consensus in artistic, as in social, settings was the order of the day, unity was difficult to ensure due to high levels of disaffection among modern dance choreographers. Nevertheless, both the concerted efforts made by the dance establishment to appear unified on aesthetic matters, as well as the high level of cultural capital bestowed upon modern dance artists during the postwar period, masked underlying conditions of instability and anxiety for all dance artists.

In this environment, many emerging and established dance artists initiated a period of reassessment, targeting the strictures of the dance form with which they identified. Apparently, rather than serving as an inclusive umbrella for their artistic endeavors, universalism proved too narrow an organizing principle for an increasingly diverse community of choreographers. As a response, dissenting choreographers sought to modify, even to re-invent, modern dance and compositional practice in order to place their work in line with their evolving aesthetic and cultural sensibilities.

Caught within racially and sexually coded conventions that designated appropriate form and subject matter, for instance, choreographers such as Merce Cunningham and Pearl Primus searched elsewhere. Both became increasingly interested in plumbing the expressive and aesthetic potential of ordinary movement and situations. In their lights, the dancing body was defined by its very movement, and not, therefore, relative to a normative standard or type suggested by a given character or role. Cunningham wrote in 1952 of his work within a milieu of like-minded artists like John Cage, Robert Rauschenberg, Jasper Johns, James Waring, and Paul Taylor thus: "There has been a shift in emphasis in the practice of the arts of painting, music and dancing during the last few years. There are no labels yet, but there are ideas. These ideas seem primarily concerned with something being exactly what it is in its time and place, and not having actual or symbolic reference to other things. *A thing is just that thing*" (quoted in Vaughan 1997, 86; emphasis mine). Cunningham's statement stressed that action is something *as it is*, not as it refers to something else, thus underlining the efficacy inherent in movement to serve as a mode of instantiation.

Likewise, a 1949 trip to Africa highlighted for Primus the phenomenological "effectiveness" of movement in a ritual context. As I detail in chapter 4, in letters she sent to various U.S. critics, and which were subsequently published in mainstream press outlets like the *New York Times*, the *New York Herald Tribune*, *Dance Observer*, and *Dance Magazine*, she recast her own work (Martin June 28, 1949; Terry May 20, 1949; Primus 1949, 1950a, 1950b, 1951; Hering 1950). She rejected the term "primitive," which she and others had formerly used to describe it, and embraced instead the term "basic" (quotation from Primus 1949, 147; see also Kowal 2007). And she noted that in ritual, form and function were essentially related in the pursuit of a specified goal—transformation. As she put it, "For those of us who are performers this is really one of the greatest classrooms, for the true dance aims at effect—the rapid movement is suddenly halted—the spinning dancer suddenly stops still before the chief, and the woman in the trance suddenly screams through the stillness. . . . No theatre has produced anything like those of Mushenge or Benin—designed for effectiveness!" (Primus 1949, 147).[11]

Cunningham and Primus neither theorized their experiences in exactly the same terms nor did their theories lead to parallel aesthetic results. Yet there is an undeniable similarity between both choreographers' conceptions of the moving body as constitutive. The comparison between them suggests that the artistic investment in questions of movement's efficacy extended beyond the milieu surrounding Cage and Cunningham. Other artistic constituencies that operated outside the objectivist aesthetic shared in the cultural work of reconsidering the uses of the body—and specifically, movement—not only to artistic but also to social and political ends. This comparison also posits the usefulness of action as an interpretive lens, leading both to an unexpected juxtaposition of choreographic projects and a new historiographic account of their meanings.

In standard accounts of postwar modern dance, which situate it within the larger history of the Euro-American avant-garde, *action* is typically deployed to advance a narrative about the renewal of an artistic vanguard. In this context, contributions like those of Cage, Cunningham, Alwin Nikolais,[12] and Paul Taylor are seen as singular in the field, taken as primary evidence of an aesthetic of "objectivism" (Morris 2006) or the discovery of "new ways to foreground the medium of dance rather than its meaning" (Banes 1987, xvi).[13] Objectivist experimentation is therefore a seminal and transformational episode that facilitated "the transition from the old to the new modern dance" (Johnston 1965, 167; Copeland 2004, 8) and a sign that a "'new' modern dance [had] emerged from the experimentalist ferment of New York's 'downtown'" (Garafola 1988, 177).[14]

Known for its aesthetic militancy "against interpretation,"[15] the Judson Dance Theater, positioned in the context of the 1960s, functions as the logical conclusion to this story, as objectivism's presumed beneficiary and successor. It is also regarded as primary evidence that objectivist choreographic practices ushered in an artistic sea change that took (post)modern dance to another level of artistic and political engagement (Banes 1983, 1987, 1993, 2003).

Gay Morris's recently published book, *A Game for Dancers: Performing Modernism in the Postwar Years*, maintains this version of events inasmuch as it supports her argument that objectivism's "consonance" within the postmodern dance field ushered in an aesthetic revival. As she argues:

> Until the 1950s, modern dance defined itself as a genre that sought to communicate emotional essences. To use John Martin's term, modern dance was "expressional" ([1939] 1965). Its techniques and point of view were based on those founded by the pioneers of the 1920s and '30s. For modern dance to achieve a *renewal*, somehow those original assumptions had to be challenged without also destroying modern dance itself. It is no secret that by the end of the 1950s "objectivist" modern dance was declared the new vanguard. (2006, xix; emphasis mine)

According to Morris, objectivism "succeeded over competing strategies" of choreographic expression, allowing a "renewal" that did not "destroy modern dance itself" in the process. At the same time, it helped to preserve the field's "semi-autonomy" from potentially co-opting cultural and capital forces (2006, xix and xvii).

Given such an approach, it seems reasonable that the story of postwar dance would end here. Yet objectivism is neither the field's only legacy nor the sole basis for the invigoration of modern dance during the 1960s. Looking at the postwar period in hindsight, important projects on modern dance during the 1960s and 1970s suggest as much (Gottschild 1996, 47–58; Foster 2002a and 2002b, 31–43; Franko 2005). Looking beyond the formation of the avant-garde, they have revealed the heterogeneity of the postwar choreographic field and its artistic practices, as well as the multidirectional politics of cultural exchange. Minority artists seen as having been deferential to the status quo or peripheral to its reappraisal, as well as vernacular cultural practices portrayed as having been marginal to its formation, are acknowledged for their contributions (Malone 1996;

Perpener 2001; Chatterjea 2004; DeFrantz 2004; Manning 2004; Shea Murphy 2007; Kraut 2008). Conversely, tacit appropriations by white artists of techniques, movement material, and expressive modes stemming from minority communities are being brought to light (Manning 2004; Shea Murphy 2007).

Dance scholars Brenda Dixon Gottschild and Susan Foster have addressed the importance of historiographic framing and its bearing on the interpretive result, in particular when viewing dance practices through constructs like the avant-garde, or the theatrical, which have typically been affiliated with the white West.[16] Likewise, scholars in the fields of art history and performance studies have also begun to reconsider the usefulness of the avant-garde as an interpretive lens as it has traditionally been constructed. As James M. Harding and John Rouse ask, "Which history? Constructed at whose expense and based upon whose exclusion? In almost any other scholarly context, these questions would seem obvious. But bringing them to bear in this context finally opens the door to a consideration of avant-garde gestures emanating from cultural contexts beyond the borders of a conventional Eurocentric history of the avant-garde and beyond the suggestion of their European origins" (2006, 13).[17]

Similarly *How To Do Things with Dance* shifts the focus away from the "ascendance" of objectivism as the pivotal outcome of the postwar years in modern dance, and opts instead for a more inclusive account of the aesthetic array as defined by action. Within this conceptual rubric, I consider the works of postwar choreographers across the artistic and racial/ethnic spectrum as equally important and consequential, not as they fulfilled the historic aims of the (white) avant-garde per se, but as they reconceived the practice of modern dance making and doing through a common investment in the constitutive power of the body. The result is a story about a heterogeneous community of artistic practitioners and audiences heralding under the banner of modern dance, as well as an account of their diverse movement ideologies and practices which generated a plurality of artistic results.

Among the members of this group, however, change came at many costs and risks. In the cultural environment of domestic containment, in which diverging from the status quo implied abnormalcy at best, and political subversion at worst, artists, like the majority of their audience members, avoided taking obvious stands against the accepted. They also routinely denied the influence of social or political matters or they declined to speak about their work in these terms. We should not equate artistic disavowal with cultural irrelevance. Rather than mounting overt critiques of the aesthetic or social status quo, choreographers used action to defamiliarize the ordinary. Sometimes the point was to make the ordinary appear strange; other times, it was to make what appeared strange seem more ordinary. In either case, however, choreographers deployed action both to question artistic and social conventions and to substantiate possibilities for difference.

As might be expected, moreover, their expressions of dissent bore a hallmark of containment: ambivalence. Work that rejected certain aesthetic conventions or conceptions of reality often reinforced others. Invariably, as each choreographer investigated the potential for movement practices to embody subjective experiences beyond what was given or accepted, each exerted whatever advantage he or she had in ways that served that choreographer's work and/or career. Within this group, hegemonic forces that upheld dominant social standing (i.e., white, Christian, heterosexual) remained operative, counterposing conditions of alterity and privilege one against another. Such contradictory, and in many ways discrete, experiences associated the lives of modern dancers in New York City with those of many other Americans. All of them, in varying ways, struggled to live and to make sense of lives that deviated from what was considered normal while seeking security in association with the dominant culture. In this sense, their common labor constituted "a plurality of resistances, each of them a special case" (Foucault 1990, 94–95).

Chapter 2 examines how choreographers like Martha Graham and José Limón, who upheld established ways of doing things in modern dance, deployed movement to reveal what they saw as the restrictive and compromising effects of normalization pertaining to gender construction. I focus on their dances *Night Journey* and *The Moor's Pavane*, respectively, which were performed on international tours, to investigate the grounds for a central irony within postwar establishment modern dance: How could universalism elevate the form for the purposes of exemplifying American cultural values, while, at the same time, providing cover for the artistic expression of skepticism about its enshrined institutions like matrimony? Their dances upheld ideologies of universalism in politics and in modern dance at the same time as they "spoke out" against normativity, and, ironically, its political uses, in their critiques of marriage. As precursors to action, they used narrative constructs to respond to forces of normalization, harnessing their critiques of matrimony on canonical literary works and heroic figures whose stature, by chance or by design, blunted the force of their criticism. By contrast, the choreographers whose work I investigate in the balance of the book moved away from this narrative-driven mode of expression that channeled emotion through the impersonation of monumental surrogates. Although action as it was manifest in postwar choreography spanned the gamut from dancers dancing roles to dancing as themselves, what made it different from these precedents was its emphasis on the body itself's role in constituting change as both a critique of the status quo and an alternative assertion of being.

Anna Sokolow, the focus of chapter 3, used her piece *Rooms* to recast the terms of the critical debate about her work while, at the same time, making a profound statement about the postwar human condition. Juxtaposing "portraits" of New York City apartment dwellers, the dance reveals a collection of lonely lives. Thus, *Rooms* went against the popular mythology of New York City as the postwar "culture capital of the world," a cosmopolitan center of excitement, élan, and creativity, and revealed it instead to be akin to an "urban suburb." In this sense, Sokolow's realization is shown to be in kind with those of left-leaning social scientists, who saw in the postwar corporate and social economies the potential for widespread, and hidden, experiences of isolation and alienation. Yet the trajectory of *Rooms* extended further than these studies in its generalized, and therefore subtle, critique of the culture of domestic anticommunism, portrayed as a communal impulse turned inward; here people act as though they fear association or even affiliation with one another, sowing a breeding ground for deep-seated isolation, even solipsism.

Chapter 4 examines the artistic and political implications of Pearl Primus' 1949 trip to Africa through an analysis of the statements she made (some published) about the trip on her return. For largely racial reasons, Primus faced critical hostility toward her work in the mid-1940s. She saw her trip as an opportunity to reframe the critical discourse that surrounded her. I focus in particular on the artistic, cultural, and political meanings of Primus' "diaspora discourse"—both written and embodied—which expressed the contradictions of her self-perception while also leading to an investigation of choreographic "effectiveness" (Clifford 1997, 244; Primus 1949, 147). Implying the capability of concerted movement to accomplish transformative ends in the context of ritual, Primus' theorization of "effectiveness," or choreographic efficacy, contributed to the contemporaneous reappraisal of modern dance practice around action. This chapter also addresses various implications of Primus' deployment of primitivity in accounts of her experiences in Africa, even as she adopted other terminology to describe her own work.

Chapter 5 develops the idea of dance movement as constitutive through an investigation of Merce Cunningham's and Paul Taylor's interest in using found, or preexisting, materials in their choreography. Embracing the idea that any movement could be adapted for use in modern dance, both choreographers assumed the role of scavengers looking around the city for choreographic material and subject matter. While Cunningham was drawn to the emerging ballet vernacular of George Balanchine for use in his chance-driven compositions, Taylor gathered ideas from pedestrians on the streets. In both cases, however, "finding" served as a route by which to explore alternative constructions of danced—and lived— subjectivity as composed moment-to-moment rather than predetermined by a given role or normative type.

Chapters 6 and 7 pair examples of action that exerted themselves outside the immediate space of the theater, substantiating the role of the body in the work of social change. Chapter 6 illuminates the contributions of Talley Beatty, Katherine Dunham, and Donald McKayle to the formation of the postwar black public sphere. Grounded in the blues aesthetic, their work conjoined the expressive and the political, embodying blackness in ways that challenged aesthetic and social conventions concerning what black bodies could be and do. Focusing specifically on their work in the context of the intensifying civil rights movement and the emerging strategy of direct action protest, I investigate the extent to which dance was not merely a reflection but rather an agent of transformation. Chapter 7 looks at similar strategies in the choreography of Anna Halprin, highlighting an "operational" similarity between her artistic practices and the sit-ins. Clearly, the protesters in Greensboro and Halprin faced different constraints to their freedom. Yet both deployed tactics of defamiliarization not only to challenge what was conventionally deemed "ordinary" or "natural" but also to re-pattern habits of body and mind with the goal of mobilizing participants for change.

Throughout this book, my goal will be to show how modern dance artists participated alongside other Americans in the postwar cultural work of "world-making."[18] At stake for them, as for other Americans, were prevailing conceptions and practices of lived experience. Suggesting that doing something on stage was tantamount to, or at least a rehearsal for, doing it in the world, their dances substantiated the emerging body politic in unexpected and transformative ways. Against long odds, dance makers used their work to actualize unusual possibilities for being by "doing" them in dance, deploying action to blur boundaries between the theatrical and the real so as to engage audiences nearby and far-flung in a shared endeavor to make meaning of their individual and collective experiences.

SETTING THE STAGE

Modern Dance Universalism and the Culture of Containment

I N 1946, Martha Graham was invited by the Circle of International Artistic Exchanges to perform in an International Festival of Music, Theater and Dance in Paris at the Theatre des Champs-Elysées. Organizers planned the festival in conjunction with the opening session of the United Nations Educational, Scientific and Cultural Organization (UNESCO). Formed in 1946 to represent governments not individuals, UNESCO had been charged by the United Nations (UN) to foster global peace and security (Ninkovich 1981, 94). To the dismay of many, including Walter Terry, dance critic for the *New York Herald Tribune*, Graham had to decline the invitation since neither the U.S. government nor UNESCO would provide money for travel (Terry 1946).[1] Graham's predicament was a supreme irony to Terry, as it seemed fitting that one of America's preeminent modern dance choreographers should participate in a meeting of this nature, at a venue of international stature. Following the war, the world was newly receptive to American art including modern dance. "Ballet Theatre's recent success in London and the requests of the French Circle for American Artists would suggest that the time is ripe for such exchanges and that other nations are eager to experience, after a long hiatus, the products of American art," Terry argued. Graham's appearance in Paris could help unite a divided and fractious world. He reasoned,

> [S]ince all men no matter how poor or of what color or faith, possess a body and since dance is the art governed entirely by the possibilities and limitations of this common denominator, it would seem that the activity of dance should be a major factor in Unesco's cultural functions. . . . From personal experience, I can tell of the unifying factor of dance. An alien tongue, an alien faith or alien customs can be annoying or bewildering, but when the possessor of those alien properties commences to dance, accent is perforce thrown upon the common denominator of the human body and for the duration of the dance one is aware of that property which is common to all. (1946)

Terry's conviction reveals the degree to which modern dance exponents thought their and dance artists' work vital to the project of global reconstruction in the wake of World War II. According to Terry, Graham was not merely an entertainer or cultural ambassador. Rather her work demonstrated the role of the body as a medium of cross-cultural exchange—and even encounter—the very grounds on which interpersonal communication, a precondition for global unity, might be cultivated. Consistent with the historic premise within the field of modern dance that the dancing body conducted avenues of kinesthetic empathy that were conducive to human understanding, Terry's rationale also presaged the particularities of postwar ideologies of universalism. Specifically, these sought in new ways to strike balances between the artistic and political demands placed on artists in an era of heightened global anxiety and increased American internationalism.

Perhaps this balancing act was nowhere more evident than in the participation of modern dance artists and their supporters in the U.S. government's international touring program under President Dwight D. Eisenhower, founded on the universalist assumption that "all men everywhere are basically like ourselves, that they are animated by substantially the same hopes and inspirations, that they all react in substantially the same way in given circumstances" (George Kennan quoted in Gaddis 2005b, 27). Called "The President's Emergency Fund for International Affairs," beginning in 1954 the program earmarked $5 million for American participation in trade fairs, exhibitions, and tours of performing artists, aiming to halt the propagation of communist ideology with a strategy of cultural dissemination all its own (Hixson 1997, 136; Von Eschen 1997; Prevots 1998; Klein 2003). In *Dance for Export*, Naima Prevots outlines the politics of dance in the context of the touring program administered through ANTA, bringing important formerly classified documents to light. Michel Foucault "defines a relationship of power . . . as a mode of action that does not act directly and immediately on others [but that] acts upon their actions: an action upon an action, on possible or actual future or present actions" (1994, 340). Drawing on this definition, this chapter moves beyond Provots' illustration of artistic and political cooperation in its investigation of a cultural dynamic of provocation and counteraction. I argue that these were, alternatively, actions exerted on choreographers by forces of normalization, and actions by choreographers, and the members of the dance community, in service of such forces. My study illuminates a deeper and more fundamental ideological coordination of governmental forces both within and outside the dance field. At the same time, I investigate the tension within the modern dance community about the overt politicization of dance.[2]

Examination of these power relations in the context both of the international touring program and the emerging atmosphere of domestic anticommunism also reveals how governmental and artistic programs collided within what Christina Klein has called the "global imaginary of containment" (2003, 22–23). Domestic anticommunism imposed and impinged upon artistic expression, not only as it was issued by governmental proxy by the ANTA-appointed Dance Panel (which allocated money through the Emergency Fund), but also more diffusely. Ultimately, I hope to show that the postwar coupling of art and politics was neither simple nor particularly convenient. Cold war suspicion of art that appeared to have political content exerted pressure on artists and critics to insulate their practices within a discourse of artistic autonomy. Government officials and their representatives in the dance community looked past choreographic content that might have been seen as critical of dominant cultural values, extolling its meanings on the basis of its "universalism." And, at the same time, the same tenets of universalism used to promote modern dance as a medium of human commonality were deployed to contain "alien" bodies abroad, through the touring program, and at home, in bias-tinged deliberations about funding. Study of the formation of universalism in postwar modern dance, and its significance in the context of the touring program, begins to illuminate the contradictory politics of difference within the modern dance field. It also brings to light the ways these politics resonated with more broadly construed postwar social and cultural relations.

Reading Graham's Invitation to UNESCO

Graham's invitation is evidence of the growing impression that she was the preeminent American choreographer in modern dance. According to a 1947 profile in the *New Yorker*, "by the mid-thirties, Miss Graham was well on her way to becoming a national institution" (Gibbs 1947, 32). President Franklin D. Roosevelt asked her to perform at the White House in 1937 (Graff 1997, 121). As Ellen Graff assesses, "In a time when American solidarity was essential, Graham's work confirmed the uniqueness of the American experience" (129). It was not until 1944, with the premier of *Appalachian Spring*, and her notably successful New York season in 1945, however, that mainstream critics and the public at large recognized the breadth and depth of her appeal.

Set to Aaron Copland's Pulitzer Prize–winning score, *Appalachian Spring* depicted the marriage of a young frontier couple, a Bride danced by Graham, and a Husbandman danced by Erick Hawkins, the man whom Graham would marry in 1948.[3] The work was so popular during Graham's 1945 New York season that she had to extend her run by one week. Even detractors, like the music critic for *Newsweek*, who had often admonished Graham in the past for the obscurity of her work, recognized the accomplishment of her newfound accessibility. "Theatrically and musically, it was by all odds her most successful season," the critic opined. "Having previously suffered righteously (and starkly) for her Art, Miss Graham has now busted loose with a seventeen-piece orchestra and some new sets . . . [G]oing to see Martha Graham has become fashionable, everybody who is Anybody thronged in droves" ("Aaron and Martha," 107). The reviewer for *Time* magazine concurred, "What was happening in the newest Graham dance-drama was comprehensible even to the bored businessman: a bride (Graham) and her groom (Erick Hawkins) built their house in the clearing of a Pennsylvania forest; they had a baby; they entertained a band of Shakers (who shook away their sins in a frenzied religious ceremony). No one was mystified for a moment" ("Purely Symbolic," May 28, 1945, 60).

According to these critics, Graham's work was a success not based on aesthetic criteria but because it was "comprehensible," in other words, obviously relevant to viewers' lives.

Symbolizing the return of the American GIs after the war, including the imminent postwar marriage and baby booms, *Appalachian Spring* appeared to usher in an era of normalcy to a world torn asunder by war. The Japanese attack on Pearl Harbor had marked a turning point in the nation's history. It challenged the public's aversion to intervention in conflicts on foreign soil because it had brought war to the nation's geographical doorstep. In a fireside chat on December 9, 1941, President Franklin D. Roosevelt intimated as much when he said of his decision to commit American troops to the Allied forces, "We don't like it—we didn't want to

FIG. 1.1 Martha Graham and Erick Hawkins in Martha Graham's *Appalachian Spring,* 1944. Photo by Arnold Eagle. Reprinted courtesy of the estate of Arnold Eagle and Jerome Robbins Dance Division, The New York Public Library of the Performing Arts, Astor, Lenox and Tilden Foundations.

get in it—but we are in it and we're going to fight it with everything we've got." At the outset Roosevelt knew that his goals were twofold: "We are going to win the war, and we are going to win the peace that follows" (Roosevelt quoted in Gaddis 1972, 1). Winning the peace required a decisive victory—the defeat, disarmament, and occupation of the Axis nations (2). The massive mobilization of citizens, and the significant disruption to the nation's way of life over the course of the conflict, had a profound effect on public opinion on the eve of peace. In May of 1945, the month of Graham's successful New York season, Americans saw an end to war. On May 8, Germany had surrendered and on May 23 the Allies bombed Tokyo, killing 83,000 people. By September, after the atomic bombing of Hiroshima and Nagasaki, the war was over.

In this cultural climate, Graham had found a winning formula with *Appalachian Spring.* Its portrayal of a pioneer union captured the hopes and dreams of many Americans at war's end, namely to bring the soldiers home so that family life could resume again. In extended movement soliloquies, Graham as the Bride displays mixed feelings about her ensuing marriage. In one, she anticipates her impending marriage with a dance of jittery expectancy. In another, her darting back and forth among various lead members of the cast portrays her as unsettled about what might be expected of her once she is married. My retrospective reading of the piece, suggesting its feminist undertones (as I will investigate further in chapter 2), is not conveyed in contemporaneous accounts of the piece, which overlooked what I see as obvious references to the Bride's prenuptial anxiety. Graham herself glossed over her subtle critique of matrimony with program comments that hinted at what she anticipated would be the work's widespread relevance and use toward national healing and unification, commenting, "I used my grandmother's stories of the pioneer days . . . to build the framework of the nation. Spring is purely symbolic of the springtime of the nation. That is why the set is so simple with no green leaves" ("Purely Symbolic," 1945, 60).

The social pertinence of Graham's work is also reflected in glowing critical accounts. *New York Times* critic and longtime Graham supporter John Martin stated, "After the long, lean years of struggle, she sells out the theatre now the day the tickets go on sale, and in the audience every third person is a symphony conductor, a dramatic star, a sculptor, a novelist or somebody else of distinguished achievement in the arts" (Martin 1944a, 20). Graham also captured the attention of the national press corps, some of whom had been skeptical about the relevance of her work in the past. Over the next few years, profiles in national magazines like the *New Republic* 1945 and 1948, *Time* 1945 and 1947, *New Yorker* 1947, and *Life* 1947 extended the spheres of her name recognition and attested to her stature among modern dance choreographers. As *Life* magazine put it,

> Twenty years ago a most determined-looking young woman with only $11.25 in her purse rented a theater and attacked Broadway with an unfamiliar idea: that the dance was not merely a form of entertainment but a highbrow art capable of expressing the deep psychological subtleties of the human mind. Today Martha Graham's psychological ballets pack Broadway houses, [and] keep highly critical dance audiences in a state of furious absorption. By unanimous opinion of New York's leading ballet critics Martha Graham is the foremost figure in the world of U.S. dancing. ("She Is Priestess," 1947, 101)

Returning to the significance of Graham's invitation to UNESCO, her recognition attested not only to her postwar cultural profile but also to the heightened status of the artistic milieu that coalesced in New York

City after the war. Enriched by the artistic and intellectual culture brought by European émigrés just before and after World War II, and nourished by a vitalized group of American artists, by 1945 New York had supplanted Paris as the cultural center of the world (Wallock 1988, 9; Polcari 1991, 23). In this cosmopolitan environment, artists "devised a new language of expression: abstract in form and international in aesthetic" (quoted in Wallock 1988, 11; see also Ashton 1972; Ashton in Wallock 1988; Polcari 1991; Harris 1993). In the area of the performing arts, the city itself provided a fertile medium. Completed in December 1943, for example, City Center became the first and foremost performing arts complex in the country (Marquis 1995, 9). Dance prospered in this environment: dancers formed institutions and institutional alliances and produced work for a growing and appreciative audience (Garafola 1988, 157).

Finally, Graham's invitation reveals the heightened sense of American internationalism after the war, the perception within and outside the country that the nation and its citizens had a role to play in securing world peace and security. In the immediate postwar years, public discussion about the nation's responsibility to take the lead in foreign affairs was commonplace and widespread. An article published in the *New York Times* in December 1945, assessed what the United States had learned in "the hundred days since v-j Day." "The question of America's role in the world has become increasingly insistent," it continued. "As a result of its decisive part in the war, the United States is involved in world affairs as never before in its history" ("Our World Role," 1945).[4]

After Pearl Harbor, "American policy makers sought security through involvement, not isolation" (Gaddis 1972, 353). The establishment of the United Nations, an international security agency, like the formation of UNESCO, signified the hopes of many to avert another world war by the institutionalization of collective, multilateral internationalism. Before the war's end Truman prepared to hand over responsibilities for resolving the war to the United Nations Organization (UNO), so that its members could take over for the "Big Three," the United States, Britain, and Russia, the Allied victors in the conflict.[5] American aid to Western Europe and Japan was another ingredient in the drive to stabilize these regions after the war. To some, victory proved America's world dominance, thereby justifying its claim to empire.[6] Power, through military and economic strength, begot security and peace.

The atomic bomb complicated the picture, especially in a world dom- inated by two superpowers, the United States and the Soviet Union. "At a time when delegates of fifty-one nations are gathered in London to chart UNO's first General Assembly meeting scheduled for January . . . in the minds of all, though not on the agenda, was the world's no. 1 problem— the atomic bomb" (Cantril 1945). The bomb forced the United States to think globally. Securing world peace could not be handled unilaterally but demanded the formation of a "collective security organization" that could function as the League of Nations never did or could (especially because the United States never joined), as a body that could exert multi- lateral pressure on any aggressor. This could also serve as both a physical and symbolic place where nations could form lasting partnerships, not just because they now had "common enemies" but also because they "could build friendly relationships which would survive victory" (Bald- win 1945, 4).[7] The West's commitment to global cooperation extended all the way to the Soviet Union. In spite of suspicion about soviet ambitions for Eastern Europe and fear about the growing membership in the Com- munist Party across the European continent, U.S./soviet negotiation pro- ceeded in good faith in 1945 (Leffler 1992, 5–8).

Amidst these good intentions, the chance the USSR could acquire the technology to build and detonate an atomic bomb and use it to advance its global aspirations, sowed pessimism among U.S. officials. Late in 1945, General Eisenhower said as much in comments made following the U.S. atomic bombing of Japan: "I would have said yes, I was sure we could keep the peace with Russia. Now I don't know . . . People are fright- ened and disturbed all over. Everyone feels insecure again" (quoted in Alperovitz [1965] 1985, 2).[8] The detonation of bombs on Hiroshima and Nagasaki—on August 6, 1945, and August 9, 1945, respectively—initiated a period of national reckoning.[9] That said, over time, as Americans came to terms with their fear about nuclear annihilation, they also began to accept the reality of the bomb and even embrace it as a guarantor of their security (Boyer 1994, 25–26; Henriksen 1997, xx).[10]

The Uses of Universalism in Postwar Modern Dance

Although, it bore the hallmarks of postwar internationalism, Terry's belief in the ability of modern dance to transcend typically insurmountable human boundaries owed to assumptions within the form's overriding universalist ideology. At its inception at the turn of the century, "human emotion assumed a central importance as subject matter [in modern dance] . . . because specific human situations and feelings emblematized a universal human condition" (Foster 1986, 150; see also Foulkes 2002, 132–33).[11] John Martin's *Introduction to the Dance* (1939), a seminal text of the interwar years, similarly professed this view. Martin argued that dance "employed as its medium a material that is closer to life experience than that employed by any of the other arts, namely the movement of the body in its reactions to its environment." Through the phenomenon of "inner mimicry," a kind of "sympathetic awareness," "all types of gesture and facial expression convey meaning to us automatically because we have felt similar muscular experiences ourselves and recognize the postural attitudes and their emotional connotations as having happened to us" (48). Or, as choreographer Doris Humphrey put it as late as 1956, "I [have] something personal to say in dance [and I] make it of universal interest" (Doris Humphrey quoted in Terry, 1956a).

Continuous with this tradition, after World War II exponents like Terry deployed a language of universalism, emphasizing the close affiliation of all forms of dance with the common human condition of embodiment. What was different, however, was the postwar emphasis on the uniqueness of modern dance as compared with other dance forms in its articulation of a "basic" language of the body, and an adamancy that, due to its essential "humanness," the form could communicate absent political ideology across human divides (geographical, national, linguistic, racial, and religious). Consider Martin's writings during the postwar period, which emphasized the role of communication in the formation of a global human community. Whereas, in its explanation of "kinesthetic sympathy," Martin's *Introduction to the Dance* (1939) had deployed universalism to theorize the transaction between the dancing body and viewers, *The Dance* (1946) went further in distinguishing modern dance from other forms of dance due to its "basicness." Calling "basic" the "common impulse to resort to movement to externalize emotional states which we cannot externalize by rational means," Martin held that such an impulse was common to all dance practices regardless of their function, formal qualities, or country of origin (9–10).[12] That said, Martin recognized distinctions among the forms spawned by these common impulses: "Geography, climate, race, religion, social environment, physique, dress, cultural tradition, historical background, and the very passage of time itself, all affect the ways men move and, more particularly, the ways they translate movement into dance" (12). Singling out modern dance, however, from numerous other dance practices, Martin claimed its singularity in the manner of its communication. "Because of the inherent contagion of bodily movement, which makes the onlooker feel sympathetically in his own musculature the exertions he sees in somebody else's musculature," he asserted, "the dancer is able to convey through movement the most intangible emotional experience." For this reason, he contended, the term "modern" to describe "modern dance" was a misnomer since "there is absolutely nothing modern about modern dance." To the contrary, modern dance was "virtually basic dance, the oldest of all dance forms" (105).

Comparable strategies were at work in Margaret Lloyd's *The Borzoi Book of Modern Dance* (1949), which stressed the artist's role in what was seen as a global reconstruction project. Like Martin's, Lloyd's account of postwar modern dance was predicated on a comparison with dance during previous eras, marking a changing climate for and in dance.[13] Whereas the circumstances of the Depression era and World War II appeared to her to circumscribe the purview of modern dance universalism, albeit in different ways, the postwar years suggested the possibility that modern dance could transcend concerns of history, nation, economy, race, and politics. Claiming that "the radical American modern dance [had been] . . . interracial from its start," Lloyd noted that at the present time, "it becomes more international, with no loss of patriotism, as it becomes more liberal, as it leaves the confines of early modernism, narrow national and *class* consciousness, for the timeless, universal realm of dance, and the one world of people" (Lloyd, 186, italics in original). It was modern dance's "correlation with humanity" that ensured its "special impact." She explained, "Despite its contemporaneity, it does not hesitate to look backward for the fundamental links between other ages and ours. It looks forward with prophetic discernment; inward to what is going on in human consciousness; it embraces the thoughts and activities of mankind. Modern dance is world conscious, concerned with social, national, and international problems, as well as with those of personal relationships" (186).

A pair of editorials by Gertrude Lippincott, published in *Dance Observer* in 1948, exemplified a similar logic (1948a and 1948b). Decrying the overt "prostitution of art for political purposes" (1948a, 44), both compared explicitly the plights of the artist or intellectual under democracy and under communism. Both editorials affirmed the idea that "great" art was "non-political." In her words, "To say that an art form, a structure of sound or notes is 'decadent' is nonsense. Music is non-political . . . really great music transcends national and political boundaries and appeals to all mankind" (1948a, 45). The second editorial, in particular, lamented the political content of the Wroclaw World Conference, assembled "by certain French and Polish intellectuals for the purpose of forwarding peace among nations." Citing an account by Julian Huxley, Director-General of UNESCO, who attended the conference as one of its five chairmen, published in the *New York Herald Tribune*, Lippincott related, "the great majority of the speeches were either strictly Marxian analyses of current trends, or else polemical attacks on American or Western policy or culture" (1948b).[14] Lippincott was disappointed not only that the event took such a negative political turn but also that it was politicized at all. "In the last analysis," she wrote, "a scientist is not a German, Russian, or American; he is an *internationalist*. The same fact holds true for an artist, although an artist may show more national peculiarities than a scientist" (117). In the metonymic relationship dance set up between the dancing body and the collective body of humanity, it was thought to foster unity around the world, thus furthering the aims of the state in embodying the integration of the artist within a broadly conceived human community.

More than either of the other critics, Lippincott deployed a capitalist subtext to conjoin the ideologies of universalism and freedom as they applied to the American artist. In "Freedom in the Arts," for example, she responded to the soviet censure of "three of the most distinguished composers of modern times, Shostakovich, Prokofiev, and Khatchaturian, announcing that their music was 'decadent, bourgeois, and undemocratic'" and "smelling strongly of modern bourgeois music of Europe and America." Lippincott saw in these events an opportunity to comment about what she believed was a paradox inherent in state funding for the arts and about whether "great" art could be political at all. Lippincott argued for a silver lining in the lack of U.S. subsidization of modern artists. Holding up as counterexamples the censorship of the soviet composers and the use of art as propaganda by fascists in Germany and Italy during the war, she contended that, even though "we do not give the artist any special position . . . in America, the artist is free to produce what he feels is right and true. His monetary rewards are often negligible, and he many never receive great public acclaim. *But this very neglect may well be a blessing in disguise, because no artist can ever serve any master other than himself*" (1948a, 44–45; emphasis mine). In her drafting of the image of the unsubsidized American artist as penniless but free from state suasion, Lippincott lent credence to anticommunist arguments both about the liberating effects of a free-market economy and the universalism of arts under capitalism.

Although without the explicit capitalist overlay, choreographers too enlisted the implied relation between universalism and artistic autonomy to lend credence to their practices. Graham's comments in a 1947 article are a case in point: "I am interested only in the subtle being, the subtle body that lies beneath the gross muscles. Every dance is, to some greater or lesser extent, a kind of fever chart, a graph of the heart. I do not compromise ideologically and I have never considered my dances in any way intellectual. Whatever theory may be read into them proceeds from the material and not vice-versa" (Graham quoted in Robert Horan 1947, 4).

Similarly, in introducing a Canadian Broadcasting Company's telecast of *The Moor's Pavane* in 1955, José Limón explained, "You will find that we have things to say there about love and jealousy, tenderness, foolishness, all of the emotions that you will find in the great tragedy, stated in a different way, not with words but with gestures. A person not understanding one single English word would be able to tell . . . about Othello . . . merely by seeing how the human body functions" (Limón, 1955). Both Graham and Limón theorized the efficacy of the modern dancing body in essentialist terms, as emanating from the body's very physicality—its core properties or, in Graham's words, "the subtle body lying beneath the gross muscles." In fact, they imagined modern dance as bringing out these qualities as dimensions of life experience that were distinctly human (i.e., part and parcel of inhabiting a human body).

It is important to flag here what these accounts establish about postwar dance universalism as compared with earlier formulations. What is evident are the various strategies of distancing the postwar period from that of the 1930s. Martin, for instance, accomplishes this through a repositioning of postwar modern dance practice outside of historically and culturally contingent artistic movements and instead within a realm of the transcendent. The contrast between Martin's postwar writing to that of the

1930s brings these differences into relief. His work in the 1930s envisioned dance practice in a historically specific way, as a reconciliation between the demands of art and political propaganda.[15] As he put it in 1933, "There can be found many adherents to the belief that art and propaganda are irreconcilable, but with the new vistas that have been opened by the modern movements in the arts this position becomes ever less tenable. Indeed, it is becoming more and more evident that art to be genuine cannot escape being propaganda." This acknowledgment of the intersection of "modern movements in the arts" and the political realm stands in sharp relief to his 1946 stance. Calling modern dance a "common [human] impulse," he effectively repositioned modern dance practice outside of these historically and culturally contingent movements and instead within a realm of transcendent universalism (1946).

Lloyd, Graham, and Lippincott, too, in various ways took pains to distinguish postwar modern dance from previous iterations, in this case emphasizing the postwar artist's autonomy from the political realm. Whereas Lloyd differentiated between the "narrow national and class consciousness" of the Depression era "revolutionary dance," and "the timeless, universal realm of dance, and the one world of people," Graham emphasized her creative process as "proceeding from the material and not vice-versa." Whereas Lippincott did not make an explicit historical comparison, her pronouncement that "no artist can ever serve any master other than himself" clearly weighed in on the side of artistic autonomy. Martin himself was not immune to this approach either. In his 1944 profile of Graham, for example, he characterized the choreographer as a "strict taskmaster and a laborious worker, demanding infallible accuracy and control of the body at all times," Martin was quick to point out that "her style of movement is not an arbitrary invention which she has thought out and standardized' it is rather a spontaneous development." Quoting Graham, "It fits me . . . like my skin." Martin took pains to show that Graham's expression of her body, as analogous to the collective human body, did not require the artist to subordinate her individual identity to an incorporative human community. In fact, Martin contended the opposite, that the refinement of dance technique and choreographic vision to express the interior life fed the artist's sense of autonomy.

On further examination, in the context of postwar internationalism, articulations of universalism in modern dance appear to be both opportunistic and compelling. On the one hand, the belief that modern dance could transcend difference on a global scale gave credence to the professional aspirations of members of the modern dance field, who sought to legitimate and institutionalize modern dance practice. While this had been a long-standing project, efforts during the postwar period intensified due to increased and broadened public interest and monies made available to cultural institutions after World War II. In line with these trends, modern dance artists founded dance schools to provide first-rate training of increasingly codified dance techniques, formed patronage allegiances with colleges and universities and local theaters, and toured nationally and internationally, some funded by the U.S. government (Prevots 1998; Martin 2000; Morris 2006). This allowed dance artists to cultivate broader and more diverse audiences, both at home and abroad, through company touring, miscellaneous public appearances, and contributions to publications within and outside of the dance field.

On the other hand, the characterization of modern dance as a "human common denominator,"[16] as well as the coupling of the personal and the collective, revealed a common assumption among critics and practitioners that modern dance was capable of addressing a fundamental issue of the time—the meaning of the individual human life in a world decimated by war and the Nazi holocaust and precariously poised on the threshold of nuclear annihilation. The belief that dance artists could unify diverse peoples through the "universal" language of human movement complemented the prevailing public view that the United States needed to play a leadership role in world affairs. Dance could ensure for the world's citizens what their leaders could not—avenues of communication leading to recognition and understanding. However, as much as international humanism was premised on the idea that unity could be reached through appeals to common experience, artists and their boosters were nevertheless careful to emphasize that such demands did not compromise individual volition or subordinate artistic intention to a more broadly conceived body politic.

Containing Dance Abroad

Such ideologies and applications of universalism were not limited to the modern dance field during the postwar period. Universalism also became the government's predominant approach to foreign policy with the goal of communist containment. In surprising and troubling ways, the disciplinary practices of modern dancers aligned through a common ideology of universalism with dominant, and exclusive, cultural notions about the nature of humanity as it was constructed in foreign and domestic policy circles.

As it had come to define postwar modern dance practice, universalism came to govern the U.S. approach to communist containment after 1949. The Truman Doctrine,[17] articulated by President Harry Truman in a 1947 address to Congress, featured components of the two competing schools of thought on foreign policy at the time, realism and universalism.[18] Whereas realism dominated Truman's approach between 1947 and 1949, events in 1949, specifically the communist domination of mainland China and the Soviet Union's detonation of an atomic bomb, called into question the realist wisdom of allowing any pocket of communism to flourish in the world for fear that it would proliferate beyond any country's or coalition's control. At the same time, these events gave new cause for fighting a war of ideas, and prompted Truman, who was already predisposed to universalism,[19] to reconsider Kennan's approach to containment. Accepting Kennan's resignation, the president appointed Paul Nitze to his post, and asked him to reevaluate U.S. foreign policy. Nitze and a small group of colleagues responded with the National Security Report of April 1950, NSC-68 (Nitze 1950).[20] "A broadly construed mandate" (Gaddis 2005b, 88),[21] the document made three recommendations aimed at combating the spread of communism across the world: (1) building national strength culturally, militarily, and economically; (2) leading the world by example; (3) precipitating political revolution or "a fundamental change in the nature of the Soviet system" (42). Citing the USSR's aspirations to become the global hegemony, as well as its "development of increasingly terrifying weapons of mass-destruction," the report warned, "every individual faces the ever-present possibility of annihilation should the conflict enter the phase of total war" (38). As the only other world superpower, the United States had a responsibility to the world to stop the "further extension of the area under the domination of the Kremlin." "It is only by developing the moral and material strength of the free world that the Soviet regime will become convinced of the falsity of its assumptions and that the pre-conditions for workable agreements can be created" (43).

The speech, in which the president appealed for aid to Greece and Turkey in order to stop soviet encroachment, constructed the global struggle for democracy in terms that shared a basis of belief with universalism in modern dance. Seeking to win congressional and public support for a heightened U.S. presence in Europe, the president cast the conflict as a choice between two "ways of life," one, "based on the free will of the majority," and another "based upon the will of the minority forcibly imposed upon the majority" (Truman quoted in Gaddis 1972, 351).[22] Truman's threat of U.S. unilateral intervention was decidedly realist, in that it sought to maintain balance within the world order through diplomatic or military counterforce in order to prevent any one country from becoming too powerful (Gaddis 2005b, 28). Yet his rhetoric suggested the universalist underpinnings of his policy in its assumption that both the cause of freedom, and the common desire for democracy among peoples living under the soviet system, would overwhelm the forces of communist encroachment into Western Europe.

According to Christina Klein, a "global imaginary is an ideological creation that maps the world conceptually and defines the primary relations among people, nations, and regions. . . . It creates an imaginary coherence out of the contradictions and disjunctures of real relations, and thereby provides a stable sense of individual and national identity" (2003, 22–23). Klein argues that there were two defining global imaginaries that coexisted during the early cold war years: one organized around containment and the other around integration. Whereas the global imaginary of containment "imagined the Cold War as a crusade against communism and invited the American people to join in," the global imaginary of integration "encouraged Americans to 'look outward,' . . . representing the Cold War as an opportunity to forge intellectual and emotional bonds with the people of Asia and Africa" (23).

Whereas policy positions like NSC-68 demonstrate the application of universalism to the global imaginary of containment, the government's creation of coordinated propaganda programs in the early 1950s evidence a complimentary program of integration. In April 1950, the same month he received NSC-68, Truman announced the "Campaign of Truth" designed, as he put it, to win "a struggle above all else, for the minds of men."[23] He continued, "Unless we get the real story across to people in other countries we will lose the battle for men's minds by default" (Hixson 1997, 14).[24] Based on the universalist assumption that, if given a choice, people across the world would prefer freedom over tyranny, the effort promoted the cross-cultural dissemination of American cultural products, and, by extension, values and ideas. These would not only convince global audiences of the merits of democratic capitalism but would also provide fodder for the instruments of communist persuasion.

Eventually, in 1953, President Eisenhower consolidated these projects and powers in the United States Information Agency (USIA) to coordinate all of the government's information programs (Hixson 1997, 26; see also Elder, 1968, 32–36). According to Theodore C. Streibert, its first director, "Our mission is to show the peoples of other lands by means of communication techniques . . . that our objectives and policies are in harmony and will advance their legitimate aspirations for freedom, progress and peace, meaning that we are trying to identify ourselves with the aims and aspirations of these other people so as to establish a mutuality of interest" (Streibert quoted in Prevots 1998, 12–13). The president's Emergency Fund for International Affairs, established in 1954, was similarly integrationist (Hixson 1997, 136). It allocated monies for similar purposes—participation in trade fairs and exhibitions, and the sponsorship of tours of performing artists. The point was to showcase American cultural achievement as a way of countering the soviet contention that the United States was "a nation of materialists interested primarily in mass production products" (quoted in Hixson 1997, 137; see also Prevots 1998, 13; Martin 2000, 217).[25] Modern dancers were some of the first beneficiaries of the Emergency Fund (Prevots 1998).

Appointed by the Department of State, members of American National Theater and Academy's (ANTA) Dance Advisory Panel played a key role in determining which choreographers and companies would be sent abroad on State Department–sponsored tours.[26] The "Dance Panel," along with other panels for theater and music, functioned in concert with other arms of the U.S. government's project for cultural diplomacy (Prevots 1998, 37–45). In minutes from one of the first meetings, member H. Alwyn Inness-Brown reported a meeting with Eisenhower in which he stated "he was 100 percent behind the program" (April 7, 1955). While the State Department usually "decided which countries and geographic areas were important to American foreign policy and would benefit from an American cultural presence," its decision about whom to send was influenced both by the United States Information Agency, which coordinated embassy requests, and the panels, which recommended particular performers or groups (Prevots 1998, 41).

According to formerly classified minutes taken during panel meetings spanning from December 1954 to April 1962, choreographers and dance companies were selected on a variety of bases, yet all were subject to the collective wisdom of panel participants. Although composition of the panel changed slightly over the years, in general members represented a gamut of involvement in dance from choreographers like Doris Humphrey to critics like Walter Terry and Margaret Lloyd, to patrons like Bethasbée Rothschild and Lucia Chase, to impresarios like Lincoln Kirstein. The panel's originally stated aim, as stated in 1955 (the second year of the panel's existence), was to "bring the very best in entertainment" (April 7, 1955, 2). A year later, the panel formulated a policy of sending "the most representative" and "first-rate" groups first, like the companies of José Limón and Martha Graham (March 10, 1955). Concerns mentioned included making sure tours would not come at the expense of the dance companies themselves—that the government could cover the full cost of the tours, including all company and orchestra members (March 10, 1955). Members also discussed the advantage of longer tours that would enable companies to "give enough performances that the general public is about to see them, and allow enough time so that they can spend some time with the natives" (May 5, 1955).

The panel selected Limón as the first to represent the United States on a monthlong tour of Latin America from December 1954 to January 1955.[27] The Mexican-born choreographer, who was fluent in Spanish, seemed ideally suited to act as a cultural deputy at two important meetings, the conference of the Inter-American Economic and Social Council in Rio de Janeiro, and the UNESCO conference that followed in Montevideo. In addition, Limón performed in São Paulo and Buenos Aires (Martin, November 14, 1954). Programs were drawn from a repertory of fourteen pieces including *The Moor's Pavane* (1949), *La Malinche* (1949), *Ode* (1954), *The Exiles* (1950), *The Visitation* (1952), and *Concerto in D Minor* (1945). The company also performed pieces from artistic director Doris Humphrey's repertory including *Night Spell* (1951), *Ritmo Jondo* (1953), *Ruins and Visions* (1953), *Day on Earth* (1947), *Story of Mankind* (1946), and "Variations and Conclusions" from *New Dance* (1935) (Martin, November 14, 1954).

By most accounts the tour was a success in introducing Limón to Latin American audiences and in whetting their appetite for American modern dance. As Martin proclaimed in comments about the performance in Rio, "They liked it; they loved it; and, from this point on, everything was clear sailing." He continued, "By the end of the third week, the company had invitations to visit virtually every country from Spain to Iceland. If the State Department has its way, most of the invitations will be accepted, beginning next fall" (Martin, January 23, 1955). While not so soon, the State Department sponsored the Limón company on another tour, this time to Poland in 1957. Quite popular there, his last performance in Warsaw drew 20,000 people. As one reviewer commented about his run in Pozan, "It is not important whether we are for or against expressionism in dancing. . . . One must state that Americans have shown themselves to be of the highest class" ("Limón Ends Polish Trip," October 23, 1957). Judging from this account from Pozan, Limón's tour was successful in propagating not only the ideology and practice of modern dance universalism but also the benefits of capitalism through modern dancing bodies "showing themselves to be of the highest class."

Graham was the next choreographer sent abroad. She and her company toured Southeast Asia between October 1955 and February 1956, performing works from her present repertory including *Appalachian Spring* and *Night Journey*. Although she had preferred to return to Europe (where she had traveled in 1950, to London and Paris, and in 1954, to London) the offer of government sponsorship convinced her otherwise (Prevots 1998, 44). In Asia, Graham's company performed in Myanmar (then Burma), India, Pakistan, Japan, the Philippines, Thailand, Indonesia, Malaysia (then Malaya), Sri Lanka (then Ceylon), Iran, and Israel (46–50; see also Dance Advisory Panel minutes, January 19, 1956). Graham's trip was tracked through the dance press, which quoted reviews by foreign critics as well as excerpts from letters Graham had written to the editors of *Dance Observer* during her trip. From Madras, India, for example, Graham wrote to editorial staff of *Dance Observer*, "Dancers speak only one language . . . that of inner experience; and that makes the fundamental language of the world" (Tassovin 1956, 41). And from Dacca Pakistan, Graham related, "The fact that this is a Moslem state makes it possible for us to have about 25 women in the audience of the native populace. Some wear the big veils still, with a small decorated little window for eyes . . . I cannot get over the sensation of otherness which I do not have in the Buddhist countries. There is a fierceness here, and to go on the streets is strange in that there are no women, or few" ("News Items," February 1956, 25).

While in her correspondence Graham reflected on her perceptions of foreign peoples and her impression of their opinions about her and her work, coverage in *Dance Observer* highlighted the ways in which Graham's performances redeemed negative impressions of the United States. In its "digest of newspaper clippings and letters from . . . Graham's tour," the magazine featured this extended quotation from William D. Hull, Fulbright Visiting Lecturer in American Literature at University of Ceylon: "Except for the works of William Faulkner," he observed, "the Graham dance is the clearest incarnation of that inner, often unrevealed to the rest of the world, American spirit that has shaped the core of my country and has kept and is keeping, its material prepossessions from swamping it. Hers is religious dancing, if to be religious means always to be searching to renew one's sense of the ultimate source of human growth and victory, so that one may not conquer but become one's self" (Tassovin 1956, 41). Another example is the account of the *Hindustani Standard*'s report of one performance in Calcutta, India, in which famous Indian choreographer Uday Shankar was seen seated "in the front row of performances shouting 'Bravo, Bravo!'" The magazine also quoted Shankar as saying that *Appalachian Spring* was a "much needed corrective to be set against the picture of the fat, well-fed, cigar-smoking American" (41).

Graham's tour was also touted by U.S. officials as having made inroads in the effort of winning the war of ideas because of its universal appeal and ability to "speak" in a language common to all. In testimony before the Senate Committee on Foreign Affairs February 21, 1956, Theodore Streibert, head of the United States Information Agency (USIA), remarked, "The enthusiastic reception which has been accorded touring American dance companies is added proof that dance is a language in itself which can transcend national boundaries and native language barriers." Noting that Graham's tour of South Asia had ended successfully he said, "Although modern dance, as such, was practically unknown in many countries in which the company appeared, the public acceptance and enthusiasm for the company's performances were immediate and overwhelming." His testimony also included extensive accounts from foreign sources or Americans living abroad. Some, like this account from the U.S. Embassy in Tokyo, were similar in their focus to that of *Dance Observer* in highlighting the benefit of seeing quality modern dance. According to the embassy staff,

> Miss Graham's presence was a revelation to the Japanese. Her work disclosed a theater of drama and emotion the Japanese thought Americans could not create. Her austere presentation of human emotions moved then to comparisons with the highly developed Japanese theater (Noh and Kabuki) rather than with the Japanese dance alone. The uniquely American aspect of her art with its original choreography, music, costuming and stage settings was eloquent ideological testimony of American's cultural depth and vitality. The Japanese had to see this creative genius and sense its dramatic and emotional appeal to acknowledge its existence. (Streibert 1956, 25)

Streibert's presentation also made it appear as though sending modern dancers abroad had led to gains on several fronts in the war of ideas. Quoting from a review from the *Times* of Indonesia he related, "If ever this paper came perilously close to forgetting its policy of leaning neither to the East nor the West, it was during the Martha Graham week, because this talented woman presented something of the United States that we could wholeheartedly approve of. We, for one, hope that it will be made possible for Miss Graham to be with us again soon; if not, we shall construe it an unfriendly act on the part of the United States" (Streibert 1956, 25).

Similarly he relayed an upbeat report from the American embassy in Rangoon estimating that during Graham's five-day run nearly 4,000 people attended each evening. According to Streibert, "The Embassy indicated that it was particularly fortunate that the Graham company performed there so shortly after the visit of the soviet leaders Khrushchev and Bulganin, as it kept very favorable publicity about the United States on the front pages of the Burmese newspapers and showed that our country had not lost interest in Burma" (1956, 25).

Yet not all the press coverage was positive.[28] An account of Graham's reception in Singapore by *The Free Press* disclosed that Graham had "considerably curtailed both her troupe's personnel and material . . . on the premise that we who live here are restricted in acquaintance with Western cultural values" ("News Items," 1956, 24). And in its synopsis of "new items" from the tour in March 1956, *Dance Observer* reported "press opinion" in New Delhi, India, "that showed sharp divergences of taste." Whereas the *Times of India* described Graham as having "what is more lasting than beauty, more gracious than grace—the quality of sudden vision and sustained recollection," the critic for *The Statesman* found fault with both *Appalachian Spring* and *Night Journey*. Of this first, he wrote, "The fault may be mine, but there must be something wrong with a gesture language that escapes one's grasp so totally." Of the second, he expressed dismay at the "wrong conception to show the lovemaking between mother and son on stage" ("More News Items," 1956, 41). While vague in detail, these reports suggest both that the Graham company might have tailored their program according to their assumptions about particular cultural audiences, perhaps guessing wrong in the case of the performances in New Delhi, and that not everyone who saw the performances perceived either the form or the content in the same terms as did their promoters.

Accounts of Limón's and Graham's tours, by the artists themselves and their proxies, are vivid examples of the troubling compatibility of universalism in postwar modern dance with the political aims of the U.S. government's war of ideas. Showcasing the accomplishments of American dance artists, the tours aimed to demonstrate the superiority of American artistic ingenuity, the seriousness of artistic pursuit, and the autonomy of the artist under a capitalist democracy. Fundamentally suspicious of alliances between art and politics, the Dance Panel ironically "got behind" the touring program because it featured choreography they deemed "universal" and, therefore, transcendent of politics, even as it was being put to explicit political uses. Ironically, the reporting in *Dance Observer* of statements from foreign press outlets complicated the dance establishment's integrationist story line heralding the compatibility of universalism with the diversity of the world's people.

Contrary foreign accounts of the tours, in fact, begin to reveal cracks within the discourse of integrationist universalism, exposing the subtext of containment that permeated its ideology and practices, and undermining claims that dance could operate independently of politics as well as establishment paeans to global unity. According to Foucault, "Power exists only as exercised by some on others, only when it is put into action, even though, of course, it is inscribed in a field of sparse available possibilities underpinned by permanent structures" (1994, 340). In line with state exertions of power through its information programs, universalism in postwar modern dance offered a theory and a system of disciplinary practices through which representatives of the state, like Streibert, members of the modern dance establishment, and even foreign proxies like Shankar or U.S.-sympathetic news organizations, could conduct the cultural work of containment.

In part these were "dividing practices" (Foucault 1994, 326), meant to objectify difference and divide the familiar from the "alien" based on normative notions of the human. This is well illustrated in Graham's account of her experience in Pakistan: on the one hand, her impression of the "fierceness here," as well as her surprise that there were only "about 25 women in the audience of the native populace," and that "some wear the big veils still, with a small decorated window for eyes," and, on the other hand, her perception of her own "otherness" in Muslim countries as compared with Buddhist ones. It is also revealed in Graham's decision to change her concert program, as was the case with her performance in Singapore, to suit what of "Western cultural values" she believed audiences were prepared to see.

In part, these were tactics of elision, which, in spite of overtures to the recognition of cultural diversity and tolerance, sought to erase difference in the cause of global unity. Consider, for example, universalism's central presumptions, that the dancing body was both a medium and metaphor for a global constituency (Martin), or that modern dance facilitated a cross-cultural encounter, absent politics, that rendered "alien" bodies familiar to one another (Terry). As Graham put it in her posting from India, "Dancers speak only one language . . . that of inner experience; and that makes the fundamental language of the world." Or as Streibert exclaimed, "The enthusiastic reception which has been accorded touring American dance companies is added proof that dance is a language in itself which can transcend national boundaries and native languages." Accounts such as these were founded on the belief that, by the postwar period, modern dance had developed in such a way as to transcend its very disciplinary and historical particularities. Exponents used this idea, in turn, not only to elevate their own dance practices over others they perceived to be more culturally and/or historically bound, but also to dismiss the contributions of so-deemed cultural others to the formation of modern dance and to see as inferior the myriad forms engendered by their work. Other tactics of elision, such as Lloyd's proclamation that modern dance had been "interracial from the start," or unqualified narratives of the form's progress, in her case, toward "world consciousness," provided pithy tropes and compelling thematic avenues by which to sidestep the history of racism within the history of the form itself.[29] Still other strategies of elision are seen in exponents' accounts of the moment of audience reception. Couched in essentialist terms, as an "inherent contagion of bodily movement" or "the most intangible emotional experience" (Martin), these strategies associated modern dance with experiences of ritual or differently reached transformation. Moreover, as we will see throughout this book, such strategies also silenced the voices of diverse and/or dissenting dancers and dance makers both outside and within the modern dance community for whom this description rang false.

As much as it suggested an accommodation of heterogeneous approaches to dancing and dance making, universalism in postwar modern dance was far from inclusive. Its integrationist discourse, founded upon the new American internationalism, belied a dominant privilege that undercut the dance establishment's aspirations of tolerance through its various acts of containment. According to the premise that the white Western subject was the normative embodiment of universal human experience, the artistic establishment, through the Dance Panel's mandate, exerted universalism in various ways through its system of aesthetic and formal prerogatives. All of these could be mapped onto various constituencies, either in the global context, denoting, for example, distinctions between "modern" and "ethnic" or "ethnological" dances, but also in the local context of the American modern dance community along racial, ethnic, or sexual lines. Nevertheless, regardless of their context, these prerogatives designated what was "familiar" and what was "alien," what was "human" and what was "nonhuman," what was "universal" and what was culturally particular, and what was "modern dance" and what was not.

Containing Dance at Home

The same forces of containment exerted through postwar modern dance universalism abroad were similarly applied at home, translated through McCarthyist anticommunism. Events of 1948 "suddenly opened wide gaps in the [Truman] Administration's anti-communist program" (Free-land 1972, 341). These events included the indictment of Alger Hiss, who served as Assistant Secretary of State for the Far East and who had "personally delivered the UN charter to President Truman," on perjury charges related to his testimony to the House Un-American Activities Committee (HUAC) (Fried 1990, 18); and the U.S. withdrawal of military aid to China following the resignation of Chiang Kai-shek. In turn, these events fanned the fires of eroding public trust in the government's effectiveness in containing the spread of communism at home and abroad. Senator Joseph McCarthy's February 1950 speech in Wheeling, West Virginia, just one month after Hiss had been convicted, capitalized on the situation.[30] McCarthy stated, "I have here in my hand a list of 205 members of the Communist party who today are in high offices in the State Department making U.S. policy, and they are known to Secretary Dean Acheson" (quoted in Ewald 1986, 7).[31] Although McCarthy admitted that the State Department "knows of no Communists who are presently employed," as Stephen Whitfield relates, "the damage had been done. A single perjury conviction was to have enormous repercussions in aggravating the public concern that growing Soviet power had already provoked" (1996, 29). This speech ushered in the era of domestic anticommunism, "a political phenomenon that extended well beyond the antics of Senator McCarthy—indeed beyond the boundaries of conventional politics" (Fried 1990, 9; see also Schrecker 1994, 1).

Klein speaks to the cultural impact of domestic anticommunism through "the global imaginary of containment," which, she argues, "translated anticommunism into a structure of feeling and set of social and cultural practices that could be lived at the level of everyday life." She continues, "Fear served as the emotional glue that held this imagined world together: fear of Soviet expansion abroad, of communist subversion at home, of nuclear war. The logic of containment rendered deviance in all its forms—sexual, political, behavioral—a source of anxiety and an object of investigation" (2003, 36). As I will discuss later in this chapter, as well as throughout the book, the politics of domestic containment also had a significant if diffused impact on postwar modern dance production and reception. This is seen specifically in the ways dance artists negotiated relationships between personal, formal, and political commitments in the context of their aesthetic practices. Of concern here, however, are the ways in which the projects of state anticommunism and modern dance universalism co-incided in Dance Panel actions concerning funding and touring.

As formerly argued, while universalism implied that all modern dance forms, and dancing bodies, were equal in their ability to express the human condition through the movement, in reality this was not the case. The double standard that operated within modern dance universalism permeated Dance Panel meetings. Clearly members valued certain choreographic modes over others, deeming inadequate those that did not meet their standards and dismissing others that blatantly challenged their principles. In myriad ways, these determinations, which conveyed establishment privilege, performed the work of normalization. Affiliation with the powers of the state not only legitimized and lent consequence to panel decisions, but provided new terms on which to police dance practices as well as the authority to penalize those choreographers whose work fell short of the mark.

Minutes of the panel, which recorded discussion of requests by choreographers for government funding for tours abroad, provide a vivid example of these operations. While members expressed their opinions through comments about "quality" or "method," their conclusions revolved around their narrowly construed concept of dance modernism. Of the choreographers I am examining in this book only two, Limón and Graham, were selected to represent U.S. interests abroad before 1961. These were choreographers whose work members agreed was most exemplary of modern dance. African American Alvin Ailey was funded and sent to the Far East in 1962, but only after several rejections and extensive discussion about the merits of his aesthetic. Susan Manning rightly argues that Ailey's funding is likely explained on the basis of his acquiescence to the establishment's reigning aesthetic, fusing, in Manning's words "black self-representation and mythic abstraction" (2004, 186). Moreover Katherine Dunham, Anna Sokolow, Pearl Primus, Merce Cunningham, and Alwin Nikolais were all ultimately denied funding. Talley Beatty never applied and Donald McKayle, who had toured with Graham in 1955, was approved by the panel for funding but was never sent abroad through this program (Prevots 1998, 107–8).

Prevots' analysis of the sociopolitical implications of the panel's rejections, especially as they pertain to the applications of African-American choreographers, is astute. She shows that, in the cases of those like Dunham and Primus, whose funding the panel denied, and of those like Ailey, whose funding the panel delayed, members acted ambivalently.[32] Cognizant of the significance of sending black choreographers and their companies abroad in light of the nascent mobilization for civil rights, the panel appeared to look favorably upon the applications of choreographers of color. According to Prevots, "there was no specific pressure from the State Department, the USIA, or ANTA to include black artists, nor was there any pressure from any particular panel members. What seems to have prompted the inclusion of African-American artists in the program was a growing awareness of their importance and the importance of their heritage to American dance" (1998, 94).

Yet there are unmistakable and salient parallels between the way in which the U.S. government handled its "negro problem" abroad and the dance panel handled its "negro problem" at home. As Thomas Borstelmann has demonstrated, "the Cold War focus on the ideals of democracy and freedom assured that racial exceptions to the American practice of those principles would receive careful attention" (2001, 74). In its efforts to cultivate the world for democracy, the racial double standard that existed across the United States, either institutionalized through Jim Crow or de facto segregationism, became the government's "Achilles heel" during the postwar years (Von Eschen 1997 109–44; Dudziak 2000; Borstelmann 2001, 45–84). To foreign peoples, segregation and racial prejudice across America ran contrary to American overtures to "freedom" and "equality." To counteract this impression, the government employed so-called communication techniques, coordinated among information and education agencies, seeking to "turn the story of race in America into a story of the superiority of democracy over communism as a system of government" (Dudziak 2000, 15). This included sending black performers and performing companies abroad (Von Eschen 2004) as well as disseminating countervailing information through educational programs and brochures (Dudziak 2000, 47–78; Klein 2003). Likewise, the deployment of universalism within modern dance as a tactic of elision glossed over a troubled racial history while, at the same time, advancing narratives that represented the opposite.

African-American artists did make significant inroads to equality within modern dance during the postwar years. As Manning argues, the period saw the "disappearance" of the term "Negro dance," convening "a time when the divided historiography of modern dance and black concert dance was beginning to give way to an intercultural historiography" (2004, 179). And yet, even as they found increasing professional opportunities and critical receptivity to their work within the dance sphere,[33] they faced blatant hostility and prejudice in the world at large. Nowhere is this more apparent than in Donald McKayle's anecdote of his experience catching a cab home from the hospital after the birth of his first daughter. Having recently arrived from an ANTA-sponsored tour of Europe and the Middle East as a member of the Graham dance company, McKayle was rebuffed by a driver as he tried to hail a cab outside Mount Sinai. The driver passed by McKayle to pick up Stuart Hodes, a white member of the company whose daughter had been born within days of McKayle's. When Hodes invited McKayle and his wife to share the cab, the cabbie explained "Thought you were going to Harlem." As McKayle relates, "We chose to shun him silently. Cuddled together against the blustering winter wind, we started our journey home and our new lives as parents" (2002, 111). Equal to Hodes in the context of the Graham company, his body an analogous conveyer of American universalism through the idiom of modern dance, McKayle's experience with the cabby also served as an ironic indicator of how arbitrary his status as a black man could be depending on who was looking.

Not as blatant as McKayle's experience with the cabby, and in spite of the progress African-American dance artists had made within the field of modern dance, they still faced prejudice often masked under debates about authenticity or quality. Consider the Dance Panel's handling of deliberations concerning Dunham and Primus. Both artists applied and were rejected numerous times by the panel on the grounds that their work under consideration for touring was substandard. In Dunham's case, prior to panel consideration of the appropriateness of her work for state-sponsored international touring, the artist had already experienced the scorn of government sanction. Dunham's *Southland*, which enacted a racially motivated lynching in the American South, aroused the ire of American officials on its premier in Santiago, Chile, in 1951 (as further discussed in chapter 6).[34] In Hill's words, "While reprisal on the part of the State Department was indeed insidious, it was at first invisible. *Southland* was immediately suppressed in Santiago: the company was forced to leave within days. There were no more reviews; nothing more was written, and nothing was publicly said; what followed was a cold and sustained silence" (2002, 304–5). Performed for the last time in Paris in 1953, the work nevertheless gave Dunham a reputation as a political liability. On an extensive tour with her company of South America in 1954, Dunham's opening in Montevideo coincided with that of Limón (a concert that had been funded by ANTA). That night, "the American Embassy hosted a cocktail party for Limón, but did not invite Dunham" (Prevots 1998, 103; see also Hill 2002). Moreover, American officials convinced Dunham's impresario to attend Limón's performance rather than hers (Hill 2002, 309).

These experiences caused Dunham to question the fairness of Dance Panel deliberations. After several rounds of rejection and tours to Australia, New Zealand, and the Far East in 1956 and 1957, in 1958 she petitioned the panel for additional consideration. According to minutes, members agreed that "Miss Dunham is a great artist and a great showman, and should be given the fullest consideration." Yet some, specifically Alfred Frankenstein, expressed reservations based on his attendance at a recent concert in which Dunham "had become theatrical in the cheapest sense. There was no authenticity; it was night club material" (Dance Advisory Panel Minutes, March 20, 1958). Panel members agreed to revisit the issue after having attended another of Dunham's performances. Incensed, Dunham fought back in an interview published in *International Variety* magazine that May. "The State Department has given us no recognition whatsoever, and it is becoming increasingly difficult for me in giving interviews to canny press to cover up for what could look like discrimination to the rest of the world" (Dunham quoted in Prevots 1998, 104). In spite of its purported sensitivity to issues of racial equality, the panel never did fund Dunham.

Nor did it fund Primus, who received similar treatment. Like Dunham, Primus had traveled extensively, in her case for a year in 1949 to Africa where she visited and studied over thirty ethnic groups (as discussed in chapter 4). On her return, Primus suspended many of her artistic activities in favor of lecture demonstrations, although she continued to perform in venues like Greenwich Village's Café Society ("Genuine Africa," 1951, 98).[35] When considering Primus' applications, panel members commented that her work was "far too untheatrical, and the company was amateurish. Also, Miss Primus is about thirty pounds overweight. On this basis the project was not acceptable to the Panel" (Dance Advisory Panel Minutes, December 22, 1955).

The cases of Dunham and Primus demonstrate ways in which racial double standards pervaded panel deliberations on the applications of black artists. Their applications tended to be turned down on the grounds that their work did not meet the panel's standards of quality (the work was either too "cheap," too "untheatrical," or too "amateurish"). By contrast, submissions by white choreographers were dismissed on aesthetic grounds (too "confusing and abstract," too "'confusing and depressing"). These determinations suggest that panel members thought the balance of work submitted for consideration by black choreographers did not even meet their bar for rejection on aesthetic grounds. By contrast, the panel's response to white artists like Cunningham, Nikolais, or Sokolow discloses members' anxiety about what were perceived to be more overt threats to their conception of universalist modern dance.

Discussion of several proposals by Cunningham illustrate the latter. In spite of some dissension within its ranks, the panel repeatedly turned down applications made by the choreographer on the grounds that his work "did not represent modern dance." In 1955, for example, it turned down a proposal that he be included on a tour of India, Ceylon, Thailand, and Indonesia with composers John Cage and David Tudor, even though the Music Advisory Panel had approved the total package. Cage and composer Virgil Thomson appealed the decision, which panel member Lincoln Kirstein had also protested, to no avail. Martha Hill justified her rejection of Cunningham saying that his work was "'way out on the fringes of American dance' and is confusing and abstract" while Doris Humphrey spoke about how "it is not a good idea to send someone in whom we don't believe" (Dance Advisory Panel Minutes, October 13, 1955). Because "the Panel does not approve of what he does artistically with other dancers," members resolved to ask him to "consider going without the company." Although it "asked John Cage to present a new plan for a recital demonstration on contemporary music, in association with Merce Cunningham, with an accent on music," Cage, Tudor, and Cunningham ultimately were not funded (ibid.; see also September 14, 1955, and November 17, 1955).[36]

Later, in 1958, the panel again turned down applications by Cunningham as well as Alwin Nikolais for similar reasons. The Dance Panel's justified its 1958 refusal of Nikolais' work by the following statement: "His use of the body is inhuman. He used it as a 'mobile,' completely motionless at times. As a single attraction it is not representative of dance in general" (Prevots 1998, 59–60). Margaret Lloyd protested the decision in a letter she wrote in lieu of her attendance at the panel meeting in 1958. She advocated that "Alwin Nikolais and Merce Cunningham [be considered] as possible dancers who might tour for the program, even though they might be regarded as too avant-garde and mystifying. They both have excellent companies and their works pique the imagination and these artists present views of dance and its endless possibilities for development." She argued, in conclusion, that it was important to sponsor "those artists who are adventuring on a cultural level beyond easy grasp. Good thing for any public to have to reach once and a while" (Lloyd quoted in Prevots 1998, 59, source not cited).

It should be pointed out that Anna Sokolow, a Jewish-American choreographer, was also rejected for touring even though her work more closely conformed with dance establishment expectations of form. Nevertheless, the panel denied Sokolow funding on the basis of her work's content. While members expressed "the highest respect for her as an artist," they thought key works in her repertory were unsuitable for foreign consumption. Terry commented, "her work is good and very exciting, but certain of her chief works ('Metamorphosis' and 'Rooms') would escape foreign audiences. They are stimulating to Americans but they are confusing and depressing to an audience who have nothing to compare them with" (Dance Advisory Panel Minutes, December 22, 1955). Because her work was rejected on aesthetic grounds, Sokolow appears to have met the panel's standards of quality assumed of white artists. This demonstrates that in the eyes of panel members, her work was "modern" and not "ethnic," or, more damningly, "revolutionary." If anything, had she been privy to deliberations, she may have seen a silver lining in this assessment, as we will see in chapter 3, as it represented acceptance by members of the artistic establishment that had been withheld during the 1940s. Like all of the other choreographers rejected for touring by the panel, Sokolow was seen by the panel to make work that in one way or another called into question hegemonic cultural values and the dominant vision of the nation. Yet, as we will see in the next chapter, which looks at ANTA-featured choreography by Limón and Graham, this was not a litmus test for funding.

Conclusion: Converging Ideologies of Universalism— Some Contradictions

Study of the formation of postwar dance universalism, as well as its operation within the context of the touring program, reveals the degree to which the ideology of the modern dance establishment and the state had converged by the 1950s. Artists and dance critics/theorists contributed to a contradictory postwar project, a project that simultaneously extricated modern dance practices from their political genesis in the 1930s and reconstructed them in ways that matched the contradictory concerns of the postwar sociopolitical hegemony. A high point of state sponsorship of modern dance, inclusion in state-sponsored touring bestowed upon modern dance artists and upon the form itself a sense of cultural legitimacy that had long been pursued. Modern dance and American dominant culture had finally meshed.

That said, the touring program was an unlikely pairing of art and politics. Support for the employment of modern dance in state affairs did not happen automatically or without anxiety. During the postwar era, under McCarthyist anticommunism, Depression era coziness between the artistic and the political presented a problem both for government officials and for artists and their supporters. In spite of efforts to the contrary, residue of Depression era debates about the relation of art and propaganda colored the dialogue. To counteract suspicion of politicization, dance artists and exponents deployed universalism, arguing that modern dance was a universal and, therefore, transcendent human language not beholden to any socially or culturally contingent commitments, and that it derived from the material of universal human experience. As much as it mitigated fears about the exploitation of artists for political gain, this formulation also represented a thematic coupling that was advantageous to the aims of containment: "freedom" as paramount to the creative process as it was to democracy. In these ways, universalism in modern dance aligned with hegemonic cultural constructions and applications of containment in the struggle to "win the minds of men." Establishment modern dance flourished in this climate inasmuch as it secured a cultural foundation on which to build itself as an institution.

Yet Dance Panel deliberations disclose an atmosphere of contention within the modern dance field as artistic challenges to established modes of doing—by those within its ranks as well as from choreographic upstarts—opened a rift that had aesthetic, cultural, and political implications. Under these conditions, members of the Dance Panel took on the responsibility of policing the boundaries of modern dance from within, acting to rein in difference of all stripes through its pecuniary mandate. What was considered "modern dance" was also what was thought to be most representative of American cultural values. As the balance of this book will bear out, a signifier of a more encompassing social dynamic of provocation and counteraction, the coordination illustrated here between artistic and state apparatuses constituted both a consolidation of power relations (agon) *and* an impetus for the mobilization (antagonism) of the "whole social body."[37]

[2]

PRECURSORS TO ACTION

Martha Graham and José Limón

CHAPTER 1 examined ways in which universalism in modern dance harmonized with the national project of communist containment in the early cold war years. Coordination occurred within the context of the international touring program, funded under President Eisenhower's Emergency Fund for International Affairs, aimed at "winning the minds of men" through the promotion of American cultural values as conveyed through the work of performing artists. Additionally, as I have explained in the previous chapter, the project was conducted through the deliberations of the ANTA Dance Panel, a decision-making body comprised of members of the American dance establishment, charged with evaluating and selecting applicants for funding. In spheres foreign and domestic, representatives of the U.S. government and their proxies performed the cultural work of containment—aimed not only at communists, or so-thought communist sympathizers, but diverse groups of Americans whose lives did not comply with normative standards. Within both artistic and political contexts, choreographers José Limón and Martha Graham were designated as standard-bearers: they and their work were seen to epitomize universalism in modern dance and to promote integrationist international relations.

This is not the whole story of modern dance during the postwar years, however. At the same time that modern dance came to prominence as an American cultural institution, aligning itself with hegemonic formations of containment, modern dance artists negotiated containment's repressive cultural effects. This chapter begins to assess the effects of the culture of containment on artists and the work they produced during the postwar years, in this case its impact on members of the dance establishment Martha Graham and José Limón, the first modern dancers to be sent abroad under the Emergency Fund. I look specifically at Graham's *Appalachian Spring* (1944) and *Night Journey* (1947) and Limón's *The Moor's Pavane* (1949), all of which were performed on international tours.[1] Apparently, each piece fulfilled the criteria for selection for touring, embodying universalism in penetrating, archetypal character studies thought to have transcendent cultural significance. Moreover, as discussed in the previous chapter, each exemplified an artistic process that valued autonomy over political content, thereby coupling notions of "freedom" in art and democracy.

This chapter endeavors to read these works against the grain already established—as precursors to action that used the dancing body to gainsay the governmental apparatus of containment by critiquing one of its prized institutions during the postwar years, heterosexual matrimony. In the context of the forces of normalization within the domestic culture of containment, these dances clearly illuminate the difficulties of marriage. Both Graham and Limón enlisted the ambiguity afforded by both the medium of movement and modern dance universalism (specifically its adaptation of canonical literary texts) to contradict conventional wisdom that marriage was a "natural" institution between a man and a woman. Yet in all these cases, strained, or even toxic, marital relations are indicated as symptoms of a more endemic cultural problem: the rigorously prescriptive environment surrounding gender formation. The portrayal of troubled marriages is, therefore, a means to related ends: the substantiation of alternative kinds of masculinity and femininity as embodied by the characters. Ironically, when seen in this light, modern dance universalism offered cover for the embodied expression, if opaque, of oppositional ideals, even as it supported an alignment between the ideologies of the dance establishment and the state.

Normalcy and the Domestic Culture of Containment

Domestic life during the postwar years was a time of enormous transformation, out of the "hot" World War II and into the "cold" war against communism waged abroad as well as at home. Widespread fear about the implications of significant social change for gender roles and family life caused a palpable and prevalent anxiety among Americans (Chafe 1991).[2] The maintenance of traditional values, as well as a focus on the importance of individual adjustment, became ways that people mitigated their unease.[3] Sociologists David Riesman's *The Lonely Crowd* and William Whyte's *Organization Man* made these social trends widely apparent, in

1950 and then 1957, respectively. Both documented the impact on individuals of societal pressures to conform—the necessity people felt to regulate idiosyncratic impulses and sublimate their personal needs to those of a group to feel as though they belonged. They also depicted the daily-life plights of people who struggled to define themselves amidst social forces hostile to their growth and self-realization. According to Riesman and Whyte, many people sought comfort in living within extremes. When faced with conflict, they adjusted. When confronted, they sublimated personal goals, feelings, and desires for the good of the group. Mastering the art of self-regulation, they strove above all to cooperate with others.[4]

The repressive cultural climate of the early cold war years reinforced this tendency toward conformity. In this environment, difference was mapped onto broader concerns about antidemocratic subversion. A comment by then FBI director J. Edgar Hoover[5] illustrates containment's applications in the sphere of gender normativity. In response to the question of whether the American people should "change our sex standards," he replied, "It is important to the very future of our national life that we hold fast to our faith. Man's sense of decency declares what is normal and what is not. Whenever the American people, young or old, come to believe that there is no such thing as right or wrong, normal or abnormal, those who would destroy our civilization will applaud a major victory over our way of life" (quoted in "Must We Change Our Sex Standards?," June 1948, 6).

The impact of the culture of containment on domestic life cannot be underestimated (E. May 1988, Chafe 1991 Spigel 1992). Cold warriors, like Hoover, cast the nuclear family and its members as key players in the national project of ensuring stability. The family symbolized the nation's "way of life"—in economic as well as political terms—a primary weapon against the presumed tyranny of socialist and communist governments (E. May 1988). During the postwar "baby boom," between 1945 and 1962, both men and women married earlier than they had previously: the average age of marriage for women was twenty and for men twenty-two (Weiss 2000, 17). Jessica Weiss argues that "the youthful ages of marriage that characterized the late 1940s and early 1950s heralded a shift from prewar assumptions about the place of marriage in the life cycle" (17). She adds that in many cases, social prescriptions against premarital sex hastened the decision to marry early, "Youthful marriage relieved women of the burden of setting the limits on premarital sexual exploration, worry over pregnancy, and loss of reputation" (25). Driven by these social forces, the number of marriages increased dramatically during the war years (1,452,394 in 1944) and peaked after the war (2,291,045 in 1946) (Weiss 2000, 22), as did the number of live births, which numbered 3,817,000 in 1947 compared with 2,939,000 in 1944 (Carter, et al., "Table Ab11–30").[6]

At the same time as society enthroned gender ideals as realized in marriage, it disparaged all kinds of gender or sexual deviance, attaching a stigma even to being single (Breines 1992). "In a 1957 study by the University of Michigan, an astonishing 80 percent of adults said that a woman must be sick, neurotic, or immoral to remain unmarried" (Steinhorn 2006, 7). Put into the language of the time, "the unmarried individual occupied a position in society generally considered by social theorists as dysfunctional in the social structure, a position that was out of step with the normative pattern of living."[7] According to Barbara Ehrenreich, in an age when "adult masculinity was indistinguishable from the breadwinner role, then it followed that the man who failed to achieve this role was either not fully adult or not fully masculine" (Ehrenreich 1983, 20). Interpreted as a sign of immaturity—which, at the time, was one euphemism for homosexuality—a person's decision to live outside of marriage caused great suspicion (Ehrenreich 1983). An unmarried person's nonconformity, or adoption of characteristics or proclivities associated with someone of the opposite sex, was seen as a symptom of social maladjustment or worse, arrested or deviant psychological development.

Policing of sexual difference escalated along with concerns about homosexual invisibility, raising the question of whether it was possible to discern a person's sexual identity on the basis of appearance, behavior, or marital status (D'Emilio 1983, 1989; Berube 1990). The culture of domestic containment raised the stakes for nonconformist behavior, equating sexual difference with communist subversion (Whitfield 1996; Johnson 2004). A comment by Senator Kenneth Wherry of Nebraska baldly illustrates: "you can't . . . separate homosexuals from subversives . . . . I don't say every homosexual is a subversive, and I don't say that every subversive is a homosexual. But a man of low morality is a menace in the government, whatever he is, and they are tied up together" (quoted in Whitfield [1991] 1996, 43). As Stephen Whitfield has observed, "in an era that fixed so rigidly the distinction between Communist tyranny and the Free World, and which prescribed that men were men and women were housewives, perhaps only one peril seemed, if anything, worse than Communism"—homosexuality (ibid.). Bigotry and ignorance concerning homosexuality bred widespread discrimination against gays and lesbians during the postwar years, and held in place "the matrix of religious beliefs, laws, medical theories, and popular attitudes that devalued and punished [them]" (D'Emilio 1983, 40).

Modern dance makers experienced the effects of containment on multiple fronts. In the first place, as I have discussed in chapter 1, the culture of anticommunism necessitated that artists cultivate a remove from the political sphere. In *The Borzoi Book of Modern Dance* (1949), Margaret Lloyd spoke to this point:

> There are no reds in modern dance today. Once there were left-wingers who, with bare feet thrust up from the ankles and fists doubled out from the wrists, outdid dancing with polemics. "Dance is a Weapon" was their battle cry. . . . Their ardor was restrained by progress (their own, not the world's) as they learned to distinguish between political diatribes and dance—long before it became dangerous to follow any but the two-party line. Now, of course, the left wings are all tucked out of sight. Only right wings (with liberal spread) are to be seen. (173–74)[8]

Lloyd's description of the political heyday of modern dance is striking, as much for its depiction of the forces inherent in the severing of the alliance between dance and the radical left as for its nostalgia. Apparently sympathetic to the politics of the Workers Dance League and groups like it, Lloyd depicted the problem of form and content as one that was eventually resolved to the idiom's advantage—"progress . . . in learning to distinguish between political diatribes and dance." Lloyd's account is a useful indicator both of the chilling effect of domestic containment on artistic political ardor and of the move toward the "liberal" center among artists who increasingly disavowed their former political leanings or removed themselves from the political arena altogether.

Dance artists also experienced containment in terms closer to home, as its ideology impinged upon their personal lives. According to standards at the time, many modern dancers, like many other artists, lived unconventional lives. Most did not marry, and, if they did, tended not to have children. Others had lovers out of wedlock, affairs that were sometimes homosexual. Take Martha Graham and José Limón for example. Graham did not marry dancer Erick Hawkins (many years her junior) until she was in her early forties (in 1948), although they had been lovers since the mid-1930s and living together secretly for several years before (de Mille [1956] 1991, 255–56, 283). They separated two years later and Graham never re-married (299–300).[9] Limón lived communally during the 1930s with Doris Humphrey, Charles Weidman, and Pauline Lawrence (Humphrey had a long-distance marriage) (Foulkes 2002, 36). He and Weidman were lovers, and, even after he and Lawrence married, they still lived with Humphrey and Weidman until Weidman left for a love affair with a man in 1939 (95). Given the circumstances of their lives and the decisions they made, these and other modern dancers, as Americans whose life choices were markedly different from the norm, had a lot at stake in the public debate about gender roles and sexual identity and how these factors played into discussions about national security. Few were outspoken on these issues; instead, they enacted their opposition more or less in their embodied practices.

Martha Graham's Feminine Mystique

Graham's 1945 New York season received rave reviews, owing much to *Appalachian Spring* (1944), which portrayed a pioneer wedding accompanied by Aaron Copland's Pulitzer Prize-winning score. As I argued in chapter 1, *Appalachian Spring* resonated with the societal desire to bring closure to the war years. Its enactment of a wedding was a harbinger of the reunions to come, a return to what some would call "normalcy." In its representation of a wedding, Graham's work signified normalcy in a recognizable package—two young white Americans marrying.[10] Gearing up for the return of GIs from battlefields abroad, Americans at home enshrined anticipated reunions in images of young married couples and young families. Represented prosaically in advertisements for everything from appliances to television, for example, normalcy was figured in pictures of a (white) nuclear family engaged in an activity at home (Spigel 1992).

Besides the factors addressed above, the idealization of the nuclear family during the postwar period owed a great deal to the legacy of World

War II. The disruption of the war had significantly altered the fabric of American family life and contributed to changing notions about sex roles. Military conscription fractured families and drained the male labor force, a loss felt especially in industrial sectors of the economy such as the metal trades, aircraft production, shipping, and munitions production. Male exodus, along with wartime production needs, required the employment of a large number of white middle-class women, many of whom had never been employed outside of the home (Hartmann 1982, 21).[11] The jobs they took, especially those in professional fields or in durable goods manufacturing, were often unionized and likely higher paying than were the usual female occupations in light manufacturing, office administration, teaching, nursing, retail, and domestic service (Honey 1984, 19–24).[12] But women's home front labor, especially when it involved a woman filling a man's job, was predicated on the assumption that it would be temporary. As documented by Maureen Honey, in addition to being wartime bread-winners, white middle-class women also maintained their role as home-makers (132; see also Hartmann 1982, 23).

The war's interference in family life continued during the years of re-conversion. As part of the national effort to return to prewar normalcy, most of the white middle-class women employed in men's jobs during the war left them following the Allied victory over Japan. As one article, "What's Become of Rosie the Riveter?," pointed out, "Since v-e Day, about a million women production workers have left the nation's aircraft plants, shipyards, ammunition factories and other industries that pro-duced so prodigiously for war." Addressing Rosie's fate, journalist Frieda Miller imagined a variety of outcomes for the women workers:

> Some of the former riveters and other industrial workers, wearied by the long grind of forty-eight hours and more per week and the excru-ciating task of producing for war, are taking well-earned rests before putting out feelers about post-war jobs. Still others, particularly a num-ber of young women whose husbands have been demobilized from the armed services, have no definite plans. At the moment, they are waiting to see how their veteran husbands fare in the readjustments to civilian life. (Miller 1946, 21)

Much of Rosie's fate depended on how much money her ex-GI husband could bring home. According to Miller, if a husband could find a job that would pay enough to support a family, then "the former Rosies will at least have the chance to devote their entire time to homemaking and some of them are sure to take it." But if for some reason a man did not assume the role of breadwinner, for example if he decided to take advantage of GI Bill benefits to pursue an education or start a business, then "the wife may find her paycheck badly needed" (Miller 1946, 21).

Views like Miller's, which encouraged women's departure from their wartime jobs, were common. So were images in advertisements portraying ecstatic white women as soon-to-be brides and aspiring (or failing) housewives who seemed as wedded to their homes and to their accoutrements as they were their husbands. In one shown in figure 2.1, a bride and a woman who appears to be her mother (she is wearing an apron) stand before a new Kelvinator refrigerator as the ad exclaims "Here's the refrigerator for the brides of the year? . . . Of course you want a Moist-Master refrigerator" (*Good Housekeeping*, June 1947, 289). In another shown in figure 2.2, a bride sits on a sofa admiring a new Presto pressure cooker as her adoring husband reads the enclosure, "Presto cookers make Lucky Brides Happy Homemakers" (*Good Housekeeping*, June 1948, 294). Ads like these, which aligned the products of a newly invigorated capitalist economy with a woman's success in marriage, contributed to the public discourse that allied the institution of marriage with the consumption of durable goods and, at the same time, located the female consumer in the home.

Such entreaties, however, did not ensure a majority of middle-class women's exit from the full-time labor force, nor did they dampen their general enthusiasm for work outside of the home. In spite of the large number of women who ceded their jobs to men on their return, the total number of women (in all racial categories) employed outside of the home in 1945 was still greater than in 1940. That many women continued to work reflects the degree to which the war had altered permanently their aspirations. Even if women justified in economic terms their decision to continue working in some capacity, they had evidently become accustomed to the fulfillment of life outside of the home (Hartmann 1982, 24; see also Kessler-Harris 1982).[13]

Graham's *Appalachian Spring* enacted in embodied terms the cultural debate surrounding the middle-class white women's postwar role, exploring the problems convention posed to women's autonomy in the context

of Graham's onstage and offstage relationship with Hawkins, who she cast
as the Husbandman. Here Graham uses three solos to indicate the Bride's
inner life. Set against a tableau of the other characters posed in stillness,
together they represented the Bride's inner dialogue.

Just prior to the wedding scene, the first soliloquy embodies the Bride's
contemplation about the impending event. In excited anticipation, she
gestures toward and shuttles back and forth between cast members situated in various "zones" around the space. The Husbandman stands at a
fence downstage left; the Preacher holds the congregation ladies in rapt
attention at center stage; and the Pioneer Woman rocks on a chair on a
"porch" at stage right. In their spatial separation, the individuals and the
group seem to represent social entities, family, church, and community,
respectively, as well as the parts of the Bride's superego that she must in-
tegrate prior to becoming a married woman in the community. This sense
of self-integration gets played out on a physical level, through the Bride's

deference toward each entity. Several times she pays her respects to the congregation ladies and the Preacher with bowing gestures. She dances to the Husbandman and looks at him adoringly; then she goes to the Pioneer Woman and mimes exchanging, rocking, and caressing a baby. Her acknowledgements are also expressed in the back and forth nature of her movement, sending her body toward one zone only to redirect it toward another.

This soliloquy leads into the wedding scene. The cast folds into a ceremonial procession with the Bride and Pioneer Woman leading, the Husbandman and the Preacher following, and the congregation ladies coupled behind. The Bride and Husbandman join hands and kneel before the Preacher for his blessing. The wedding scene concludes with the Bride and Husbandman's rousing duet to the Shaker hymn "'Tis a Gift to be Simple." Conveying a joyous occasion, the dance celebrates their marriage by highlighting their partnership. In solo variations, each plays off the other, the Bride skipping, hopping, and swinging and the Husbandman dancing an exuberant jig. In the reprise, they dance together, each drawing on the movement vocabulary of the solos and ending in a twirling embrace.

In spite of these ecstatic expressions, contemporary viewers cannot miss the Bride's apparent ambivalence toward the prospect of marriage and children apparent in her second soliloquy.[14] To a tremulous musical passage, the Bride choppily retraces the journey of her first soliloquy, indicating the various pulls on her being. At times, she literally returns to the places on the stage where the others are or were standing and performs a reprise of the original gestures (like rocking the baby), this time in the absence of the others. In a more amplified embodiment of "back and forth" that evokes a sense of indecision rather than integration, she cycles on and off balance with momentum that sometimes carries her into a spin. This passage ends when she goes to the Pioneer Woman's chair, spins it around, then sits on it. She crosses her legs and bounces one of them up and down nervously. As if in response to her unease, her husband comes up behind her, and with a grounding motion brings his hands just above her eyes. His presence seems to draw her into the fold; she happily leaves her post to join him in a reprise of their earlier celebratory dance to the Shaker hymn. Expressed through their unison and symmetrical movement, she is now included in his and the community's circle again.

The third soliloquy concludes the piece. As the cast holds in tableau looking upstage (their backs to the audience), the Bride moves downstage, kissing her hands and extending them to the audience. Offering a sense of praise and resolution, the soliloquy suggests that now the Bride is prepared to encompass all that is and will be required of her as a married woman in this community. The section ends as the Husbandman comes up behind her and "covers" her; he cradles her hands in his and brings them to her heart, embracing her at the same time. In a romantic moment, she turns and clasps his face in her hands.

In the Bride's apparent decision to put her anxiety to rest through her

FIG. 2.3 Martha Graham and Erick Hawkins in Martha Graham's *Appalachian Spring*, 1944. Photo by Arnold Eagle. Reprinted courtesy of the estate of Arnold Eagle and Jerome Robbins Dance Division, The New York Public Library of the Performing Arts, Astor, Lenox and Tilden Foundations.

reliance upon her husband, Graham offered audiences a return to the status quo through the alignment of traditional gender roles.[15] In this sense, the dance portrayed the dominant social imperative for women to give way to the returning GIS—indeed, to mend their lives and lead the way toward prewar normalcy. Nevertheless, as William Wyler's popular film *The Best Years of Our Lives* (1946) illustrates, adjustment to life after war was far from simple. It portrayed these challenges in its examination of the "rehabilitation" of three veterans who return home only to find their community in the throes of peacetime conversion. The film follows the reintegration of the servicemen through the renewal of their relationships with wives and girlfriends. As they struggle to reckon with war-related injuries both physical and mental, they must also reacquaint themselves with their families and gradually reenter the lives they left behind. Each couple must reestablish its terms of engagement; both the men and women resist the loss of autonomy that partnership brings. While they seem ill-equipped to handle the transition, their wives and girlfriends, endowed with extraordinary powers of patience and understanding, bend over backward to create a place for them. The movie ends with one wedding and the promise of another, thereby foreshadowing the prosperous baby boom years to come. Yet even though the marriage of the lead characters—Homer and Wilma—establishes the beginning of their life together, thus symbolizing renewal, it does not ipso facto resolve the other problems that the movie has introduced, such as the pressures of conformity, male dissatisfaction with work, and thwarted female ambition. The movie reveals compromises made by real men and women seeking security at war's end. As William Graebner points out, "Obsessed with security from the middle of the war years through the 1950s, Americans— both men and women—willingly surrendered independence and autonomy for the certitude of a stable future" (Graebner 1991, 14; see also May 1988, 10–14, 87–94).

Several years before *The Best Years of Our Lives*, *Appalachian Spring* performed this peacetime turn to family and community, and likewise exposed its inherent problems. Even though Graham's Bride ultimately seemed to quell her fears about marriage by turning to her husband, the work nevertheless enacted the Bride's apprehension about her impending marriage. Even though the ending of the piece offers convention itself as a solution to the Bride's anxiety about according with the norm, the work nevertheless renders such fears legitimate through the Bride's substantial embodiment of them. Thus, through the Bride's soliloquies, Graham posed questions to convention: Were marriage and motherhood a woman's ultimate goals, their most supreme accomplishments? Was autonomy possible in marriage? What was the role of family, community, or religion in a couple's intimate life? Was domestic life a source of peace or cause of anxiety?

Although Graham had personal reasons for these questions, they were also on the minds of other Americans at war's end. Similarly even as Graham nodded to convention in *Appalachian Spring*'s optimistic portrayal of courtship and marriage, through her Bride Graham challenged contemporaneous notions about female subjectivity and autonomy. Assessing *Appalachian Spring* in this light, I contend that its subject posed more opposition to the dominant culture than others have maintained. That is, the work confronted tradition by questioning the benefits of matrimony at a time when marriage as a social convention was being enshrined as part of the nation's drive to normalcy (E. May 1988). I contend that, through the Bride's plight, Graham performed a kind of public contemplation on the issues she found troubling about marriage, including female subordination and loss of autonomy. In this way, the work introduced themes that Graham would take up later in darker domestic studies like *Cave of the Heart* (1946) based on Medea and *Night Journey* (1947), an adaptation of the Oedipal tragedy.

Importantly for the argument of this book, the piece also exemplified the kinds of thematic, aesthetic, and epistemological polarities that could exist within one work of dance—dynamics of provocation and counteraction within and among different registers of signification. On one level, Graham's work epitomized universalism in modern dance—situating the subject of the Bride, and the event of her marriage, not only as a metaphor of renewal for the country but also as a metonym for "human" experience. On another level, Graham used the work's very universalist premise as a point of departure for the expression of the Bride's particular difference, seen in her physicalization of ambivalence toward the prospects of being married. Still on yet another level, the work's very kinesthetic economy of objection, as embodied by the Bride's ambivalence, undermined the authority of the normative forces within it, as signified by both the members of the community and the purported outcome of the dance—the Bride's resolution to marry, culminating with her marriage to the Husbandman.

In much the same manner, Graham's *Night Journey*, premiered in 1947, also took up the story of a marriage, this time through the bittersweet portrait of a woman's misplaced desire for the man she has taken as her husband. This man, of course, is Oedipus, the newly anointed and unwitting king of Thebes who has murdered his father, Jocasta's former husband, as he attempts to escape the outcome of a prophesy that he will, in fact, murder his father and marry his mother. Like *Appalachian Spring*, *Night Journey*, which told the Oedipal drama from Jocasta's point of view, had personal import for the choreographer (Banes 1995, 157). The year after its premier Graham and Hawkins were wed.[16] Yet, even though Graham made the dance at a moment in her life that held romantic promise, in many ways the dance itself depicts the underside of female commitment. It portrays a woman whose destruction is inextricably linked to her biologically determined roles as wife and mother.

Departing from the play's original plot, Graham presented the story as a series of flashbacks beginning the moment before Jocasta hangs herself as punishment for her crime of incest.[17] Graham's choice for an opening conveyed to audiences that her interpretation of the story would be different in that it tells the story through the eyes of Jocasta, rather than those of Oedipus. Yet it also highlighted the significance of Jocasta's ultimate fate: at the end of what is to come, the only option she has is to kill herself. Of this moment in the dance Graham wrote, "Now Jocasta kneels on the floor at the foot of her bed and then she rises with her leg held close to her breast and to her head and her foot way beyond her head, her body open in a deep contraction. I call this the vaginal cry; it is the cry from her vagina. It is either the cry for her lover, her husband, or the cry for her children" (Graham 1991, 214). The premise is that just before she commits suicide Jocasta reflects on the events of her life, searching for signs that she first overlooked but that might have revealed Oedipus's identity to her. The information she seeks, however, emanates from the parts of her distinctly female anatomy, signs of her biologically determined roles.

Graham stripped the play down to a series of scenes beginning when Oedipus reenters Jocasta's life: his arrival in Colonus, his coronation, their marriage and its consummation, their realization of their incest, Jocasta's

FIG. 2.4 Martha Graham in *Night Journey*, 1947. Photo by Philippe Halsman / Copyright Halsman Archive. Courtesy of the Jerome Robbins Dance Division, The New York Public Library of the Performing Arts, Astor, Lenox and Tilden Foundations.

suicide, and Oedipus's self-blinding. Without spoken text to help viewers follow the story, the dance's characters make it legible. For example, Graham typecast roles to make characters' appearances accord with audience expectation. Accentuating the main theme of incestuous sexual desire, she cast herself, a mature dancer, as Jocasta, and Hawkins, her significantly younger husband-to-be, as Oedipus.[18] Costuming provided additional information as to the nature of their onstage relationship. Jocasta wears a sleek, long-sleeved black dress, ornamented with intricate brocade and a large beetle-shaped brooch pinned onto her chest. Her seductive attire emphasizes her sexual desire (and desirability), while the brooch suggests its lurid and insidious nature as well as the inevitability of her son's demise. Oedipus appears similarly regal and alluring in a dark robe (which he eventually takes off to reveal his robust physique) and briefs (which emphasize the muscularity of his legs and buttocks). The decoration on his costume makes it clear that his desire for Jocasta has consequences. A cord motif running around the outline of his cape, reminiscent of an umbilical cord or a rope, indicates its incestuous nature as well as the way Jocasta will end her life. According to Graham, "The umbilical cord is . . . [Jocasta's] savior, her companion, her reason or the evidence for her passage into the world of death, of forgetfulness where memory exists no more and the terrors of memory have no place" (Graham 1991, 216).

The movement themes amplify what is evident from the characters' appearances, that Jocasta and Oedipus are essentially biologically different, and that their tragic union is fated. Jocasta is a woman whose "female intuition" has failed her—she "clutches at her breasts, her abdomen, her arms, making almost impatient little up-and-down motions of one foot in recognition and revulsion of her own desire"; she "crosses her hands over her groin—a gesture ambiguously suggesting both shame and the recollection of sexual ecstasy" (Siegel 1979, 203; Banes 1995, 159). These gestures also imply Jocasta's vulnerability (marked as feminine), perhaps to offset Graham's obvious physical strength in performing the role. Similarly, Graham marks Oedipus as masculine through a series of "phallic gestures" that assert his manliness (Siegel 1979, 156 and 204). His movements are impulsive and forceful, qualities that refer to his impetuous murder of his father as well as his haste in marrying Jocasta and assuming his father's place in his parents' marriage bed. These, along with a series of

FIG. 2.5 Martha Graham and Erick Hawkins in Martha Graham's *Night Journey*, 1947. Photo by Philippe Halsman / Copyright Halsman Archive. Courtesy of the Jerome Robbins Dance Division, The New York Public Library of the Performing Arts, Astor, Lenox and Tilden Foundations.

"lovemaking duets" combine to convey his sexual prowess as well as the passionate nature of his liaison with Jocasta (Banes 1995, 161).

As in *Appalachian Spring*, Graham's constructions of main characters Jocasta and Oedipus appear to have accorded with conventional notions of gender normalcy. Expressed through costuming, movement vocabulary, and character interaction, these constructions depended on recognizable signs of femininity and masculinity on the one hand, and on the accentuation of gender difference on the other.[19] In these ways, Graham's constitution of male and female characters resonated with the social preoccupation with traditionally drawn masculine and feminine ideals. Within the prescriptive discourse of normalcy, in which heterosexuality was assumed to be a compulsory element, categories of masculinity and femininity were constructed around historically specific assumptions about the interpretation of behavioral signs.[20] A set of standards existed by which a person's outward appearance and behavior could be judged by a viewing public. The point was to establish signs for determining whether or not a person's demeanor conformed to conventional expectations of that person's gender.

In articles published in popular magazines, for example, writers constructed essentialized masculine and feminine ideals intended to prove the innate correctness of normative assumptions about gender attributes. In one article *Newsweek* contributor Elizabeth Dunn began with the premise that "by the time I was ten I knew that men are strong, self-controlled, logical, realistic, accurate about facts and almost invariably right." As this childhood intuition stood to reason, she used personal experience to certify its claim. This came in the form of her husband, "a charming but sedentary fellow" who epitomized masculinity because he screwed the top of the thermos bottle on so tight that "it had to be sent back to the factory to be opened again" (1948, 64, 65). *Look* magazine contributor Russell Lynes measured a woman's femininity to the extent it made men behave like men: "a lady is a woman who makes a man behave like a gentleman" (1958, 19). Other articles attempting to refute essentialist logic had the result only of strengthening conventional arguments about gender difference. Marybeth Weinstein's *New York Times Magazine* article entitled "Woman's Case for Women's Superiority," for example, enumerated the ways in which women surpassed men in the areas of patience, memory, cleverness, diplomacy, management, and tact, attributing women's superior skills to their experiences in the home as daughters, wives, and mothers. "Women are cleverer than men and would make better generals," she contends, "[because a] girl is born knowing things a man doesn't learn until he has a marriageable daughter, who, with her mother, is set on conquest." By comparison, actual "complex military maneuvers such as strategic retreats and diversionary tactics are as child's play" (1955, 26–27). Meaning to acknowledge women's singular strengths, Weinstein's reliance upon stereotypes only strengthened other arguments that men and women were different from each other and therefore not equals.[21]

Contrary to these normative versions of gender, in significant ways Graham's characters ran against the grain. In their embodiment of females who appear to have the power of self-possession and the ability to reflect on the decisions that they make, *Appalachian Spring* and *Night Journey* offered alternatives to typical deterministic notions about how women were, or should be, other directed, thereby performing a public critique of conventional gender roles especially as they were constituted in marriage. While characters like the Bride and Jocasta appear to fit the ideal mold in the ways in which they defer their own authority to their husbands and seem to accept their biologically/socially determined fate as wives and mothers, each exhibits power, desires, and self-determination. Graham's Bride, while doe-eyed, takes the time to reflect on what she is about to do, and we see her thinking process as she attempts to resolve some issues that she has with her impending marriage. Likewise Graham's portrayal of Jocasta defied normative expectation not only because she has unwittingly committed incest, but also because she pursues her own sexual desire (Burt 1998, 50; Banes 1995, 160–63). Besides, the visible age difference between Graham and Hawkins added a naturalistic dimension to the spectacle of their pairing.[22] According to Ramsay Burt, in Graham's oeuvre, she is among a series of "powerful and dangerous heroines," such as Medea (*Cave of the Heart*, 1946) and Clytemnestra (*Clytemnestra*, 1958), who embodied "threats to the family home" (Burt 1998, 46).[23] Through these and other heroines, Graham actualized the possibility of female autonomy and desire. Her believable portrayals of women who chafed against accepted definitions of gender identity served as models for real women who questioned what it meant to be female in the postwar years.[24]

In many ways, her characters' experiences presaged Betty Friedan's highly influential book *The Feminine Mystique*, published in 1963. Here Friedan unearthed what she called "the problem with no name," a woman's gnawing feeling, often manifest in depression, that she has compromised her autonomy and personal satisfaction in pursuit of a gender ideal (Friedan [1963] 1983). Friedan's protagonist was the suburban housewife, a woman "buried alive" in her tract house, the victim of watching the world pass by her picture window (336). Although she looked perfectly content having achieved the American Dream, in her heart she knew that the dream was, in fact, a trap. If she sublimated her needs in the desires of others then she "forfeited" her own self-development. If she loved others by "merging her ego" with them, then she risked losing her self-definition (323). Pursuit of the ideal had lessened the burden of her existence, because it made her decisions seem like foregone conclusions. But its ultimate costs were enormous.

José Limón's "Virile Dance"

Choreographer José Limón's 1948 article "The Virile Dance" lamented the history of "superfluous men" in dance and presented an alternative vision of the male dancer. Included in the former category were "effeminate adjuncts and supports of the dazzling ballerina," "creatures of exquisite romantic fantasy," or entertainers, who "gravitated to more lucrative aspects of the dance" like musical comedies or dance films. Limón's alternative he deemed "men of caliber and dedication," who must "affirm man's sanity and dance it." Implied in this comparison is a critique of the ballet tradition, which, for the most part, relegated men to partnering or character roles, and to entertainment-oriented dancing, which featured virtuosity over substance. But the article was also meant to counter some typical assumptions—that dancing was womanish and male dancers effeminate. To the contrary, Limón argued that concert dancing was a "virile" occupation. "In a society desperately in need of all its art and artists," he wrote, "the art of the dance offers a rare opportunity for those with the vision of its ancient grandeur to speak of it anew" (Limón 1948, 21; see also Sorell 1966, 82–86).

Limón's article was part of an enduring effort to recruit male dancers and legitimize the role of men in concert dance, begun by choreographers Ted Shawn and Charles Weidman, critics Martin and Terry, and groups such as the New Dance Group, all of which had promoted an image of male dancing that countered effeminate stereotypes (Foulkes 2002). Leading an all-male group of dancers, Shawn, for example, highlighted the "virility" of dancers' bodies by presenting them engaged in physical labor or sport—thus amplifying their masculinity in the absences of women or the pretext of heterosexual relationships. Like Shawn, Limón sought to demonstrate that dancing did not emasculate men; however he did so not through spectacles of machismo but in the representation of exceptional men, heroes, who faced extraordinary challenges or obstacles.[25] As Ann Murphy notes in her essay on Limón and Lucas Hoving (who danced with Limón for over a decade), "[they] expanded the terrain of modern dance by giving unprecedented richness not only to male expression but to men in relationship to one another" (2002, 59). Except in dances like *The Traitor* or *The Emperor Jones* in which there are no women, Limón's heroes also asserted their maleness in the context of relationships with female characters.

Limón's essay, specifically its attempt to carve out a niche for virile men in dance, also resonated with the contemporaneous discourse about gender, specifically societal concern about what was then called "gender convergence." In scholarly circles this term stood as the preferred explanation for nontraditional gender practices (Breines 1992, 30). Sociologists David Riesman, William H. Whyte Jr., John Seely, R. Alexander Sim, E. W. Loosley, Jules Henry, and Talcott Parsons in particular looked at changes in homes, schools, and workplaces, attempting to explain the popular perception that gender roles were becoming less and less distinct. In the popular discussion, the social scientific idea of gender convergence was embodied in the personae of the "he-woman" and the "she-man." While the she-man assumed the role of the domineering woman (the overbearing wife, mother, or secretary), the he-woman assumed the role of the browbeaten man (the pushover father or husband or the "organization man").

The overworked male was a version of the female-dominated male; whereas the latter was emasculated by the expectations of the women in his life, the former succumbed to the pressures of the workplace and of the organization. Riesman's depiction of the other-directed individual and Whyte's organization man embodied this male type. The requirements of postindustrial society had shaped him; his life was dictated by the bureaucracy of corporate capitalism and consumption, not by adventurous entrepreneurialism and production. In other words, through deindustrialization, the rugged individualist had been lost to the compliant, other-directed organization man. In the directing of his attention outward, expressed in his yearning to belong and in his concern with public opinion, the organization man seemed to have become more like a woman (Whyte 1956, 6; see also Riesman [1950] 1977). Even the ambitious man felt the "tyranny of public opinion." At least this was the claim of a 1958 article in *Look* magazine in which writer William Atwood probed the reasons behind frequently cited Census Bureau findings that one fourth of married women would be widowed between the ages of fifty-five and sixty-four and would live another sixteen to twenty-three years.

Atwood inferred that a man's desire for outside approval of his actions and decisions could cause his early death. As he explained, "unlike older traditional societies, there is no point at which he may say, 'I've made it. I've gone as far as I can go. Now I can relax.'"[26]

The figure of the aggressive woman was the feminine counterpart to the he-woman; however, whereas the he-woman often invited sympathy, the she-man summoned disdain. A 1949 *Reader's Digest* article typified the kind of scapegoating she suffered. Here, longtime foreign correspondent Leland Stowe wondered why foreigners idolized contemporary American women as feminine ideals, when, in his view, they were embarrassments. According to him, there was near "general consent" abroad that, compared with all the world's women, "America's Eve" was the best looking, the most modern, among the best dressed, and possessed of "a remarkably fine figure" and "exceptional intelligence." In Stowe's eyes, however, the American woman wasted all of her attributes: "[she] is . . . the most spoiled and self-centered woman in the world; the most aggressive; the most unhappy and dissatisfied" (1949, 49). In her self-centeredness and her moxie, the modern woman appeared to have usurped the qualities formerly associated with American men. Still, like the organization man, she seemed to lack the inner drive and vision of the American pioneer, which rendered her feckless and discontent.

Both personae appeared in a 1958 *Look* magazine feature story, "The American Male: Why Do Women Dominate Him?: Does he like petticoat rule, or has it been forced on him by the stronger sex?" In the article, writer J. Robert Moskin attempts to account for "recent scientific findings" that show "that in the years since the end of World War II, [the American male] has changed radically and dangerously; that he is no longer the masculine strong-minded man who pioneered the continent and built America's greatness." According to Moskin, "from the moment he is born, the American boy is ruled by women"—from the hospital nurse to his mother. In this picture, the submission of the female-dominated man did more than make him seem "feminine"; it literally emasculated him (77–80).

The discussion about gender-specific types is evidence of a widespread societal investment in defining and debating parameters for gender normalcy for white, middle-class Americans. As the personae of the he-woman and she-man were drawn from the world, they suggest that some men and women in their daily experience of gender defied conventional thinking about it. And the hostility expressed toward these figures in their portrayals in scholarship and in the popular discourse shows the extent to which they had become focal points for cultural animus and unease surrounding issues of gender and sexuality.

In the context of this debate, therefore, Limón's writing on "The Virile Dance" advocates for a place for a man's man in the presumably effeminate world of dance, countering the likely assumption that men in dance were necessarily she-men. In his choreography, Limón, like Graham, drew on traditional definitions of gender and gender difference to construct his characters. Nevertheless, there were some variations between the ways in which these types were rendered. Graham's men and women occupied separate spheres of a shared movement vocabulary (while the movement is stylistically and technically similar, men and women often do different steps), whereas Limón's dancers most always did the same steps. In Limón's work, gender was marked in terms of appearance, in contrasts between the physiological attributes of male and female bodies (like size, physique, and strength), which were amplified by gender-specific costuming, and in terms of space (the space inhabited by individual bodies, spacing between or among bodies, or groupings).

In this sense, Limón's approach to gender was as much a way of differentiating among characters as it was a way of keeping up appearances. According to Foulkes, Limón "sought out equal pairing with women on stage and off to deflect attention from [his and Charles Weidman's] relationship" (2002, 95). Even after Limón married Pauline Lawrence in 1941, and therefore could substantiate his own heteronormativity in the fact of his marriage, he still favored these heterosexual pairings.[27] Yet matching men and women in relationships of equivalency did not close avenues of representation in which he could enlarge the expressive possibilities for the male dancer, especially in his partnership with Hoving. As Ann Murphy contends,"José and Lucas . . . found an ambiguity and passion together which translated into potent male-duets that were neither the dances strictly of lovers or of bodies (José and Lucas were both bisexual, married men), but something in between, something polymorphous and androgynous" (2002, 66).

Limón investigated the intricacies of intimacy in *The Moor's Pavane*, an adaptation of Shakespeare's *Othello*. Commissioned by the Connecticut

College American Dance Festival and set to music by Henry Purcell it took Limón nearly three years to complete (Owen 1999, 119).[28] Stripping down the play, Limón built the dance around the relationships among its four principal characters, Othello, Desdemona, Iago, and Emilia. "Going to the play's basic dilemmas rather than by trying to duplicate its actions," the dance does not reproduce scenes in the play or follow the twists and turns of its narrative; rather it represents "a process of deterioration, perhaps several interrelated processes" (Siegel 1979, 169). It does this by concentrating on the marriage of Othello, a Moor, and his noble wife, Desdemona. A crisis occurs between them when Iago (who is a soldier under Othello's command and also his friend) tells the Moor that his wife is having an affair with his best friend and lieutenant, Cassio. Provoked by Iago and plagued by doubt about his wife's fealty, Othello eventually murders Desdemona then kills himself (although Limón does not represent Othello's suicide). These "processes of deterioration," therefore, are embodied through the disintegration of the relationships among the characters.

The piece opens on a quartet in which the four main characters dance in a circle, their hands joined.[29] The women, played by Betty Jones (Desdemona) and Pauline Koner (Emilia), wear period-inspired costumes, dresses with tight bodices and full skirts that bare their chests and shoulders. Desdemona's is all white, a sign of her radiant innocence. The men's costumes are also of the Renaissance; both wear tuniclike cloaks, tights, and ballet slippers although Othello's cloak stands out because it is full-length and black. While Othello's racial otherness is not emphasized, it is not ignored either as Limón's casting of himself, a Mexican-American, as Othello, and the color of Othello's costume make evident.[30]

Soon the group separates into gender-similar pairs that move in canon with one another. The couples weave in and out, alternating variations on the same phrase. Ostensibly sharing the same steps, a contrast in levels distinguishes the men from the women. The women lunge and lower themselves to the floor, while the men, who form the center of the group, reach their bodies toward the sky clasping each other's hands. This formation establishes the links between the members of the gender-similar couples. It also makes the men appear to tower over the women, marking the superiority of their size and strength. In constant metamorphosis, the composition of the pairs changes again. This time Othello and Desde-

FIG. 2.6 *Left to right*: Pauline Koner, Lucas Hoving, Betty Jones, and José Limón, circa 1949, in José Limón's *The Moor's Pavane*. Photo by Walter Strate. Courtesy of the José Limón Dance Foundation.

mona lock in an embrace while Iago and Emila look on, thus confirming the bonds between the men and their respective wives.

An aside, in which Iago isolates Othello, sets the wheels of the plot in motion (depicted in figure 2.7), changing the dynamics of the group and introducing dramatic subtext. Standing behind Othello and clutching his shoulders Iago whispers something to him, in one ear and then the other. In disbelief, Othello turns to face him. Then he chases Iago upstage. For a moment all are still as Othello dances alone. His torso contracted in pain, he brings his hands to his eyes then sends them out (this motif suggests that knowledge involves both seeing and blindness). Compositionally Limón's use of the aside is akin to Graham's decision to tell the story of *Night Journey* as a flashback. It helps motivate what happens through the introduction of Othello's psychic conflict. On the one hand, it isolates Othello in his doubts thereby driving a wedge between him and Desdemona, who will be kept in the dark about his suspicions; on the other hand, it demonstrates the complicated intimacy between Othello and Iago, who are both rivals and confidantes, their connection at once cemented and polluted by Iago's betrayal.

Like the opening quartet, the dance that follows is constructed around relational ideas, on the one hand, solo, duet, trio, quartet, and on the other, one person set against three, two set against two, and four together. It is through the transformation of groupings that Limón unfolds a complex web of connections. Limón builds his choreographic structure on Purcell's music, which alternates theme and variation, and the form of the pavane, which allows for same- and opposite-sex coupling. Furthermore, the pavane, as danced by the entire group, functions as a constant in the midst of the emotional turmoil.

Besides these methods, in large part Limón trades on gendered stereotypes to portray his characters and their relationships. Although distinct from each other, each couple's emotional dynamic is stereotypically familiar. Iago and Emila are flirtatious and conniving—their seduction of one another coasts on the waves of fall and recovery, motion and stillness. At times, Emilia flaunts herself, raising her skirt coyly and glancing over her shoulder at Iago. As Murphy observes, "although she begins as a pawn of her indifferent husband, she ultimately controls and lustily taunts him with the handkerchief which she has stolen for him" (2002, 69). Fixated on the handkerchief that Desdemona holds out from her position downstage, Iago and Emilia pursue each other as they devise a plan to steal it. They will use it as evidence to prove to Othello that Desdemona has betrayed him. Throughout their duet they give each other knowing looks. Contrary to Murphy's interpretation, I see Iago as the one more in control. While it is true that Emilia entices him with promises of getting the handkerchief, that it takes such an insidious promise to lure him at all suggests his power in the relationship. At times, Iago seems so intent on destroying Othello and Desdemona's marriage that he ignores Emilia. She gets involved in the plan to get his attention. Furthermore, that she must resort to a sexualized self-presentation to win his favor makes her seem all the more conventional. His response to her, a gently possessive clutch just under her right breast, makes it clear that he is in a position to take advantage of her charms.

In contrast, the interaction between Othello and Desdemona is freighted, weighed down by the imbalance of power and knowledge between them.

FIG. 2.7 Lucas Hoving and José Limón circa 1949 in José Limón's *The Moor's Pavane*. Photo by Gerda Peterich. Courtesy of the Jerome Robbins Dance Division, The New York Public Library of the Performing Arts, Astor, Lenox and Tilden Foundations.

Plaintive, deferential, and adoring Desdemona repeatedly reaches out toward Othello. Sometimes, these efforts are met with an embrace, but more often they are rebuffed leading her to clutch herself or clasp her face. True to convention, she appears other-focused—whatever the problem she wants to make it all right. He, on the other hand, is brooding and remote, alternating between tenderness and aggression. While the lovers often move in mirror images of each other each person seems closed off. Othello is isolated in his suspicions whereas Desdemona is secluded by her ignorance. Yet ultimately he has more room to maneuver as his movements have a greater spatial and dynamic range than do hers.

Othello's dominance is most evident in their final duet, a masterful portrait of anguish through a series of ambivalent gestures and holds (suggested in figure 2.8). The couple comes together momentarily after dancing with the others. Then Othello recoils, grabbing himself, his arms around his own waist. Desdemona is visibly upset; she hunches over then unfolds, bringing her hands up to her eyes and radiating them out, a variation on an earlier motif. Turning toward her, Othello responds. Cupping her face with his hands he brings her toward him to kiss her. Then, as if he is going to strike her, he raises his arms over his head, joining his hands. Instead, he gently grabs her hands to twist her around in a slow turn. This motion ends as he throws her hands downward. He recoils again. This time, she follows, attempting to reassure him. They join as he lowers her in a dip onto his knee. As she leans back, her head dangling, he encircles her chest with one forearm and supports her back with the other in an ambiguous hold that makes it look like he is either about to embrace or strangle her. He lets her go, she reaches out for help, but he pursues. Othello murders Desdemona as Emilia and Iago, who are now center stage, block the act from view.

At the same time as Limón amplified Othello's virility in the depiction of his power over Desdemona, he complicated this picture by exploring the potential of his charged and notably physical relationship with Iago. As the aside establishes early on, the men are passionate antagonists (Siegel 1979, 173–74). The duet portrays a gamut of emotions, from playful cooperation, shown in the jumping sequence, to hostility, expressed as the men shove and pull each other. What is remarkable is the extent to which the men use each other's weight as force for their own mobilization. This is especially clear in a dynamic series of balances in which, clasping the other's hand, each brushes a leg into arabesque. This leads the partners into the jumping sequence that Siegel describes, portraying their interconnection through their shared momentum. The duet ends as the men fight for advantage. One moment, Othello subdues Iago by standing over him and pinning him with a bent leg; another, Iago jumps onto Othello's back and rides him as the encumbered Othello strides toward stage right.

According to Burt, "the choreographed encounters Limón devised between Othello and Iago . . . can be interpreted as sexual and homoerotic" (Burt 1995, 126–27). These encounters include not only the ones I have described but also several others in which Iago taunts Othello with the handkerchief that he and Emila stole from Desdemona. At one point "Iago gets down on his hands and knees and arches his back as he twice rubs the handkerchief against his own body from his crotch up to his face" (Burt 1995, 126–27). Burt reads this gesture as Iago's implication that he has slept with Desdemona (a departure from the original plot in which Desdemona is accused of having an affair with Cassio). More important, however, was its homoeroticism. "The manner in which Iago conveys this draws Othello's attention to the sexual attractions of Iago's own body. He is thus revealing himself as a (male) erotic object to Othello's (male) gaze, thus evoking the forbidden realm of homosexual sexuality" (Burt 1995,

FIG. 2.8 Betty Jones and José Limón, circa 1949, in José Limón's *The Moor's Pavane*. Photo by S. Enklemann. Courtesy of the José Limón Dance Foundation.

126–27; see also Murphy 2002, 66–67). This moment is emblematic of a larger representational strategy at work in Limón's dances, in which he and Hoving charged moments of "passionate counterpoint," using dramatic conventions borrowed from the classical ballet (Murphy 66–67). Burt cautions against reading Limón's portrayal of "suppressed homoeroticism" as "an expression of Limón's sexual orientation." Rather, he sees it as a sign of Limón's embrace of modernism ("it was the universal, humanistic ideologies of modernism that restrained Limón's work from recognizing and dealing with these issues directly"), and of a culturally rampant homophobia, both of which made it difficult for men to be intimate with each other, as lovers or even friends (Burt 1995, 127).

That said, in the context of the contemporaneous debate about gender normalcy, it is impossible to ignore the ways in which Limón's interpretation of Shakespeare's play, as a quartet among four friends and as two sets of duets (one set is opposite-sex married pairs, the other is same-sex pairs), situates front and center the question of intimacy, between the men and their wives, most importantly that of Othello and Desdemona, and between the same-sex partners, Othello and Iago first and foremost, and, to a much lesser extent, Desdemona and Emilia.

In spite of the particular conflicts that drive the interaction among members of the main couples, in many respects all share one important theme: an interplay between intimacy and power. What sets Othello's relationship with Iago apart from his relationship with Desdemona is a power differential. Duets between Othello and Desdemona highlight Othello's physical power—this is the literal power he has over her, even though his actions are dictated by what he believes she has done to him. As the end of the dance makes clear, Desdemona's life force can be extinguished with one act of brute strength. Both Foster and Foulkes have argued that the focus on virility among male concert dancers and choreographers was a way they counteracted common assumptions that dancing made them less masculine (Foster 2001, 160–161; Foulkes 2002, 79–103). In this sense, Othello acts both on his own behalf, in the context of the story, and as a proxy for Limón. His strong and decisive action conveys that he will not be pushed around by his wife or meddling friends, and it demonstrates that dancing is not and never was for sissies.

Interestingly, Othello's dancing with Iago, in its enactment of a relationship of male equals (if not in terms of rank, than in terms of size, strength, and dancing ability), provided an opportunity for Limón to negotiate the emotional and physical dynamics of such a match-up before a viewing audience. In this light, Iago's tormenting of Othello can be seen not only as a power play that might eventually end Othello's marriage to Desdemona, but also as an erotic provocation. In terms of intimacy and power, Iago's is an act not only of ambition but also of jealousy: He wants Othello for himself. Regarding Othello, he turns against Desdemona not just because of what he fears she has done to betray him and tarnish his reputation, but also because she stands in the way of the one he really wants, Iago. Or, if he does not want Iago explicitly, Othello murders Desdemona as proxy for that aspect of himself that he does not want to expose: his desire for another man.

Read both within and outside of the parameters of the story of Othello, Limón's latent love triangle couches a chilling statement about the difficulties of marriage. *The Moor's Pavane* served as a public site in which to represent the charged life of physical and emotional intimacy, both between a man and his wife and that man and his confident.

It is likely that the work's very availability to counterreading brought diverse audiences into the theater.[31] While the work fulfilled the demands of modern dance universalism in its adaptation of a classic story, it also portrayed a conflict to which many viewers could relate, regardless of their sexual orientation. For instance, George Chauncey has documented a growing interest in the iconography of masculinity among young male homosexuals in the postwar period. As he puts it, "The transformation in gay culture suggested by the ascendancy of gay was closely tied to the masculinization of that culture. Jeans, T-shirts, leather jackets, and boots became more common in the 1940s, part of the 'new virile look' of young homosexuals" (1994, 358). Chauncey's research suggests that Limón's focus on virility expressed a nascent sexual consciousness in which homosexuality and masculinity were not opposed to one another. As he has shown, by the 1940s "growing numbers" of gay men adopted a "self-consciously masculine style" signifying that their homosexual practices "no longer seemed to require the renunciation of their masculine identities" (1994, 358). Limón's images of masculinity legitimized the male body in dance by contradicting assumptions of its effeminacy. His images also spotlighted the male body in motion negotiating a space for male-to-male intimacy, contributing to the production and circulation of homoerotic images consumed by members of a gay subculture that grew significantly after the war (D'Emilio and Freedman 1997, 289).[32]

Conclusion

In dances that suggested the problems and, in some cases, failings, of matrimony, Graham's and Limón's presented individual characters as exemplars of the universal human condition. The stories they sought to portray relied upon the dramatization of gender differences to render their particular meanings clear to audiences. Audiences could "read" the central dramatic conflict in the ways the main characters related to one another, or conveyed their feelings through body language. Drawn from normative stereotypes in their construction, their main characters seemed plausible, legitimate, and safe vehicles for audience empathy.

Yet, paradoxically, inasmuch as these works traded on dominant cultural constructions, they indicted its reigning ideology of gender roles. To this end, both choreographers deployed the medium of movement to their advantage. While their characters and their situations appeared to manifest normative experience, characters' actions called into question the logic of matrimony and its inherent power relations. With the Bride and Jocasta, for example, Graham fashioned feminized women of determination and consequence, whose bodies who did not look the part of "she-men" but wielded power in the world nonetheless. Limón's male characters betrayed the feminine attributes of psychological and emotional depth, yet they were not afraid to commit decisive acts. Furthermore, both choreographers envisioned new roles for men in dance: Graham, by turning the gaze on some male characters thus making them objects of desire, and Limón, by enacting complex webs of intimacy spun with ambiguous bonds that introduced the possibility of same-sex desire. Operating in a world in which individuals navigated their lives depending on the stable truth of the visible, as precursors to action Graham and Limón used movement to challenge some of its core contentions about the ways that men and women looked and acted.

In an essay on "passing," Linda Schlossberg observes that "at the most basic level, we are subjects constituted by our visions of ourselves and others, and we trust that our ability to see and read carries with it a certain degree of epistemological certainty." On one level, social life depends on the assumption that to see is to know; we trust our eyes to perceive what is real and what is true and to help us discern what is false. For these reasons, "passing," or the misrepresentation of reality to portray oneself as one is not, "becomes a highly charged site for anxieties regarding visibility, invisibility, classification and social demarcation. . . . because] [i]t disrupts the logics and conceits around which identity categories are established and maintained" (Schlossberg 2001, 1).

Seen in terms of strategies of passing, Graham's and Limón's dances posed threats, if opaque, to prevailing ideologies of legibility that relied upon the assumption that difference could be discerned through the interpretation of a person's appearance or behavior. In contradictory ways, their dances exemplified how it was possible for people to hide or obscure their difference from the norm, to "pass" as "normal" by exhibiting qualities known to meet the viewing public's expectations of normalcy, while at the same time embodying ideas that undermined them. This is particularly significant given both the conventional wisdom that the body was a "human common denominator" and the domestic culture of containment. The idea that the body's movement could reveal as well as conceal truths terrified those who placed a high premium on discernment.

By the late 1940s, as the threat of communist subversion intensified along with imperatives to "contain" it, the equation of seeing and knowing took on an even heightened significance as people looked to markers of normalcy or aberration for clues about how to classify each other (Nadel 1995; Foreman 1997; Abrams and Hughes 2000). Indeed, with so much riding on the relation between outer and inner, a fear of cover-up pervaded cold war social relations, as evidenced especially in the era's preoccupation with the supposed link between antidemocratic subversion and "sexual perversion." Consequently, much cultural attention went to policing the boundaries of normalcy to prevent blurring of or transgression from rigidly defined gender and sexual lines.[33] Since it challenged masculine and feminine ideals, sexual difference was seen during the cold war as an equal if not greater threat to the nation's stability than even antidemocratic political philosophies and organizations.

Legibility formed the basis of debates about subjectivity in modern dance too. Graham's *Appalachian Spring* and *Night Journey*, and Limón's *The Moor's Pavane*, signaled the modern dance establishment's move toward choreographic legibility in the postwar years. These adaptations of canonical literary works could be "read" as one would read literature through conventions of plot, character, symbol, and subtext. Within these conventions, Graham and Limón used dance movement to "express . . . an inner compulsion," as John Martin had put it. In other words, they aspired to give form to human emotion, making visible what was obscure to the ordinary, nonartistic eye. While this move to legibility made modern dance more accessible to broader audiences, it also proved that the idiom was up to the task of representing enduring stories of human history, including those that shed light on vexing issues brought by the end of the war and that were commonly brushed under the domestic rug.

[3]
ACTION IS ORDINARY
Anna Sokolow

Western Man in the middle of the twentieth century is tense, uncertain, adrift. We look upon our epoch as a time of troubles, an age of anxiety. The grounds of our civilization, of our certitude, are breaking up under our feet, and familiar ideas and institutions vanish as we reach for them, like shadows in falling dust.

(Arthur Schlesinger Jr. [1949] 1998, 1)

A NNA Sokolow's *Rooms* (1955) was one of the most psychologically pen-etrating and visually arresting choreographic works of its time. It portrayed individuals who live in close proximity to one another and yet cannot make a connection, atomized subjects living amidst the masses in mid-century New York City, members of "the lonely crowd" in America. Through a series of portraits, composed of solos and several group sections, performed to Kenyon Hopkins' jazz-based score, the work offered glimpses into the pitiable side of the human condition—isolation, self-absorption, desperation, obsession, longing—as embodied by city dwellers. Unlike Sokolow's Depression era work, which owed to a social realist aesthetic in its depictions of classic scenes from the economic class struggle, *Rooms* was more general in its indictments, and therefore more suggestive of the plights of everyday people, regardless of their socioeconomic identities. The premise was that its characters live feet away from each other in the same New York City apartment building and yet feel isolated and alone. As Sokolow put it, "[*Rooms*] reflects the tiny awful loneliness of people shut up in their rooms in a place like New York" (Sokolow quoted in Hering June 1955b, 36).

For Sokolow, an early proponent of Revolutionary modern dance, the work and its success marked the culmination of a decadelong personal and artistic reassessment and experimentation in which she readapted her mode of trenchant social critique to the various demands of the times. The same critics who had faulted Sokolow's work in the immediate postwar period for its aesthetic and political anachronism now hailed her achievement with *Rooms*, in spite of what John Martin, a reviewer for the *New York Times*, called its "monotony of key, its excessive length and half a dozen other objections that can be raised against it" (Martin May 16, 1955, 26). Martin, for his qualms, deemed it "one of the best pieces of the season in its own special way." "On a theme of urban loneliness and isolation," he commented, "Miss Sokolow shows us a set of eight commonplace individuals, involuntarily grouped together, pretty well unaware of one [an]other's existence, and each with an obsessive problem. . . . it is another of those studies in quiet desperation, done in half light, mostly in slow motion . . . [and] its ultimate aim seems to be to induce you to jump as inconspicuously as possible into the nearest river" (May 16, 1955).

While Sokolow's work conformed to the expressive economy advocated by the modern dance universalists (kinesthetic empathy), in many ways it announced its departure from artistic convention. Stripped of some of the trappings of modern dance universalism—mythic, archetypal, legendary, or heroic figures facing a defining conflict—its protagonists were ordinary New Yorkers engaged in their everyday lives. Set pieces amplified this atmosphere of the mundane: a bunch of chairs that dancers moved on- and offstage, their numbers reduced, multiplied, and recombined for each section. Finally, the piece had no climax, no possibility for catharsis. Instead its anticlimax underlined the individual's existential struggle to make meaning in the context of the day to day.

Investigating the dance alongside two comparable and contemporaneous formations—intellectual accounts of subjectivity and the built environment of New York City—this chapter focuses on *Rooms'* quiet yet direct protest. This came in the form of its embodiment of alienation—consciousness without agency, isolation in the midst of a crowd, residence in a human-created hell. Likewise, in the spirit of Sokolow's postwar work, this chapter enlists the dance to reveal conditions for postwar New Yorkers that were commonly attributed to suburbanites: anonymity, homogeneity, conformity, and estrangement.

A Childhood in New York City

Sokolow drew inspiration for the piece from her lifelong experience as a Jewish New Yorker. In a profile written about Sokolow in 1955, Doris

Hering identified what appeared to her to be one of the central ironies of *Rooms*: How could such a stark denunciation of city life have been choreographed by someone who "deeply loved the city—who would never choose to live anywhere else—who is truly happy and creative only when surrounded by New York's concrete and soot" (Hering June 1955, 36)? The answer to such a question has several layers, some of which can be unearthed through a brief discussion of Sokolow's early life and work as an artist.

The third-born child of Russian immigrant parents, Sokolow grew up in New York in tenement houses on the Lower and Upper East Sides of Manhattan. When Sokolow was three, her family moved to New York from Hartford, settling on St. Mark's place in what is now known as the East Village. Her early years were all but stable. Like many male Jewish immigrants, her father, Samuel, who had been trained in Russia as a Talmudic scholar, had trouble adjusting to life in the United States. When her father's attempts to secure an occupation failed, Anna's mother, Sarah, took on the breadwinner role, working from dawn until dusk as a seamstress in a garment factory. When he soon became gravely ill with the early stages of Parkinson's disease, her mother was forced to commit him to a charity hospital where he spent the rest of his life. Samuel's departure from the home forced Sarah to bring Anna's infant sister, Gertie, to a Jewish orphanage, as there was no other family in New York to take care of her. Anna, who was around four years old at the time, attended a preschool in the neighborhood, while her older brother, Isadore, and sister Rose attended a public elementary school. Eventually Isadore dropped out of high school so that he could take odd jobs to contribute to the family's income (Hering June 1955b; Warren 1991).

In spite of these hardships, some of which were simply part of living in New York City itself, the city in turn gave Anna much in the way of enrichment. As Hering put it, "For some, this urban environment would have been an adversary. For Anna Sokolow it has done two things. It has given her a deep and sure insight into all kinds of people. And it has given her a sense of place-belonging" (Hering June 1955b, 36–37). While Sokolow's "deep and sure insight into all kinds of people" would surface later, in her choreography, her sense of belonging in the city was evident early on. She believed that the city was a learning ground. Here she could avail herself of the accessible and affordable opportunities it offered for self-improvement and entertainment, and she could observe myriad examples of humankind in the people she encountered every day.

Sokolow began dancing as a young child at the Emanuel Sisterhood of Personal Service, a settlement house near her apartment building where she and her sister Rose studied fine art, theater, and dance. Founded mostly by affluent American Jews, settlement houses like the Emanuel Sisterhood helped recent immigrants assimilate to American culture, providing after-school programs for children of working mothers in which children could take classes including those in the fine and performing arts. "The development of new dance in America . . . was indebted not only to descendents of the Duncan and Denishawn traditions, but to a generation of immigrant children educated in the settlement houses" (Graff 1997, 18; Tomko 1999; S. Jackson 2000, 7–13). Settlement houses employed modern dance artists to teach young children as they waited for working parents to pick them up after school. Choreographer Helen Tamaris remembered the classes at Henry Street Settlement House on New York's Lower East Side thus, "The dancing was called interpretive dancing. We danced in a large room—with transparent red gold curtains. On the walls were pictures of dancing girls by Botticelli, in long draped costumes—with garlands of flowers in their hair. I loved the soft lights and the little framed pictures in silhouette over the piano [of] little figures leaping over each other. . . . This was a new world far away from the wild life of the streets" (Tamaris quoted in Graff 1997, 18–19).

When she was fifteen, Sokolow too began taking dance classes at Henry Street on scholarship. She now lived with her sister Rose and her family in a loft (after having been kicked out of her house by her mother because she had said she wanted to become a professional dancer). At Henry Street, directed by Alice and Irene Lewisohn (whose family of means came from Germany), Sokolow studied with some of the most innovative teachers and artists in modern dance at that time including Blanche Talmud, Bird Larsen, Michio Ito, Benjamin Zemach, and Louis Horst (Rossen 2006). According to Rebecca Rossen, "Here, ideologies of reform and acculturation mingled with dance technologies to mold American bodies out of Jewish bodies. The Lewisohns' programs became unique sites for the transformation of first-generation daughters of working-class, Eastern European immigrants into the first (or at least second) generation of American modern dancers" (2006, 150).

FIG. 3.1 *Left to right*: Elsa Pohl, Anna Sokolow, and unknown dancer as "Beauty, Reason and Folly." Emanuel Sisterhood (1922). Photo by Hiram Myers. Courtesy of the Sokolow Dance Foundation.

It was at Henry Street that she met the young Martha Graham and composer Louis Horst. Soon she joined Graham's first company, yet she felt most engaged in Horst's choreography classes. For the early modern choreographers these classes seemed essential if they were ever to compose their own work. As choreographer Sophie Maslow, another member of Graham's company, recalls, "We all studied choreography with Louis. It never occurred to us not to. If we wanted to dance away from the Graham company, what would we dance if we didn't create the dances ourselves? There were no solos to be learned like variations from *Swan Lake*, and we certainly were not going to do excerpts from Martha's works" (Warren 1991, quotes Maslow on 23).

Eventually Horst asked her to be his assistant, a choreographic apprenticeship of sorts. "He had not only introduced a world of music to her (she first heard Gershwin, Poulenc, and Scriabin among many others from his keyboard) but he also had led her, through music, to an understanding of some of the most basic tools of her craft" (Warren 1991, 25).

Sokolow's Revolutionary Dance

In 1937, Sokolow gave a lecture at the New School,[1] in which she made a distinction between modern dance, which she said was inherently revolutionary because it "has broken from the classic, using new techniques, new forms, new subject matter," and what she called "the revolutionary dance movement," "which allied itself with the point of view of the revolutionary class itself—which, today, is the working class"[2] (Church Dec. 1937). On the one hand, Sokolow's political consciousness had been fostered by her mother, a socialist and an active International Ladies Garment Workers Union (ILGWU) member who, like many Eastern European immigrants to the United States, "transformed [her] religious zeal into energy to fight for social change" (Warren 6). On the other hand, it was nurtured by the dynamic political atmosphere in New York City, one of the hotbeds of leftist political activity (Graff 1997, 6; Denning 1997). According to Graff, "This geographic intimacy was convenient for socially conscious dancers, and the collision of the two revolutionary worlds sparked an explosion of choreographic activity. The antiacademy and antielitist basis of modern dance fit nicely within the mission of proletarian culture, just as the proletarian worker proved an eager student and enthusiastic audience for the emergent art" (7).

Immersed in the turbulent and politically charged atmosphere of the Depression era leftist movements, Sokolow embraced their causes as her own, creating socially trenchant works that struck a delicate balance between the sometimes contradictory commitments of art and politics. At the same time, she contributed to the efforts by Jewish modern dancers to the formation of universalist dance modernism. As Naomi Jackson notes, "radical dance was a kind of Jewish dance" (2000, 176). She continues, "[Jewish dancers] from socially conscious backgrounds were passionately engaged in redefining these entities, even as they joined them. It was not a straightforward matter of assimilating to American culture but of reshaping art and society in line with egalitarian views at the root of Jewish ethics and the historical experience of persecution" (177).

Sokolow's first forays into the choreographic arena came under the aegis of the Workers Dance League, an organization she helped to found in 1932 along with Edith Segal, Miriam Blecher, and Nadia Chilkovsky.

With its motto, "The Dance Is a Weapon in the Revolutionary Class Struggle," its mission was to make accessible dance training and performances to workers in New York City (Warren 1991, 34; Graff 1997, 7–8). Contributing to a choreographic collective, Sokolow, alongside these choreographers and others, presented her work as part of group evenings and even political rallies (called Spartakiades), sometimes before thousands of workers. Reviewing one such evening for the *New York Times* in 1934, John Martin found Sokolow's work to hold the most promise. "Miss Sokolow handles a group like an experienced choreographer," he commented. "[S]he has a fine, solid grasp of the elements of form, her technical requirements are high, and she rarely lets external bits of propaganda get in her way" (January 21, 1934, X8).

Whereas Martin usually expressed skepticism about the extent to which art could do political bidding, on recognizing the accomplishments of Sokolow and others he tentatively reconsidered: "The function of art is not to bring us merely up to the point of common experience," he wrote, "but rather to start from common experience and lead us into a fuller sense of the underlying realities involved."[3] In other words, good art should not merely represent what we already know about the world or what we thought was "real." Instead it should "defamiliarize" reality by illuminating what lay under it, so as to make visible, and palpable, truths about the world that viewers might rather ignore or gloss over. In practice, this choreography of socialist realism[4] demonstrated many of the same characteristics of Bertolt Brecht's "epic theater," which, in his words, "involved . . . a technique of taking the human social incidents to be portrayed and labeling them as something striking, something that calls for explanation, [something that] is not to be taken for granted, not just natural. The object of this 'effect' is to allow the spectator to criticize constructively from a social point of view" (Willett [1957] 1964, 125).

Sokolow shared Brecht's intention of raising viewers' consciousness about the compromising conditions of contemporary life in the hope of prompting collective action toward social reform. In *Strange American Funeral* (1935), for example, Sokolow adapted a poem by Michael Gold (with music by Elie Seigmeister) about a steelworker "caught in a flood of molten ore—whose flesh and blood turned to steel" (Martin, June 30, 1935; Gilfond, May 1936, 54). Similarly *Case History No.—* depicted the human toll of poverty and urban decrepitude in the form of a delinquent and "defiant" youth (Church, March 1937, 41).[5] In her review, Marjorie Church attempted to tease out the ways in which Sokolow's work cultivated an activist's point of view: "By her work, one is aware that she desires, not to extol the virtue or deplore the plight of workers, but to speak of and to working class audiences, in terms of their own experiences and with clear delineation of relationships and contradictions in that experience. By the very juxtaposition of these contradictory elements, a comment is evolved and a direction indicated" (Church, April 1937).

Sokolow's objective, to use modernism as a vehicle through which to represent class-based humanitarian issues, coincided with that of other artists working toward the causes of what was called the Popular Front. Representing the internationalization of left-wing movements for social and class justice, it was a mobilizing construct around which proponents could unite in the cause of resisting oppressive power structures around the world, most clearly manifest in fascism (Fer et al. 1993, 256–57). It is not surprising then that Mexican painter and activist Carlos Mérida greatly admired Sokolow's work, some of which, like *Slaughter of the Innocents*, later called *Madrid*, had a Latin American import.[6] On seeing a performance in 1939, Mérida offered her an artistic residency and performances in Mexico (Warren 1991, 81–82). On the invitation of the Mexican administration of President Lázaro Cárdenas, Sokolow extended this residency, living and working in Mexico for nearly two years and collaborating with other artists who were equally committed to revolutionary art as she was.[7] These were momentous years in Mexican history, during which, under Cárdenas (1934–1940), the country began to pursue the social program envisioned by earlier revolutionaries (Folgarait 1987, 12).

Sokolow's almost decadelong involvement in the Mexican artistic community sustained the significance of her revolutionary dance during the years in which modern dance in New York City underwent a sea change. Mexico's progressive movements reached their height of activity and impact under Cárdenas during the pre- and early war years, encouraging artists to work in the same political spirit. By comparison, the Popular Front all but dissolved in New York leading up to the war, as members of the left wing incorporated themselves into broader political circles prompted by offshore events, such as the militarization of Germany, the German occupation, the formation of the Axis power coalition, and U.S. entry into the war following the Japanese attack on Pearl Harbor (Denning 1997, 3–50). Likewise choreographers in New York felt a need to assess the ways in which their work might better address the emerging sociocultural conditions of such events. In the modern arts, including dance, nationalism became the rallying call of the day as artists redirected their attention toward the support of American troops fighting abroad and the cause of unifying the nation (Kowal 1999; Manning 2004; Morris 2006).

At the same time, choreographers began to adopt noticeably different modes of representation as well as subjects for choreography, on the one hand embracing the lyricism afforded by the increasing number of ballet-trained dancers in their ranks, and, on the other, looking for subject matter that spoke to the new nationalism. This change can best be exemplified in works like Graham's *Frontier* (1935), *American Document* (1938), *Salem Shore* (1943), and *Appalachian Spring* (1944) (Graff 1997, 105–31; Manning 2004, 115–77). These works, and others like them, glossed over markers of racial, ethnic, and class differences in order to emphasize the universality of seminal American experiences through characters who negotiated the treacherous terrain of belonging to a nation. Although not all revolutionary choreographers fell into aesthetic line, there was certainly an expectation among critics that they would, or should. While Sokolow's experience in Mexico nurtured her in many ways, personal, artistic, and political, it set her out of step with the modern dance community in New York. As Hering put it, "By one of the many contradictions that have flavored Miss Sokolow's career, as her prestige in Mexico increased, her reputation in New York declined. She became almost a stranger in the dance world of her own country" (Hering 1955b, 37).

The Problem of Coming Home

Between 1939 and 1948, when she was commuting back and forth to New York from Mexico, Sokolow's stature in the New York modern dance community changed significantly. Whereas once critics had found her work full of promise, now they called it "outdated." In one account of Sokolow's first concert back in New York, Mary O'Donnell described a scene in which "Hundreds of Anna Sokolow's staunch admirers thronged the Theresa L. Kaufmann Auditorium to sit or stand but above all to welcome Miss Sokolow upon her return from Mexico and to assist at such a gala occasion in the dance world." Yet, on seeing the concert, O'Donnell wondered what all the fuss was about. "It would be gratifying to be able to record that the recital was worthy of the high-spirited anticipation which preceded it," she wrote. "Such unfortunately was not the case" (1940, 55). In her 1942 review of another one of Sokolow's rare New York appearances, Lois Balcom was more specific in her criticism. While she praised Sokolow for her expression of "vivid lyricism" she charged that, on the whole, her work "still seems reminiscent of a stage which modern dance once passed through but has now for the most part emerged from-the stage of fixed gaze and unrelieved persuasive movement when tenseness in body pattern was made to served for high emotional tension in the dancers themselves" (quoted in Warren, 100). On Sokolow's 1943 concert, Balcom commented similarly, "The Sokolow program, 'takes one back,' back to a clearly delineated and easily 'datable' period in modern dance-the 1930s. . . . This is not a happy outcome for a young artist of Anna Sokolow's creative promise. Perhaps she has remained away too long, or perhaps it is merely that invention does not always keep pace with conviction" (Balcom January 1944, 9).

Edwin Denby, critic for the *New York Herald Tribune*, reached similar conclusions about the anachronism of Sokolow's aesthetic in 1943, although attributing the problem to a lack of artistic maturity: "the old numbers dealing with such themes as slum childhood, juvenile delinquency, or Loyalist Madrid—numbers that once seemed natural as adolescent reflections—now, seen in an adult atmosphere, look artificial and false to their terrible themes" (1986, 181; other similar reviews are found in Warren 1991, 101–3).[8]

By all accounts, this was a difficult period for Sokolow, one in which she had to adjust herself and her work to the circumstances of life in New York, as well as to public interest and concern about the Jewish Holocaust. As Jackson points out, "The increased intersection of Jewish interests with modern dance focused the challenge to a purist, apolitical definition of modern dance, reframing it as an expression of social/ethnic/political consciousness and as a hybrid style with disparate influences" (2000, 187). What this meant was the Jewish modern dancers adapted themes and subject matter that had always been the province of Jewish concert dance to the requirements both of universalist dance modernism and the postwar ethos. Sidestepping the overt socialist content of Revolutionary dance, their dances drew on the "two principal sources" from which to create "Jewish dance," identified by John Martin in a review of a concert by Benjamin Zemach: (1) "the actual physical movements of the Jewish folk in their daily life and . . . their religious practices, such as those especially of the Chassidic sect," and (2) "the characteristic daily movement . . . described as the 'rhythm of city living'" (quoted in Jackson 2000, 179).

Sokolow's *The Exile* (1940), *Songs of a Semite* (1943), and *Kaddish, The Bride*, and *Images from the Old Testament* (all 1946), as well as Sophie Maslow's *The Village I Knew* (1951), illustrate the first case in that they were strongly and obviously identified with Jewish religion or culture.[9] Sokolow's *Rooms*, however, falls into the latter category, with its representation of Jewishness by proxy, through the embodiment of "the rhythm of city living" (N. Jackson 2000, 179). According to Warren, Sokolow reinvested in the resources of her own life, "returning to Judaism for inspiration," and thereby "reestablishing continuity with the world of her childhood through her art." "Now the process of turning her life experiences into the expressive language of dance was once again unfolding" (1991, 105).[10] Adversity prompted the choreographer to enlarge and explore the parameters of her life experience and artistic imagination and to become more introspective in her work (103).

At the same time, Sokolow investigated modes of expression and choreographic venues that fell outside the purview of modern concert dance. These included choreographing for the Broadway stage, in projects like Elia Kazan's *Street Scene*, a Broadway musical redux of "Elmer Rice's 1929 Pulitzer Prize winning play" set "in a crowded tenement section of the Lower East Side of Manhattan" (Warren 1991, 107), teaching movement for actors as a member of the faculty at the newly formed Actors Studio,[11] and traveling to Israel in 1953 for a residency with Inbal, a Yemenite dance company. In all of these arenas, she focused on finding a movement idiom to express the emotional experience of the everyday. As she put it, "I like to dance about people . . . how they feel, what happens to them" (quoted in Goodman 1947, 15). In her teaching at the Actors Studio, for example, Sokolow applied her own work of "searching for truth" to the problem of so-called method-acting, to train actors to render characters through the plumbing of their most significant personal experiences (Warren 1991, 115–16). Similarly, in working with the Inbal group, she helped company members find a sincere and effective mode of choreographic expression. In the words of Sara Levi Tanai, then director of Inbal, "[S]he tried to understand our world, which was so far from her own experience . . . to understand the essence of our works, our spirit, and our style. . . . When she understood the source of our inspiration and what we were trying to say, she helped us free ourselves to be more able to say it" (Tanai 1955; see also Hering June 1955b).

The Culture of Consensus

In many ways, both in its content and political slant, Sokolow's postwar reassessment resonated with the work of contemporaneous social scientists, who were likewise compelled to reexamine their governing assumptions against the social, political, and economic realities at mid-century. Daniel Bell, John Kenneth Galbraith, David Riesman, Arthur Schlesinger Jr., and William Whyte, for example, all reappraised what they had inherited of leftist political thought, prompted by the global and domestic consequences of World War II. On a worldwide scale these included the devastation of Western European cities, economies and social fabrics; disillusionment and cynicism brought by both the holocaust and the detonation of the nuclear bomb on Hiroshima and Nagasaki; soviet totalitarianism and postwar expansionism; and the simmering cold war. Domestic conditions included the boom of the consumer economy, the standardization of goods and services, the postwar wave of suburban development, and, finally, home front anticommunism.

Acknowledgement of changing historical conditions led each scholar, in one way or another, to note "a disconcerting caesura" between the older generation New Deal liberals and the "new generation, with no meaningful memories of these old debates, and no secure tradition to build upon" (Bell [1960] 1962, 404).[12] As Schlesinger offered, one's political philosophy "need not invoke Marx at every turn in the road, or point its prayer-rug to Moscow" ([1949] 1998, 156). Similarly, Bell, a self-identified "radical intellectual who had articulated the revolutionary impulses of the past century and a half," declared that "ideology" as Marx had defined it, was now an outmoded and bankrupt concept (256). Instead Schlesinger, Bell, and the others looked to the individual, not the mobilization of the masses through organized political movements, as a vehicle for social change. As

Schlesinger put it, "The consequence of this historical re-education has been an unconventional rejection of totalitarianism and a reassertion of the ultimate integrity of the individual" (ix).

In making such contentions, social scientists brought on themselves a burden that prompted their own scholarly investigations—finding new and meaningful ways of negotiating the tension between individual responsibility and collectivism. What was the individual's obligation to self, family, community, society, and world? And to what extent did such obligations hinder individuation, on the one hand, or compassion for others, on the other? If individuals were the world's last great hope, what kinds of challenges stood in the way of their self-realization, autonomy, judgment, or potency? The desire for power, the pull of societal convention, or the yearning to belong to a group, for example, could drive a person to conform blindly to the expectations of others. These tendencies seemed particularly threatening under the specter of communism, which gave rise to fears that susceptible Americans might fall under its ideological sway. These were not unlike the questions that motivated Sokolow in her dances "about people . . . how they feel, what happens to them."

As it had in *Rooms*, anxiety about conformity motivated scholarly works, each painting a picture of postwar individuals as followers who sublimated their personal desires to accommodate or adapt to what they perceived as the conventional wisdom or standard. In *The Lonely Crowd* ([1950] 1977), David Riesman observed a greater societal tendency to seek approval than to act autonomously, to conform and adjust rather than to assert difference. He named such behavior "other-directed" and postulated that "the other-directed man simply does not seek power; perhaps, rather, he avoids and evades it. . . . In a sense, he would rather be right than be president" (239). In this way, conformity placed freedom at risk: "The idea that men are created free and equal is both true and misleading: men are created different; they lose their social freedom and their individual autonomy in seeking to become like each other" (307). William Whyte articulated similar concerns in *The Organization of Man*, which criticized the "collectivization" of American society embodied in the image of the "organization," the manifestation of a mass need to "belong" (1956). He urged his readers to be aware of and not fall prey to conformists in their midst. "Listen to them talk to each other over the front lawns of their suburbia," he implored, "and you cannot help but be struck by how well they grasp the common denominators which bind them" (4). For his part, Galbraith, in *The Affluent Society*, examined the draw of consumer culture and the cause and effect relationship between the mechanics of the mass market and the proclivity of Americans to want to be like each other. Manipulated by the exigencies of the marketplace, individuals' "wants were increasingly created by the process by which they are satisfied" (1958, 158). Such an environment produced consumers, people whose sense of individualism was expressed in the ability to acquire mass-produced material objects, and who felt accomplished in satisfying externally manufactured "wants."

Yet for all of their cogent and pressing observations, these scholars set the bar low in their recommendations and suggestion of alternatives. In fact, under the pressure of "the culture of consensus," none condemned conventionalism outright, even as they catalogued the ills of conformity. Schlesinger put this in terms of "maintaining a social dimension" (249) in which an individual's nourishment occurred in the context of society.[13] "For all the magnificent triumphs of individualism," he wrote, "we survive only as we remain members of one another" (248). Whyte too advocated "individualism *within* organization life" (12; emphasis mine). As he put it, "We do need to know how to co-operate with The Organization but, more than ever, so do we need to know how to resist it" (13). Striking this perilous balance demanded consciousness—the ability to stand at a distance from social and political authority and to cooperate with others in action while maintaining the right of private judgment (Whyte 1956, 251). For Galbraith, autonomy came in the cultivation of the ability not only to resist "contrived" wants but also to become aware of "original needs." In these ways, people could more effectively manage the demands of the market, which fueled their desire to spend money on useless objects, without getting carried away by them (1958, 153).

Perhaps closest to Sokolow's conception of the contemporary postwar subject as seen in *Rooms* was Bell's reconsideration of Marxist "alienation." Marx defined alienation as the condition in which individuals, who have become objects by "losing control of the process of [their] work and of the product of [their] labor," become separated from themselves; in this case, individuals lack agency and the necessary conditions for the development of consciousness (Bell [1960] 1962 quotes Marx on 360). By contrast, Bell used "alienation" to describe a condition of separation, "Alienation is not nihilism but a positive role, a detachment, which guards one against being submerged in any cause, or accepting any particular embodiment of community as final. The individual insulated himself from conformist social pressures with critical detachment." "What is left for the critic," he wrote, "is a hardness of alienation, the sense of otherness. The claims of doubt are prior to claims of faith" (16). As we will see, however, *Rooms* reversed conditions within Bell's framework to show insulation and alienation, not as stances of critical detachment, and, therefore, advantageous to the formation of subjectivity, but as conditions of isolation. What is more, the work portrayed consciousness without real agency, enacting individual lives contained by the strictures of social life and structures of the built environment.

The Lonely Suburbanite

In many ways, *The Lonely Crowd*, and investigations like it, labored to diagnose the social problems endemic to affluent, white, middle class, mid-century American society—people who appeared on the surface to have no real problems at all. The end of the war had vitalized the American economy. Gone was the massive unemployment of the Great Depression and the disruption of the workforce of the wartime economy. By 1949, fewer than 5 percent of able (male) workers were unemployed. Many industrial workers, including blacks and recent immigrants, enjoyed increased wages and benefits and fewer work hours.[14] The economy absorbed a greater number of female workers who remained working after the war, either as primary breadwinners or supplemental earners in their homes.[15] The gross national product had risen 200 percent from 1940 to 1945 and reached $284 billion in 1950, compared with $55 billion in 1933 (Doss 1991, 333). The high employment and growth in productivity meant that there was a greater distribution of wealth among American citizens and an overall improvement in their quality of living (Leuchtenburg 1983, 50; Patterson 1996). Although between 1945 and 1959, the percentage of all Americans living in poverty declined only slightly to 22 percent, the numbers of Americans who owned homes, enrolled in institutions of higher education, and could obtain the latest products of comfort and convenience increased considerably. Optimism about productivity and the pleasures associated with consumption substituted for marked increases in class status; in effect, temporary purchasing power acted as a surrogate for sizable increases in wealth.

Such widespread affluence offered the chance for a standardization of expectation among white middle-class Americans. Leuchtenburg and others have highlighted how the "booming economy enabled millions of Americans to take part in the burgeoning consumer culture" (Leuchtenburg 1983, 55). For many, that is, those who had the means to keep up with the Joneses, "togetherness" and "belonging" became central life goals expressed through common practices of consumption (73).[16] On the one hand, standardization of mass production, the proliferation of mass media (including TV and radio), the growth of franchises, and the rise of suburban living provided the means by which anyone who could afford it could belong to the middle class and therefore live like everybody else. "With unprecedented amounts of disposable income, consumers devoted much of their time to institutions that catered to their needs and whims— shopping malls with hanging baskets of flowers and piped music, suburban department stores with civic auditoriums, supermarkets with row on row of brilliantly colored cartons" (55). On the other hand, such trends added to the feeling of a homogenized culture. Access, or lack thereof, to the amenities of a moneyed world signified difference—race, in this case mapped onto class. Increasingly, improvements in working conditions for most industrial workers, unionization, and new opportunities for their economic advancement made it less likely that workers, as Bell argued in *The End of Ideology*, would see themselves only as objects of labor (1960).[17]

Whether fair or not, many of these practices of conformity, mass production, and homogeneity got boiled down in the entity of the suburb. An expedient answer to the acute housing shortage the country faced after World War II, the proliferation of suburban development across the country provided numerous families the chance to own their own homes (Jackson 1985; Stilgoe 1988; Fishman 1987; Hayden 2003; Lewis 2004). The shortage came because of demands of returning veterans relocating after the war and was exacerbated by an unanticipated marriage boom, during and especially after, the war. Defying predictions, in 1946, for example, at the peak of the boom, the marriage rate was 2.5 times greater than expected (1.5 million marriages compared with 600,000 predicted)

("Housing: The Boom Is Over," 1951, 80). As the *New York Times* reported in December 1945,

> Home, sweet home is a nightmare crisis instead of a song for America's war-shifted millions, and their housing problem is a top priority headache in every section of the nation. . . . The scarcity picture, which has been intensified since V-J Day, is a hectic composite in which thousands of families are doubling up, living in substandard dwellings, even sleeping in cars, sheds, railroad stations, streets, garages, cellars, or trailers; or occasionally in a pup tent, school or filling station. (See also Hayden 2003, 131–132)

To fund the growth in the housing industry—10 million new units between 1946 and 1952—banks loaned generously to developers "backed by the Federal Housing Administration (FHA) and the Veterans Administration (VA)" (Hayden 2003, 132). Providing builders with loans and tax incentives while making provisions that allowed servicemen to purchase homes with no money down, the government initiated a housing boom that lasted until 1951 ("Housing: The Boom is Over," 1951; "How Long Can Boom in Housing Go On?," 1955, 76–77). Levittown, Long Island, one of the first suburban communities constructed after the war, epitomized the application of mass production on the housing industry. A 1950 *Newsweek* magazine describes the process by which "1,200 flat acres of potato farmland near Hicksville, Long Island," became one of the two Levittown communities constructed after the war:

> An army of trucks sped over new-laid roads. Every 100 feet the trucks stopped and dumped identical bundles of lumber, pipes, bricks, shingles and copper tubing-all as neatly packaged as loaves from a bakery. Near the bundles, giant machines with an endless chain of buckets ate into the earth, taking just 13 minutes to dig a narrow, four-foot trench around a 24-by-32 ft. rectangle. Then came more trucks, loaded with cement, and laid a four-inch foundation for a house in the rectangle. After the machines came the men. On nearby slabs already dry, they worked in crews of two and three, laying bricks, raising studs, nailing lath, painting, sheathing, shingling. Each crew did its special job, then hurried on to the next site. Under the skilled combination of men & machines, new houses rose faster than Jack ever built them; a new one

was finished every 15 minutes. ("Housing: Up from the Potato Fields," July 3, 1950)

When completed, Levittown on Long Island had 10,600 houses and a population of 40,000 and growing. Levittown in Pennsylvania was even larger; built on 5,500 acres in lower Bucks County, it boasted 17,311 single-family homes and over 70,000 residents (State Museum of Pennsylvania Web site).

In the public mind and practice, the suburb was more than a means by which millions of families could put roofs over their heads; the suburban house more than a shrine to the nuclear family ideal. According to Clifford E. Clark Jr., the desire to own a suburban home revealed people's private aspiration and was evidence of the "rise of an unprecedented consensus which saw affluence as the core of the new order" (1989, 171). Robert C. Wood's 1958 study, *Suburbia: Its People and Their Politics* bore this theory out. Appropriating the fashionable idea that suburbia was "a looking glass in which the character, behavior, and culture of middle class American is displayed," he turned the mirror inward to "find a man who is not appealing" (4). Like Riesman, Wood contrasted the suburbanite with the man of yore—"the stern Puritan, the sturdy yeoman, the hardworking capitalist" (4). These types now all but nonexistent, "in their place is a prototype whom it is difficult to idealize: a man without direction or ambition except for his desire for a certain portion of material security, a man so conscious of his fellows that he has no convictions of his own" (4). In suburbia, he argued, "David Reisman's lonely crowd is everywhere" (5).

To these images of suburban dystopia, the city, especially New York City, was typically counterposed as antidote. Assuming the role of "culture capital of the world" with the literal destruction of Paris and the immigration of numerous European artists, intellectuals, and philanthropists, postwar New York appeared to residents and outsiders alike to be brimming with diversity, verve, and panache. In the words of author E. B. White, a New Yorker, "The city is like poetry: it compresses all life, races and breeds, into a small island and adds music and the accompaniment of internal engines" (1949, 21–22). Or as British writer J. B. Priestly put it, "Its huge cosmopolitanism—it has more Jews than Palestine and more Italians than Naples—is untouched in the history of man. . . . The

FIG. 3.2 Levittown, New York. circa 1950. Copyright and courtesy of Associated Press Images.

ends of the earth are gathered together down one New York City side street. You can dine, drink and amuse yourself in three continents. The New York that O. Henry described forty years ago was an American City, but today's glittering cosmopolis belongs to the world, if the world does not belong to it" (1948).

According to White, Priestly, and many others, the intermingling of millions of foreign-born and native people representing so many races and creeds, made New York a permanent exhibition of the universalist phenomenon of "one world."

And yet, in spite of its cosmopolitan stature, New York was not immune to the housing problems facing the rest of the country after World War II; these were, in some ways, more acute and insurmountable for the residents of the city's five boroughs. In the postwar years, the city faced a huge influx of population, comprised not only of veterans returning from abroad who decided to settle in the city, but also similarly massive numbers of southern blacks and newly immigrated Puerto Ricans. Finding ways of dealing with this influx posed numerous challenges to city officials and residents, who, during the war years, had been focused on housing military personnel and their families (Plunz 1990, 247).[18]

Dancing Alienation

Rooms is not pretty. But it is real.

(Hering April 1958; italics added)

Defying proclamations, like those by White or Priestly, of the city's resistance to forces and problems of suburbanization, Sokolow's *Rooms* performed the city as other, bringing to light existing conditions of atomization, paranoia, dislocation, and itinerant loneliness that, conceivably, many experienced but brushed under the rug. Rather than speak out overtly about these conditions as she may have at an earlier time, Sokolow physicalized them in action. Through a movement metaphor, *Rooms* invoked the world offstage: bodies shaped by and shaping the built environment, conditions of corporeal life that had emerged both by the severe postwar housing crisis and some of its logistical exigencies.

The concept for *Rooms* grew out of early studies Sokolow conducted at the Actors Studio with students.[19] As Warren details, "Occasionally she worked with two or three couples, at other times with a solo figure. The images she gave the actors to work with were drafted from her lifetime as an insatiably curious observer in what may be the loneliest city in the world" (1991, 119). Using an interrogative method not unlike the one that contemporary choreographer Pina Bausch is known for today, Sokolow asked the actors to improvise to questions like "You're looking out the window. What do you see?" or, accompanied by a recording of Stan Keaton's song "The Nearness of You," "How does it feel to be near someone who is not there?" (Ibid.). Aza Bard McKenzie, with whom Anna created "Escape," recalls that the work took shape over a period of months during which "the roles and the characters would change or be molded in one way or another." "Anna, of course, developed the movements," she remembered, "but it was in the evolution of the relationships, the inner-content, that the actors were so valuable. What they came up with was the life that was going on inside them" (quoted in Warren 1991, 119–20). Later, when Sokolow set the work upon dancers, the piece changed slightly as its themes became more physically "elaborated" (quoting McKenzie) and movement vocabulary more refined. As described by Sokolow, "*Rooms* ends where it began. Dreams. No ending. That's the Jew in me. Ask the world a question and there's no answer. All I do is present what I feel and you answer. You answer" (quoted in Murphy [1980] 1990; italics added). Throughout, Sokolow emphasized a concept central to the theory of action as elucidated in this book—"dancing is movement" not "steps" (Sabin 1953, 36).

The work is composed of nine sections—"Alone," "Dream," "Escape," "Going," "Desire," "Panic," "Daydream," "The End," and "Alone" (a redux)—each revolving around a particular state of emotion, action, or imagination.[20] Paradoxically, the work is performed by a group of anonymous individuals, each enacting a different account of solitude. "Alone," the first section, begins in darkness, accompanied by Hopkins' fast-paced and edgy score. The lights come up as dancers enter the stage then take their seats on evenly spaced chairs. They look around slowly with glazed stares. Then, in a building cacophony, they begin to assert themselves, some standing up, some sitting up, others sitting sideways they clump, thump, kick, stomp, and slump, performing movement motifs of some of the extended phrases that will appear in their entirety over the course of the dance. "Alone" ends as each person, sitting and facing front again, leans forward as if having something to say, but not uttering a word. Here we see a group of people living in close proximity yet each in a solitary world. Although each has a story to tell—an indication of each person's individuation—no one can get in a word edgewise since everybody's talking at once. Sokolow described the section in these terms, "Each person in a chair is alone in a room, and they are looking out of the window. The room is very small and they don't know who lives next door. They don't know who they pass on the stairs going up and down. . . . [I]t's like saying alone, alone, alone, eight times" (quoted in Warren 1991, 149).

Several solo sections follow including "Dream," "Escape," "Going," and "The End"; these are interspersed with a few group sections entitled "Desire," "Panic," "Daydream," and "Alone" (redux). In "Dream," the section following "Alone," a man fights the contradictory urges of rest and mobilization. In sustained movement passages that accelerate, decelerate, or

FIG. 3.3 Beatrice Seckler in "Escape" from Anna Sokolow's *Rooms*. Photo by W. H. Stephan, New York City. Courtesy of the Sokolow Dance Foundation.

stop without warning, or in lyrical adagio phrases punctuated by impulsive halts, he expresses the unforeseen adventures of the dream imagination. "Escape" is similar in its depiction of a contradiction, this time between availability and remoteness. A woman waits, embodying the feeling of expectancy (as if she awaits a soon-to-arrive lover) by literally shivering with excitement. To pass the time, she plays a hide-and-seek game with herself around the chairs. In this, she is transported to a state of reverie; slumping down in a chair she spreads her legs and massages the floor with one foot to an internal and regular rhythm. In a gestural pantomime, she holds a mirror to her face, looking at herself and what she looks like; the mirror seems to function as a sign of what or whom is absent, as a substitute witness with whom she might confirm her feelings. In what appears to be another act of verification, she draws her hands to her face and "reads" a letter. What it says sends her in motion in a waltz with herself and a chair as a partner. In a climactic embrace, she lies atop two chairs, one leg sweeping and wrapping sensually around one of them. The section ends in the protagonist's devastation; spinning wildly and throwing down a chair, she appears to have lost her composure, then she steadies herself and stands at the back of a chair in resignation.

Isolation is the dominant theme in the duets as well; even when performers dance together one gets the sense that each is still in his or her own world, in effect, performing solo. Thus group sections amplify the theme of aloneness and anonymity by way of a metaphor of the "lonely crowd." In "Panic," for example, a man creeps around the margins of a group, represented by several cast members. As the others enter the stage to take their seats set in a cluster, the man advances toward them then quickly retreats; no one acknowledges him. At one point, he approaches each of the others standing prostrate, his upper body contracted in an overcurve, his shoulders hunched, his arms clinging to his body. In movement bursts he expresses the anxiety of paranoia. At one point he straightens abruptly and then pauses as though frozen in fear; other times he hurls himself around the space, first at each of the others and then at the floor, an action that sends him spinning out of control. His face in his hands now, he shakes his head then runs to a chair and hides. What causes this panic? Whom does he fear? Are the others on stage people he would like to get close to? Are they people who he imagines secretly watching him? While these others appear unaware of his presence, to what extent has he internalized the feeling that they are nevertheless standing in judgment of him? We never know.

"Desire" expresses estrangement through the structured couplings. Six dancers enter, three men and three women, and take their seats at chairs evenly spaced in two rows of three. Whereas in two cases, a male and female member of a couple face each other, in the third case a chair is turned clockwise so that the male member of the middle couple faces the back of the male in the couple to the right of his partner. Through this brilliant arrangement, Sokolow introduces the possibility of unrequited love, both hetero- and homosexual. Looking like sleepwalkers, dancers reach out blankly to each other, arms extended at ninety degrees forward, hands yearning. All the while, their legs slide on parallel tracks of the floor in even cadence. At another moment, the dancers lie next to each

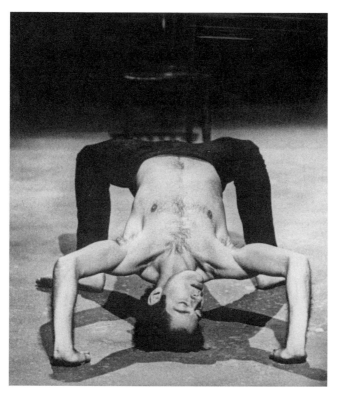

FIG. 3.4 Jeff Duncan in "Panic" from Anna Sokolow's *Rooms,* 1967. Photo by Edward Effron. Courtesy of the Jerome Robbins Dance Division, The New York Public Library of the Performing Arts, Astor, Lenox and Tilden Foundations.

other on the floor, organized horizontal to the chairs. They perform similar reaching movements with both arms and legs, suggesting the myriad ways people can come together, as well as the many barriers to closeness that keep them apart. Whereas choreographic coordination has the potential to evoke images of a coordinated human community, in this case it suggests the possibility that human beings are no better than machines on autopilot. Is love meditated? Is it unwitting? Do docile people have any desire? If so, for what? Moreover, the experience of separateness in the context of the group heightens the sense of each dancer's isolation, on the one hand, and, ironically, deadens its impact, on the other. Not having individuated themselves in any significant way, these people are anonymous; since we cannot identify with them through an experience of shared subjectivity we feel somewhat distanced from their suffering.

Although each section depicts a different scenario, Kenyon Hopkins' jazz score gives the entire work an edgy feel. According to pianist Betty Walberg, Sokolow's accompanist at the Actor's Studio, "[Sokolow] was the first choreographer in contemporary modern dance to commission a jazz score for a concert piece and to treat it as classical score" (quoted in Warren 1991, 149). For example, in "Going," a solo for a male dancer, Sokolow highlights the possibility that Hopkins' music is a kind of soundtrack for life, music that plays in a character's head. In this section, a man moves excitedly to an urban pulse, leaping, jiving, twisting, shimmying, striding, gyrating. As he dances we wonder, "Who is this man," and, more importantly, "Where is he going?" Yet, for all of his momentum, he seems stuck, and therefore "going" nowhere fast.

Sokolow's use of chairs as both set pieces and as props was novel for its time. In Walberg's words, "Now how many dances do we see using chairs?" (quoted in Warren 1991, 149). In the poetic landscape of the piece, the chairs serve multiple purposes. Throughout, they heighten the redolent contrasts between mobility and strandedness, isolation and connection, desire and revulsion. Additionally, they establish a sense of place, a local geography, through their evocation of a room arrangement. In this way, their configurations set the scene for the movement. In some cases, uninhabited chairs indicate absences. Regardless of how chairs are used in any given section, one similarity pervades throughout. All of them are the same—hard, rigid, uncompromising—yet, as though they were social architecture, each person must find ways of adapting to their structure.

Staging the Tower in a Park

But what were these urban exigencies, exactly? Sokolow has commented that her personal experiences, in particular her recollection of tenement living, served as impetus for this work ([1980] 1991). However, I would argue that the work's presentation of city life in terms of anonymity and multiplication also evoked the approach to urban housing synonymous with the postwar period, the "tower in a park." A freestanding high-rise building surrounded by open park space, the tower in a park seemed the most practical, economical, and aesthetically pleasing solution to the postwar housing crunch (Plunz 1990, 240–41). Just prior to the war, the developers of Parkchester, a Bronx housing project completed in 1940, funded privately by Metropolitan Life insurance company,[21] first seized on this idea, maximizing population in the replication of identical high-rise apartment buildings. "Its fifty-one high-rise buildings housed 42,000 persons in 12,273 apartments" (253). Removed from city subway lines and insulated from the city grid by surrounding park space, however, the project separated residents from the urban core. Moreover, its high density and homogenous design minimized the sense of harmonious diversity evoked by White and Priestly in their tributes to urban life.

While wartime construction of housing for nonmilitary personnel and their families was rare, developments like Parkchester served as models for a few publicly funded projects, like the East River Houses in East Harlem, supported by the United States Housing Authority (USHA) and completed in 1941.[22] A more modest development, the East River Houses combined six high-rise with twenty-two low-rise buildings, situated in the area of two cleared city blocks and set off of the orientation of the street gridiron (Plunz 1990, 245). Choreographer Donald McKayle's family was among the first to move there. As he recalls, "We moved into the brand new Harlem Housing Project, where we had a two bedroom apartment filled with light, overlooking tennis courts, a river view park, and a playground. . . . Everything was thoroughly modern, and all tenants had their households moved by vans that were fumigated before they were unloaded into these pristine environs. Everything was wonderful in the new neighborhood, except for one major problem, the public schools" (2002, 5).

Although, as McKayle's account makes evident, many of the development's first residents were optimistic that projects like the East River Houses would be the solution to the problems they faced in their former neighborhoods, for the most part this turned out not to be the case. As tower height increased, often so did crime.[23] Nevertheless, the East River Houses established a precedent for construction in East Harlem in which racially and economically integrated neighborhoods were demolished to make way for high-rise, "tower in the park" housing projects.[24] The Lower East Side faced the same fate, with the demolition of tenements in the 1950s to make way for similarly designed high-rise dwellings (Plunz 1990, 245).

FIG. 3.5 Image of New York City public housing circa late 1940s.

The slowdown in wartime construction of housing stock caused an acute shortage at war's end. In a report issued in December 1945, for example, the newly elected Mayor William O'Dwyer's Emergency Committee on Housing found that the housing shortage had reached crisis proportions, and would not ease for another two years. The committee, headed by then park commissioner Robert Moses, estimated that at least 40,000 families, or 140,000 people, needed "shelter," and advocated that the city spend $26 million on emergency temporary housing. This included the purchase of 5,000 Quonset huts, which could house two families each, refurbishment of "abandoned public schools" to house 15,000 unmarried veterans, renovation of existing tenement housing stock, and a readjustment of current zoning and building laws to allow for increased occupancy ("5,000 Quonset Huts," 1947).[25]

Even with the concerted effort launched in early 1946 by federal, state, and local officials, the emergency housing program yielded modest results in cities even as late as the second quarter of 1947. According to *New York*

Times reporter Lee Cooper, "From New York to San Francisco, from Milwaukee down to New Orleans, the situation is much the same for returning veterans and non-veterans. About 40 per cent of the men who were in uniform still are living 'doubled up' with friends or relatives or occupying other makeshift quarters; and nearly 25 per cent of all married veterans are without homes of their own" (May 25, 1947). He continued, "apartment houses are bulging with tenants, and most of the limited number of new multi-family buildings will bring rentals beyond the average pocketbook" (May 25, 1947). By the last quarter of 1947, suburban and outlying communities began seeing improvements, yet in cities around the country, including "Manhattan and the other city boroughs . . . residential building continued to lag far behind the general level of operation in the country," a factor cited "to prolong the shortage here" (Cooper, September 21, 1947).

It was not until December 1947, when city residents began moving into the first three large-scale government subsidized housing projects (Amsterdam Houses, James Weldon Johnson Houses, and Abraham Lincoln Houses), all in Manhattan, that City Construction Coordinator Robert Moses declared that "residential construction [had] approached a pace that gradually would ease the pressure of the housing shortage" ("Housing Shortage Easing," 1947).[26] Rents at the Abraham Lincoln Houses started at a mere $29 to $40 a month for families of seven or more. Yet due to their "tower in the park" design, these residential developments yielded the same problems as the East River Houses and others in low-income areas. In isolating their residents in towers that were surrounded by open space and oriented off of the city gridiron, they "contained" residents, closing off their access to the central core of the city, on the one hand, and concentrating the social ills of their populations in close quarters (Plunz 1990, 256).

Like the publicly funded projects discussed above, companion developments Stuyvesant Town and Peter Cooper Village were conceived to ease the city's housing shortage. Completed in the summer of 1947, they were funded privately by Metropolitan Life insurance company and intended for middle-class residents. Built on eighty acres along First Avenue between Fourteenth and Twenty-third Streets, the community boasted 11,250 units and accommodated 25,000 residents in 110 buildings (Bagli and Scott, August 30, 2006). While the communities provided residents with much needed shelter, as well as an opportunity to remain in the city at rental rates many could afford, there were other aspects of life in these projects that left much to be desired. In fact, the challenges residents faced were not unlike those confronting occupants of more heavily subsidized construction. Some might argue that the challenges were even exacerbated by the massiveness of the developments.[27]

Whereas the low-income "tower in the park" housing development had the effect of "containing" residents within, Stuyvesant Town and Peter Cooper Village insulated residents from "unwanted external intrusion" (Plunz 1990, 255–56). Moreover, the requirement of clearing land for new construction displaced thousands of people as their homes, schools, places of worship, and businesses were literally demolished. Robert Moses, who oversaw city postwar construction in his various official capacities, is as famous for what he destroyed as he is for what he built.[28] Moses' "bulldozer philosophy"—his focus on demolition and reconstruction, rather than renovation and refurbishment—"ignored the crucial requirement to improve the quality of life for neighborhood residents" (Scott 1999, 356; see also Plunz 1990, 270). His construction projects destroyed racially and economically integrated, viable communities and displaced thousands of people (Scott 1999, 356).

The postwar "tower in the park" developments, regardless of their intended residents, remade the urban fabric of the city, replacing an organic but cohesive disorganization (of people living and working together in the same settled neighborhoods) with cohesion of a different order—a macroscale superstructure of highways, bridges, and tunnels and the dispersion of micropopulation nodes into massive apartment complexes. The manner and mode of making sense of the city as a pedestrian and urban dweller, while not completely changed, had been radically altered. Moses' changes certainly added to the accessibility of New York City by car, and in significant ways enhanced the quality and affordability of life for its residents. Yet the changes also contributed to the deterioration and eventual demise of many viable and diverse neighborhoods, as residents were given incentives to move into housing projects or as they fled to the suburbs. Mobility afforded by the newly constructed highway system and automobile, new suburban building, FHA financing for World War II veterans, and the growth of the regional transportation system (trains and buses), enabled professionals to live in surrounding suburbs and commute to work. By contrast, nonskilled workers gained the least from highway building—which diverted funds from social services. For example, the number of people needing public assistance rose by 45 percent between 1945 and 1965 (Scott 1999, 356). In all of these ways, New York City became a microcosm for much of the nation at this time—a country increasingly divided by the haves and have-nots: urban areas dominated by the racially diverse working classes and suburbs dominated by affluent whites.[29]

Conclusion: The Dolorous Place

In an essay written in 1957, critic George Beiswanger cast *Rooms* as a contemporary version of Dante's *Inferno*, as both works offer "visions," in Dante's words, of "the dolorous place." "Modern man, creature of the 'lonely crowd,' empty except as he is 'other-directed'—this is his general hell. In *Rooms* we are left with that hell, as in most of the significant art of our times" (Beiswanger 1957, 22). Resonating on multiple registers, the work marked an aesthetic and political shift for Sokolow, while, at the same time, performing the struggles of the postwar subject. Adopting the "rhythm of city living" trope, Sokolow drew on her own experiences as an outsider—living as a Jew as well as an artist who had left her home only to return to a changed city. Yet, Sokolow elided these particulars in the work's abstraction of space and place, deploying action—movement, not steps—to bring to light myriad conditions of human dislocation in the context of a typical New York City apartment building.

In *Rooms*, physical space amplifies the emotional conditions inside it. Turning Bell's conception of alienation on its head, the work embodied consciousness without critical detachment, agency dictated by social and environmental structures, and mobilization turned inward as a form of emotional stasis. As an alternative to real action in the world, the characters take residence in fantasy; finding hiatus in the imagination, they construct places where there is potential for emotional fulfillment and human connection. In all, the work enacts an ontology of containment, emotional and physical. In this sense, it was emblematic of the times, as the pressures of domestic anticommunism exacerbated a more culturally generalized suspicion of difference. While the community of concert dancers and choreographers in New York City had been somewhat immune from direct confrontation by the forces of McCarthyism, dance artists still felt its repressive effects (Graff 1998; Prevots 1998; Manning 2004; Jowitt 2004). Sokolow herself was never called before the House Un-American Activities Committee (HUAC), but government investigators came to her residence to question her (Warren 1991). Primus was also an FBI target (as discussed in chapter 4). Others active in the dance community, like choreographer Jerome Robbins and choreographer and dance critic Edna Ocko, were asked to testify before HUAC, and Edith Segal appeared before a New York legislative committee (Graff 1997, 159).

Rooms manifested these effects, enacting knowledge, or "truth" as Sokolow called it, within the softer politics embedded in the actions of ordinary individuals. While formalized to a certain extent, the work's expressive language portrayed its protagonists as typical people in recognizable situations, their actions born of day-to-day challenges to sustain subjectivity and a sense of significance as a member of a crowd. In its defamiliarization of the everyday, *Rooms* not only shed light on happenings in daily life that deserved examination, but also underlined the very fact that such things warranted treatment on the stage. While heightened, the work's ordinariness—its very premise of doing life as itself—flew in the face of universalist conventions governing modern dance composition, which privileged approaches that represented individuation as a singular and solitary heroic journey to self-knowledge. By contrast, *Rooms* asserted that ordinary material, with few dramatic embellishments, offered the impetus, subject matter, and parameters for choreographed dancing, and that human experience was plural in that common experiences yielded multiple points of view.

[4]

ACTION IS EFFECTIVE

Pearl Primus

THE preceding chapter details how choreographer Anna Sokolow's postwar work, in particular *Rooms* (1952), reframed the ordinary to bring out its inherent theatricality. In this, Sokolow both marked a departure from modern dance universalism, namely its epic proportions, and rendered instead the subjectivities of ordinary people by highlighting the actions of their everyday lives. It also presents *Rooms* as having helped facilitate a shift in Sokolow's career in line with artistic, political, and sociological sea changes from the 1930s to the 1950s. *Rooms* signaled a realignment for Sokolow in its abstraction of the everyday circumstances it portrayed. Here she unmarked her work as leftist dance and adopted a more politically ambiguous yet no less critical stance. Similarly, this chapter examines the significance of the cultural work of an analogous figure in Trinidadian-American choreographer Pearl Primus, whose postwar efforts to redefine her own and modern dance practice accomplished comparable results. I argue that in the late 1940s and early 1950s Primus' written and embodied accounts of diaspora reshaped the critical debate surrounding her work, advanced new ideas about modern dance practice around the idea of efficiency, and initiated her political realignment concurrent with other black civil rights activists at the time.

Central to this account is Primus' yearlong trip to Africa in 1949, supported by a grant from the Julius Rosenwald Foundation. In Africa she studied the dance and ritual practices of at least thirty tribal groups, recording her observations in writing, on film, and with line sketches (Perpener 2001, 170; "Genuine Africa," 1951, 98–102). A PHD student in anthropology at Columbia University at the time, Primus saw the trip as a homecoming of sorts, a chance to "go back where I came from" ("Pearl Primus: Foremost Dancer," 1951, 56). Not content assuming the role only of an observer, she absorbed herself in her research, and, when allowed, participated in the dances of her African hosts (Perpener 2001, 170). During and after the trip, Primus documented her experience in essays and articles that she wrote herself and in interviews later published in the national media. Of special interest are the writings she penned between 1949 and 1950, which were published either as essays or as correspondence with members of the New York dance press, and profiles written about Primus by others that were published during the same period.[1] These publications provide a travelogue of sorts, documenting the general outlines of the journey and detailing some significant experiences along the way. Closely examining the meanings of these writings in the contexts of both postwar modern dance and the nascent civil rights movement in the United States, this chapter investigates how Primus used the public discourse surrounding her trip to initiate a forum about a range of issues, artistic, social, and political.

Moderations of her ardent advocacy of black civil rights in the early to mid-1940s, Primus' written and public statements after 1947 appear tempered by the culture of containment. Concentrating on synthesizing her humanitarian aims within the work of her artistic and scholarly production, she distanced herself from her former stance, which had positioned her ethnographic and artistic work as components of a broader sociopolitical agenda. What appears is a project of self-definition, through which Primus refigured her subjectivity and mode of artistic expression through the lens of diaspora. James Clifford contends that "diaspora discourse articulates, or bends together, both roots *and* routes to construct what Gilroy (1997) describes as alternative public spheres, forms of community consciousness and solidarity that maintain identifications outside the national time/space to live inside with a difference" (251). Likewise, Primus' diaspora discourse figured her body as a locus for contradictory experiences: perceptions of being simultaneously inside and outside, belonging to and alienated from, located within and dislocated from her cultural "homes," the United States and Africa. Primus' trip honed her sense of positionality as an ethnographer in the process of negotiating a space for participation *and* observation. For Primus this positionality worked in unexpected ways. Having embarked on the trip expecting that it would "authenticate" material for her modern dances, her fieldwork complicated the question of authenticity. Not only did she realize that her presence was vital to the conservation of traditional dance forms but also that African ceremonial practices could shed new light both on her artistic work and the project of postwar modern dance more generally speaking.

Through Primus' public discourse, the complexity of her subject position emerges, revealing a personal experience of defamiliarization. While it unsettled her, Primus' position at the nexus of the familiar and unfamiliar gave her critical leverage to examine conventional notions about modern dance practice as well as the African-American experience. Of particular interest to the scope of this book is her investigation of performative "effectiveness," denoting the efficacy of action to accomplish transformative ends. Viewing African ceremonials in relation to compositional practices in modern dance, she began to understand effectiveness as a property underlying myriad performances regardless of their stated function. Translated to her work as a choreographer of modern dance, her realizations underlined the agency and drama inherent in the actions of moving bodies.

"The Negro Dances Himself": The Aesthetic Politics of Dancing Diaspora

My claims about the transformative significance of Primus' 1949 trip to Africa rest on an account of her activities prior to that point as both artist and social activist. Against the backdrop of the internationalist Popular Front, Primus' early dances fused traditions within modern dance, namely leftist dance and so-called Negro dance.[2] Inhabiting the role of diasporic subject, Primus used her artistic work to promote ideas about social justice and as a means of performing social change.[3]

Primus began her dance training at the New Dance Group school as a young adult. A self-sustaining and interracial artistic collective formed in 1932, the New Dance Group housed a professional training program for "working-class amateurs," a performance ensemble, and a forum for the discussion and dissemination of leftist ideas (Graff 1997, 53–60). At the time she began, Primus could not afford the "extra dime carfare required to go back and forth to the dance school." "The school gave her a scholarship and paid her carfares and for lunches" (M. Carter 1944, 5).

Primus made her debut in 1943 after only two years at the school. Her program of solos spanned the Africanist gamut, from *African Ceremonial* (an adaptation of a Belgian Congolese fertility rite), to *Rock Daniel* and

FIG. 4.1 Pearl Primus in *Hard Times Blues* (1943). Photo by Carl Van Vechten. Courtesy of the Van Vechten Trust and the Jerome Robbins Dance Division, The New York Public Library of the Performing Arts, Astor, Lenox and Tilden Foundations.

Hard Times Blues (drawn from vernacular material), to *Strange Fruit* (an adaptation of Lewis Allan's poem in which Primus assumed the role of a white onlooker at a lynching). From all accounts, the concert demonstrated Primus' ability to combine Africanist vernacular and modern dance movement material to comment on episodes in the Pan-African experience (Perpener 2001, 163).[4] Her performance at Carnegie Hall later that year presented more of the same, this time in a "festival of authentic African songs and dances" organized by the African Academy of Arts and Research directed by Kingsley Ozuomba Mbadiwe and "created and arranged" by Asadata Dafora (Gordon, December 16, 1943).

How are we to understand Primus' early iterations of diaspora? Why did she elect to treat this subject matter and what were the artistic, social, and political implications of her decision? Clearly, Primus' early work inhabited the legacy of artistic precedents like Dafora, Katherine Dun-

FIG. 4.2 Pearl Primus, 1943. Photo by Carl Van Vechten. Courtesy of the Van Vechten Trust and the Jerome Robbins Dance Division, The New York Public Library of the Performing Arts, Astor, Lenox and Tilden Foundations.

ham, Josephine Baker, and Zora Neale Hurston, all of whom presented material drawn from across the African cultural continuum. Anthea Kraut has credited Dunham, Baker, and Hurston specifically with inaugurating a "historical transition from representations of black primitivity to representations of a black diaspora" in dance during the interwar period (2003, 434). Their work also had a political valence in its demonstration of complex and hybrid diasporic subjectivities. As we will see later in this chapter, these accorded with controversial research in anthropology and evolutionary biology that questioned assumptions about the singularity of black culture in the Americas (Ramsey 2000) as well as with efforts by African-American activists to align their struggles for equality with transnational movements for human rights.

Primus' choices also reflected the shifting racially coded representational conventions governing modern dance production at the time. In *Modern Dance/Negro Dance*, Susan Manning argues that the early 1940s were a transitional period in modern dance in which conventions involving "metaphorical minstrelsy" were supplanted by those she calls "mythic abstraction." During the interwar years, often in the context of leftist dance, white dancers deployed metaphorical minstrelsy to signify political solidarity that ran across lines of race or social class. They used their bodies as "vehicles for the tenors of non-white subjects" accomplished through "abstraction" or "personification" (2004, 10). This theory is illustrated in canonical works by white artists including Helen Tamaris' *Negro Spirituals* (1928) and Martha Graham's *Immediate Tragedy* and *Deep Song* (both 1937) as well as *American Document* (1938) (Graff 1997, 105–31; Manning 2004, 125–42). The availability of these expressive options, however, was not a two-way street. Convention held that nonwhite artists, including Jews, should dramatize circumstances from what was considered their own ethnic or racial background regardless of their personal experience of it.[5] Options for African-American artists were the most narrow. As Donald McKayle explains, "It was perfectly all right for white performers to be Orientals, Negroes, or just anything the convention of the work asked for—but for Negroes, unthinkable and lacking in theatrical 'verisimilitude'" (quoted in Manning 2004, 10).[6]

Manning notes a change in the 1940s. "As Negro dance achieved a new authority within black and white public spheres, modern dance redefined its whiteness." This paved the way for the emergence of what she calls "mythic abstraction," a representational convention that privileged the white body as an unmarked and universal body (2004, 118). In chapter 1, I housed this convention under the term "modern dance universalism" in order to denote the ideology implicit in viewing the modern dancing body as a metonym for the collective body of "humanity" within postwar internationalism. As I pointed out, however, in spite of its integrationist vision, universalism in modern dance, as in the political sphere, was far from inclusive. Universal in name only, it upheld the dominant privilege operative in the culture of containment of naming white Western human experiences as the norm and measuring all other experiences against them. For black modern dancers, this meant relegation to a gamut of subjects assumed to comprise their real or mythic heritage, even as they sought to redefine their purview as one of diaspora and not primitivity (Kraut 2003, 2007) These included subjects drawn from rural or urban black life including spiritual practices, protest songs, or so-called primitives—that is, tribal or preindustrial cultural traditions across the African diaspora (Manning 2004, 118). According to Manning, Dunham's 1940s performances, in particular, schooled theatergoers in the "performance of diaspora, the migration of expressive forms from Africa to the Americas and within the Americas," thereby preparing the expressive grounds for choreographers like Primus who would take up similar subjects (ibid.).

This is the cultural climate in which Primus produced her work, and in which it was received by audiences and critics. Evidently, diaspora provided Primus with a body of culturally relevant material with which to work, under the auspices of "Negro" dance. It also served as a point of entry into the artist's work for (white) dance critics. Yet the choice to "dance diaspora" did not preclude critics from defining her work in reductive racial terms, from setting a bar for "authenticity" that did not exist for white choreographers within modern dance universalism, or from imposing expectations of "originality" that were consistent with the elevation of artistic autonomy within modernism. Nor did it decrease the pressure on Primus, either to anticipate what critics might find lacking, or to redress that lack in rigorous creative research.

Speaking to the issue of Primus' critical reception, accounts of Primus' early performances situated them squarely within the contradictory scope of "Negro" dance. John Martin, for example, reviewing her first concert for the *New York Times*, lauded her ability to fulfill his conflicting demands, "It would be hard to think of a Negro dancer in the field who can match her for technical capacity, compositional skill and something to say in terms that are altogether true to herself both racially and as an individual artist," he proclaimed, continuing "if ever a young dancer was entitled to a company of her own and the freedom to do what she chooses with it, she is it" (February 21, 1943). Applying what appears as a checklist, Martin underlined Primus' gifts as technician, choreographer, and public intellectual yet positioned them within the limited scope of *"being true to herself both racially and as an individual artist"* (emphasis mine). Likewise, in a column published in late 1943 in *Mademoiselle* magazine, Martin called Primus "already somebody to be reckoned with." "No other Negro dancer has yet appeared with anything like her artistic range or her innate equipment," he wrote. *"Her great gifts are racially rooted, but not bound by any means to mere topical treatment. . . .* She has tremendous dramatic power, the gayest kind of comedy lilt and a technique that fairly bowls you over" (November 1943, 203; emphasis mine). Similar assumptions are evident in a 1943 profile in *Vogue* accompanied by a full-page spread, "At twenty-three, this young New York dancer, strong, powerful, and always dramatic, has *fused in her work her whole background*: her Harlem life, her telephone operator days, her studies with those two famous teachers, Martha Graham and Charles Weidman, her jitterbugging at Harlem's Savoy Ballroom, and her investigations into African tribal dancing as part of her psychology studies" ("People Are Talking," 1943, 48; emphasis mine).

In these accounts, both Martin and the writer for *Vogue* attempt to strike a balance between Primus' race and her artistry, as if the two were mutually opposed and needing reconciliation. This is most pronounced in Martin's writings, summarized in his statement that "her great gifts are racially rooted, but not bound by any means to mere topical treatment," but also in effect in the profile's observation that she "has fused in her work her whole background."

In different ways, these writings also introduce the critical tension between what were seen as salient components of any postwar modern dance: originality and authenticity. Neither mutually exclusive nor fused, these were interrelated elements within the formula by which dance critics appraised the artistic work before them. Whereas "originality" referred to an artist's treatment of a subject, authenticity denoted the subject being treated. In theory these appear to be clear distinctions, but in practice they were not, either as they got worked out on the stage or as they emerged in the dance critical discourse. As we saw in the last chapter, for example, Anna Sokolow's work in the early to mid-1940s was impugned on both counts. Here is a reprise of Edwin Denby's assessment of a 1943 concert for the purposes of demonstration: "the old numbers dealing with such themes as slum childhood, juvenile delinquency, or Loyalist Madrid—numbers that once seemed natural as adolescent reflections—now, seen in an adult atmosphere, look artificial and false to their terrible themes" (1986, 181). Denby's review seems to place a heavy burden on Sokolow to be original in its observation that work that once "seemed natural" now "looked artificial and false to their terrible themes." In this sense, Denby's characterization references not only his but the general conclusion among critics that Sokolow's treatment of her material in the early 1940s was outdated. However, Denby's claim that her "numbers" "look[ed] artificial and false" also spoke to the critical expectation that artists would make work that "rang true" to audiences. Truth being a relative term, critical entreaties to verisimilitude were complicit in upholding the forces of normalization at work in the culture of containment.

"I Want My Dance to Be a Part of the Conscience of America"

When Primus first burst onto the modern dance scene,[7] most critics accepted the validity of her material under the auspices of diaspora (its "authenticity") and focused more on how she could make her work "original." Although unlike predecessors Dunham or Hurston, both ethnographers who drew their material from field study in the West Indies, at the time of her debut Primus had spent most of her life in New York City and had no firsthand knowledge of the African cultural continuum save her own experiences as an immigrant growing up on the Westside of Manhattan.[8] Primus' actual distance from her material posed no problem for Martin, who commended her debut on both counts of originality and authenticity: "If Miss Primus walked away with the lion's share of the honors, it was partly because her material was more theatrically effective, but also partly because she is a remarkable gifted artist." He noted Primus' use of "genuine primitive movement" in *African Ceremonial*, and deemed *Rock Daniel!* and *Hard Times Blues* "original choreography of tremendous impact" (February 21, 1943). For other critics, originality trumped authenticity in their estimation of Primus' work. Reviewing the African festival at Carnegie Hall, Eugene Gordon of the communist *Daily Worker* perceived Primus' "belated entrance [at Carnegie Hall] was like a blast of cold air in a stuffy room. The audience awoke, bestirred itself and sat on the edge of its seat." While Gordon had no illusions about the authenticity of Primus' performance—she performed an "imaginative interpretation of African dances"—what mattered more to him was that she "introduced something-different" into what had, at the end of the evening, become "a monotonous . . . repetition of detail" (December 16, 1943). Similarly, Edith Segal of the *Daily Worker* applauded Primus' work for its political acuity: "Here was the longed-for experience in the theatre, when form and content are perfectly merged," she wrote, "when artist and audience come together in a common emotional, intellectual, and spiritual union" (1944, 11). Additionally, in her own comments about her work *Strange Fruit*, Primus saw no disconnection between her black female body and the role she was playing as a white male. "It dawned on me that if I could isolate a person from a lynch mob, I would have a different character from the brute who participated in the crime. People don't commit horrible crimes like this when they're alone and sober." She continued, "In mobs, you have the mass mind to treat. . . . [M]y dance shows a member of the mob as he leaves the scene of the crime. . . . He looks back at the black body hanging by its neck and reviles himself for what he has done" (Primus quoted in Carter 1944, 5).

Others, however, like Lois Balcom of *Dance Observer*, viewed Primus' decision to present cultural material as subject matter as an obstacle to her development as a "modern" dancer. As she reasoned, "Of course, the African heritage enters into her attitudes, her insights, her ambitions, and her dance movements; nevertheless, what she knows about tribal ceremonies she has learned actually from books. With the trustworthy intuitions of her blood to guide her, her interpretations achieve a closer approximation of authenticity than would those of a white dancer—but they remain approximations" (December 1944, 123).

For Balcom, the attempt to represent her "African heritage" stunted Primus' artistic growth. In striving to stage "authentic" primitives that she could only "approximate," she was diverted from "the modern dancer's prerogative . . . to offer an individualized expression, experimental in form, concerned with the significant aspects of the changing world" (123). Likewise, a review published in *Dance Observer* of a May 1946 performance criticized Primus for her "theatricality" and "exhibitionism." "Of all the primitives," the reviewer claimed, "*African Ceremonial* still is tops. It is the most unadulterated on the list. As for the rest, what could be beautiful savagery descends to blow-by-blow repetition of uninspired torso and hip flexions." The writer continued, "Miss Primus . . . faces a problem in avoiding clichés of her own making. Perhaps she should dig deeper into discovery of movement" ("Pearl Primus," June 1946).

These reviews appear to have tipped the balance toward the valuation of originality, encouraging Primus to view her material as a means to a modernist end, and thus advocating movement invention and manipulation. Others, however, held Primus to what appeared to be her stated intention: adapting culturally specific movement practices for the stage. For example, consider a review that appeared earlier that year in *Dance Observer* comparing Primus' *Dance of Beauty* to a "1930s" film of a "Belgian expedition to the Congo," which featured "a brief sequence of Watusi dancing." Measuring Primus' dance against the portrayal of Watusi dancing in the film, the critic found her work lacking in verisimilitude, stating, "The first few moments of her dance—a figure regally white-robed, in a firm stance, giving an illusion of height, with an impulse of movement, balancing, moving almost without moving—raised the awakened hope. But soon everything was otherwise. The dignity failed, the promise was broken, the figure disrobed, the dance insulted itself. It ended with ridiculous head-rolling: a picture of a slap happy doll baby" ("Pearl Primus," February 1946).

Clearly reductive in the worst way, such reviews bring to light essentialist contradictions within universalist dance modernism as they circumscribed the artistic practices of African-American artists and placed them in an awkward position "between representing the race and articulating an individual vision" (Manning 2004, 175; see also Perpener 2001).

Richard Green presents another angle on the problem of authenticity for Primus, inherent in the fact of her body as a representational signifier. According to Green, Primus' "Negroid" appearance, "her facial and body characteristics" placed her outside the set of "theatrical convention that privileged first and foremost white women and then mulattos." As a result, "Primus' body represented an(O)ther dark site for the projection of primitive fantasies" by white onlookers, on the one hand, and "embodied the suffering and injustices that others could only attempt to portray," on the other. He summarizes, "Her representation of Negro problems operated not only on a thematic level but also on a physical one. As an authentic Negro, the distinction between actor and role collapses in Primus" (2002, 123).

Whether driven by the contradictory critical discourse that surrounded her work, her sense of her role as "'artist ambassador' for her race" (Lloyd quoted in Green 2002, 122), or her own ethnographic bent, it is clear that Primus took the question of the authenticity of her material seriously, going to great lengths to get closer to her subject matter. Margaret Lloyd's account of Primus' creative process leading up to the creation of *Afri-*

can Ceremonial, one of her first dances, is a case in point. According to Lloyd,

> [Primus] visited libraries and museums, consulting all the pictures available, taking two or three lines from one book and half a line from another, slowly piecing together a dance. She had to watch, in adapting her source material, to keep each tribe and each dance of each tribe separate. When a dance was finished she checked it with her African friends, many of them students at Columbia, who were not dancers but knew the tradition so thoroughly that they could detect the slightest error. Then she checked the rhythms with the two native drummers—Norman Cole, a doctor and dancer, too, who came from Africa with Asadata Dafora, and knows all the intricacies; and for the West Indian dances, the Haitian, Alphonse Cimber, equally versed in Caribbean ways. They corrected and instructed her in the fine details. (1949, 269–70)

On a similar mission, in 1944, Primus took her first trip to gather material from field study, spending several months traveling across the southern United States disguised as a sharecropper. She picked cotton and attended "sixty-seven . . . shabby little churches, as well as open air revivals and 'spur-home' prayer meetings," studying the religious practices of rural blacks ("Pearl Primus: Foremost Dancer," 1951, 56). When asked by a reporter why she could not find material for her dances by visiting churches in New York City, she stated, "I've studied churches up here and could get my material from them, *but I want more authenticity*." When asked why she needed to travel incognito, she replied, "because if people know that I'm 'a somebody,' they won't act naturally" (Carter 1944, 5).

Through her statements, Primus expressed why she felt compelled to visit the historic region where Americans of African descent had been enslaved until 1865, and forced to abide by "Jim Crow" laws, which proscribed "separate but equal" accommodations for people of color thus legalizing forms of discriminatory segregation, since the 1890s. That said, at first glance Primus' assertion that her experience of African-American life down south, in spite of the fact that she was traveling in disguise, would be more "authentic" than the experiences she might have if she ventured as "herself," or attended revivalist churches in black sections of New York City, appears naïve. Yet Primus' desire to conduct fieldwork that would provide the knowledge necessary for her to embody her informants' experiences deflects the impact of this criticism, as does her consciousness about how, if passing as a southern black, she would be forced to submit to the injustices of the region's Jim Crow laws in order to accomplish her artistic and scholarly ends. As she put it, "I'm militant and I don't tolerate racial abuse, but there is food for me in the South and I'm not going to let my personal scruples stand in the way this time. I'm going to comply with all their Nazi-like rules because I hate to let people know who I am" (Carter 1944, 5).

"Shocked," "deadened," and "saddened" by the experience, she later commented that the trip was necessary "in order to know my own people where they are suffering most" (Lloyd 1949, 275; 'Pearl Primus: Foremost Dancer," 1951, 56). As she expected, the trip fueled her artistic and political fires, leaving her a rich palette of emotions and images from which to work. Distancing herself from the issue of originality, and aligning herself with the matter of authenticity, Primus commented on her intentions in an interview published on her return, "I am not trying to create something new in the dance. . . . I am only attempting to present the Negro in his own true light, as he was in the past in Africa and as he is now, a member of a fighting democracy" (Segal 1944, 11). She continued, "In America's bosom we have the roots of Democracy, but the roots do not mean there are leaves. The tree could easily grow bare. We will never relax our war effort abroad but we must fight at home with equal fierceness. This is an all out war; we will not stop fighting until everyone is free from inequality" (ibid.). And, as she told the Afro-American, "I know you can't solve the race problem by dancing, but each of us must try, in his own way, to contribute to interracial understanding. Only when this is achieved can America enjoy a real democracy to the benefit of its people" (Carter 1944, 5).

Pursuing authenticity through fieldwork gave Primus a platform for work that was more strident in its condemnation of racism in a U.S. context, including *Motherless Child* and *Slave Market* (both 1944) set to African-American spirituals. Yet she did not abandon her other more internationally drawn material. Primus composed her solo concert debut at the Belasco Theater on Broadway in December 1944 around existing solos as well as adaptations of traditional dances from Haiti and Africa (Prickett 1998, 644–47). She and several others danced, while a narrator, "seated at the foot of the proscenium, attempted to tie the various numbers together into a kind of over-all picture of the Negro" (Martin October 5, 1944).

In *The Souls of Black Folk*, W. E. B. Du Bois noted a "double consciousness" in black cultural and expressive practices—"two souls, two thoughts, two unreconciled strivings . . . in one dark body, whose dogged strength alone keeps it from being torn asunder" (Du Bois quoted in DeFrantz 2004, 64). Primus' early work manifests this dichotomous quality in its attempts to unify the aesthetic, the cultural, and the political in one body. Her critics' difficulty in understanding the multilayered significance of her danced embodiments of diaspora points to the fact that there was no easy fit between Primus' artistic goals and the critical expectations for black concert dance. Yet Primus' work, as well as her statements about it, resonated beyond the parochial politics of dance modernism.

The ideas Primus embodied in her work ran parallel to those of the leading black intellectuals and activists of the day, specifically that the dancing body could enact a continuity of exchange among peoples of African descent, and that strengthening connections between blacks in the Americas and those in Africa could boost the African-American community's estimation of the value of its cultural forms.

Beginning in the 1920s, Franz Boas had challenged the notion that race was a biologically determinate category of human difference and therefore could not serve as the basis for prejudicial social practices based on racial difference (Borstelmann 2001, 27). Dunham's fieldwork in the Caribbean in the mid-1930s, and the subsequent publication of her essays demonstrating the endurance of African cultural retentions across the diaspora, had a marked impact on midcentury scholarly thinking about diasporic cultural transmission in the Americas (Ramsey 2000). Also funded by a Rosenwald Foundation Fellowship, in 1935–36 she traveled to Haiti, Jamaica, Martinique, and Trinidad, spending most of the time in Haiti. Dunham's 1941 essay, "The Negro Dance," based on fieldwork in Haiti, traces the transmission of African spiritual dance practices to the new world (2005). When African ritual practices came in contact with Christianity, and as their practitioners were forced to renounce their former spiritual beliefs, she hypothesized, these ritual practices changed, as did the intention behind them. Both became secular. Yet, she argues, even though Pan-African dances may not look exactly like those in Africa, or may not be done for the exact same reasons or achieve the same ends, they are still Africanist in that they demonstrate similar formal characteristics, "While, during the cultural segregation, the African traditions were more modified here than elsewhere, those which persisted now have a sound functional relationship towards a culture which is contemporary, rather than towards one which is on the decline; and, therefore, such traditions as have been retained are assured of survival as long as the large, strong cultural body of which they are a part survives" (quoted in Clark and Johnson 2005, 225). Moreover, she contends that the fusion of Africanist elements in African-American culture with those of other American cultural practices accounts for "vigorous" "re-emergence" of new cultural forms.

In focusing on cultural retention as expressed in cultural practices, Dunham's research underlined the value of the legacy of Pan-African cultural production for American blacks. In particular, her findings countered previously accepted assumptions that being black in America was like being a member of any other of the country's ethnic groups, "[t]he same pattern, only a different shade!" (Herskovits quoted in Ramsey 2000, 199).[9] Prior to Dunham's fieldwork, and the subsequent publication of her findings, scholars like Dunham's mentor at Chicago, Melville Herskovits, believed that assimilation to U.S. culture had diluted the expression of Africanist cultural elements in the cultural production of American blacks. Dunham's research led Herskovits to revise his contentions and develop a theory of "New World Africanism," which asserted that Africanist features had indeed been retained in the cultural practices of people of African descent across the Americas (Ramsey 2000, 197–200). This reversal brought Herskovits' position more in line with leading African-American scholars, like W. E. B. Du Bois, Langston Hughes, Countee Cullen, and Arthur Huff Fauset, contributors to Alain Locke's pivotal volume, *The New Negro* (1925), which, according to Ramsey, "connected contemporary African diasporic cultural expression and political ideology to a refigured African present and past" (Ramsey 2000, 199).

Dunham's research also added a voice to the growing chorus of scholars who asserted that race was a matter of cultural practice (what people did and with whom they identified and spent time under social circumstance), not biology. Such shifts in intellectual formulations of race as a marker of cultural, not biological, difference bolstered the claims of activists in the nascent civil rights movement in the years leading up to and after World War II; they legitimated their claims that racism and racial prejudice were arbitrary, based solely on skin color, not on fundamental human differences that could justify, or even warrant, unequal social and juridical treatment (L. Baker 1999, 194–207).[10]

Activist and entertainer Paul Robeson (later joined by activist Alphaeus Hunton and scholar W. E. B. Du Bois), for example, founded the International Committee on African Affairs (ICAA, later to become known as the Council on African Affairs, or CAA, in 1942) in 1937 based on these assumptions. Its mission both educational and political, it sought to inform African-Americans about Africa while also "support[ing] the political liberation of the colonized African nations, and improved economic and social conditions on the African continent" (Von Eschen 1997, 20–21). Building diverse coalitions along the interests of American blacks, and lobbying members of Congress for their support, "the new CAA embodied a militant and explicit diaspora consciousness, accompanied by a distinct shift to autonomous black leadership" (20). As such it galvanized civil rights activism around global anticolonialist and antifascist movements; as *Chicago Defender* columnist John Robert Badger put it in 1942, "[We] recognize that our own status is connected with that of other submerged peoples, especially those of Africa and the West Indies, where the issue of race has been injected into politics and forms an ideological pillar of the repressive structure of world imperialism" (Badger quoted in Von Eschen 1997, 41; Badger, 1942, 15).

A similar politics of diaspora emboldened activists Walter White and A. Philip Randolph in their drive to garner equal opportunity for black citizens in the defense industries and armed forces. In 1941, for example, they threatened the Roosevelt administration that they would organize a march of 100,000 African Americans on the Mall in protest of discriminatory practices of the U.S. Defense Department. In Robeson's words, the rally would send "a mighty blow on the side of real democracy for our people here as well as our brothers on the continent of Africa" (Robeson quoted in Von Eschen 1997, 103). Several days before the rally, the president responded with Executive Order 8802, a provision stipulating an antidiscriminatory policy "in the employment of workers in the defense industries or Government because of race, creed, color, or national origin" and forming a Fair Employment Practices Committee for oversight (quoted in L. Baker 1999, 193). The CAA did succeed, however, in demonstrating support for their policies later that year, when their "Big Three Unity" rally, held in Madison Square Garden, brought 18,000 people together under a banner of civil rights for black Americans formulated in a language of anti-imperialism (Singh 2004, 102).

Not merely a factional group, therefore, the CAA's politics articulated the position of the majority of American blacks, who "strongly supported the independence of colonies in Africa and everywhere else. They understood . . . that the status of people of color in the United States could not be separated from that in other parts of the world" (Borstelmann 2001, 41; see also Plummer, 1996, 85–86; 163–65). The same went for the majority position regarding U.S. involvement in World War II. As Rayford Logan, professor of history at Howard University wrote in 1944,

> In normal times the great masses of Negroes, North and South, accept more or less silently the not too violent disregard of what they more or less vaguely consider their constitutional and legal rights and the equally nebulous ideals of the Declaration of Independence. But when our nation goes to war to assure the victory of the "democracies" over the "fascist" nations, we naturally become more insistent that democracy, like charity, should begin at home. (7; for more on Logan see Plummer 1996, 101)

Logan's comments illustrate the opportunity black activists saw in the U.S. justification for its entry into the war. According to Thomas Borstelmann, "By framing their war propaganda as a struggle for democracy and against the Third Reich's racist tyranny, the Western Allies opened themselves to intensive critiques of their own colonial and segregationist practices" (2001, 29).[11]

In this context, Primus' comments before and following her 1944 trip down South clearly capitalized on the rhetorical and real weaknesses of the U.S. government's case for war. Like other black activists, she deployed a diaspora discourse in order to link the civil rights movement in the United States to global struggles against tyranny. Her association of white supremacists in the South with Nazis in Germany in comments to the *Baltimore Afro-American*, for example, made analogous the apartheid dictated by Jim Crow and the Nazi's policy of ethnic cleansing. She demonstrated a similar political consciousness in her comments to the *Daily Worker*, first in the identification of her artistic subject matter as "the

Negro in his own true light, as he was in the past in Africa and as he is now a member of a fighting democracy," and second, in her evocation of a metaphor of democracy as a tree with roots but no leaves. With these statements, she traced the lineage of American blacks to Africa thus linking the nascent struggle for civil rights to the historic and global struggle against colonialism. At the same time, she indicated her position that democracy in the United States would never survive if it did not extend to all of the nation's citizens, just like a tree could not survive without its leaves. In fact, influential books by scholars Ashley Montagu in *Man's Most Dangerous Myth: The Fallacy of Race* and Gunnar Myrdal in *An American Dilemma*, published in 1942 and 1944, respectively, argued similarly, underlining the "paradox" of American democracy, a system that could support a discourse of "freedom and justice for all"—what Myrdal called "the American Creed"—on the one hand, and racial prejudice, on the other (Myrdal [1944] 1962, 4; see also L. Baker 1999, 194).

At the war's end, the black justification for civil rights in the United States remained largely the same; yet other factors galvanized activists' resolve as the movement gained a larger popular following as well as broader political and public notice. First, the experiences of soldiers returning from war paved the way for interracial respect and understanding. "[B]lack soldiers [were] less willing to return home and quietly accept their prewar status as second-class citizens" (Borstelmann 2001, 42). Similarly, for many white soldiers, fighting side by side with black comrades as well as the specter of Nazism (that was, in part, founded upon an ideology of racial discrimination) shed a critical light on the racial apartheid at home (Von Eschen 1997, 42). Second, after having sustained their critique of racism throughout the war years, the black public became more resolute in its conviction that the status quo in the United States was untenable and unacceptable (Borstelmann 2001, 41). Success of anticolonial movements abroad strengthened the justification of civil rights at home in the context of a government billed on democracy (41). Walter White, executive secretary for the NAACP from 1931 to 1955 and war correspondent for the *New York Post*, put it this way in his 1945 *A Rising Wind*:

World War II has given to the Negro a sense of kinship with other colored—and also oppressed—peoples of the world. Where he has not thought through or informed himself on the racial angles of colonial policy and master-race theories, he senses that the struggle of the Negro in the United States is part and parcel of the struggle against imperialism and exploitation in India, China, Burma, Africa, the Philippines, Malaya, the West Indies, and South America. (144)

White cast the racial predicament for a postwar United States in stark terms. The country could maintain its "policy of appeasement of bigots," thereby "court[ing] disaster," or "live up to her ideals and thereby save herself and help to avert an early and more disastrous resumption of war." He continued, "A wind is rising—a wind of determination by the have-nots of the world to share the benefits of freedom and prosperity which the haves of the earth have tried to keep exclusively for themselves. That wind blows all over the world. Whether that wind develops into a hurricane is a decision which we must make now and in the days when we form the peace" (155).

Due to the broadening black political consciousness, membership in civil rights organizations like the NAACP increased ninefold between 1940 and 1946 (Borstelmann 2001, 41–42). Although organized protest against racial inequality had risen in the period just before the U.S. entry into the war (e.g., A. Phillip Randolph's planned protest on the Mall and the "Big Three Unity Rally"), it had mostly stilled during the war years. After the war, mobilization of black citizens began again with renewed fervor, this time through the publication of written petitions and appeals to global policy-making entities within the UN. In 1946, for example, the National Negro Congress (NNC) (through the National Lawyers Guild) drafted a petition on human rights violations in the United States, "deplor[ing] poverty, poor schooling and housing, and high black mortality rates" and "describ[ing] peonage and the persistence of lynching" (Plummer 1996, 171). The NNC sent the petition to the UN Secretariat and a copy to President Harry Truman along with a "cover letter rebuking him for his reversals of Roosevelt's [civil rights] policies" (ibid.).[12] Similarly, in 1947 the NAACP penned *An Appeal to the World: A Statement on the Denial of Human Rights to Minorities in the Case of Citizens of Negro Descent in the United States of America and An Appeal to the United Nations for Redress* and sent it to John P. Humphrey, director of Human Rights at the UN Division of the Secretariat. The document, written by scholar/activists W. E. B. Du Bois, Milton

Konvitz, and Rayford Logan, and attorney Earl B. Dickerson, "detailed the history of racial discrimination and its current social, political, and economic impact on black Americans" (Plummer 1996, 181).

Given her outspokenness on these issues during the war years, Primus was uncharacteristically silent regarding racism at war's end, at least as far as statements to the popular press went. The only comment I can find in which she stated a position that linked her artistic and political work along racial lines is a comment published in a small profile in *Time* magazine in 1947, two years prior to her trip to Africa. "What I try to express in my dancing is the culture of the Negro people," she commented, continuing, "I am not preaching a 'back to Africa' movement. I am simply trying to show the Negro his African heritage and make him see that his culture had a dignity and strength and cleanliness. . . . I don't know yet what I have to say about my own life or place in my own land. But some day I hope to be able to say, 'This is my expression, this is what I have to say'" ("Little Primitive," 1947, 44).[13]

While uncharacteristically oblique, Primus' comments appear to temper the tone of formerly strident statements. They also modified her former positions. First, in claiming that she "was not preaching a 'back to Africa' movement," she distanced herself from organized efforts made in that name. Second, in stressing her intention of "expressing . . . the culture of the Negro people," "showing the Negro his heritage," she aligned herself with a broadly conceived humanistic endeavor that could not be reduced to politics alone. That is, she sought to make the past useable for black Americans by underlining the existence and value of black cultural practices. Her pledge, to "make [American blacks] see that [their] culture has a dignity and strength and cleanliness," associated her work with the objectives of an increasingly outmoded ideology of racial uplift, which, in Kevin Gaines' words, "represented the struggle for a positive black identity in a deeply racist society, turning the pejorative designation of race into a source of dignity and self-affirmation through an ideology of class differentiation, self-help, and interdependence" (1996, 3). The project of racial uplift was associated with the cause of advancing the interests of American citizens of color, and yet it was not necessarily affiliated with organized political movements against racism.

Analogous to Sokolow's generalized critique of the ills of postwar social relations *Rooms*, Primus' circumspection on these matters might in part be attributed to the change in the U.S. political landscape at midcentury, President Truman's issuance of the Truman Doctrine in 1947, and the pressures of domestic containment. Black activists, who had formerly pledged their allegiance to the radicalized internationalism of the left wing, now rallied around the American flag (Von Eschen 1997, 114). In an environment not unlike the one Americans lived in after 9/11, political dissent was seen as the subversion of democratic principles that formed a bulwark against, in this case, the spread of communism. On arriving home from Africa, Primus herself became a target of government scrutiny and incrimination for her former affiliation with communist party members and for a performance at a 1945 campaign rally for Benjamin Davis, a black communist candidate for city council in New York City (Associated Negro Press, undated, cited in Manning 2004, 181).[14] As a result, in 1952 the FBI revoked her passport.[15] Paradoxically, the fact of Primus' postwar silence, or her hedging at best, on these matters makes it difficult to estimate the extent to which the cold war red scare had an impact on her beliefs, or at least on her expression of them.

Reading the Letters Sent Home

Primus received a fellowship to travel to Africa by chance. Originally she had applied to the Rosenwald Foundation for a grant to form a small company and produce a new work. However, when the president of the foundation saw her perform in Nashville, Tennessee, he decided to change the terms of her application. According to Margaret Lloyd, "When he learned that she had never been to Africa, he felt that steps should be taken at once, that the Rosenwald Foundation owed it to themselves and to the world to send her to study the authentic forms at their source" (1949, 265).

In excerpts of the first two letters she wrote home, one to Walter Terry and published in the *New York Herald Tribune* and the other to Martin of the *New York Times*, Primus wrote of her mission as primarily ethnographic. As much as she thought she was in Africa to authenticate her own adaptations, she soon learned that in order to do so the dances she wished to study needed to be reconstructed first. "Dance in Nigeria is in a deplorable state," she commented. "People are ashamed to dance their native dances, jitterbugging and ballroom dance have swept the country. But I have witnessed dances which will perish with the dancer. . . . It is

FIG. 4.3 Pearl Primus "Packing for Africa," circa 1949. Photo by Rosalie Gwathmey. Courtesy of the American Dance Festival Archives.

my duty to preserve their flavor, to reproduce them for the Western mind, to bring beauty into our narrow world" (May 20, 1949).

She continued, "I am fortunate to be able to salvage the still existent gems of dance before they, too, fade into general decadence. In many places I started movements to make the dance again important. Ancient costumes were dragged out, old men and women-toothless but beautiful with age-came forth to show me the dances which will die with them" (May 20, 1949).

Nevertheless she cultivated a remove from her hosts, revealed in a tone one might expect of a foreign tourist, "Nigeria was quite an experience. My memory will never let go the happiness, the misery, the laughter, the tears, the illness, the dancing, the friends—the filth, dirt, disease. . . . I did not stay in any mansion but in homes where water was unboiled, fruit unwashed, where there were insects and dust, but I survived" (1949).

Excerpts of the letter written to Martin reveal a deepening conscious-ness about her position as outsider: "What strange adventures lie ahead are as unpredictable as those I have already had," she mused. "I have passed through all the stages from hysteria to near death, but the people loved me with a fierce, possessive love. They spoiled me in their own strange way, they dropped to their knees before me, they named me into their tribes, and when they saw me dance, they swore I was juju woman indeed."

Primus is treated as a stranger by her Nigerian hosts, but they also accept her as one of their own. Yet, from an artistic standpoint, Primus realizes she has much to learn from the Nigerians: "from them I learned the inner con-versation of muscles and the enjoyment of subtle movements" (1949).

In a letter published in *Dance Observer* six months later, Primus re-vealed the deepening stakes of her visit as she felt transformed by her ex-periences: "Tonight I write by the light of a tiny lantern and a sputtering twig dipped in palm oil. The village is Kahnplay [Liberia]—hamlet of Paramount chief Mongrue. He has adopted me as his daughter and to use his own words 'Whatever I have is yours for you are my child—you call me father'" (Primus 1949, 147).

She continued, "Now I am being prepared for initiation into the *Sande*, one of the most powerful of the female cults in Africa. The members are marked down the back and over the shoulder down the front to the pubic region. I shall plead for fewer cuts—though the design is beautiful I don't think I could endure all. Unfortunately I am sworn to secrecy and there-fore cannot tell you too much" (Primus 1949, 147).

Absorbed in her research, and literally adopted by her hosts, her danc-ing had taken on new meaning as she found new reasons to move. "This is a new life for me," she wrote. "I have been amazed and overjoyed, for when the spirit entered me the reason for the dance became the reason to move. I danced as I have never danced on the stages of America. Myself was transformed; yet underneath all this a deep process of analysis was taking place" (Primus 1949, 147).

The letters are evidence of Primus' commitment to documentation and analysis.[16] She writes to record what she has seen, done, and learned not only for her own purposes but also for those of her hosts, whose feelings about dance were changing due both to the disintegration of colonial rule and to the westernization of various areas of the continent. The first-person narrative voice, therefore, becomes a lens through which she can convey to readers the details of her experiences and their bearing on their lives.

But they also complicated the existing critical debate about Primus' artistic work that hinged on matters of authenticity. What appears most pressing for Primus to communicate is the irony she perceives in her situation. Primus herself, an American, whose broader culture brought the Nigerians the jitterbug—a symbol of the demise of their traditional dancing practices—was also the person who could make dance relevant again for her African hosts. "Coming home" to Africa, therefore, was not what she expected, as she assumed responsibility for doing what she imagined Africans could do for her, authenticate traditional dance practices. Yet her homecoming seemed to accomplish something else as well. Not only did the recognition of her abilities and adoption into various and sometimes highly differentiated groups give her a deep sense of belonging. It also allowed her to work through her complicated diasporic subjectivity. What was once a more cerebral understanding of her position within an African cultural continuum became basic to her conception of self.

Primus' realizations had sociocultural and political implications that reached beyond the circle of her readers. In her documentation of the cross-fertilization of Africanist dance practices, Primus contributed to the broader and long-standing discussion about cultural retention across the African diaspora begun by scholars like Dunham more than a decade earlier. Her accounts of her literal adoption by her hosts, on the one hand, and ability to "pass" as African on the other, contributed to contemporaneous scholarship by Herskovits and others that rethought the lines of transmission and retention across the African diaspora. Moreover her sense of her own responsibility to preserve African traditional performance undercut the perception shared by some American anthropologists and the public alike that the diaspora illustrated a cultural continuum in which African practices were the most authentic and African-American ones the least (Dunham 2005; Ramsey 2000). Instead she put forth the idea that diaspora was not a one-way route; rather its exchange was fluid and multidirectional.

Finally, Primus' reflexivity about her own subject position vis à vis that of her informants accomplished something that was both rhetorical and philosophical.[17] It allowed her to reframe her own modernist dance practices in the terms that she derived from her observations of and participation with her African hosts. As much as she was transformed by her experiences, she continued to mine them for information about her work as a dancer and choreographer, effectively maintaining an awareness of her difference even as her experiences blurred the boundaries of her subjectivity. As a result, she secured the purchase to reconsider what was meant by "primitive" by examining the inherently dramaturgical nature of tribal theater. Taking back her use of "primitive" to categorize African dance forms, she replaced it with the term "basic." As she explained, "Here form and function are intricately related and dependent on one another: This is a course in choreography. The basic patterns of life—the circle which is the embryo—the force of the straight forward line which is birth—the spiral, the Xing, the jagged line which denote growth and struggle—the return of the circle again—the shrinking of the circle to a tiny speck and the dropping of that speck into the vastness of eternity which is death" (Primus 1949, 147).

Rather than view African dances as crude or even unsophisticated she saw them as seminal and therefore generative in her thinking about the art of movement. This led her to another realization; that she might characterize what she had witnessed as a theater of efficacy in which intensity came in the pursuit and achievement of a desired and verifiable result. "For those of us who are performers this is really one of the greatest classrooms, for the true dance aims at effect—the rapid movement is suddenly halted—the spinning dancer suddenly stops still before the chief, and the woman in the trance suddenly screams through the stillness. . . . No theatre has produced anything like those of Mushenge or Benin—designed for effectiveness!" (Primus 1949, 147).

Teasing out the elements of theatrical "effectiveness," Primus defined her own perspective on postwar dance modernist practice. Study of African ceremonial performances underlined both the functional side of dance performance—to effect transformation—and what Richard Schechner would later call "the efficacy entertainment braid": "Efficacy and entertainment are not so much opposed to each other; rather they form poles of a continuum" (2003, 130).

In her investigation of performative "efficiency," Primus complicated the critical discourse surrounding her work, thereby countering arguments made by Balcom and others that in adapting African dance forms for performance she was holding herself back from becoming a good choreographer of modern dance or making a cliché of her own work. Instead she emphasized that the study of African dance practices led her, and could lead dance modernism, in new aesthetic and theatrical directions by plumbing the potential of action.[18]

Primus' thought on these matters came to fruition in an essay she published on her return in *Theatre Arts* magazine in December 1950. Entitled "Earth Theatre," it imagines a new theater in which modern dance and dramatic artists might reinvest their efforts: "And so the earth becomes the stage: the curve of endless skies the backdrop. The setting is the jungle itself with its giant trees and twisting vines; the bald tops of mountains, with their rocky fingers jutting out, form the wings. The props are made from the bones and hair of the earth. And the actors are merely men and women!" (41).

She continued, "It is not theatre in our sense of the word—not a place where people go and pay for an evening of entertainment. Yet I was never before so aware of the magic of theatre as during the long year I spent among the people of the jungle" (41).

The essay outlined the importance of the body in African performance, claiming that "drama," the word Primus uses to describe the genre of the performances she witnessed, centered upon the physicality of the performers themselves, actors or dancers who were "called 'the play.'" Transcending a purely symbolic capacity, these actions resonated in the realm of the real. As she put it, "In the hands of the finest 'plays' one becomes soft clay, moulded into anything desired. This art of the theatre is so highly developed in the medicine men and women that they have often been known to drive the evil spirit out of the body by just performing before an ill person" (41). Underscoring evidence of an African cultural continuum, Primus found an analogy for this kind of efficacy in African-American religious practices, in "old revival churches of our south." "Here a single figure, armed with the poetry of language and a compelling magic, sweeps his singing audience from the wonders of Creation to the vision of terrible Judgment" (43).

Choreographing Memory: Writings of the Return Home

Melvin Dixon draws on Pierre Nora's notion of *lieux de mémoire*, or sites of memory, to make a connection between the black writer's evocation of memory and the larger African-American project of re-presenting the past. Authors of vernacular fiction use "strategies of recollection" and a means of "transmit[ing] Afrocentric wholeness in our heritage" (1994, 19). In this case, "wholeness" comes from the citation of memory as a kind of history; documentation serves the function of performance in oracular culture. The speaking of memory through written enactment provides accounts of experiences that had been neglected, overlooked, or suppressed, thereby "authorizing" the unauthorized. "Memory becomes a tool to regain and reconstruct not just the past but history itself" (18–9). Evocations of place are central to the pursuit of "wholeness" in "enlarg[ing] the frame of cultural reference for the depiction of black experience" for individuals, groups, and communities (20). According to Dixon, "By calling themselves to remember Africa and/or the racial past, black Americans are actually re-membering, as in repopulating broad continuities within the African diaspora" (21). What is more, for the literary artist herself, the citation of memory becomes a "stage or site on which the drama of self-acquisition is played" (21). The performance of memory through written documentation, therefore, is central to the constitution of the authorial subject; it allows the subject to coalesce through a personal-made-universal construction of race and place. It is a citation and a situating of the subject as both an individual and a member of a simultaneously national *and* transnational racial community.

Dixon's notions resonate strongly in Primus' artistic and scholarly work following her trip to Africa. For example, in an article that she published in *Vogue* in 1950, Primus employed memory not only to document her experiences in Africa, and to portray their significance to various audiences, but also to substantiate and authorize her evolving diasporic consciousness. The essay performs a travelogue of embodied transformation. In the first place, the body, which has been transported to a faraway and foreign place senses that it has, in fact, "returned home": "I stood there till the sun had burned through to my bones. I stood there thinking. I looked at my skin . . . at my bare feet . . . I lifted my arms and prayed. There among the swaying palms in the quiet of the Congo I prayed and I felt my lips quiver as I held back a shout. I knew then that I had not gone to Africa to study something, for I had become part of that something. In me were the singing and the drumming . . . in me the hopes . . . the dances . . . the sorrow and the laughter of my people" (1994, 99).

In the second place, she has returned to New York only to feel estranged: she experiences a diasporic disembodiment in which her body is in one place and her mind another. "Sometimes a strangeness creeps through me, even as I sit in the crowded New York subways and see the stations come and go. My mind records only the swaying palm trees and red earth roads which lead to the heart of the Bush. Peace seems to envelop me, my eyes close upon New York; and once again I am a wanderer. I am *Omawale*, child returned home."

In Dixon's terms, Primus' recollection was both a "retelling and a restaging"; she uses the rendition of memory—the formal composition of its account in written language—not only to reframe but to reconstruct her experience in Africa. Here she represented a complicated account of transformation. Whereas prior to leaving she assumed that her trip would accomplish a personal pilgrimage, her experiences in Africa not only changed her objectives but also changed her in ways she could not have anticipated. Furthermore, Primus' recollection, or retelling, accomplishes a restaging of the actual experience both to demonstrate to readers that hers is an original story and also to "write [her]self into the larger history of the race" (Dixon 1994, 26).

Yet this article also illustrates the complexity of Primus' diasporic subjectivity. This is seen in the passage cited above, in which she constructs herself in New York as both here and not here, and in Africa as there and not there—a "wanderer"—as well as in her deployment of a primitivist discourse that portrays her as outside the cultural practices she claimed to have made her own.

In one passage, for example, she tells the story of having been awoken one night to the "sound of drums." Lured by the beating, she "crept like a thief," going "from tree to tree in the direction of the drums." As "the drums grew louder, I shut off my [flash]light and went from shadow to shadow. Suddenly I was there," she recalled. What she discovered was a "tiny village" in a clearing. Around a small fire, "women were dancing as I had never seen before." She continued, "Men were sitting smoking, their long pipes seemed attached to their mouths. The drummers were singing a chant counter that of the women. They were dancing, but not as I had seen it before . . . *not the performance . . . the real dance.* Their hips were swaying and their breasts were tight" (Primus, October 15, 1950, 145; emphasis mine). Having been "assured" by her hosts that "there was no dance at night," Primus was faced with a quandary. Should she reveal herself in order to participate, thus disclosing her deception to her hosts? Or should she remain concealed, in order to witness the event in secret? Fighting with herself about what to do, she elected to remain hidden.

In her words, "Oh, I wanted to fling myself among them but the suddenness would have frightened them. I am forbidden to witness anything without the administrator present. . . . The low fire distorted the faces and the shapes. I watched till I felt tears running down my face. Slowly I disengaged myself from the scene and again hugging the shadows of the black night, I crept back to the house" (145).

Memories can be hazy, short on detail and malleable to suit the purpose at hand. Primus performed these qualities of memory through her primitivist rhetoric, presenting Africa as a unitary idea. Primus' portrayal of this moment is rife with what must have been stereotypical images of Africa in the minds of her American (Western) readers. These included her depiction of the participants in the ceremony women with "tight breasts," men smoking pipes that "seemed attached to their mouths," and drummers chanting. Primus' distinction between "the performance," which she had been allowed to see, and "the real dance," which she had viewed covertly, worked to support an essentialist and hierarchical account of foreign dance practices that valued as authentic those forms not meant for outsider consumption and viewed as spurious those presented in the company of others. In recalling this memory in these terms, Primus aligned herself with Western, not Third World, interests in ways that would appear to undercut her more encompassing project, to complicate contemporary notions of Africa, and to define herself and her work in complex terms, as well as undermine her authority as an ethnographer.

It is also likely that her primitivist discourse had sensational value as well, attracting readers to her story and keeping their attention. The representation of Primus as a Western primitive in the popular press supports such an interpretation, as do the ways she fed this evolving image. Consider a profile that appeared in *Ebony* magazine, which had a primarily black readership, in 1951 ("Pearl Primus: Foremost Dancer," 1951, 54–58). Depicting Primus as a classic overachiever, "billed as America's foremost Negro Dancer," the article described her as a "sturdy, squat ball of dynamic energy who is currently writing three books, studying for her PHD at Columbia University, and interpreting in a spectacular fashion Africa's tribal dances which she saw and studied during a year of travel in the

FIG. 4.4 Pearl Primus in the Belgian Congo, 1949. Photo by A. Da Cruz. Courtesy of the American Dance Festival Archives.

jungles of the Dark Continent" (54). While the author made a concession to Primus' version of the trip as a "return home"—"She saw Africa not as a tourist but as an American Negro returning to the source of her culture" (54)—on balance s/he portrayed the journey in sensational terms. Consider this passage:

"Pearl went native effortlessly. She found a striking kinship with the tribes of the steaming interior where it got so hot her hair grease boiled up in bubbles. She braided her hair native style, went bare footed and bare breasted. Wherever she stopped she ate and lived with the tribes, asking no favors or conveniences. . . . Today she is slowly ridding herself of the tropical diseases which were part of the high price paid for her epochal look at the Dark Continent" (54).

If this article is any indication of Primus' persona in the black press, it is clear that such outlets portrayed her as a Westerner who "went native effortlessly." Rather than countering such claims as being misguided, Primus herself fueled these sorts of perceptions to promote her work and claim a mantle of authority based on her apparent authenticity. In 1951, for example, after a performance at Café Society, she stated to a reporter from *Time* magazine, "Everything I do is consistent with what I saw in Africa—except for wearing a bra. I have to make that concession to our modern standards" (98).

In aligning her with dominant American culture, might such evocations of the West/non-West binary have afforded her the political cover necessary to conduct and disseminate her pathbreaking research, even at the cost of eliding the complexity of her subject position? Or did such portrayals, in the scope of her whole project, serve further to represent her multilayered subjectivity and public persona? Although it is difficult to answer these questions definitively, due to lack of information and the opacity of the sources that exist, it is likely that Primus understood the calculus of her choices, believing that they buttressed rather than diminished her authority, furthered rather than obstructed her objectives.

Consider the *Vogue* article. In admitting to having become aware over the course of her stay that she had not been privy to everything, she demonstrated sensitivity toward the breadth and complexity of traditional practices—not all were meant for show, not all served the public purpose of entertainment. That she took risks in witnessing a secret ceremony highlighted her intention to present as full a picture as she could of tribal life, rather than remaining satisfied treating performances offered up to her (Western) consumption. Moreover, while the story revealed her knowledge that her ethnographic work was not comprehensive, it underscored the great extent to which Primus was a valuable source of information, simply because she had gotten closer to these myriad and diverse cultural practices than had most Westerners. In this sense, her introduction of unauthorized material into the American cultural imaginary built bridges between her American readers and her informants in Africa even as it reified conventional cultural divides.

Conclusion: The Effectiveness of Doing

As I have argued here, in performing living history, Primus sought to ensure the survival of Africanist practices by sharing her experiences with new audiences who could help keep them alive. Her writings, in particular, highlighted the process of formalizing her endeavors through embodied memory. They did not simply represent what she remembered but demonstrated to her audiences *the doing* of how and what to remember. In this, Primus accomplished what she billed as a dual artistic and educational mission: she aimed to recast the image of Africa, and African Americans, in the minds of readers, even as she harnessed them onto troubling and enduring stereotypes. During the postwar years, her cultural work stood out because it heightened the connections of American blacks to Africa—embodied in her own experience of travel. This diverged from the general postwar trend among black activists of neutralizing the importance of the international stage for the cause of black civil rights in the U.S. And yet, Primus' textured, and, at times contradictory, portrayal of her trip signaled that this was not an easy relation.

Lowrey Stokes Sims argues that whatever the benefit to their artistic practices, the use of the primitive by black modern artists like Primus nevertheless reinforced and perpetuated normative social relations under colonialism (Sims 2005, 87).[19] Yet the politics of such deployments are far from simple. On the one hand, diasporic artists are exemplary cosmopolitans who must navigate multiple worlds at once, and whose art work negotiates various (and sometimes irreconcilable) commitments personal, social, and aesthetic. Their artistic practices are forms of cross-cultural translation, embodiments of the dynamic intertwining of a multicultural, often multiracial, subjectivity. On the other hand, they are consummate outsiders. Neither complicit in the colonialist power relations of primitivism, nor "primitives" themselves, they must reconcile these competing subject positions in their artistic practices. According to Sims, a silver lining appears in mediating such contradictory demands:

> Whereas [white] modernists are usually cast as having a "sense of alienation from the rise of the corporate industrialized state," for black artists modernism affirmed the notion that a black individual could be an agent of change or transformation. Whereas for white artists modernism "was reflected in the breakdown of the representational and the familiar in literature and art," for black artists that rupture represented a potential revolution in self-definition and self-image as they assumed the role of proactive rather than reactive agents in contemporary society. (2005, 87)

Politically temperate and ambiguous as they were, thus marking Primus' circumspection under the culture of containment, her accounts of her trip reveal a fascinating project of self-definition in which Primus assumed a "proactive rather than a reactive" stance that had aesthetic, theoretical, and historical implications. On a personal level, dancing diaspora, as well as using writing to work through its implications, were constitutive in that they served as labor in which Primus sought to resolve the contradictory nature of her self-perception. Responding to and reframing the debates about her work she left behind, which had been driven by the dichotomy of originality/authenticity, her comments had a constitutive angle as well, in casting her artistic practices in terms of her deepening sense of her own embodied subjectivity. Continuous with the history of dance modernism, Primus used her knowledge of African performance to refresh wearied traditions and invent new ones. As part of a larger modernist movement that, according to cultural critic Kobena Mercer "was always multicultural" (2005, 148), her encounters, real and embodied in her writings and dancing, provided new subject matter and prompted artistic invention in areas of representation. Like other modern artists, Primus used an encounter with "the primitive," in this case African people, to prompt herself into thinking about what she was doing in invigorating ways, and as justification for going against convention. Her experiences in Africa gave her license to refigure her own body, trained in modern dance techniques, and to rethink her previously held assumptions about movement and choreography. Through the lens of her fieldwork, Primus challenged, and thus destabilized, more broad-based critical assumptions about the uses of ethnographic dance material by black choreographers. Studying African dance forms, viewing performances, and talking with her informants gave her ideas about how meaning could be connected to "doing" itself—how movement was inherently dramatic with no narrative overlay or emotional motivation. Thus, her theorization of "effectiveness" underlined the inherent efficacy of any action regardless of its stated function in ways that contributed to the reinvigoration of dance modernism at midcentury.

In short, Primus' accounts of her trip offer a fuller picture of postwar diasporic subjectivity as a condition of defamiliarization: the feelings of belonging and not belonging to peoples and places she desired to call "home." Throughout Primus' work, one senses that her performance of sharing secrets was also a performance of silence—suggesting that there were other secrets she had elected not to share. Such strategies constructed her not as Westerner, or African, but as someone in between.[20] Moreover, her silence marks the shifting political economy of the American left during the early cold war years and indicates what was to come in the U.S. civil rights movement, when the actions of individual bodies alone and together became a powerful impetus for the cause of social change.[21]

ACTION IS FINDING SUBJECTIVITY

Merce Cunningham and Paul Taylor

The new painting has broken down every distinction between art and life. . . . What matters most is the revelation contained in the act.

(Harold Rosenberg quoted in Hilton Kramer 1999)

Painting relates both to art and life. Neither can be made. (I try to act in that gap between the two).

(Robert Rauschenberg 1959)

Not satisfied with the suggestion through paint of our other senses, we shall utilize the specific substances of sight, sound, movements, people, odors, touch. Objects of every sort are materials for the new art: paint, chairs, food, electric and neon lights, smoke, water, old socks, a dog, movies, a thousand other things which will be discovered by the present generation of artists.

(Allan Kaprow 1958; emphasis mine)

CHARACTERIZING the movement in the visual arts left in painter Jackson Pollock's wake, critic Harold Rosenberg and artists Allan Kaprow and Robert Rauschenberg addressed the potential of art to spark change through the juxtaposition of the real and the imagined. They envisioned artistic action not as a means toward "suggestion" through representational mimesis, but as a constitutive endeavor unto itself, serving as both a segue between contingencies in art and life and as an act of discovery or revelation. Redefining the artistic act had consequences for viewers too. If artistic action was to "find" objects in the world and redesignate their uses, the viewer's was to participate in the work of making meaning, which included reconsidering assumptions about the nature of life and art and the relationship between them.

Drawing on this context, this chapter examines the significance of kinesthetic acts of the imagination that likewise investigated the possibilities of "finding," or conditions of "foundness" as forms of artistic "fieldwork." These licensed art making and subject formation in ways that troubled artistic and social status quo. I focus on the early work of two choreographers, Merce Cunningham and Paul Taylor, who deployed foundness both in their literal use of "scavenged" materials and as a governing trope through which to conceptualize the meanings of their work. Stripped of the universalist trappings of heroism, collective significance, and claims of transcendence, "foundness" led to the mobilization of a more elemental yet integrated self, "not just a body but a whole person" (Cunningham quoted in Belgrad 1998, 162). It also manifested seemingly stable binaries (like real and imagined, normal and strange, cogent and absurd, and known and unknown) as fluid, enacting ontologies that complicated conventional conceptions of identity.[1] For these reasons, Cunningham's and Taylor's artistic results registered in more ways than one, as forms of action that both *were* different and *looked* different than the norm. Their practices of foundness asserted the wholeness and completeness of any body, demonstrated the body's intrinsic capacity for movement, and rendered the world as strange. Resonating with contemporary biological and social scientific findings that posited the mutability of identity, these practices contributed to emerging formations of counternormative subjectivities, albeit under cover of stylization. They also functioned as forms of aesthetic and social agitation, defamiliarizing the everyday in terms of what people "should" look like and how they "should" behave.

That said, it would be inappropriate to read Cunningham's and Taylor's significations as wholesale indictments of prejudice—sexual, racial, or otherwise. For one reason, their privilege as white males worked to their advantage. It allowed for tactics of elision identified with modern dance universalism, which glossed over difference with the goal of cultural integration, on the one hand, and for presenting expressive opportunities that were not available to choreographers of color at the time, on the other. This is not to say, however, that just because Cunningham and Taylor reproduced some of the dominant power relations inherent in modern dance universalism in their work, they were not subject to their effects—namely the forces of normalization associated with the culture of containment. This is made clear here by discussion of the critical discourse that surrounded the choreographers and their work, which took modern dance universalism as proxy for normativity.

For another reason, the very components of their approaches limited the trajectory of their actual political import. It was easy, for example, for audiences to write off their real significance, first of all because the artists themselves did, and, second of all, because their work looked so fabricated. Speaking to the first point, as Cunningham put it in comments about *Suite by Chance* (1953): "the meaning of the dance exists in the activity of the dance. A jump means nothing more than a jump" (Vaughan 1997, 69). Speaking to the second point, foundness had the effect of severing links between a dance and the world by dint of the inscrutability of the compositions it produced. Herein lay the paradox of representing otherness yet doing so in ways that rendered it illegible as a substantiation of "real" difference or social change.

In laying out the objectives of this chapter, it is important also to say what they are not. As discussed in the introduction, the utilization of "found" material is typically associated with "objectivism," an expressive mode that "foreground[s] the medium of dance rather than its meaning" (Banes 1987, xiv). Approaches like Cunningham's and Taylor's are coupled with other choreographers, like Alwin Nikolais, whose work appears in kind.[2] This historical focus on objectivism draws a distinction between representational mimesis or meaning-driven work, and the assertion of art and artistic processes for their own sake. Objectivism is seen as primary evidence of an avant-garde shift in modern dance. As I have argued, groupings like these not only have the potential to perpetuate Eurocentric dance historical mythologies but also to elide other kinds of juxtapositions that could yield meaningful results. Rejecting the tendency to see "objectivism" as an across-the-board announcement of an emerging (and restrictive) artistic vanguard, I focus instead on the particularities of artistic strategies within it—in this case, those which deployed finding or foundness as an artistic action of world-making.

In this light, Nikolais' work would be shown to be very different in kind than that of either Cunningham or Taylor due to its utopianism. As I have argued elsewhere, Nikolais' choreographic objectivity led to works that enacted a similar kind of ontology of difference (in Martin and Gitelman 2007). His practices distanced the artist from his work while at the same time yielding "strange" results (dancers whose appearances and actions challenged notions both about what was "dance" and about what was "human"). These practices also promoted the autonomy of individual dancers, who exercised their own movement prerogatives in response to a given movement problem or set of contingencies. However in Nikolais' case, objectivity led to artistic results so far out of the realm of the ordinary as to suggest worlds unto themselves. Nikolais' visions signified real possibility inasmuch as they replicated orderly and plausible systems of meaning. Their legitimacy, therefore, came as a result of their implied comparison: Why couldn't the real world be more like the imagined one? Having similarly dispensed with the goal of representational legibility, Cunningham and Taylor went further than Nikolais in rendering unusual, but more readily recognizable, conditions of doing and being through the utilization of "found" materials, the very trappings of the everyday. Reframing movement material extracted from a social or cultural context, Cunningham and Taylor, like Primus and Sokolow, highlighted the efficiency of movement as a form of action to corporealize conditions of being. In different ways, each choreographer, therefore, demonstrated real functions for movement beyond representation.

The "Ready-Made Self"

Cunningham and Taylor were not alone in their idea to investigate the capacity of the commonplace to both license innovation and give form to emerging conceptions about being in the world. Allying themselves with composer John Cage and with visual artists Marcel Duchamp, Robert Rauschenberg, and Jasper Johns, they generated ideas about dancing that led to unexpected discoveries about structure, subject matter, and meaning.[3] Like the other artists in their milieu, they used foundness to call into question the nature of the real, or the "given," as well as its bearing on individual autonomy. They did this through the application of artistic strategies that, in various ways, distanced the artists from their artistic products while, at the same time, heightening their sense of freedom in the creative process. Foundness served as the rationale by which each artist justified his artistic prerogative as a willing acceptance of given structures or rules, which, paradoxically, he had assigned or imposed (by chance) on himself as a means of governing his artistic practices.

French dadaist and expatriate Duchamp provided both a precedent and impetus for these endeavors in his deployment of foundness through the "invention" of "ready-made" sculpture. Clearly, Duchamp meant his work to be incidental, not monumental. With his ready-mades—akin to visual puns—Duchamp posed challenges both to conventional aesthetics and normative social relations by using humor to blur the boundaries of life and art. Specifically relevant to this chapter, Duchamp's *Fountain* signified an alignment between the homosexual and the avant-garde. As Paul Franklin contends, "*Fountain* begins another story in the history of art, a story that tells the tale of serial production not only as a form of avant-garde artistic production but also as an analogue to homosexual reproduction," which called into question both the primacy and the priority of heteronormative mimetic relations (Franklin 1999, 258–59).

Duchamp's ironic irreverence, often tinged with sexual innuendo, tickled the intelligence of artists and audiences alike.[4] Yet the debate about the work's meanings within the canon of art history suggests that not all viewers read *Fountain* the same way. Its very qualities—its irreverent material reality—directed audiences away from questions about the artist's personal life toward the immediate pleasure of "getting" the joke. Moreover, the "ready-made" implied that the artist was not solely responsible for making meaningful art. Art did not "exist as veracity, truth" (Duchamp quoted in Tomkins 1980, 128). Instead the artist and the onlooker shared the responsibility for making meaning. "The artist performs only one part of the creative process. The onlooker completes it, and it is the onlooker who has the last word" (Duchamp quoted in Tomkins 1980, 128).

As Paul Franklin contends, *Fountain*'s multivocality, its suggestion of difference through the multiplicity of innuendo, introduced the possibility of a queer reading while at the same time offering other routes of comprehension. With such methods, Duchamp contributed to a larger artistic effort, the attempt to repudiate habit—in the words of nineteenth-century French writer and anarchist Jules Laforgue—"The idea of liberty would be to live *without any habits*. Oh, what a dream! What a dream! It's enough to drive you crazy! A whole existence without a single act being generated by habit. Every act an *act in itself*" (Seigel quoting and translating Laforgue, 1995, 117; emphasis mine).[5] Duchamp's application of Laforgue's ideas to the realm of art making "opened the way to a lighter, more elemental kind of selfhood" that enabled the artist "—at least in imagination—to transcend the limits that any and every culture imposes on its members" (13).

Drawn to the work of Duchamp, Cage, who was Cunningham's life partner and often collaborator, examined the potential of foundness as it applied to the making of art and as a metaphor for life practice. Seeking similar results as Duchamp, Cage tapped into other resources such as Eastern forms of philosophical and spiritual thought, particularly Hinduism and Buddhism. He hoped to accomplish in his music what these processes brought about internally: to "wake [us] up to the very life we are living" (Cage quoted in Tomkins 1976, 100). From Hindu philosopher Ananda Coomaraswamy, for instance, Cage appropriated the idea that art should "imitate nature in her manner of operation" rather than by a holistic verisimilitude. In other words, art did not have to look like the real as long as it referred in some way to the process by which the real was constituted. From Gita Sarabhai, a student from India who studied with him in the mid-1940s, he learned that the purpose of music was "to sober and quiet the mind, thus rendering it susceptible to divine influences" (Cage quoted in Tomkins 1976, 98–99). And for several years, Cage regularly attended the weekly lectures of Dr. Daisetz T. Suzuki, who taught a course on Zen Buddhism at Columbia University. Suzuki's lectures led him to thinking about the artistic process as a kind of "listening."[6]

In spite of their methodological and ideological differences, Cage concluded that, when coupled, psychoanalysis and Eastern forms of spiritual meditation were processes through which the individual could reach a deeper awareness and appreciation for daily life.[7] These became the impetus for routes of creative investigation driven by playfulness and curiosity, on the one hand, and by the need for personal recuperation, on the other. At this time in his life, Cage was filled with sorrow in response to the horrors of the war as well as due to the dissolution of his marriage (Katz 1999b, 235; Rettalack 1996, xlv). Eastern forms of thought and practice also sparked Cage's novel approach to the artistic process. By the 1950s, for example, Cage combined Duchamp's ideas about the "ready-made" with the divining system represented in the ancient Chinese text *I-Ching* or *Book of Changes*.[8] Rolling dice, tossing coins, or employing other chance operations, Cage's method generated both the rules for and the results of his procedures. In this, he intended to preserve in his work the quality of spontaneity while at the same time reining in its devolution into anarchy. Cage described his artistic process as "purposeless play" (Cage quoted in Tomkins 1980, 69).[9] Contending in *Empty Words* (1979) that chance operations are not mysterious sources of "the right answers," he asserted, "They are a means of locating a single one among a multiplicity of answers, and, at the same time, of freeing the ego from its taste and memory, its concern for profit and power, of silencing the ego so that the rest of the world has a chance to enter into the ego's own experience (Cage 1979, 5).

Cage's interest in the East followed a general trend among intellectuals and artists to forge relationships with Asia through the appropriation of "things" Asian. As Christina Klein argues, "Middlebrow culture brought these alliances to life by translating them into personal terms and imbuing them with sentiment, so that they became emotionally rich relationships that Americans could inhabit imaginatively in their everyday lives" (2003, 8). But investment in the East in the realm of cultural production also accomplished other forms of cultural work under the purview of containment, "helping to construct a national identity for the United States as a global power" (Klein 2003, 9). For Cage, as for Cunningham, the East served multiple purposes along these lines, providing personal insight into selfhood that served as alternatives to Western notions, generating structures for artistic production and meaning making, and lending an integrationist internationalist perspective to their work. At the same time, the artists' derivation and deployment of these ideologies and practices on their own terms asserted their Western privilege while, at the same time, lending an aura of the exotic to their avant-garde productions.

Cage's conception of foundness operated also to make meaning of and to signal his own difference. It did so in establishing a central paradox in which chance generated both the parameters (the rules) for artistic production and their outcome (results). In her work on Cage, Joan Retallack has identified a distinction between contradiction and paradox that will be operative here. Whereas contradiction "takes place within closed systems" and connotes "unified and coherent sets of interlocking definitions and laws," paradox "operates outside of the internal consistency of any given set of rules." Moreover, "while contradiction leads to logical gridlock, shutting the system down and sending us to ferret out our mistake, paradox reveals insufficiencies of limiting systems in a complex world, catapulting us out of a system into a new realm of possibilities" (1996, xxvi). Here chance engendered "given" conditions for art making, which the artist would "find" and contend with. Cage imagined "finding" as working in concert with the values of Zen Buddhism, to attune the artist's consciousness so as to "free the ego" from subjective desires and expand his or her awareness of the surrounding world. But these relations also served as a meta-phor for an ontology of difference in their assertion that conditions for living were given, as they were for art making, then found. In other words, the choice to be or to do something that ran counter to the norm did not come first; it came as a result of something that was given at the outset.

"Free and Discovered Rather than Bound and Remembered"

In different ways, Cunningham and Taylor applied the principles yielded by Cage's experiments, asserting how artistic action could exist independently of the artist even as it functioned as a metaphor for that artist's own social and subjective reality.[10] In this case, regulatory operations, like chance or other kinds of imposed constraints, produced unexpected results and secured a space for artistic freedom, albeit a bounded one. Foundness as applied choreographically provided a haven both for the expression of nonconformity and for its concealment.

For Cunningham, Cage was the motivation for nonconventional choreographic practices. The two met in the late 1930s at the Cornish School of the Arts in Seattle, where Cunningham was a student and Cage an accompanist. Vaughan writes that Cage made an impression on Cunningham during a series of composition classes in which Cage introduced structures for collaboration that allowed "the dance and the music [to] be composed at the same time rather than one waiting for the other to be finished. . . . [I] was teaching the dancers to compose, using percussion instruments" (Cage quoted in Vaughan 1997, 17).

Cunningham moved to New York in 1939 to join Martha Graham's company, and Cage followed several years later, with his wife, Xenia (Tomkins 1976, 94–95).[11] In the early 1940s, while still a member of Martha Graham's company, Cunningham began experimenting with choreography.[12] Soon after moving to New York, he started taking class at George Balanchine's School of American Ballet (SAB). As early as 1942 Cunningham started searching for alternatives to the dance languages he was learning at the Graham studio and at SAB. He cut down on the number of ballet classes he was taking before company class and rehearsal with Graham. Instead, alone in his loft, he began investigating his own capacities for movement and exploring other approaches to dance making. He recalled

> I began to fear that the Graham work was not in lots of ways sufficient for me. I suppose it came about from looking at other dancing and being involved with the ballet—something about the air, and the way she thought about dancing. So I began to do this thing I do of giving myself a class every day, and trying to experiment and push further. I don't mean to say I knew everything, because I didn't, but I would do what I knew, and then push beyond that, and see what else I could find. (Cunningham quoted in Vaughan 1997, 26)

Urged by Cage, in 1942 he presented his choreography on a program with fellow Graham Company dancers, Jean Erdman and Nina Fonaroff. According to Erdman, the wife of mythologist Joseph Campbell, "it was John Cage's idea that we do a concert together. He and my husband were eager to have us get out from under Martha's thumb . . . So at their prodding we started" (Erdman quoted in Vaughan 1997, 26–27).

In 1944, Cunningham joined Cage again for a concert presenting six dance solos and three pieces of music. Cunningham "dates his beginning from this concert" (Vaughan 1997, 29). *Root of an Unfocus*, performed at this concert, warrants particular attention as it embodies a paradox that characterizes Cunningham's early aesthetic practices. It embodies how, by imposing limits on his creative process, Cunningham licensed his autonomy.

The premise of the work is as follows: "The dance was concerned with fear. It began in conscious awareness of something outside the individual, and after its passage in time ended in the person crawling out of the light" (Cunningham quoted in Vaughan 1997, 29). Even though Cunningham established a narrative premise for the work—that it would express fear— its structure was anything but conventional. Rather the dance had a mathematical framework consisting of "three large sections, each section according to its tempo structured in lengths of 8–10–6 beats. The time structure was a square root one so Section I was 8×8 in length, Section II 10×10, Section III 6×6. The dance was five minutes long ($1 \frac{1}{2}' - 2\frac{1}{2}' - 1'$)" (Cunningham quoted in Vaughan 1997, 30). The structure was integral to the communicative intention of the composition. It "allowed for [the expression of fear] in a way that [he] felt more conventional structures, [e.g.,] theme and variations, ABA, would not" (Vaughan 1997, 29).

Cunningham's recollection of *Root* minimized the importance of its emotional content, focusing instead on the novelty of using a temporal structure—like the fixed parameters of a radio show—to allow the composition's independence from a musical score. As he recalled,

A lot of modern dance people in the audience liked [*Root*] because it seemed to them to be tied to an emotional meaning. . . . They thought it had to do with fear. It had nothing directly to do with fear as far as I was concerned. *The main thing about it—and the thing everybody missed— was that its structure was based on time, in the same sense that a radio show is.* It was divided into time units, and the dance and the music would come together at the beginning and the end of each unit, but in between they would be independent of each other. This was the beginning of the idea that music and dance could be dissociated, and from this point on the dissociation in our work just got wider and wider. (Cunningham quoted in Tomkins 1976, 244–45; emphasis mine)[13]

Clearly *Root* marked Cunningham's departure from establishment modern dance, a turn away from the dominant aesthetic vision which saw the stage as the extension of the artist's inner life and the dance as a poetic metaphor interpreting life's meanings.[14] His memory of audience misinterpretation gave credence to his perception that what he was doing was new, simply because it seemed beyond the comprehension of most audience members. The memory also illustrates the centrality of foundness in his early thinking. What was "found" in this case, was a "structure based on time." While in one sense this structure was "given," in that each artist agreed on its imposition on their creative processes from the outset, it became "found" in the process of making the piece as all of the collaborators discovered ways of reckoning artistically with its limits.

This approach allowed each artist to work in collaboration with and also independently of the others. Having agreed upon the terms by which they would compose the piece at the outset, each artist used the rules to promote conditions of artistic nonintention. As compositional principles that operated independently of the artistic process of each, the rules led to unpredictable results. Yet, at the same time, such a process separated the elements of regulation—or the rules—from what they allowed—individual choice. In all of these ways, foundness engendered a way of working that would have future significance. It suggested that through acts of self-regulation, an artist could simultaneously exercise freedom of choice and restrict the degree to which his or her work would reveal information about him or her, all without seeming to be hiding anything.[15]

Cunningham continued to explore ways in which elements of the "found," like rules governing chance or pedestrian gestures, could lead to unexpected aesthetic results. Of these works, *Symphonie Pour Un Homme Seul* (1952), commissioned by conductor and composer Leonard Bernstein,[16] is worth noting. Created for the Brandeis University's Festival of Creative Arts for a cast including both trained dancers and untrained students, it used chance to determine the length of time devoted to any event or group of events, and utilized "found" movement (actions from everyday life) like washing hands, combing hair, running, walking, filing nails, and doing various popular dance steps. According to Vaughan, the piece marked the first time "everyday gestures were used in performance simply as movement—that is to say, without mimetic significance" (Vaughan 1997, 64). Through the paradox of the found, Cunningham had realized his ideal—*to make movement itself the subject of dance.*

Three essays Cunningham wrote between 1951 and 1952 fleshed out these ideas. "The Function of a Technique for Dance" (1951) argued that moving was the most important ingredient of dancing, not dramatic acting or technical display. "The dancer [must] strive for complete and tempered body-skill, for complete identification with the movement in as devastatingly impersonal a fashion as possible. Not to show off, but to show; *not to exhibit, but to transmit the tenderness of the human spirit through the disciplined use of the human body*" (quoted in Vaughan 1997, 60; emphasis mine).

As he had done in the process of composing *Root*, Cunningham elaborated the ways in which imposed limits (discipline) could yield freedom: "[T]he final and wished for transparency of the body as an instrument and as a channel to the source of energy becomes possible under the discipline the dancer sets for himself—the rigid limitations he works within, in order to arrive at freedom" (Vaughan 1997, 60).

For Cunningham, disciplinary structures also served as alternative ways of structuring both the artistic process and its results. "Space, Time and Dance" (1952), an indictment of establishment modern dance, detailed these ideas. It laid out what Cunningham saw as the "flat contradiction of the modern dance." "Agreeing with the original modern dance mission of discovering new or allegedly new movement for contemporary reasons," he thought it contradictory that those in the establishment did not "feel the need for a different basis upon which to put this expression" (Cunningham in Vaughan 1997, 66). With their "use of psychology as a tremendous elastic basis for content," the traditionalists seemed "mainly content to indicate that either the old forms are good enough, or further that the old forms are the only possible forms" (Vaughan 1997, 66). Could dance be "modern" if it was not experimental?

As an antidote, he stressed focus on moving itself, rather than a "push" for meaning. "We don't have to worry ourselves," he wrote, "about providing relationships and continuities and order and structures—they cannot be avoided. They are the nature of things. . . . *if a dancer dances, everything is there*" (Vaughan 1997, 66; emphasis mine).[17] Again Cunningham returned to the liberating potential of structures inherent to the dance medium itself: space and time. Choreography structured around time in turn produced "a space . . . in which anything can happen in any sequence of movement event." This method encouraged the independence of the choreographer, who was free to organize a composition in any way he saw fit. It also ensured the autonomy of both dancer and musician who created work apart from each other, and yet whose work was ultimately "connected at structural points" (ibid.).

Between 1951 and 1952, Cunningham generated compositional techniques that ran along the same lines, employing, as Cage had, the *I Ching* or *Book of Changes*.[18] Flipping coins and consulting the book's hexagrams, he organized the sections for *Sixteen Dances for Soloist and Company of Three* into a sequence, each of which enacted an emotion from the Indian classical theatrical vocabulary. Remy Charlip, who collaborated with Cunningham on the piece and also danced in it, wrote this about the experience, "Mr. Cunningham's arrangement of the sequence of dances was based on the conviction that it is possible for anything to follow anything else, and the actual order of events can be chanced rather than chosen, *the resultant experience being free and discovered rather than bound and remembered*" (Charlip quoted in Vaughan 1997, 62; emphasis mine).[19]

Clearly, these operations exerted the artists' Western prerogative, affording and even facilitating the use of culturally and historically specific materials out of context. To Cunningham and Charlip, however, these Eastern sources represented the means by which to reject artistic convention and license greater autonomy, "free and discovered rather than bound and remembered." This feeling of autonomy was heightened as both artists realized the potential inherent in the decision to disregard a rule, result, or operation. As Cunningham recalled, although the sections were "separate entities, we were beginning to use 'poetic license' in disregarding connecting points within the dances" (Cunningham quoted in Vaughan 1997, 58–59).[20]

David Vaughan encapsulated the significance of Cunningham's innovations in an analogy he drew in a 1957 essay on "non-objective choreographers." Here Vaughan distinguished between two ways of waiting for a friend on a street corner in a big city. In the first case, "you" wait expectantly, your "impatience growing [when] he does not come. You see everyone and everything in a *not*-relation; everything and everyone is *not* the person you await. Finally he arrives, and you find he's not late at all. But your anxiety has kept you from seeing and has created more nervousness" (emphasis original). By contrast, in the second case, "you . . . wait without expectation, intention or anxiety." In Vaughan's lights,

> Now this is theatre. Visually aware, you see that each individual passing is walking, or standing still, is different, that he moves differently, that the store fronts are different as different people standing looking into the windows; that without any intention of being self-expression, each person is extraordinarily so. Each *action*, as it happens, and as you are aware of it, is absorbing. It doesn't make much difference whether your friend arrives on time or late. You have been a spectator in the audience, using your faculties as you watch the players in *action*. (emphasis mine)

In the first case, waiting is burdened both by the worry that plans and intentions might not materialize and by the task of differentiating between what or who is not the friend. In the second case, waiting is made pleasurable by an openness to the world and what is happening in it. Indeed surrounding action is absorbing for its own sake, in the context of the street as a stage.

An "ABC" of Bodily Movements

Although not referring to Paul Taylor directly, the thrust of Vaughan's essay captures the substance of his work as well. Like Cunningham, Taylor was fascinated with foundness, yet he took the literalness of Cunningham's approach one step further in his investigation of posture as "an ABCs of bodily movements" (P. Taylor 1987, 76; Kowal interview November 7, 2007). While pursuing a career in the world of establishment modern dance, Taylor was also intent on finding alternatives to its expressionist prescriptions.[21] A 1953 performance of Cunningham's *Sixteen Dances for Soloist and Company of Three* had piqued his interest in chance as a means of motivating the creative process. Hoping to learn more about it, Taylor spent the summer of 1953 with Cunningham and his fledgling company at Black Mountain College and continued rehearsing with him into the next year. In 1954, after a frustrating experience in *Dime a Dance*, Taylor decided to leave the group. Like everyone else, Taylor had learned all of the parts of the dance so that if his name were randomly paired with a phrase during the performance he would be prepared. During the performance, however, the object denoting Taylor's part was never drawn, forcing him to sit in the wings until the end (P. Taylor 1999, 51; see also 46–47).

This frustration with chance aside, Taylor sought ways of depersonalizing choreography through other compositional methods that could objectify the creative process. Although his goal was not unlike that of Nikolais, whose multimedia compositions fulfilled a predetermined abstract idea that thereby circumvented the choreographer's inner life, Taylor's methods of achieving it were notably different. In association with choreographer James Waring, with whom he participated in a loose performance collective called Dance Associates,[22] in collaboration with visual artist Rauschenberg, whom he had met by coincidence in 1954, and in conversation with Cage, Taylor began thinking in terms of "found" movement.

While Cunningham had declared that any movement could be dance, Taylor translated this dictum more strictly. Unlike Cunningham, whose search for movement led him to the School of American Ballet among other places, Taylor "went out and looked around the streets" (P. Taylor 1987, 76).[23] While Cunningham experimented with how dance could serve as a metaphor for ordinary movement like walking, running, jumping, standing, and so forth, Taylor took a more literal approach, looking to extract this movement and transpose it directly into his work. As he recalled,

Everywhere the city's inhabitants are on the move—objects just waiting to be found, make-dos of an untraditionalized piebald nation, milling and walking, sitting in vehicles or on benches, tearing after a bus, some drunk and lying flat out. Lines of restless people at banks, theaters, and rest rooms. Wads crammed into elevators or spaced artistically on subway platforms or leaning against skyscrapers. They are standing, squatting, sitting everywhere like marvelous ants or bees, and their moves and stillnesses are ABCs that if given proper format could define dance in a new way. (P. Taylor 1987, 76)

Through these observations, Taylor discovered that posture and gesture could be the foundation for a new dance vocabulary. Gradually, he "amassed a collection of natural postures, stick-figure drawings which fell naturally into five stacks—ones of legs standing, squatting, and kneeling and two other categories of arm and head positions"—and stored the drawings in his empty refrigerator (P. Taylor 1987, 76–77).

In its application of foundness, Taylor's work demonstrated more affiliation with the artistic practices of visual artists Robert Rauschenberg and Jasper Johns than it did with Cunningham's choreography by chance.[24] For Rauschenberg, for example, work was finding materials to incorporate; this was the main event, not the finished product. Rejecting conventional definitions of the artist as creator, he fashioned himself in Duchamp's image, as a scavenger and combiner of ready-made objects. For his "combine" paintings, for example, he collected and reassembled diverse discarded materials from paint, to junk, to taxidermied animals. So poor he could not afford to spend money on materials, Rauschenberg took pleasure in being resourceful, in using what was available—be it sounds of the street, discarded clothing, bicycle reflectors, newspapers, or a stuffed billy-goat—in interesting and even astonishing ways (Kotz 1990). Duchamp's example gave Rauschenberg (and Jasper Johns for that matter)[25] "permission to use non-art materials in incongruous and seemingly random juxtapositions" (Sandler 1988, 148). Juxtaposing found articles from daily life, he achieved the shock of the new by recontextualizing the old. As it had for Cage, Cunningham, and Taylor, the process of contending with found materials added an element of the unexpected to Rauschenberg's artistic process. The nature of what he found challenged his imagination. "It is hard to paint nothing," Rauschenberg commented. "A picture is an object, a whole, that isn't just waiting for someone to express anything. It is finished before it is painted" (Rauschenberg 1959, 58).[26]

If Taylor's utilization of posture as "found" movement for choreography was analogous to Rauschenberg's artistic combinations of junk, Taylor's challenge was to make postural movement look interesting and "natural" at the same time. He did this through "stylization," asking trained dancers to execute material in ways that looked as ordinary as possible (Kowal interview November 7, 2007). For *7 New Dances* (1957), for example, Taylor and his dancers underwent a process of "unlearning dancerly habits" because, as he put it, "the natural movements, when done in a dancy way, looked unnatural." This meant that the performers had to stop themselves from identifying with movement, refraining themselves from investing given phrases with emotional significance or from using them as the bases on which to construct a character. Paradoxically, getting the performance of the postures to seem natural required that the dancers invent "a new, yet equally stylized" manner of doing them. Instead of investing movement with feeling as they had been trained to do, they practiced executing it with an air of neutral detachment and matter-of-factness (P. Taylor 1987, 77). To "look natural" they adopted a contrivance of neutrality.

Cultivating the dancers' "ordinary" presence was only the beginning of Taylor's efforts to construct normalcy as aesthetically interesting. Soon, he discovered that idiosyncratic phrasing could add dynamics to movement sequences composed of ordinary postural elements. He set the sequences to uneven counts—much like syncopation—imposing a varied rhythmic structure on usually mindless actions like standing, sitting, and walking. Mastering Taylor's phrasing required an extraordinary amount of the dancers' attention and coordination; they had to override their habitual postural phrasing patterns in order to adapt to the imposed rhythms. Speaking of the challenge, Taylor recalled that "learning these counts was like memorizing a page of numbers in a phone book" (1987, 77–78). "Since each posture tended to get blurred when executed consecutively," Taylor surrounded each one with stillness to create a more visually stimulating effect. Again, the choreographer's aesthetic prerogative denaturalized the experience for the dancers. "The sequences took little physical exertion, made it impossible to rely on our muscle memories, and were difficult to remember. By isolating the postures in stillness, we were left with no chains of uninterrupted movement." Stillness posed another problem. Not only did the dancers have to "discover how to hold still and yet remain active in a way that looked vital," but also they had to check their propensity to move. "For dancers whose training had been in movement," Taylor remarked, "this was like a springtail losing its tail, or a snail losing it pace" (ibid.).

"Dancing Is a Visible Action of Life"

Through different compositional routes involving foundness, both Cunningham and Taylor conceived their dancing and dance making in terms of action, suggesting that any movement, done by any person, could serve as material for a dance composition.[27] Statements of their difference from the dance establishment, these artistic practices of action also made manifest experiences of alterity that both supported and clashed with aesthetic and cultural norms. This section examines these contradictory dynamics through close readings of individual dances, and, when applicable, accounts of their reception.

Indeterminacy in Cunningham's work offers an interesting place to begin, in the ways that it led to the reproduction of cultural norms, on the one hand, and posed challenges to them, on the other. As I have discussed, Cunningham's employment of indeterminacy, including but not limited to procedures of chance, yielded idiosyncratic results within the creative process. In turn, these results, or guidelines for action, provided the choreographer with parameters in which to exercise artistic prerogative.

In self-performed solos, Cunningham used these practices to ensure his own actualization in the process of meeting the physical demands of tasks he had determined by chance. He saw an opportunity in performance to direct mind and body to the same goals; in his physical and mental concentration he harnessed a potentially subjugating consciousness in the work of self-constitution.[28] Dancing solo, and therefore outside of any social context that would be suggested if other dancers had been on stage with him, Cunningham positioned himself in direct relationship with the audience members watching him dance, thus confronting directly their expectations.

Speaking about *Untitled Solo* (1953), one of the works in Cunningham's *Solo Trilogy*, Carolyn Brown, a founding member of his dance company, underlined Cunningham's early emphasis on the meaning of movement *as it is*, not as it *referred* to something else. In her words, his solo is "not

FIG. 5.1 Merce Cunningham in *Untitled Solo* (1953). Photo by Louis A. Stevenson Jr. Courtesy of the Merce Cunningham Dance Foundation.

about something but is that thing. It tells no story, but is dynamically the raw, direct, immediate essence—a reality" (quoted in Vaughan 1997, 78). In a trilogy of physically demanding solos, which included *Untitled Solo* (1953), *Lavish Escapade* (1956), and *Changeling* (1957), Cunningham discovered what his body could do given imposed temporal and spatial constraints. The artist created portraits of embodied subjectivity, constituting himself moment by moment as a man apart from conventional conceptions of masculinity.

In *Untitled Solo*, set to a score by Christian Wolff, Cunningham generated movement phrases for the arms, legs, head, and torso, which, in his words, "were separate and essentially tensile in character, and off the normal and tranquil body-balance" (Vaughan 1997, 78). Then he used chance to "superimpose" these phrases on his body (each having its own rhythm and time length) so that each body part or portion would fulfill its movement obligation independently of the others and yet simultaneously (ibid.). Cunningham's challenge as a performer was to make physical sense of the phrases when they were combined, especially given Wolff's rhythmically complicated score, which contrasted with the intricate cadence of the movement phrases' sequences. In other words, the structure of the work forced him to contend with whatever phrase structure the chance operations generated; he had to "find" what had been "given" by these operations. The same went for *Lavish Escapade*, as illustrated by Cunningham's extended commentary about the process of making and performing the work:

> Very often, you did something slow with your arm, for example, and something rapid with your feet—but the arm had to do something large against this—and this set up a kind of opposition. . . . And also the juxtapositions, because of the chance thing, of getting from one thing to another, just the getting to it, and I didn't do anything about that other than go there as directly as I could—that in itself was part of the drama . . . It wasn't a question of technical problems, jumping, or multiple spins, or things like that, but the positions were so awkward, to do fully and then get to the next one, and do it fully, to do them so that they made some kind of dance sense. (Vaughan 1997, 88)

Carolyn Brown has commented that in some cases, "some of the final movement superimpositions were so difficult he was never able to realize them completely" (quoted in Vaughan 1997, 103). *Changeling*, the third dance in the trilogy and similarly "characterized by contorted body positions," had the same result (as shown in fig. 5.2). It was nearly impossible for Cunningham to do. Nonetheless, Cunningham recalled that he could succeed in making the solos look natural with more rehearsal. In his

FIG. 5.2 Merce Cunningham in *Changeling* (1956). Photo by Richard Rutledge. Courtesy of the Merce Cunningham Dance Foundation.

words, "all three succeeded in becoming continuous if I could wear them long enough, like a suit of clothes" (ibid.).

All three solos confronted expectations of normalcy, setting the dancer apart because of the ways he looked and acted. Costumes for each of the works, for example, confounded expectations about the dancer's gender identity. In *Untitled Solo*, he wore tattered rehearsal clothes, in *Lavish Escapade* a "union suit in multicolored stripes with one very long leg" (Vaughan 1997, 89) that he had knitted for himself, and in *Changeling*, a tight-fitting knit bodysuit accompanied by a knitted skullcap on his head. These were not typically "male" costumes that emphasized the dancer's virility through the accentuation of his strength or exposure of masculine-identified body parts like the chest, buttocks, and thighs. Rather, these costumes accented their arbitrariness both in their specific relationship to a given dance, and in their contribution to any governing thematic. They appeared to have been pulled out of a grab bag. Thus, they marked the performer as strange, in their tatters, structural idiosyncrasies (one leg of the union suit was cut off), or their general difference from other kinds of costumes or street clothes that might mark the performer as a man. The performer's movement followed suit. Cunningham's solos were expressions of deliberate awkwardness, attempts to make dance out of material that was nearly impossible to execute at all, gracefulness aside. Choreographed by chance, and presenting the dancer alone, they allowed Cunningham to sidestep narrative contingencies involved with relating to other dancers—for example, how to partner a woman without implying a romantic relationship or the implications of dancing with another man. Outside of a normative context, the solos also begged questions like "who is this man, why is he dancing, what is he doing, why does he look like that?"

To some members of the establishment, like Louis Horst, the answers to such questions were alternatively amusing and horrifying. As Horst remarked after a performance of *Lavish Escapade* in 1957, "Merce Cunningham's *Lavish Escapade* was a marvelous solo. It was waggish. It was humorous. It was, at times, mimetic and, at times, deeply probing psychologically. Specifically, it set forth the complete deterioration of an individual who tries, tries again, but never quite succeeds. Generally, it had as its core the behavior patterns of a profoundly disturbed personality. It was imaginatively conceived and engrossing" (February 1957).

In Cunningham's terms, action conveyed what can be a daily struggle for dancers, to know the body moment to moment, and, in this, to figure out what is possible to do given physical and compositional constraints. As he put it, "The dancer spends his life learning, because he finds the process to dance to be, like life, continually in process. That is, the effort of controlling the body is not learned and then ignored as something safely learned, but must and does go on, as breathing does, renewing daily the old experience, and daily finding new ones" (1951 in Vaughan [1997], 60). Here, the body in the here and now meets the material that has been given as dance. Such performances manifest a kind of being that had not been predetermined by a given role in a story but discovered and constituted moment to moment, in the act of dancing. Moreover, Cunningham's construction of self absent legible markers of his masculinity emphasized an alternative kind of identity expressed through the phenomenological fact of his male body dancing.

Cunningham was aware of what he was doing in terms of subject formation. For instance, he compared his dancing to "naked energy"—"a whipping of the mind and body into an action that is so intense, that for the brief moment involved, the mind and body are one" (Cunningham [1952], in Vaughan 1997, 86). Paradoxically, however, I would also argue that the moment of actualization functioned at the same time to distance the performer from the world because it defined his existence exclusively in terms of what happened on stage.[29]

In many ways, it was more challenging for Cunningham to achieve the same effects in the context of group works. In their very composition, such works necessitated that Cunningham dance in relation to others, and thus engage in relationships that had a bearing on his danced embodiment of subjectivity. Cunningham used procedures of indeterminacy to mitigate the significance of social relations within each piece.

In *Summerspace* (1957) (shown in fig. 5.3), the decision by Rauschenberg to clothe all of the performers in modeled unitards minimized distinctions among them. Cunningham's treatment of movement material had the same effect; phrases were generated by chance, recombined, and assigned to performers regardless of their gender. The focus on virtuosic physicality also generated possibilities for partnering that highlighted physical and choreographic dimensions such as support (weight exchange, holds, lifts), spatial relationships (level, position on the stage), and timing (unison, canon, stillness), and minimized the significance of gender difference on the stage. This is not to say that in *Summerspace*, men and women were interchangeable, or that chance enabled Cunningham to erase all signs of gender difference. Whereas indeterminacy could be a great equalizer, in making available tactics of elision, it also had the potential to generate compositional possibilities that were, perhaps, undesirable to the choreographer's overall concept of a given piece.

One of the puzzling things about Cunningham's work from this period is the appearance that he applied indeterminacy selectively, in ways that seem inconsistent with his stated working method, to avoid choreographing certain situations, like male/male partnering, for example, or to select others (heterosexual partnering). *Summerspace* exemplifies Cunningham's maintenance of convention in decisions about partnering which are clearly evident in traditional handholds, opposite-sex pairing, and the absence of same-sex pairing (which one would assume might occur if the

FIG. 5.3 Carolyn Brown and Viola Farber (standing) in Merce Cunningham's *Summerspace* (1958). Photo by Richard Rutledge. Courtesy of the Merce Cunningham Dance Foundation.

choreographer had strictly applied the results of chance operations). To counter the significance of these heteronormative markers, Cunningham applied techniques from his solos to group settings, deploying what Roger Copeland has called "the atomized body," a construct that first appeared in *Untitled Solo* in which he used chance to generate separate movement phrases for different body parts and then faced the challenge of integrating them in the moment of execution. In group works, then, "everyone on stage . . . is always a *soloist*" (Copeland 1994, 189).

Antic Meet (1958) (as shown in fig. 5.4), more obviously than any of the pieces discussed so far, incorporated literally "found" material to parody contemporaneous and historic movement idioms, such as classical ballet, athletics, vaudeville, and Graham technique. Cunningham drew his title from the idea of an "athletic meet," and sought to contrast "'clichés of vaudeville and various styles of dancing take [*sic*] the place of contests'" (Vaughan 1997, 103).[30] In its incorporation and reassignment of found movement vocabularies and styles, the piece honed a point of view on the past, highlighting the contrivances of the objects of its critique. In a vaudevillian solo, for example, Cunningham (wearing white workman's coveralls) rolled up his sleeves and performed a light soft-shoe number, dragging his feet across the floor. Movement material combined steps of lilting, jumping backward, and ankle spiraling, with a finale of grandly presentational high kicking. Similarly, in "bacchus and cohorts," Cunningham used "borrowed" movement and design elements to poke fun at Graham. Wearing an oversized sweater with many long sleeves but no exit for his head, Cunningham "danced" among a corps of four women wearing voluminous, and antiquated, crinolines. Spoofing staples of Graham's movement vocabulary, like cupped hands gesturing to their foreheads, the corps surrounded Cunningham as he searched for a way out of his sweater. In these sections, the work performed a doubleness, holding up found idioms as examples of pretentiousness or objects of ridicule at the same time as it asserted their potential as resources for movement invention, all situated equally within the composition. It also allowed Cunningham to present himself, as he had in his solos, as an other. The first section, for example, enlists him as a participant in an "entrance parade" playing the role of outsider, a clown "who has fallen in love with a society whose rules he does not know" (Vaughan 1997, 107). Compared with much of his other work of this period, the piece received a warm reception by critics, who were amused by its antics. As Doris Hering of *Dance Magazine* put it, "In his new work, *Antic Meet*, Mr. Cunningham used his own supremely elegant idiom to poke fun at other dance and movement languages. And he made it seem as though all the other kinds of dance were out of tune and only his comments had absolute pitch. . . . We can't wait to see it again" (Hering, October 10, 1958, 33–34).[31]

Some, like Foster, have argued that Cunningham's group dances highlight the ways in which he adjusted results generated by procedures of indeterminacy, using markers of heteronormativity as a shield for his homosexuality (2001, 177). This is likely true. However I also think it is important to recognize how Cunningham's group dances, especially *Antic Meet*, substantiated alterity, even as they masked it. Amplified as a kind of double sign of his strangeness, for example, Cunningham's solos within group work set himself apart—in establishing his difference from other dancers, he also emphasized his departure from normative constructions of masculinity by posing himself against the norm embodied by the others. What is more, just as Cunningham's body (its appearance and ac-

FIG. 5.4 Merce Cunningham and Remy Charlip in *Antic Meet* (1958). Photo by Matthew Wysocki. Courtesy of the Jerome Robbins Dance Division, The New York Public Library of the Performing Arts, Astor, Lenox and Tilden Foundations.

tions) signified his difference from company members, company members' bodies, in the scheme of Cunningham's choreography, served in kind. Even in more balletic works like *Summerspace*, ambivalent portrayals of "men" and "women" set everyone apart both from heteronormative constructions in both establishment modern dance (e.g., the works discussed in chapter 2 by Graham and Limón) and certainly in the domestic culture of containment.

Choreographing Posture as Action

Like Cunningham, Taylor deployed foundness to defamiliarize the expected, emphasizing as Cunningham had the instability of constructions of both sociability and society. Taylor's posture-based work, however, went further than that of Cunningham in utilizing ordinary movement (action) to highlight elements of everyday life that people typically glossed over in the course of experience. As he put it in an interview, "I wanted . . . not just to broaden the range of what dance could be, but hopefully to show people how just ordinary life was something to really look at" (Kowal interview November 7, 2007).

7 New Dances (1957), an evening-long suite, exemplifies this approach of "transforming ordinary gestures for the stage so that they read from a distance" (Kowal interview November 7, 2007). Performed with three female dancers, the piece tested Taylor's resourcefulness with found movement and a limited palette of postural possibilities. In *Epic*, for example, Taylor stood in a dark business suit executing variations on actions of standing, lunging, kneeling, and walking, accompanied by the recorded sound of a telephone operator's voice announcing the time every few seconds. In *Resemblance*, also a solo, Taylor performed phrases of walking while a dog sitting on the stage looked on. *Duet* was more stripped down. The curtain went up on Taylor, standing in a business suit, and Toby Armour, sitting in a cocktail dress, each of whom remained stationary for four minutes.

In presenting male and female dancers whose costumes emphasized their gender identities, these pieces appeared to be making statements about the clarity of gender difference. However, the pedestrian movement the dancers performed had no gender-specific import. Performed with a matter-of-fact intent, these actions revealed nothing about the dancers' identities. Taylor achieved his effect regardless of who was doing what. Nikolais had attempted to erase most, if not all, signs of gender difference in his portrayal of the body as an object. Cunningham had minimized the significance of gender difference either by appearing alone or exaggerating certain attributes through parody. By contrast, Taylor juxtaposed, recombined, and re-situated "found" material in unusual ways to thwart viewers' assumptions about the meanings of what they were seeing. For instance, while costumed in stereotypical garb (e.g., business suit and cocktail dress) that signified gender opposites, dancers either performed movement that was not gender specific (as in *Epic*) or remained still (as in *Duet*). These juxtapositions configured unexpected relationships between visual signs (the performers' appearances and behavior) and their referents.

Each dance suggested a social situation, however the dancers' neutrality and relative lack of interaction stressed the audience's role in "completing" the work. To liquidate content, Taylor, like Cunningham, employed stillness and idiosyncratic phrasing as tactics of defamiliarization to interrupt the flow of movement. Yet unlike Cunningham, who used procedures of indeterminacy both to license and to justify incongruities among disparate compositional elements, Taylor let his choices stand on their own. In setting up loaded scenarios but not delivering on them as expected, *7 New Dances* suggested that connections between what someone looked like and how they acted could not be predicted; to the contrary it was constituted moment to moment in performance, as it was in everyday life. The dance also embodied the troubling possibility that, within any moment of social intercourse, there were multiple possibilities for action, reaction, and perception; signifiers of meaning could be read in varying ways by different audience members depending on their point of view. Reality, therefore, was a subjective construction.

3 Epitaphs (reset in 1960 from an earlier version Taylor choreographed in 1956), *Fibers*, and *Insects and Heroes* (all 1961)[32] highlight different but related strategies Taylor developed of using foundness not only to disrupt social processes of gender assignment but also to manifest ontologies of alterity in the postwar years. Unlike the early work of Cunningham, which has been well documented in existing literature, Taylor's work from this period is relatively unknown, and rarely seen unless one visits his archive. For this reason, I have provided ample description in order to support my claims about each piece.

A study of posture and gesture, *3 Epitaphs* (as shown in fig. 5.5) performed the travails of androgynous humanoid creatures set to American folk music. Both costumes and choreography work together to emphasize the mutability of identity. The dancers are dressed from head to toe in dark knits (designed by Robert Rauschenberg); even their faces are covered with hoods adorned all over with bicycle reflectors that look like compound eyes. By rendering them faceless, and accentuating the muscular contours of their bodies, the costumes make the dancers look practically identical aside from size and weight variations. The performers lumber about, torsos hunched. Rhythmic and repetitive, their dance portrays the performers as equal and, in a sense, interchangeable, members of a group. Their movement vocabulary combines whole-body postural gestures with nonliteral motifs—for example, the spinning of the forearms from the elbows, or the inclination of the head. Taylor's frequent use of movement canons, when one dancer performs a phrase and others repeat it, evokes a feeling of imitation rather than of theme and variation. Due to their seeming predilection for imitation, along with their lightly lum-

FIG. 5.5 Paul Taylor Dance Company in *3 Epitaphs* (1956). Photo by © Jack Vartoogian / FrontRowPhotos. Courtesy of the American Dance Festival Archives.

bering movement quality, the dancers appear monkeylike. Much of the time, they pal around the stage in groups or by themselves; their interaction is informal and unmotivated by gender-driven narratives. Even the partnering reveals little; the lifts involve minor weight exchanges requiring relatively only slight upper body strength. Although facilitated with different visual and kinesthetic strategies, this piece had the same effect as *7 New Dances* in suggesting that it could be performed by any group of dancers, regardless of gender or racial identities.

3 Epitaphs sparked a heated debate among members of the modern dance establishment. In an interview, Taylor recalled Martha Graham's reaction in which she chided, "Naughty boy, we don't cover up their faces."[33] Yet others were clearly drawn in by Taylor's humor. "Mr. Taylor weaves his images with that strange blend of humor and solemn detachment that one often finds in children," remarked the reviewer for *Dance Magazine*. "It is not the humor of dramatic situation but of visual incongruity" ("Review of Paul Taylor's Three Epitaphs," 1956).[34]

If *3 Epitaphs* deployed foundness to accentuate a strange but homogeneous likeness among performers, *Fibers* (1961) (fig. 5.6) used it to evoke a comparably unfamiliar world. As in the former, *Fibers'* choreography, set design, and costumes worked together to produce this effect.[35] The set was simple: a large tree is at stage right, whose branches—made of material strips or "fibers"—cascade downward. The dancers' costumes, designed by Rouben Ter-Arutunian, displayed a similar motif. With fabric "fibers," or strips, decorating their bodies, the men looked like strange gladiators. On their chests, each wore a modified harness: pads over the sternum and nipples were threaded with fabric strips that wrapped around the rib cage. Their briefs were similarly designed: straps extended to the back from patches placed at the hips. Straps, secured by vertical patches, wrapped around the men's limbs as well, but left room for their joints to move. On their heads, they wore helmetlike creations; skull caps, from which fabric strips interwove, creating face masks. The women's costumes bore the fiber motif as well, but theirs were not as elaborately constructed as those of the men. They were clothed in white leotards and tights, each leotard decorated with a few thin black cords that extended diagonally from each side of the rib cage, across the hips, and toward the lower back. On their heads were "bonnets" made of fabric strips that attached at the back.

Due to their difference in styling and construction, the costumes distinguish between the men and the women. However, the distinctions displayed did not fall along traditional lines. For instance, the women's hair, an attribute commonly associated with femininity, was covered by the bonnets. What is more, Taylor declined to mark the women in other traditional ways, as they wore neither dresses nor skirts. Like their female counterparts, the men's appearances were strangely ambiguous. In a departure from traditional dance costuming, the men did not bear chests or wear shirts but instead displayed bodies adorned with fabric straps. Thus, the costumes obscured, rather than maintained, conventional gender categories. In fact, one could argue further that because gender or race were not marked in recognizable ways, the distinctions between them referred to the experience of alterity in general.

The choreography of *Fibers* added to the feeling that the world presented on stage is alien. The dance opens with a duet by two men. While the first kneels by the tree, another enters, performing an explosive phrase of twists and jumps. Soon, the first joins the second in motion; although

FIG. 5.6 *Left to right*: Maggie Newman, Paul Taylor and Linda Hodes in Paul Taylor's *Fibers* (1961). Photo by Bill Schipp. Courtesy of the Jerome Robbins Dance Division, The New York Public Library of the Performing Arts, Astor, Lenox and Tilden Foundations.

they proceed in unison or in canon, their phrasing is impulsive, which makes it seem as though their dance progresses in fits and starts. For this reason, it is difficult for us to anticipate what they will do next. As the men stand face to face, three women enter. At this point, the dance becomes more complex. Dancers come in and out of solos, pairings, and groupings. Often the movement of one person or group contrasts with that of others, so that members of the company appear to be moving independently of each other rather than in concert. When seen in relation to the stationary tree, the juxtaposed groupings evoke a sense of foreground and background on the stage. Dancers seem to come in and out of focus, making us aware of the difficulty of attending to more than one thing at the same time. During one moment, for example, one of the men cowers in the foreground, his body curled like a snail's shell. As he struggles, face down, to lift himself off the ground, a man and a woman dance exuberantly behind him. The contrast of the man and the couple divides our attention: should we focus on his poignant solo or on their virtuosic duet? Additionally, the hybridized movement vocabulary adds to the sense that this dance, like its performers, is difficult to categorize. It is a combination of ballet steps, such as extended leg gestures and intricate jumps, with Tayloresque modifications such as postural gestures, a "v"-like arm position, and a parallel leg stance.

Insects and Heroes (1961) (fig. 5.7 and fig. 5.8) combines the oddity of

3 Epitaphs and *Fibers* yet sets it in a social situation just removed from ordinary life. The curtain opens to reveal an empty, vaguely lit stage set designed by Rauschenberg.[36] Upstage is a wall of nine translucent sliding screens; each screen is a door to a small, closetlike chamber. One at a time, lights appear at the top of each chamber. They illuminate dancers, in silhouette behind the screens, who seem unaware of the audience. Separate and compartmentalized, as though in apartments, some look as if they are dressing while others tentatively explore their cells. Their gestures are self-referential or halting, giving them a reflective effect. Without any ado, a human-sized black creature, with long prickly bristles extending from its bodysuit, moves slowly across the stage, sliding its feet across the floor. When the "insect" exits, the dancers, some in black leotards, others in white or black/white combinations, appear from their chambers one by one. Each joins in a lively petite allegro begun by the first entering man. Unlike the introspective insect, they are confident. With expansive arm gestures, they open themselves to the audience. Their buoyant steps are meant to dazzle us. Thus begins the dance in which Taylor proposes that "in each man lives an insect and a hero" (Lennon 1962).

The entrances and exits of the dancers and the insect punctuate this dance comprised loosely of scenes. The lack of definition between the sections underscores the dance's general ambiguity. Also puzzling is the relationship between the dancers and the insect. Although at times the insect seems to have a discernible effect on the ensemble, its effect is inconsistent. Once, its presence seems to agitate the performers, causing their movement to hasten with urgency. In another scene, it seems to paralyze them slowly until they "freeze" into sculptured poses. These moments stand out due to their apparent causal clarity; however, they are exceptions. Much of the time, the dancers ignore the insect, never making eye contact with it. While the creature seems more aware of its human counterparts, shuffling around them as they dance or standing to watch them, it never directly engages them.

Although diffuse, antagonism shades a few memorable exchanges. During a duet by the two men, the insect observes, standing behind them with its arms raised. Their movement brings the men head to head as if opposed. Then, with the insect standing over them, they crouch covering their heads as if cowering during a civilian bomb drill. In another scene, a woman dancing alone is abruptly ushered back to her compartment by

FIG. 5.7 Paul Taylor Dance Company in *Insects and Heroes*. Photo by Rouben Ter-Arutunian. Courtesy of the Jerome Robbins Dance Division, The New York Public Library of the Performing Arts, Astor, Lenox and Tilden Foundations.

a man once the insect appears on stage—although there is no reason to believe that the insect will harm the woman, the man's anticipatory action seems a sign of his assumption of the insect's perniciousness.

Clearest is the distinction between the insect and the dancers, first telegraphed by the insect's strange costume. Movement differences add to this effect: while the insect's movement is limited to scuffling and hopping, the dancers share technically challenging and lyrical movement phrases. Finally, the segregation of the space accentuates the separation between the insect and the dancers. In all but the last scene, the insect is relegated to the space on or offstage, while the dancers are always "on" stage, either inside or outside of their compartments. Even though the dancers sometimes seem at odds, their conflicts are always resolved; those dancers left out or alone eventually end up in the fold. This is not true for the insect, who never makes inroads into the community.

The last scene amplifies the theme of difference. In obscuring darkness, the dancers stand in a clump. The creature waddles onstage and matter-of-factly pulls a sheet out of its costume. Blankly, two dancers use the sheet to cover the insect. Then they lead it to a dark compartment, slide the door closed, and join the others. The dancers do not acknowledge the significance of their action to us, or to each other; in this way, their action is made to seem insignificant. Behind the screen, the insect is ostensibly out of sight and out of mind. Now the dancers join together in variations of the

FIG. 5.8 Paul Taylor Dance Company in *Insects and Heroes*. Courtesy of the Jerome Robbins Dance Division, The New York Public Library of the Performing Arts, Astor, Lenox and Tilden Foundations.

signature movement phrase, carving and shaping the space. As the dance winds down, one by one the dancers return to compartments behind the screens. Again in silhouette, they resume their personal gestures. The lights slowly fade but the palpable eeriness accompanying uncertainty remains.

Assuming the work rendered a dream, reviewers were content to chalk its oddity up to fantasy. Doris Hering and Robert Alhen both focused on its dreamlike quality. In her review, Hering described the dance as a "delicious dream conjured up by Mr. Taylor" (Hering, October 1962). Although in her appraisal of the festival's program she had railed against dances by Merce Cunningham, Anna Sokolow, Jack Moore, and Ruth Currier for "transgressing" the line between "theater," "dance," and everyday life, she was satisfied by Taylor's composition. "What did it all mean?" she wondered. "For some reason that was not important," she decided.

"After all, how often is one privileged to gaze upon a dream?" Calling the dance a collection of "surrealistic dance sketches," Alhen, like Hering, had been pleased by the work's effects and had not pushed toward an interpretation of its meaning (Alhen 1962).

Not everyone who saw the dance discounted its social commentary. Peter Lennon, a London critic who saw the work performed in Paris in 1962, saw a "clear enough pattern of introduction, combat, insect epidemic, struggle and final, understated release: the sea-urchin, defeated . . . sheds its foliage and becomes a struggling human being." He interpreted the "swishing, elegantly repulsive sea-urchin" as a symbol "of one's daily nameless (or misnamed) fears and persecutions," writing that "one could also accept it as representing the beast, so to speak that is in all of us" (Lennon 1962). Unlike those of the American critics, Lennon's interpretation spoke directly to Taylor's intention—to invite the possibility of seeing the strange as commonplace. As he explained, "in spite of what one might think, this work is neither facetious, nor is it self-consciously bizarre; it is curiously normal" (ibid.).

These critical accounts suggest that, like those of Cunningham, Taylor's dances used ordinary action both to expose and closet difference. A case in point, *Insects and Heroes* deployed movement to mark clear distinctions among dancers, distinguishing between men and women, for example, or humans and the insect. Nevertheless, even though these differences appeared when bodies (and their movement) were juxtaposed one against another, no dancer was particularly bound by "nature" to perform a particular role or movement vocabulary. In this sense, difference was shown both to be culturally constructed in terms of type, and also highly individualized, suggesting that a person's appearance is not a certain indicator of identity or potential for movement.[37]

Wholeness, Mobility, and Mutability

The idea of having your own body and its activity be the material—that was really tempting.

(Rauschenberg quoted in Tomkins 1980, 104)

Rauschenberg observed a fundamental difference between the mediums of painting and movement. Painting, he thought, was a "fixed" medium, "made out of its external materials," whereas dancing was a "total medium," in which the "the body and its activity" served as "the material of the composition" (quoted in Tomkins 1980, 104). Several contentions are operative here: first is the body's given potential for action; second is that the content of a dance is rendered both in and through physicalized movement; and third is that, due both to these characteristics and to its basic animatedness, the medium of dance is "unfixed." In sum, dance possesses an inherent potential to disrupt and destabilize on levels both personal and social.

Cunningham spoke to the possibility that dance could effect personal change in this reflection on the ontological significance of his chance operations: "I began to use random methods in choreography to break the patterns of personal remembered physical co-ordinations [so that] . . . the resourcefulness and resiliency of a person are brought into play. Not just of a body, but a whole person" (Cunningham quoted in Belgrad 1998, 162).

The interruption of practices or processes of normalization, and their replacement by new patterns, movement material, and physical directives, forged spontaneous modes of being and doing. Both Cunningham's *Root of an Unfocus* and Taylor's *7 New Dances* are cases in point because of the ways in which the choreographic methods were aimed at "repudiating habit" (Laforgue). In this sense, artistic processes defamiliarized performers' ingrained movement patterns, pathways, and impulses; necessitated that they shed them; and led them to physicalized reconstitutions.

These practices of foundness dismantled some of universalism's core premises, and, as a result, substantiated counternormative subjectivities as expressed in dance terms. For example, the imposition of structural or procedural obstacles to the generation or performance of movement material—a means of working against ingrained tendencies—countered universalist claims that every form of dance sprung from the same "basic" impulses (J. Martin). Practices that "brought into play" "the resourcefulness and resiliency of a person" asserted the capacity of each body to attend to specific challenges set in its way, thus resisting the universalist mindset to make every "body" an emblem of a common (and totalizing) humanity. Finally, the defamiliarization of conditions in and through which dance could emerge departed from universalist notions that all dance sprang from and represented "intangible emotional experience" (J. Martin).

Foundness, in all of its iterations, implied a social dimension as well, in affording, and thereby asserting, the mutability of identity as constructed moment to moment. This idea resonated with sexologist Alfred Kinsey's contemporaneous research on male sexuality. Kinsey's *Sexual Behavior in the Human Male* (1948), for example, challenged the prevailing belief that homosexuality was a psychological symptom. He found that sexual experimentation among men was widespread and that same-sex encounters were fairly commonplace. According to Kinsey, at least 37 percent of adult males had, during their lifetime, at least one "homosexual" encounter in which they had achieved orgasm (1948, 623). Kinsey asserted that "there were no homosexual persons, but only homosexual acts" (Kinsey quoted in Robinson 1989, 67). Kinsey's focus on the importance of *what people did*, as compared with *what they "were"* in psychological terms, underlined the significance of action to the formation of identity (in this case, sexual) in ways shared by Cunningham's and Taylor's work.

Yet Kinsey and the choreographers diverged on the matter of the significance of choice. Kinsey, for instance, explained a person's attraction to members of the same sex in terms of individual taste or the happenstance of sexual experience. "This problem is, after all," as he put it, "part of the broader problem of choices in general: the choice of the road one takes, of the clothes that one wears, of the food that one eats, or the place in which one sleeps, and of the endless other things that one is constantly choosing" (1948, 661). By contrast, Cunningham's and Taylor's work emphasized that the choices in life were not ubiquitous but limited by a priori conditions, given by governing procedures, found, and then acted upon. In other words, whereas autonomy was a central principle in all accounts, Kinsey imagined an unlimited palette of choices while the artists imagined a more restricted one.

In other ways, Cunningham's and Taylor's artistic practices engaged with other findings in the social and biological sciences addressing the significance of mutability among seemingly stable identity categories of "sex" and "race." A brief genealogy of the historical and cultural economy of visible difference in the United States leading up to and including the period of the cold war provides a necessary backdrop. In an American context, difference tends to have racial connotations (Outlaw 1990). In the nineteenth century, for example, biological scientists embraced the idea that "race" was "a gathering concept for morphological features that were thought to distinguish varieties of *Homo sapiens* supposedly related to one another through the logic of a *natural* hierarchy of groups." They believed that "the behavior of a group and its members was determined by their place in this hierarchy" (1990, 64). These precepts legitimated legalized enslavement in some regions and justified widespread discrimination of people of African descent whose appearance varied from that of the white majority. In this case, people assumed that "race" was a stable category, and could, therefore, designate visible morphological markers distinguishing one person from the next (ibid.). Such constructions of blackness not only rationalized widespread racial prejudice but also fed the white imaginary. As author Toni Morrison puts it, "Nothing highlighted freedom—if it did not in fact create it—like slavery. Black slavery enriched the country's creative possibilities. For in that construction of blackness and enslavement could be found not only the not-free but also, with the dramatic polarity created by skin color, the projection of the not-me" (1992, 38).

At the same time, scientific and social constructions of "race" served as models for the emerging science of sexology; "race" became a convenient analogy for sexologists' attempts to discern gender difference (Stepan 1990; Somerville 2000). Siobhan Somerville points out that "[c]omparative anatomy, which had been the chief methodology of nineteenth-century racial science, gave sexologists a ready-made set of procedures and assumptions with which to scan the body visually for discrete markers of difference" (2000, 25). Racial and gender differences were mapped onto each other as mutually supportive signs of normalcy or abnormalcy (Somerville 2000).[38] Scientists' opinions varied in the particular morphology of gender difference, but, according to Somerville, "the underlying theory remained constant: women's genitalia and reproductive anatomy held a valuable and presumably visual key to ranking bodies according to norms of sexuality" (27). In these ways, science substantiated racial and sexual hierarchies, upholding the norm as truth and the deviation the inferior copy, and giving credence to the assumption that to see difference was to know difference.[39] What seemed to be a correspondence of observed characteristics of racial or gender difference based on physical appearance or behavior were culturally constructed assumptions.

By the late-nineteenth and early-twentieth centuries, the "discovered" so-called intermediate types—the person of mixed race or mulatto, or the "sexual invert"—became exceptions to the rules, destabilizing the mimetic binary in their refusal to fit into one category or another. They occupied a precarious and contradictory place in the social imaginary: while some deemed the two analogous examples of sexual degeneration, others saw the mulatto as evolutionary evidence of varied human sexual practices (Somerville 2000, 33). At the same time, people began questioning the scientific explanation of racial difference. As Michael Banton and Jonathan Harwood have asserted, systems of racial classification caused as much confusion as they did clarity, "no one was quite sure what races were to be classified *for*. . . . The same object may be classified differently for different purposes. No one can tell what is the best classification without knowing what it has to do" (quoted in Outlaw 1990, 64).[40]

In response, scientists in the early twentieth century focused as much on cultural practices (actions and associations) of individuals and communities as they did on visual appearance, making the study of "race," "sex," or "gender" as much a social science as a biological one.[41] Such theories, offered as explanations of "intermediate types" of human beings who unsettled mimetic binaries in defying simple categorization, proposed that identity was not simply something that someone was born with, it was something that cohered over time, through personal associations and practices (Somerville 2000, 33–4). In kind, Cunningham's and Taylor's turn to action emphasized the contingency of individual experience, while, at the same time, underlining the potential for fluidity in the formation of the self. In science and in dance, normalcy was not a putative matter but depended on circumstantial contingencies and individual responses.

Susan Foster has argued that in his "focus on movement and in the individual response to and interpretation of that movement, Cunningham found protection for his homosexual identity" (2001, 174). She continues, "Cunningham's closet . . . fractured bodies into parts of equal significance and value so that individuality could be defined by the activities, all of equal value, in which the dancer was at each moment engaged" (ibid.). According to Foster, as much as it altered standing conceptions of modern dance practice, Cunningham's "determined inquiry into physicality" had adverse effects: sustaining the guise of "nonsexual dancing instigated by the earliest modern choreographers" and "sustaining its inherent racism" (175). Foster's basic claims are true (the same could be said about Taylor), but they lack a nuance afforded by greater cultural depth. Thus, it would be a mistake to leave the argument here.

In chapter 1, I investigated the cultural and aesthetic significance of the convergence between universalism in modern dance and the U.S. foreign and domestic project of communist containment, ending with the case of the international dance touring program under President Eisenhower's Emergency Fund for International Affairs. While both the federal and the dance establishment lauded artistic "freedom" as primary evidence of the superiority of democracy as a system of government, members of the Dance Panel, acting as proxies within the U.S. government's struggle to "win the minds of men," policed boundaries of normalcy within the modern dance field, conjoining aesthetic and social standards. In Cunningham's case, the panel rejected repeated applications for touring in the 1950s on the grounds that his work was "'way out on the fringes of American dance' and is confusing and abstract," calling him "someone in whom we don't believe" (chapter 1). Although not as vehemently, in the early 1960s panel members expressed similar views about Taylor's work, calling it "avant-garde" and "anti-dance" (Prevots 1998, 64–65). It was not until 1962 that the panel deemed either Cunningham or Taylor worthy of funding. Clearly, panel members perceived Cunningham's and Taylor's artistic practices as threats not only to accepted ways of making and doing dances, but also to normative epistemologies.

Such views were perpetuated outside the confines of the Dance Panel's classified meetings within the dance field and society at large. Chapter 2 focused on the ways in which societal anxiety about antidemocratic subversion were mapped onto conceptions of normalcy, which, in turn, reinforced social tendencies toward conformity. In this context, constructions like the nuclear family served multiple practical and ideological purposes, as a framework for understanding social relations and gender differences, on the one hand, and as a bulwark against communism, on the other. Within the modern dance field, universalism provided a comparable gold standard in its provisions for the designation of normalcy, albeit in dance terms. Graham's *Night Journey* and Limón's *The Moor's Pavane* offered counternormative perspectives on heteronormativity through investigations of the institution of matrimony. Yet, because they fulfilled prescriptions for universalism, they were seen by members of the dance establishment as exemplary conveyers of "American" artistic values. In this case, aesthetics trumped content as grounds for establishment support.

By contrast, Cunningham's and Taylor's transgressions—on the levels of aesthetics and content—made them subject to establishment invective. Significantly, objections to their work functioned as proxies for a generalized yet latent homophobia, couched in aesthetic terms. This occurred even within a professional field in which many homosexuals played important roles—even as detractors. Louis Horst's review of a 1951 concert exemplified establishment response to early work by Cunningham, whom he called "still one of our potentially great young dancers, preferring the ignominy of experimentation to the easy success of brilliant performance in the works of Martha Graham." Responding to *Sixteen Dances for Soloist and Company*, Horst complained that the "few threads of continuity" never crystallized into an apparent theme. Patronizingly, he suggested ways the choreographer could help the audience appreciate the work. "Why not call the piece Voyage of the Hero, Transformations of the Hero, etc.," he offered, "rather than objectively, non-committaly, and with confusion cryptically naming it *Sixteen Dances for Soloist and Company of Three*?" (1951, 41). Among establishment critics, Hering's positive response to *Antic Meet*, which I have previously discussed, was a notable exception. Here it appears that Cunningham's use of parody, and the literal incorporation of a variety of dance forms, blunted criticism of the work's nonsensical incongruity.

Taylor faced even more blistering scorn. Most reviews of *7 New Dances*, for example, expressed outrage. Martin of the *New York Times* walked out of the theater early in the performance. Horst authorized *Dance Observer* to leave a blank space where his review of the performance would have been.[42] Walter Terry, one of the only critics to remain in the theater wrote, "Paul Taylor . . . seemed determined to drive his viewers right out of their minds (or out of the theater). Before cracking up completely, several persons left, but I managed to stick it out for five of the seven numbers" (Terry October 27, 1957). Terry's main problem was Taylor's use of stillness, "The core of dance, is action. . . . [Whether] cerebral, emotional, visceral or spiritual action is the source of inspiration, it must be channeled into overt action—formal rhythmic, meaningful—if it is to be called dance" (ibid.).[43] Reviews of a 1957 concert by the production collective Dance Associates, in which Taylor participated, sparked a similar reaction. Doris Hering of *Dance Magazine* called the group the "*enfants terribles* of the concert world," noting that "their perversities sometimes turn out to be as self-deluding as Dada" (February 1957, 12). The concert provoked the same response from Lawrence Witchel, reviewing for *East* magazine, "There are moments in my life when I come to the momentous conclusion that I HATE the entire Avant-Garde Art world. Dance Associates provided one of the more unforgettable of those moments" (Witchell December 13, 1956; emphasis in original). Witchel expected content, but what he got was "nothing." Singling out Waring's *Two Duets from Work in Progress*, for example, for "express[ing] . . . the most definite idea of the whole evening," he railed, "some very sensual movement is created, but like the essential idea they go no place and do nothing, and as a result leave the spectator with nothing" (December 13, 1956).

Surely there were critics who appreciated Taylor's work, yet these were of an avant-garde persuasion. Responding to *7 New Dances*, Kolya Tcherny, of the *Village Voice*, for example praised Taylor for his "magnificently restrained, poetic, often transcendingly beautiful dances." Anticipating the rancor of her counterparts representing other press outlets, she declared, "Mr. Taylor is to be congratulated for his courage and thoroughness in presenting a neglected aspect of artistic form in the theater. He will doubtless have to pay dearly for having done it" (1957). Likewise, Marianne Preger, who danced with Cunningham, praised Taylor, Waring, and their associates, exclaiming, "What an afternoon of luxuriant theatricality! Messrs. Taylor and Waring provided one of the most vigorous, varied, and exciting dance programs that I have seen in many a moon . . . This program was the stuff of which the future of modern dance is to be made" (1956).

Save for the praise of like-minded boosters, Cunningham's and Taylor's projects flew in the face of artistic and governmental projects of containment, both of which depended on stable categories of identity to distinguish friends from enemies. In the governmental realm, fear of putative difference as a sign of communist subversion was rampant. As a result, government officials as well as members of the general public reverted to thinking about difference in binary terms. As one government official put it in an interview with the notorious red baiter, Senator Joseph McCarthy, "If you had been in this work as long as we have been, you would realize that there is something wrong with each one of these individuals. You will find that practically every active Communist is twisted mentally or physically in some way" (quoted in Johnson 2004). Scientific research detailing the centrality of individual choice in identity formation, for example, or instances of gender or racial mutability, failed to promote greater public tolerance of diverse sexual practices or gender and racial identities; instead they seem to heighten the stakes for those upholding reified categories (D'Emilio 1983, 37).[44] Traditional ideals and cultural stereotypes acted as thresholds of normalcy, litmus tests of whether someone counted as a threat or not.

The same was true in the field of dance, although in this case anxiety about difference (i.e., racism and homophobia) was communicated in aesthetic terms. A majority of critics found fault with Cunningham and Taylor on two counts: impenetrability and the choreographers' and their followers' insularity (both of which coded for homosexuality). Reviewer Nik Krevitsky, for example, complained that "Cunningham . . . view[ed] his art as a special thing for himself and his associates," not "a social thing [that] can communicate to even the interested group who came to see the performance" (all quotes appear in Krevitsky February 1951). Witchel took similar issue with the Dance Associates, whom he charged, "start off with the premise that they are not to be accepted, that what they are doing is supposedly new and different and is to be completely beyond your comprehension." He continued, "They have not taken movement and delved into its ideas and complexities and arrived at a new Art form, but have let their instincts and impulses, without the discrimination necessary to newly create, dictate their gyrations. They have struggled to find within themselves impulses that appear to be different and daring, and have by doing so bypassed the inherent profundity of dance and left themselves with only the superficial" (December 13, 1956).

Conclusion

Study of Cunningham's and Taylor's investment in action during the postwar years illuminates how alignments of power within the fields of modern dance and society were complex and often contradictory. Their work allowed for a consolidation of dominant aesthetic and social relations through the exercise of racial privilege, on the one hand, and pioneered the grounds for establishing meaningful modes of embodying a generalized alterity, on the other. Under the multilateral pressures of aesthetic and cultural forces of normalization, what others have deemed forms of closeting were also, I contend, bold assertions of difference. True, both choreographers' racial identities made some of universalism's tactics of elision available. This is most clearly seen in their methods of equalizing the importance of all bodies in a given piece—thus glossing over gender or racial differences—and in their emphasis on the potential of movement to function as an abstraction, thus minimizing the significance of who was performing and in what context. Yet, importantly, their dances also rendered the body's capacities both for subject formation and for mobilization, conditions necessary for the action of the "whole social body,"[45] as we will see in the next two chapters.

THE USES OF ACTION 1

Talley Beatty, Katherine Dunham, and Donald McKayle

There comes a time when every human being must protest in order to retain human dignity.

(Katherine Dunham, quoted in Hill 2002, 219)[1]

Now is the time to move. This is no time to talk; it is a time to act.

(Dr. Martin Luther King Jr. quoting the
Reverend L. Roy Bennett 1958, 46)

I N 1959, Donald McKayle and his company performed *Rainbow 'Round My Shoulder* on national television. The piece portrayed the lives of black men on a chain gang, road builders who break up bedrock with their pickaxes in preparation for laying blacktop; men whose own road leads nowhere, only to more backbreaking labor. To words sung by Leon Bibb, it told a tale of futile lives, dead-end dreams, and stillborn desires, memorializing, through danced embodiment, the loss of the men's birthright: vitality, dignity, and potency. According to McKayle, *Rainbow* represented "punishment [that] does not fit the crime. Sometimes the crime was just being a black man and doing what you weren't supposed to do" (speaking in Reinhart 1990). The dance, therefore, brought into the light of day an unacceptable and untenable situation, representing the historic institution of racial prejudice as wrought on the bodies in question through compulsory labor. In contradictory ways, the dance embodied the condition of the men's restraint in shackles and chains, and, at the same time, their physical and spiritual agency and resistance to the powers that be. McKayle used the conceit of the dance to construct black men whose coordination, might, and imagination, as capacities for meaningful action, transcended their given status as second-class citizens. With this approach, McKayle's work took the challenge of actuality to a new level.

The dances of Cunningham and Taylor had offered the possibility for real significance in their presentation of dancers as the "authors" of their own actions through the guise of foundness. Yet, seen in the context of the early civil rights movement, McKayle's cast appeared to perform a protest in which their actions were "made 'visible' side by side with the[ir] characters in a Brechtian way" (Schechner 2003, 127). As Richard Schechner has put it, "Where distancing is used a definite social or political consciousness is engaged and the appeal of the performance is not to people as individuals but as participants in larger social units" (ibid.).

Throughout this book, I have presented case studies in which modern dances accomplished acts of social and cultural change by challenging normative distinctions between the symbolic and the actual. They not only represented conditions of alterity but enlisted bodies to constitute new ways of being and doing in postwar America. Intensifying this argument, this chapter examines the political efficacy of McKayle's *Rainbow* as revealed by two contexts, linked together in the blues aesthetic: modern dance precedents by McKayle himself, Talley Beatty, and Katherine Dunham, and the history of African-American protest at mid-century. In this light, I contend that McKayle's work made manifest an emerging cultural ethos that saw embodied performance not only as a reflection of cultural transformation but as a vehicle for or substantiation of it. [2] *Rainbow 'Round My Shoulder*, in particular, refuted a world that would punish men on the basis of the color of their skin, while, at the same time, reconstructing and empowering the black male body through the medium of modern dance.

Setting the Stage

National television coverage enhanced the social dimensions of the piece. Premiered at the 92nd Street YM-YWHA's Kaufman Auditorium, a central venue for modern dance in New York City, *Rainbow* attracted the attention of a representative for *Camera Three*, the CBS Sunday morning show, who called McKayle the next morning asking if he would adapt it for television. [3] This was not McKayle's first such request. A 1952 opportunity to televise *Games* had ended in disappointment when the producers and sponsors of CBS's *Omnibus* asked him to change the lyrical accompaniment and alter the mixed-race casting, even after having issued him a contract for the appearance (McKayle 2002, 49–50). By contrast the offer to perform *Rainbow* on *Camera Three* had no stipulations owning to the program's "secular" and "broad cultural" mandate (117). Something had happened during the seven-year interim that transformed what had once been squeamishness by television executives to broadcast modern dance with explicit racial content into interest. Clearly the acceptance of McKayle's work in this context illustrates the significant inroads made by both modern dance artists and African Americans in securing a public for their expression. In the lights of this book's argument, I would also contend that McKayle's favorable experience in 1959 signaled a broader cultural understanding of the body's role—in this case, as mediated in modern dance—in the formation and mobilization of the postwar body politic.

My argument is strengthened by McKayle's invitation to present another work on *Camera Three*, along the lines offered him by show producer, Jack McGiffert: "pungent ingredients: vibrant group dancing, vital pivotal characters, choral singing surrounding rich solo voices, and an American story that reached the heart" (McKayle 2002, 120). He delivered with a restaging of *Her Name Was Harriet* (1952), now titled *They Called Her Moses*, a work that, like *Rainbow*, aimed at the issue of racial prejudice, this time through the story of the life and death of underground railroad conductor, Harriet Tubman, and characters McKayle imagined as her friends (ibid.). In an interview, McKayle remembered something that made the television performance of this work all the more poignant and meaningful for him. At the conclusion of the live broadcast in which the piece was performed, news anchor Walter Cronkite cut into a newscast on sit-in protests that were sweeping over the South (Kowal interview September 22, 2006). As McKayle recalled, "it was a time of great change and people putting their lives on the line to effect that change. I thought the dance was part of that in its own way" (quoted in Morris 2006, 157–58). Beginning on Monday, February 1, 1960, coincidentally the night after Alvin Ailey's world premier of *Revelations* in New York City, the sit-ins and the wave of demonstrations they sparked, both galvanized a national movement for black civil rights in the United States and signified a fully corporealized cultural turn to action.

An example of "nonviolent direct action," the sit-in, like the work stoppage and the boycott, employed Mohandas Gandhi's techniques of "passive resistance" to expose and oppose existing social conditions, acting as an alternative to legal or legislative avenues of political intervention

(King 1958; Gregg 1959; Waskow 1966; Mayer [1962] 1990).[4] Mohandas Gandhi's practices of *Satyagraba*, or passive resistance, had demonstrated the political efficacy of "non-cooperation," or the conscientious refusal to obey the law or to abide by dehumanizing custom, as a strategy of resistance (Gandhi 1951, 73–110; Jack 1956, 59–65). Stemming from *Satyagraba*, King's use of direct action protest further actualized this approach, transforming the sphere of the commonplace—personal routines, everyday places, the justice system, interpersonal relationships, the national media and so forth—into a site of resistance through nonviolent acts of defamiliarization (Kowal 2004, 149).[5] However, the sit-in differed from comparable forms of protest in one crucial respect: While boycotters or strikers made their point through concerted absences, sit-in activists exerted pressure by insistent presence, occupying spaces from which they were usually prohibited. Sit-in activists put themselves center stage instead of removing themselves from the scene. Recognizing the success of direct action in Greensboro, other protesters around the state and the region during the next few months and continuing into the next year adopted similar tactics, staging read-ins at public libraries, kneel-ins at segregated churches, walk-ins at theaters and amusement parks, and wade-ins at segregated pools and beaches (Chafe 1980, 137; Bloom 1987, 157).[6]

In Greensboro men and women put their bodies on the line to protest the effects of racial prejudice on their daily lives, prompting many others around the country to do the same. As I have argued elsewhere, while the protests had not been conceived by a choreographer or carried out by professional performers, they were nevertheless "staged" to achieve maximum coordination, visibility, and impact (Kowal 2004). As in the case of McKayle's *Rainbow* or *Her Name Was Harriet*, events that might have found only a limited local audience received mass notice through television broadcasts. In all categories but one (choral singing), the sit-ins provided a real version of the elements that attracted audiences to McKayle's dance works: "group choreography," sympathetic and compelling lead characters, and "an American story that reached the heart."[7] Although performed under notably different conditions, and carrying varying risks for participants, McKayle's dances and the Greensboro sit-ins were analogous in their demonstration of the capacity of black bodies to engage in resistive acts by occupying real public spaces (the Walgreen's department store, television airwaves, and, by extension, a place in the cultural imaginary) and of the public's readiness to make meaning of such acts in their roles as actual and de facto participant observers.

The Resistance in Giving Voice

In this case, the convergence of life and art was predicated on the historical formation of the black public sphere through the blues aesthetic, enactment by and mobilization of black bodies refusing to comply with the given. A hallmark of the African-American expressive tradition, the blues aesthetic takes as interrelated the artistic, the social, and the political, and sees as continuous acts of "giving voice" and resistance. Houston Baker, for example, defines the blues aesthetic as including but not being limited to the musical idiom, the blues: "[T]he blues are a synthesis (albeit one always synthesizing rather than one already hypostatized). Combining work songs, group seculars, field hollers, sacred harmonies, proverbial wisdom, folk philosophy, political commentary, ribald humor, elegiac lament, and much more, the constituted an amalgam that seems always to have been in motion in America—always becoming, shaping, transforming, displacing the peculiar experiences of Africans in the New World" (1984, 5).

Building on Baker's research, other scholars of black expressive culture have adopted a more phenomenologically based paradigm, or the term "black and blues ontology," to illuminate the lived dimension of such aesthetic convergences. According to Beverly Skinner, "A black and blues ontology aggregates the concepts of blues aesthetics and black aesthetics in an overarching vision in which musical forms, folk art, and other expressivities within a culture are political, subversive, critical, and didactic." Conceived as a resistive practice of the imagination, "a black and blues ontology re-constructs an oppressive, inequitable political, social, economic environment and denounces it by playing on and with the inconsistencies and vagaries emanating from that environment. The resulting artistic expressivities counteract the enervating effects of oppression and paradoxically energize the oppressed, reaffirming their humanity" (1998, 1000).

Skinner's account stresses the closeness of art and life. Artistic "reconstruction" represents the real in order to make a comment about it. It also "counteracts" the real not only in its denunciation of racist systems of oppression but also in its dignification of the black experience. Her theory also provides a continuum by which to compare art making, in this case compositions of modern dance, and nonviolent direct action protests, shedding light on their compatibility as forms of black expressive culture that possess formal and intentionally communicative elements. Protests can be seen to have aesthetic components, and modernist dance practices to have political ones. While mining these kinds of alignments has more or less been my methodology all along in this book, highlighting expressive coordination between black concert dances and civil rights protest tactics underlines their real-world significance. If, as I have shown in other chapters, artistic practices provided the means of expressing, envisioning, and embodying counternormative ontologies, then, in these cases, actors (artists/protesters) did so at grave physical and personal risk. When art and life collided in this way, stakes were raised both for actors and onlookers, and the potential for on-the-ground benefit was both greater and more obvious.

Genealogies of Protest

Although genealogically related in the blues aesthetic, or black and blues ontology, concert dances and political protests were more *and* less aligned over the decades of the early twentieth century. As grounding for the consideration of the analogy of *Rainbow* and the sit-ins, this and the next section establish a genealogy of embodied precedents: forms of black political mobilization in the early twentieth century and "protest" dances of the late 1940s, specifically Talley Beatty's *Mourner's Bench* (1949), McKayle's *Games* (1952), and Katherine Dunham's *Southland* (1951).

Much has been made of the effectiveness of nonviolent direct action in combating racism in the early twentieth century, as well as the singularity of the sit-ins in their structural and expressive departure from comparable actions like boycotts, strikes, or work stoppages. Anne Braden, for example, has argued that what made "nonviolent direct action" different from protests like rallies or marches was its "*disruption* [of] the operation of discriminatory social practices associated with Jim Crow laws" (1989, 134–35; emphasis mine). Protest tactics of this kind enacted on a massive scale individual refusals to bow to racism or to its institutionalization in segregation and served as performances of collective "non-recognition" of racist laws and social protocols.

[W]hen such tactics of resistance are used by great numbers of people at the same time they take on an additional dimension. They become a very conscious weapon of social struggle, of defying tyranny and taking the offensive against it. They are a form of attack on unjust conditions, in which the attackers use every means at their disposal—their voices, their feet, their bodies, and the mass weight of their very numbers— every means except physical violence, to destroy the system that they oppose. (134–35)[8]

While the nonviolent tactics of King and his followers have become land- marks within the history of the civil rights movement, they emerged out of what Nikhil Singh calls the "long history of black civil rights," a period "bracketed by Roosevelt's New Deal and Johnson's Great Society" (2004, 6). In the 1930s, for example, blacks engaged in "Don't-Buy-Where-You- Can't-Work" campaigns in Chicago, Philadelphia, Harlem, and Washing- ton, DC, which protested discriminatory hiring practices, especially in white-owned establishments (Meier and Rudwick 1970, 4; Singh 2004, 64). The Depression era saw other forms of black political mobilization, including the Harlem riots in 1935; the establishment of the Brotherhood of Sleeping Car Porters, a trade union organized by socialist A. Philip Randoph; and the formation of the National Negro Congress (NNC), an organization dedicated to the pursuit of black civil rights across the na- tion (Singh 2004, 64). These efforts culminated in 1941, when a group of black workers, called the March on Washington Movement (MOWM) and organized by the estimable labor leader A. Philip Randolph, planned a march on the Washington Monument to demonstrate to President Frank- lin D. Roosevelt that they would not stand for the U.S. government's discriminatory hiring and contracting practices within the growing arma- ments industries (Mayer 1990, x; Singh 2004, 64). Although they never carried out the march, the threat the group posed pressured Roosevelt to institute a federal Fair Employment Practices Committee (FEPC) to over- see employment in the defense field (Singh 2004, 64). And, in June 1942, Randoph and the MOWM organized the "Big Three Unity" rally at New York City's Madison Square Garden, attended by over 18,000 activists (102). Although some, like "MOWM youth organizer, [and] future civil rights leader Bayard Rustin would describe the MOWM as the 'symbolic inaugura- tion' of the modern civil rights era," Singh observes that "the MOWM . . .

would have been unthinkable without novel ideas and projects knitting together heterogeneous agencies of the struggle for racial equality at new scales of association and influence" (65). He continues, "The MOWM, in other words, was the culmination of a decade of political activity when U.S. blacks became fluent with the instruments and strategies of modern politics, including the press, the picket, the protest march, and the property riot—all of which fully entered the repertoire of black struggles during this period" (ibid.).

In chapters 1 and 4, I discussed how, in the early war years, the national drive for black civil rights dovetailed with global efforts to combat colonialism and fascism. These coalesced in organizations like the CAA (Council on African Affairs, reestablished in 1942). These organizations provided both a forum and a focus for the expression of what the majority of American blacks saw as the hypocrisy of the U.S. government's war on fascism abroad. The formation of other radicalized groups alongside the CAA, like the Congress of Racial Equality (CORE),[9] founded by pacifist James Farmer in 1942, as well as the revitalization of the National Negro Congress (NNC), contributed to the formation of a "black counter-public sphere" (Singh 2004, 102). Participants sent a message to their leaders and leading black intellectuals that they were out of step with the popular mind, a message that eventually sent the NAACP in a more interventionist direction just as the United States entered the war.[10]

CORE, in particular, embraced Mohandas Gandhi's techniques of "passive resistance," calling their approach "nonviolent direct action," following Gandhi's reference (Meier and Rudwick 1970, 4).[11] Putting Gandhi's philosophy in their own words this connoted "(1) the power of active goodwill and non-retaliation; (2) the power of public opinion against injustice; (3) the power of refusing to be a party to injustice, as illustrated by the boycott and the strike" (quoted in Laue [1965] 1989, 7).[12] Throughout the 1940s, CORE employed techniques of direct action in an effort to end the segregation of public facilities (those of recreation and accommodation) in the North, and of interstate bus and train lines (Meier and Rudwick 1970, 5).

In the context of the disruption and eventual dissolution of the Black Popular Front in the late 1940s, CORE's moderate approach to political mobilization must be noted. As we saw in chapter 4, prior to the articulation of the Truman Doctrine in 1947, black activists including choreographer Pearl Primus—under mounting pressure from anti-communist forces (in Primus' case, the FBI)—softened their rhetoric. For instance, just before and after her trip to Africa in 1949, Primus shifted from speaking about her choreography in the revolutionary terms of the Popular Front and the Workers' dance movement, to articulating her artistic and political objectives in terms of racial uplift, specifically her objective of making the past relevant for African Americans. Using a discourse of diaspora, she turned to a more traditional, and publicly acceptable, way of couching her work, concentrating on the promotion of black positive self-image rather than political and social advancement. Her rhetorical redirection gave voice to her evolving sense of herself as a public intellectual, and conveyed the broader meanings of her artistic practices. The work of other black public intellectuals took a similar turn in the late 1940s. Instead of mobilizing the masses in public demonstrations and rallies, it concentrated on drafting petitions (e.g., W. E. B. Du Bois' 1946 *An Appeal to the World: A Statement on the Denial of Human Rights to Minorities in the Case of Citizens of Negro Descent in the United States of America and an Appeal to the United Nations for Redress*), which outlined goals and means of pursuing black civil rights as a form of human rights as declarations to international policymaking bodies in and through the United Nations (Von Eschen 1997, 74–85; Singh 2004, 53).

The sit-in emerged from this culture of moderation, in which activists committed to pursue black civil rights through nonviolent and temperate means, even as they sought to escalate the pace of change on the ground. Combined with more typical forms of economically aimed protests like the boycott, strike, or work stoppage, the sit-in proved an effective way of achieving a measure of social justice, if not full-fledged equal rights. Channeling collective impatience with black establishment methods of pursuing change through legalistic means, the sit-in became a "new tactic" in the war against racism. In the introduction to *The Negro Revolt* (1962), Louis Lomax described the "new tactics" adopted by young protesters as well as their radicalized point of view:

> The Negro revolt involves a drastic change in our methods and ideas
> concerning segregation and established Negro leadership organizations.
> Concerning segregation, *the revolt lies in the fact that we not only have
> decided that the last vestige of that evil must be eliminated, but have em-*

braced a new methodology, and armed ourselves with new weapons in our war against segregation and all of its concomitants. And the revolt against the established Negro leadership organizations has come about because these organizations are wed to weapons which, though they accomplished some gains, have proved incapable of dealing segregation a final death blow . . . [This] is not to say that we have completely abandoned or turned against them; rather it means that we Negroes have demanded tactical changes. . . . While the established Negro leaders were still locked in the methodological debate, rank-and-file Negroes have moved on their own, employed new tactics and achieved incomparable results. (Lomax 1962, xiii-xiv; emphasis mine)[13]

Alternatively, through the sit-in, individual protesters, acting together, could register a mass refusal to tolerate prejudice; in the action of "sitting"—or inserting one's body into a problematic and compromising situation—each person, acting in coordination with others, constituted the changes sought as opposed to waiting for the court system to issue a favorable ruling. While the same claims could be made for other forms of nonviolent direct action protest, such as the boycott and the work stoppage, the sit-in of the early 1960s prompted social change by *enacting* as opposed to acting by not-acting (by removing the body from a compromising situation). In other words, rather than decline to work, or decline to ride segregated buses, sit-in protesters inserted themselves in the very places where they were not allowed or supposed to be, thereby calling into question the prohibitive conventions that had forbidden their presence in the first place. The sit-in presented an alternative reality in which blacks and whites coexisted and commingled in public spaces. It also provided a structure that could be adapted to suit the particular needs of a group of grassroots-level organizers; demonstrators needed little training[14] and therefore could be organized locally, by young people (mostly college students), independently of institutional or national support. In the context of the early civil rights movement, sitting-in, therefore, was a way of "standing up for what was right while trying to stay within the law" (Patterson 1996, 403). Thus, it appealed to ordinary people who wanted to express their anger and frustration directly, yet in a measured and nonviolent way. Martin Luther King Jr. described this method of "massive noncooperation" as one of "persuasion not coercion" (1955, 52).

The sit-in proved effective, too. By the end of 1961, nearly two hundred cities across the "upper South" had integrated a variety of public accommodations, although according to Mayer "victories in the Deep South remained rare" (1990, xviii).[15]

Forms of nonviolent direct action not only disrupted existing social, cultural, and political paradigms concerning race relations but also contributed to the formation of an invigorated black public sphere during the cold war years. Houston Baker credits the person and attributes of Dr. Martin Luther King Jr.—his "language," "voice," and "articulation"— as "capturing the peculiar agency of civil rights and the movement's effort to recapture and recode all existing American arrangements of publicness" (1995, 16). King's tactics, vision, and leadership, all grounded in his Christian ideology and spiritual practices, led other activists further to cultivate the public sphere for other expressions of black agency: "Oratory and nonviolent direct action; commitment to, and reliance upon the power of the southern black American masses; charismatic appeals to racial and religious coalition; organizational merging of the Southern Christian Leadership Conference with the struggles of the youth-led sit-ins and Freedom Rides—all of these King-endorsed strategies produced a new black American publicity" (1995, 18).

"[I]nstituting a body-on-the-line revolution," these actions inaugurated a shift in the civil rights movement in which protesters "transformed" public spaces that had formerly been inhospitable to blacks, like schools, jails, buses, libraries, and even television airwaves, into "sites for liberation" (quotes appear in Baker 1995, 18).

Reflection as Practice of Freedom: Talley Beatty's *Mourner's Bench*

Historic iterations of black concert dance also contributed to the formation of the black public sphere, in offering performances of embodied blackness that departed from both aesthetic and social conventions concerning what black bodies could be and do. In the context of the early cold war years, and their suppressive effect on black activism in the late 1940s, chapter 4 investigated Primus' use of published writing to redefine herself and her movement practices through a paradigm of diaspora. I argued that through written acts of remembering, Primus evoked a "stage, or site on which the drama of self-acquisition is played out" (quoting

Melvin Dixon 1994, 21). Similarly, Talley Beatty's *Mourner's Bench* was a dramatic, if temperate, statement of black agency. Here the citation of memory, represented by enactments of reflection, reconstructed a black-identified past in and through the performer's body, designating, therefore, the site of power in the action of the black body itself.

In the PBS video *Free to Dance*, Beatty calls *The Mourner's Bench* "a personal expression of grief," adding, "he [the protagonist] is thinking upon the events of the day, looking out, moving across the bench, looking out, moving across the bench" (Lacy 2000). Beatty began performing the solo in 1947 until it became the second section of his 1949 *Southern Landscape*, a work "inspired by Howard Fast's published history of the post-Civil War Reconstruction period in the South," which "dealt with the terrorization of black sharecroppers" (T. Ellison 1998, 49; Hill 2002, 291). Even after it got incorporated into the latter, the solo highlighted Beatty's versatility: As K. S. Bartlett, a reviewer for the *Boston Globe*, commented, the work "gave Beatty an opportunity for an important contribution both as a dancer and as a choreographer" (Bartlett 1952 quoted in Emery 1988, 286).

The solo is as striking in its introspection as it is in its display of virtuosity.[16] Accompanied by the hymn "There Is a Home in Jesus," a man sits alone on a long wooden bench, his posture erect, his focus inward. As he moves along the bench, in a series of nearly repetitive gestures, he contracts his torso, bringing his attention even deeper inside, and then releases it, his arms and his attention directed to the sky. In its contrast, this first phrase establishes the work's central motif, the act of reflection (an escape into memory and imagination) coupled with a sense of being in this world. This motif is elaborated in the next movement series, which takes place in front of the bench: a sequence of presentational leg extensions and torso tilts end abruptly as two big impulses set the dancer turning around the bench, momentum that ends as he lowers himself backward onto it. In other words, the dancer's flight into meditation is tempered, or grounded, in physical conditions—namely the solidity of the bench and the force of gravity. The next phrase, too, shares a theme of collecting in and radiating out, the dancer using the bench as his partner in his challenge to gravity. Again, his attention inward, the dancer straddles the bench, and, with his legs gripping it for support, he directs his body forward as though he's flying, his arms gesturing outward, exten-

FIG. 6.1 Talley Beatty in the "Mourner's Bench" solo from Southern Landscape at Jacob's Pillow, 1948. Photo by Eric M. Sanford. Courtesy of the Jacob's Pillow Dance Festival Archives.

sions of the impulses of his torso. The feeling of meditation and focus is renewed as the dancer steps onto the bench. With movement displaying consummate grace and strength he extends his leg in second position, then ronds to attitude, a full gesture that sends him into a 180-degree turn on the bench in arabesque. In an admirable feat of balance and control, he lowers himself to the floor, his leg in arabesque becoming the new supporting leg once it touches the ground. The piece ends with a reiteration of the dichotomy between momentum and abrupt end. Several turns in second position with his leg outstretched propel the dancer around the bench. This action ends suddenly, however, when he turns to face the audience, his whole body flattened like it is up against a wall, his arms extended out. Softening again, the dancer lowers himself onto the bench. Facing upstage, he reaches up his arms as though in an act of praise, then draws them in, gestures that cast him rolling across the bench.

Both in its amalgamation of vernacular and modern dance vocabularies and its structural formalism, *Mourner's Bench* stretched aesthetic and cultural boundaries. For example, enactments of devotion, like the expansive, outer and upward reaching arm gestures, and the pulsing of the cupped hand to the heart, situated Beatty's technical and specifically ballet-inflected phrases in an African-American expressive context, thereby constructing the performer's body as a multivalent sign evoking a condition of diasporic syncretism. In this cross-cultural context, the piece negotiates tension between being in the world of the everyday, signified by the object of the bench and the performer's navigation of it, and the departure from it, represented not only in the performer's meditative attitude and introspective gestures but also in Beatty's balletlike use of the body as an abstract metaphor of the sacred. In his 1945 essay, "Richard Wright's Blues,"[17] Ralph Ellison explains that "[t]he blues is an impulse to keep the painful details and episodes of a brutal experience alive in one's aching consciousness, to finger its jagged grain, and to transcend it, not by the consolation of philosophy but by squeezing from it a near-tragic lyricism. As a form, the blues is an autobiographical chronicle of personal catastrophe expressed lyrically" (1964, 78–79).

Similarly, Beatty's dance expresses the feeling of the blues through its performance of lyric self-restraint, a quality conveyed by the protagonist's enactment of reverence. In this case, the "mourner" escapes the world by venturing inward. He "keeps the painful details and episodes of brutal experience alive in one's aching consciousness" by finding solace in the depths within himself, discovering an inner sanctuary through which to express his faith and to experience physically the power it gives him (quoting R. Ellison 1964, 257). Yet his inward looking also locates a core from which he might radiate out. In expansive extensions of his limbs that actively shape the space around him he embodies a form of "transcendence" in which he can elevate himself apart from the lamentable conditions of the everyday. As Ellison puts it, "[T]he blues are not primarily concerned with civil rights or obvious political protest; they are an art form and thus a transcendence of those conditions created within the Negro community by the denial of social justice. As such they are one of the techniques through which Negroes have survived and kept their courage during that long period when many whites assumed, as some still assume, they were afraid"[18] (1964, 257).

If the significance of the protagonist is minimized in the context of racism, his experience of his body within the choreography of the piece substantiates an alternative reality in which the performer can experience moments of transforming self-definition. Beatty himself saw it as a "protest dance"; as he commented to Hill, "I thought everybody back then was doing protest dances" (2002, 291).

Critical reception to the piece was mixed. While reviewers noted Beatty's prowess as a performer, they questioned the treatment of the work's content. For example, a 1948 review in *Dance Observer* faulted Beatty for his "pretentious subject matter," noting "the only lightness felt was in the transparency of his choreographic efforts." It also expressed skepticism about the relevance of the work's technical demands, exclaiming, "It seems a pity that a dancer with Mr. Beatty's technical skill continues to express only his virtuosity, and to confuse exhibition with expression" ("Talley Beatty," 1948, 7). The latter comment was in line with a trend among reviewers of the time to call into question the value of ballet training for African-American performers—the convoluted logic was that classical training would inhibit their "natural" dancing ability. With respect to Beatty in particular, John Martin caused a stir when, in a 1940 review of Katherine Dunham's *Tropics and Le Jazz Hot*, he singled out Beatty for his "serious dallying with ballet technique" (quoted in Perpener, 2001, 183). Not mentioning the topic of virtuosity, a review written later that year focuses on *Southern Landscape*'s aesthetic potential. Compared with Beatty's other dances on the program, which the reviewer found derivative of Katherine Dunham's work, as well as with the efforts of "far too many good, young Negro dancers [who] are devoting themselves to making anthropology exciting," he found that *Southern Landscape*, while "rather crudely choreographed . . . does possess possibilities of future development, his dance would go beyond mere entertainment and become both more original and more meaningful" ("Dudley-Maslow-Bales Trio," 1949, 38). Yet comments like these, questioning the relevance of Beatty's syncretic choreography, underline the extent to which Beatty's work, as both dancer and choreographer, functioned as a manner of protest, enacting a corporealized experience of self-definition that introduced unauthorized knowledge into the cultural imaginary.

In *White Man Listen!* (1957), Richard Wright called the Negro "America's metaphor," explaining that "[t]he history of the Negro in America is the history of America written in vivid and bloody terms; it is the history of Western man writ small. It is the history of men who tried to adjust themselves to a world whose laws, customs, and instruments of force were leveled against them" (Fabre and O'Meally 1994, 109).[19] Wright's statement was bald in its observations about the brutal legacy of slavery for black Americans; at the same time as it indicated the conditions of diaspora, a process by which black Americans found ways of "adjusting" themselves to a culture that was mostly hostile to their presence. Recognizing the absence of this story in dominant narratives of American history, Wright was not alone among black authors and artists working in the 1950s and early 1960s to assume responsibility for the documentation of the African-American experience in their artistic works.

During the postwar period, he, along with authors James Baldwin, Amiri Baraka, Ralph Ellison, and Lorraine Hansberry; visual artists Elizabeth Catlett, Phillip Evergood, Robert Gwathmey, Jacob Lawrence, and Charles Whit; and choreographers Talley Beatty, Donald McKayle, and Alvin Ailey, among many others, used artistic practices grounded in the blues aesthetic to bring to light complexities of the black experience in America (Powell 1997, 118).[20] In his work on black vernacular fiction, Kimberly Benston categorizes such practices that "shape, transform, [and] displace," in terms of self-definition, as acts of "re-naming." He argues that a primary motivation for black authors is to cast off the names, or definitions, given them by the dominant culture and to reappropriate or change them to express an identity that is self chosen. "For the Afro-American . . . self creation and reformation of a fragmented familial past are endlessly interwoven: naming is inevitably genealogical revisionism" (Benston [1984] 1990, 152). Through these processes, the artist identifies himself both in relation and in opposition to past constructions not only of selfhood but also of cultural (or rather, familial) lineage. In the black literary tradition, (un)naming occurs in the telling of stories meant to redefine racial identity in the present by reconstructing accounts of the past; thus, a person does not simply cast off one term of identity and replace it with another. Instead, selfhood is reclaimed through self-directed, self-formulated revision.

In this light, Beatty's dance was an affirmation of black subjectivity, both in its performance of memory as an embodied condition of being, and in the protagonist's graceful negotiation of life circumstances. His dance on and around the bench signified an embrace of or at least a willingness to confront physical challenge, a metaphor for a self-defined approach to daily life circumstances. The protagonist appeared not to be one who would shrink in the face of obstacles that had been placed in his way (like the bench), but one who would discover inventive ways of surmounting them. However, if this was a form of protest, it was a self-defined oblique one. Although the protagonist's stunning actions asserted his potency as an individual, his actions were directed toward the accomplishment of technical feats in a cordoned-off and somewhat utopian realm. In these ways, Beatty's dance enacted transcendence from daily life, asserting agency through a distancing from not a confrontation with the powers that be. Like Cunningham and Taylor, Beatty used his work as an exertion of his autonomy, to procure a space beyond the reach of social prescriptions in which to fully inhabit a dancing consciousness.

Taking It to the Audience: Donald McKayle's *Games* and Katherine Dunham's *Southland*

Sometimes you get a sense of mission even before you are aware of it. An act is determined of you but you're like a sleepwalker searching for some important object, and when you find it you wake up to discover that it is the agency through which that mission, assigned you long ago, at a time you barely understood the command, could be accomplished.

(R. Ellison 1964, 17)

In a 1961 interview, Ralph Ellison looked back on the 1950s and early 1960s attempting to account for ordinary black people's motivation for carrying out acts of courage within a civil rights context. Charging "too many of us have accepted a statistical interpretation of our lives," he argued "much of that which makes us a source of moral strength to American goes unappreciated and undefined." Then he asked, "Now, when you try to trace American values as they find expression in the Negro community, where do you begin? To what books do you go? How do you account for Little Rock and the sit-ins? How do you account for the strength of those kids? You *can* find sociological descriptions of the conditions under which they live *but few indications of their morale*"[21] (1964, 16–17; emphasis mine).

Ellison's point was that, in "accepting" external, "statistical," or social scientific accounts of their experiences, many black people had abdicated to others the power of making meaning in and of their own lives. Moreover, they had overlooked a source of their "strength" as black Americans—a "morale" rooted in practices of the imagination such as expressive cultural forms grounded in the blues aesthetic. To his mind, no author's work better captured the hallmarks of such practices than that of Richard Wright: "Nowhere in America today is there social or political action based upon the solid realities of Negro life depicted in *Black Boy*; perhaps that is why, with its refusal to offer solutions, it is like the blues. Yet in it thousands of Negroes will for the first time see their destiny in public print. Freed here of fear and the threat of violence, their lives have at last been organized, scaled down to possessable proportions" (1964, 94).

According to Ellison, works like Wright's *Black Boy* (1945), while not "offering solutions," set the stage for mass action in its representation, even "organization," of black life in vivid parcels for the consumption and provocation of ready, reading audiences.

Ellison's retrospective look at Wright's *Black Boy* offers a useful temporal marker suggesting a shift in the black cultural imaginary during the postwar period, embodied both in Wright's fiction and in readers' responses to it in the late 1940s, and, as we will see, in the performance and reception of McKayle's *Rainbow 'Round My Shoulder* in the late 1950s. Two dances, Katherine Dunham's *Southland* (1951) and Donald McKayle's *Games* (1952), helped set the stage for *Rainbow* in their deployment of elements of the everyday to draw unvarnished portrayals of the endemic culture of racial prejudice in the United States. Akin to the move of "taking it to the audience," their expressive tactics, grounded in social realism, stood in contrast to the more moderate and abstractly construed

FIG. 6.2 Shawneequa Baker, Donald McKayle, Louis Falco, Jaime Rogers, William Louther, and Raymond Sawyer in *Games*. Photo © Jack Mitchell. Courtesy of the Special Collections and Archives, Langson Library, University of California, Irvine.

acts of freedom embodied in the revisionist reflection of the protagonist in Beatty's *Mourner's Bench*.

The idea for *Games* came from McKayle's personal experience and depicts the communal life of inner-city children, whose only playgrounds were city streets (McKayle, 2002, 47). It uses sung and spoken words to convey its subjects' layered emotional and social experiences. According to Marcia Marks,

> Donny was watching children in a playground, serving as a volunteer play director, when he first conceived the idea of *Games*. . . . As he watched he found himself transposed back to the street in the Bronx where he grew up. He and his friends were playing the game "White Flag." Suddenly the Puerto Rican boys began shouting "*la hara, la hara*," their word for cop. All the boys fled except one. He went back to

get the handkerchief, the white flag. The policeman caught him and began beating him up. Donny, about 13 at the time, when to the police station and defended the boy. (1963, 30; see also McKayle 2002, 46–47)

Through the eyes of young protagonists, McKayle conceives the world in terms of three themes: "Play," "Hunger," and "Terror." Each of these offered a perspective of double vision, characteristic of the blues aesthetic, through which to perceive the complicated transaction between the action that ensued onstage and the words of the sung accompaniment (Kowal 2006). McKayle used two narrative media—the dance and the song—simultaneously to unravel the story on stage and, at the same time, comment on it.[22] Through this layering, McKayle revealed how children use play to cope and contend with the exigencies of their lives, negotiating conflicting feelings like pleasure, disaffection, aggression, and fear through play acting and game playing—"the serious business of being a child" (McKayle 2002, 46). Ultimately the piece raised the question of whether or not their playing has really prepared the children to deal with the world imposed on them by racism. The piece ends as the children confront an act that has been brought upon them from the outside—the brutalization of one child, Sissie, by a police officer. Although the act occurs offstage, the child's scream and her limp wandering onto the stage confirm audience suspicions that she was beaten up.[23] The audience watches helplessly as the other children gather around and try to comfort her as she collapses and then droops limply from the arms of one of her friends.

Dunham's *Southland*, choreographed and premiered in Chile, deployed similar tactics to expose the dubious hypocrisy of white-on-black violence, this time in the context of present-day race relations within a community in the rural South.[24] The piece combined singing, dancing, and minimal speaking in a serial unfolding of scenes, some of which were concretely dramatic and others that were abstractly drawn. It began with this prologue, delivered by Dunham, "There is a deep stain, a mark of blood and shame which spreads from under the magnolia tree of the southland area and mingles with the perfume of the flowers. This is not all of America. It is not all of the south, but it is a living, present part" (quoted in Hill 2002, 293).

Speaking in the present tense, about a contemporary situation, Dunham set the scene for the action to follow. Although the piece takes numerous twists and turns, in essence it tells the story of a black man, Richard, who is unjustly accused by a white woman, Julie, of brutalizing her (she had actually been beaten up by her boyfriend, Lenwood) and who is lynched onstage before an angry crowd. In the second scene, set on a street and then in a smoke-filled café, the crowd becomes a sympathetic chorus, offering comfort for Richard's lover, Lucy, and lamenting the racially driven violence that pervades their lives.[25] Dunham used a naturalistic approach in which her "dance drama . . . recontextualized historical 'facts' and dancers' biographies, new dramatic choreography and old musical numbers, thereby enabling dancers to more truthfully internalize, or embody, the materials" (Hill 2002, 294). As Clark and Hill have pointed out, Dunham's approach was not unlike "method" acting in which there is little distinction between the world onstage and the one offstage—"the play . . . is a thinly disguised exposé of truth" (ibid.). Its resemblance to reality apparently troubled some viewers, and reprisals followed. For example, while reviewers for communist newspapers first in Chile and then in Paris, where the piece was next (and last) performed, praised the piece for its unvarnished portrayal of racism in America, representatives of foreign entities in Santiago and Buenos Aires, as well as those from the U.S. government diplomatic corps, shunned Dunham while she was abroad (Hill 2002, 309). In the 1950s, members of the Dance Panel "tentatively approved" but eventually denied her funding for state-sponsored international touring through Eisenhower's Emergency Fund (Prevots 1998, 104–5).[26]

In "The Site of Memory," Toni Morrison brings to light the common practice among African-American writers from the mid-nineteenth to the early twentieth century to gloss over the grim realities of their lives, observing that "[w]henever there was an usually violent incident, or a scatological one, or something 'excessive,' one finds the writer taking refuge in the literary conventions of the day" (Morrison 1998, 190). She continues, "In shaping the experience to make it palatable to those who were in a position to alleviate it, they were silent about many things, and they 'forgot' many other things. There was a careful selection of the instances that they would record and a careful rendering of those that they chose to describe" (191). What Morrison finds missing from these impressionistic narratives are factual details—or, in other words, a grounding in the real—the lack of which makes it difficult, if not impossible, to know what exactly happened. What she finds even more vexing, though, is a commensurate omission: the author's reflection on what an event meant to him or her or to the other people involved, insight into the world of human interior life, or what she calls "subjective speculation" (194). According to Morrison, memory, but even more the ability to imagine the inner lives of historical subjects, becomes central to the contemporary author's excavation process (192).

Counter to the impulse to use expressive culture to perform an act of "forgetting," dances like *Games* and *Southland* exemplify how, by the mid-1950s, the black tendency to repress, suppress, or omit condemnatory acts of the past had been externalized, in grievances expressed openly through significantly public actions. Using material drawn from daily life, and thus conflating the symbolic and the actual, both *Games* and *Southland* took the problem of racism to viewers. Both works turned to the not-so-distant past to "excavate" and re-present the black experience in such a way as to place the onus for white-on-black violence on the general viewing public.

In this, both dances manifest an aesthetic shift from the trope of "forgetting" and "remembering" as in *Mourner's Bench*, in which the body was the conduit through which this transaction took place, to the use of memory that situated causes for moral indignation in the everyday squarely in hands of viewers. Beatty's black everyman now had a name and lived in a particular sociogeographic environment that bore on his experience. Like the perpetrators of nonviolent direct actions, for example Rosa Parks, the woman who initiated the Montgomery Bus Boycott in 1955,[27] or the "Greensboro Four," the male college students who conducted the first sit-in at the Greensboro Woolworth's store,[28] the protagonists in *Games* and *Southland* are individualized even as they are representative members of their respective communities. The works effectively showed how racism was, at once, born on a massive scale by the collective black public, and manifest on an individual scale, as acts or threats of violence perpetrated on individuals by individuals. What is more, their mixed reception and censorship are evidence that they were perceived as threats to the status quo by individual viewers or by the audiences they represented.

Hill has argued that for Dunham, *Southland* was "both a public act and private rite de passage, affirming how dancing is a healing process as well as a political act" (2002, 290). In the story of the work, she notes not only "the consequences of social protest in the 1950s," but also "the temperament and perhaps the very soul of protest expression rooted in the African American political struggle" (ibid.). The same could be said about *Games*. Both Dunham and McKayle used their work to stand up to racist practices—defying prescriptions for black complicity—and to bring their attendant brutality into the light of day.

McKayle's Civil Disobedience: *Rainbow 'Round My Shoulder*

In similar ways, McKayle's *Rainbow 'Round My Shoulder* brought together artistic and real realms in portraying protagonists for whom the imagination was a realm of redemption. Like other forms of cultural production within a black and blues ontology, McKayle's dance represented an essentially and inherently problematic and compromising situation, but went further in embodying a condition of freedom conveyed in the act of dancing itself. McKayle's work envisioned the capacity of prisoners on a chain gang—individuals literally shackled by racism—to transcend their given status through danced embodiment.

In accomplishing this transaction, McKayle both drew on and departed from precedents. Like Beatty's *Mourner's Bench, Rainbow* distanced its characters from the particulars of the everyday. In line with the conventions of universalism in modern dance, its characters were archetypal and emblematic, inhabiting an abstractly construed place (a work site), with generalized problems that might face prison convicts, like isolation and exhaustion.[29] Moreover, the convicts satisfied the expectation in postwar modern dance that the black male dancing body be depicted as a laboring body capable of feats of brute strength.[30] In introducing a female character to serve as an object of romantic fantasy, McKayle portrayed the men as decidedly heterosexual, and undeniably sexual beings.[31] Within the restrictive aesthetic parameters for the representation of black masculinity in modern dance, however, McKayle's dance provided a more complicated model of the black male than it seemed at first glance. It shared with *Games* and *Southland* a striking expression of "subjective speculation," therefore moving beyond painting a portrait of a racially drawn

FIG. 6.3 The Donald McKayle Dance Company in *Rainbow 'Round My Shoulder*. Courtesy of the Special Collections and Archives, Langson Library, University of California, Irvine.

situation to making a comment about it. In other words, while *Mourner's Bench* condemned only through implication, *Rainbow* spared no moral indignation in its presentation not only of the results of a broken judicial and penal system, but also of the adoption of human strategies to transcend and even to protest it.

According to McKayle, the title of the piece has a double meaning, "Rainbow was the prison slang for the tool used to break rock for roadbeds. The pickaxes glistened as they were swung, sometimes creating their own fleeting rainbows, arcing spectrums of color reaching into space and quickly vanishing" (2002, 115). The "rainbow" is an instrument of imprisonment and torture. Yet, as a symbol of treasure or "holy grail" it connotes freedom.[32] Similarly, the lyrics were laced with multiple meanings. As McKayle put it, "The melody was short, spare, driving. The coded lyrics were filled with despair, but always held an ever present glimmer of hope" (2002, 115).

The first section lays out the main themes of the piece. It begins with the sounds of early morning: a dog barks, a bird crows, and the wind howls. A soloist enters to Bibb's voice, which is rich and low as he sings "Rocks and Gravel"

> Well it's early in the morning
> Baby when I rise oh wella
> Baby when I rise oh wella
> Baby when I rise oh wella
> Got the aches and pains, lordy mama
> Make a man wanna die oh wella
>
> Well it's hard and it's hard lordy rollin'
> Well it's hard and it's hard lordy rollin'
> Well it's hard and it's hard lordy rollin'
> Come on boys oh wella[33]

Flexed with exertion, the soloist's body bends, whips, twists, and punches in a driving phrasing. Drawing on traditions of work dances within black concert dance, he appears as both a laborer and an instrument, the extension of a command and the agent of its accomplishment. An ensemble of men enters, holding each other's hands as if they are chained together, their bodies sculpted by hard labor. In a canon following the phrase set by the soloist, the ensemble moves with single-minded commitment. As Doris Hering wrote in a 1961 review, "Seven men entered hand-in-hand, each dipping a shoulder as though bearing a weight. They had the rhythm of people long bound together . . . Sometimes the group sat quietly watching, sometimes they burst into a great frenzy of almost primitive dance, with shoulders and arms eloquently alive, with the tension so cumulative that they ended in a grunting shout" (January 1961a).

It appears that each man is a cog in a relentless machine, each body having no other objective but this work. Paradoxically, however, in the scheme of the piece the message is far from hopeless. Each man performing his movement in unison with others in the group, the effect is one of amplification, not diminution. As McKayle put it, "Our bodies were being used as tools, and yet an ever-present defiance colored the movement with a sardonic and seething race and a dangerous humanity" (2002, 115). The section ends as the men slump to the floor, their energy apparently spent. Yet, according to McKayle, each man's imagination performs an act of release: "The men collapsed on the ground for the midmorning break and their minds immediately filled with visions of freedom" (ibid.). Their labor has not been for naught. The men's performance of "seething race" and "a dangerous humanity" has been registered in the cultural imaginary.

An apparition in a collective dream, a female character (originally played by Mary Hinkson) enters to the song "Dink's Blues":

> I had a gal she was long and tall
> Moved her body like a cannon ball
> Fare thee well oh honey
> Fare thee well
>
> If I had wings like Noah's dove
> I'd fly up the river to the one I love
> Fare thee well oh honey
> Fare thee well[34]

She embodies a feminine ideal with her expansive port de bras, sweeping ronds, furtive posés, and sinuous torso gestures. "She entered as if lifting a slip over her head, dropping it, and stepping into the pleasure of a gentle shower, delighting in the feel of the water running down her body, anointing her limbs with scented lotion, and reveling in her own loveliness" (McKayle 2002, 115).

As Selma Jean Cohen explained in a 1959 review, "They envisioned a woman: one as a lyrical embodiment of soft but sensuous femininity; one as the jazzy girl he would date for a night on the town; one as the woman he loves and from whom he must part. In her three roles, Mary Hinkson gave a stunning performance of remarkably fluid grace and dramatic sensitivity."

Through an economy of longing the female character helps to substantiate the men's heterosexuality, while, at the same time, suggesting that they too are objects of (her) desire. Like the lyrics imply, however, Hinkson's sensual image is tempered by the reality of her inaccessibility: The "having of a gal" is undercut by the conditional impossibility of "having wings like Noah's dove." She may be "had" but she cannot be "got." As if in a separate world, she dances by herself, not acknowledging the men. And the men, in various positions on the floor, look past her too. As McKayle explains, "She was at once free, a flighted bird, and then a rooted reed bending supply in a violent storm; the sensual caresses of intimacy, and then the prison visit window clanging shut; the face in the snapshot that would never been seen again, and then the tiny disappearing figure waving farewell on the train platform" (2002, 115). Eventually, she disappears offstage.

FIG. 6.4 Donald McKayle
and Carmen De Lavallade in
Rainbow 'Round My Shoulder
(1963). Photo by Norman
Maxon. Courtesy of the
Special Collections and
Archives, Langson Library,
University of California,
Irvine.

According to McKayle, this character introduces an element of "cush-
ion" into the narrative of imprisonment; she is a recuperative force, an
embodiment of hope and freedom, even if she seems to exist only in the
men's imagination (Reinhart 1990). Yet it is clear that she is also a sign of
the men's sexual impotency, loneliness, and the futility of their desire.
These are shown in the portrayals of relationships she has with two of the
men. One of these encounters is expressed through sweeping and swinging gestures in which at times a man literally sweeps Hinkson off her feet
or cradles her in his arms. This duet seems both gleeful and sorrowful, as
the lovers, who dance in an urgent unison, seem not to see each other, as
if they exist in separate worlds. Their courtship ends abruptly as the
woman backs offstage. In the background, the ensemble amplifies the
couple's frustration, their muscles flexing as if trying to burst out of their
shackles, accompanied by the title song:

> I got a rainbow, huh
> Tied around my shoulder, huh
> I'm goin' home, huh
> My Lord, I'm goin' home

The ending of the piece reiterates the theme of racism's senseless and common brutality, foreshadowed with the verses:

> Another man done gone
> They killed another man
> He had a long chain on
> Another man done gone

We hear a gunshot, and the two members of the ensemble who had romantic duets with the female character drop to the ground. "One is lifted and carried off stage by his comrades; then the other one enters and falls and dies as the lights fade" (correspondence with the author, April 20, 2007).

Rainbow's ending makes clear McKayle's expressive intention, to portray his male protagonists as objects of social anxiety, their bodies literally chained and even hunted down, their every movement anticipated, regulated, and exploited by the powers that be. As McKayle has put it, "these human beings seem expendable" (Reinhart 1990). Like precedents *Mourner's Bench*, *Games*, and *Southland*, *Rainbow* served as an act of choreographic self-definition that communicated a point of view on its subject matter in its very treatment. As Jay Clayton argues, "the ability to tell a story is as empowering as any image of freedom contained in it" (Clayton 1993, 96–97). *Rainbow* commented on the loss of the black man's potential in a culture that likened his skin color to the commitment of a crime by casting men as laborers for social "progress" (e.g., builders of a train track that signifies the technology of modernity), without even the promise of human rights. Like its precursors, *Rainbow* enacted a critical intervention. While it did not depict subjects who actually attained dignity through self-determination, it countered the systematic social suppression of minority voices by allowing them to "speak out" in choreographed and embodied terms. The dance was "outspoken," supplying insider knowledge typically omitted from dominant discourse. In its depiction of lives lost for the progress of a society that would imprison men on the basis of the color of their skin, its story mounted a social critique just as the civil rights movement was starting to gain national ground.

Yet, even in its stark indictment of the white world, *Rainbow* was multilayered and contradictory. The depiction of the men's strength, for example, valorized their labor and displayed their capacity for action, yet it also questioned their actual productivity. Set against this ambivalent por-

FIG. 6.5 Donald McKayle Dance Company in *Rainbow 'Round My Shoulder* (1967). Photo by Stanley Levy. Courtesy of the Special Collections and Archives, Langson Library, University of California, Irvine.

trayal of outwardly expressed power, moreover, was the intimation of the condition of the men's inner lives, the camaraderie they felt toward one another coupled with the impotent desire they felt toward a female character. Although McKayle intended her character to serve as a recuperative force, an embodiment of hope and freedom even if she does exist only in the men's imagination, she also functioned to reinforce the futility of the men's lives in which their desire for her will be unrequited and unfulfilled. These complexities of the dance's meanings, however, did not undermine its impact. Like dances that had come before, *Rainbow* performed a social protest. Not only did the dance as a whole convey a situation that was morally reprehensible and deserving of condemnation, but its dancers enacted a complex condition of human agency that was at once burdened by racism and possessing of the potential for mobilization.

Reviewers of performances of the piece in 1959 and 1961 seemed strikingly attuned to its aesthetic and its message. Selma Jeanne Cohen, for *Dance Observer*, found that "[b]ecause [McKayle's] movement ideas derive from concepts of characterization, his works have a functional integrity. His new piece, *Rainbow 'Round My Shoulder*, dealt with a chain gang—their interminable labor, their dreams, their sorrows" (1959). And Doris Hering, for *Dance Magazine* observed that the inspiration for *Rainbow* "rose from the well of racial memory. . . . It came, as did Mr. McKayle's well-remembered *Games*, from a sense of injustice, anchored to hope. But like *Games*, it was no social tract. It spoke through the only language absolutely and honestly right for it—the language of dance."

She continued, "It would have been easy to make some sort of melodrama out of *Rainbow 'Round My Shoulder*. It would also have been easy to trail in the wake of the powerful choral music used as accompaniment. Mr. McKayle avoided both pitfalls. He compressed a surge of emotion into a firmly disciplined dance form. *Rainbow* was *Games* grown up" (January 1961a).

Although Cohen's and Hering's reviews still betrayed a bias for narrative-driven yet "firmly disciplined" expressionistic dances, they were a far cry from writing about black modern dance even a decade before. Their praise for McKayle's adaptation of "racial memory" for the dance stage seems not as prescriptive; moreover, both critics acknowledged the composition of the dance, its "functional integrity," on the one hand, and its dance language, on the other. In these ways, they granted him greater artistic license than that which black choreographers of the past had enjoyed.

Conclusion: Civility as a Form of Militancy

In *Blues People* (1963), poet and author Amiri Baraka wrote as follows of jazz musicians on advent of bebop:

> It was the generation of the 1940s which . . . began to consciously analyze and evaluate American society in many of that society's own terms. . . . And even further, this generation also began to understand the *worth* of the country, the society, which it was supposed to call its own. To understand you are black in a society where black is an extreme liability is one thing, but to understand that it is the society that

is lacking and is impossibly deformed because of this lack, *and not yourself,* isolates you even more from that society. Fools or crazy men are easier to walk away from that people who are merely mistaken. (Baraka 1963, 185; emphasis in original)

Baraka's insights about the generation of jazz musicians in the 1940s, specifically their awareness both of the "liability" of being black in America and of the deficit of understanding they faced from the dominant culture, sheds light on choreographic works by Beatty, McKayle, and Dunham of the same general historical period. Likewise illuminating is Baraka's idea that art could at once mark the "isolation" black artists felt from "that society," and serve to counteract that isolation through the "analysis" and "evaluation" of it "on [its] own terms." Finally, Baraka's ideas provide a framework for addressing the questions posed at the outset of this chapter, questions about the contribution of black concert dances to the formation of the postwar black public sphere. During a period of escalated racial conflict, black dance artists and civil rights protesters worked in kind to mobilize the black public.

In her 1959 review of *Rainbow* for *Dance Magazine*, Cohen recognized the potential of the work to signify in these terms, writing that "[t]he dancers were given strong, percussive movement—big, strong, masculine movement. Most often they danced in unison, or two groups mirrored each other. Their uniformity had a persistent forcefulness" (1959, 17). Although not taking the work to the social dimension, Cohen's account suggests her impression that, in this case, the amplification of individual bodies acting as one expressed the commitment of each to the benefit of the whole in ways not unlike an organized protest. Compared with *Games* or *Southland*, which were more like rallies than sit-ins in presenting issues without enacting the changes protesters' sought, *Rainbow* performed a problem and its remedy vested in the performers' capacity for action. While *Rainbow* shared with *Mourner's Bench* the presentation of protagonists who deployed the imagination as a practice of freedom—it was both a haven and a source of strength for stunning feats of physical coordination and virtuosity—*Rainbow* went further in its expression of "subjective speculation," firmly taking on the problem of white-on-black violence and the itinerant prejudice of the justice system. However, unlike the protagonist in *Mourner's Bench*, whose concerns are expressed as being internalized, the men in *Rainbow* seem to be gearing up for a bigger, more sustained, and more orchestrated fight. Ironically, while the protagonists in *Rainbow* are literally in shackles, their very physical and psychological fortitude suggests that the binds of racism will not hold them for much longer—that their "work," expressed as action, will inevitably free them. By contrast, the individuals portrayed in *Mourner's Bench*, *Games*, and *Southland*, who are "free" in this literal sense—in that they are not shackled and chained—seem more tethered to their respective realities, and their movement more contained within its representational parameters.

McKayle himself was aware of the militancy of this work. In his words,

> I am a very militant person. In fact, I was militant before militancy came into fashion . . . I knew Lorraine [Hansberry], and Paul Robeson, who was a great inspiration to us all, and Langston Hughes. And there was Harry Belefonte and Sidney Poitier, and the painter Charles White. We were all together in Harlem, and we all had our dreams of what we could and wanted to do. We also knew that we would have to go out there and create a platform for ourselves. We had to help ourselves. Nobody was going to do it for us. (quoted in Gruen, 1973)

Situated within the milieu of social-minded, activist African-American artists during the postwar period, McKayle's account that making dances was a form of "doing something" for a cause that "nobody else was going to do . . . for us," reiterates the real political significance of his work, a significance overlooked by those scholars who would align it with the more temperate statements of the modern dance establishment.[35]

[7]

THE USES OF ACTION 2

Anna Halprin

Aᴏᴏ race riots in Detroit and Watts, in 1968 choreographer Anna
Halprin[1] began a piece she would later call *Ceremony of Us*. Halprin
had been approached by James Wood, director of the Workshop at the
Studio Watts School for the Arts, who "had recently seen a Dancers'
Workshop[2] performance and felt something of the participation, freedom, and involvement between performers and audience which we create." Wood asked to collaborate with her on a piece that would include
black dancers from the school and white dancers from the San Francisco
area, and would be performed during the Los Angeles Festival of the Performing Arts. As Halprin recalled, "It was part of [Wood's] plan that
people from the Watts community would come to the Mark Taper Forum,
most of them for the first time, and mingle with the affluent whites who
attended the Mark Taper regularly. That theater, a status symbol of 'let
me in,' was to be, as Wood said, 'a tool for social change'" (1995, 152).
Although Halprin had never before worked with explicitly racial themes,
in many ways *Ceremony of Us* brought to fruition her early experiments
investigating the inherent efficacy of any body and her personal commitment to civil rights.[3] Shuttling back and forth between her company in
San Francisco and the group of dancers she assembled from the Studio
Watts School, Halprin applied techniques from gestalt therapy to facilitate
artistic and social experiments in rehearsal (J. Ross 2006, 267). Eventually
Halprin brought the groups together for ten days in early 1969, to rehearse
prior to performing in Los Angeles. As Janice Ross has argued, "As much
an opportunity for redefinition as healing, the rehearsals offered all participants the chance to examine and possibly begin to re-create not just
themselves but the racial attitudes of society." However, as effective as the
work was in bringing the disparate groups together, its ultimate result was
inconclusive. As Ross contends, "No so much a dance as a lived experiment
in attempting to erase boundaries, prohibitions, and taboos, *Ceremony of Us*

would turn out to be in equal measure both daring and timid, both a challenge to the status quo of racial stereotypes and an unwitting reinforcement of the sexual and class myths embedded in them" (2006, 271).

Merging the symbolic and the actual in the process of making and performing a dance, *Ceremony of Us* carried out the cultural work of making artistic, social, and political objectives coincide and of attempting to make them coexist. In Halprin's words, "You can separate your life from your art, but it is so exciting and full of creative possibilities if you don't" (Halprin quoted in Ross 2006, 275). The work clearly owed, in its concept and result, to precursors in universalist modern dance, the postwar civil rights movement, and the artistic experiments of the milieu in and around the Judson Dance Theater. My intention here is not to rehearse the significance of the history of the Judson Dance Theater, as others have done so eloquently and so well.[4] Instead, I wish to cast backward to the late 1950s and early 1960s and Halprin's early development as a choreographer predating Judson's most "prolific" year, 1963 (quoting Banes, 1993, 5–6). My goals are twofold: to probe the dimensions of her work that might have lent themselves to the ends realized in *Ceremony of Us* and to examine the operational basis of Halprin's early work refracted through the lens of direct action protest.

Since the late 1950s, Halprin had been exploring ways of upsetting the balance of power both within traditional theatrical settings and outside them, breaking expressive conventions and blurring lines between performers and audiences. Her pieces cultivated a sense of unpredictability that made it difficult for doers and viewers to fall into stereotypical patterns of behavior and thinking. Like Cunningham[5] and Taylor, she sought to underline the position of dancer as author through an exploration of the quotidian. Halprin, however, departed from them in her use of improvisatory methods to generate performance scores. In this, Halprin stressed the constitutive process involved in the act of moving—what she called "the unfolding" (Halprin quoted in Renouf 1963, 345). While Halprin's postwar work generated from a different root, her end results shared important characteristics of those of her white colleagues: they were nonlinear and nonnarrative, and therefore resisted viewing practices based on interpretation. Moreover, they upheld white privilege in their deployment of tactics of elision, namely by purveying what Susan Foster has called the myth of the "natural body." Like Cunningham, who incor-

FIG. 7.1 "Silhouettes on the Wall," from Anna Halprin's *Ceremony of Us* (1969). Photo by Tylon Barea. Courtesy of the Office of Anna Halprin.

porated elements of Asian cultural practices in order to "universalize physicality," Halprin plumbed the potential of the science of kinesiology to make manifest in dance terms the Sanskrit saying "see an ordinary object for the first time" (Renouf 1963, 347).[6] Commenting on the work of the generation of artists after Cunningham and Halprin, Foster's point about the racial implications of such work still stands: "the cultural distinctiveness of the exercises mattered less than the opportunity they afforded to excavate beneath normalizing habits in search of a raw and unbiased responsiveness" (2003, 58). Yet there were important cultural implications of such a position in the late 1950s and early 1960s. This chapter examines the social and political dimensions of Halprin's early work as they coincided both with the trend among dancers to assert the efficacy of ordinary movement and the growing sense among Americans of the power of movement to conduct progressive social change.

In research on the history of direct action protest, Barbara Epstein distinguishes 1960s political consciousness from that of the 1930s. "Unlike the activists of the thirties," she argues, "who gravitated to the issues of political and economic power, the activists of the sixties tended to gravitate to what seemed more fundamental issues of how social life as a whole should be organized, what ideas it should be ruled by" (1991, 38). Whereas Halprin's early work might have been premised on ideas about the body's symbiosis with nature, this did not stop her from turning the tables so as to question what was "ordinary" or "natural" in the first place. Over the course of her early career, Halprin increasingly provoked performers and spectators to examine their assumptions about art, and, by extension, the world, in a drive to transform physical and mental habits of consciousness through artistic action. In these lights, Halprin's work is not simply seen as an example of universalist appropriation in modern dance, but as having developed in correlation with an emerging cultural ethos, as idealistic and imperfect as it was, that sought to dismantle some of universalism's core applications in normativity.

This work also found expression in the cultural work of African-American artists and activists in the postwar years. In the last chapter, I related the work of Talley Beatty, Katherine Dunham, and Donald McKayle to that of the sit-in protests through their common genealogy in the blues aesthetic. In these cases, choreographed movement gave voice to experiences of racial marginalization by interrogating the similarities and differences between the real and the imagined. Pioneering a radicalized public sphere, televised broadcasts of McKayle's *Rainbow 'Round My Shoulder* and *Her Name Was Harriet*, in 1959 and 1960, respectively, and the sit-ins in 1960, made such images ubiquitous. Transposed from the local to the national stage, they were available to anyone who happened to be tuning in. Significantly, however, unlike the sit-ins, which stressed a one-to-one correspondence between the "stage" and the street (choreography *was* life), McKayle's work relied upon metaphor for its real meanings (choreography was *like* life).

This operational contrast brings out the significance of Halprin's approach, which sought more than any of the other practices examined thus far, to plumb the body's intrinsic potential for political efficacy at the same time as it used choreography to occupy and agitate. To highlight this point, this chapter looks at Halprin's early work, including *Five-Legged Stool* (1962), alongside protest tactics in the early civil rights movement, particularly in sit-ins. In Brecht's epic theater, estrangement meant distancing the viewer from the action on stage in order to provoke a critical reaction.[7] Likewise, both Halprin's work and the sit-ins deployed defamiliarization to spark action. Highlighting compromising ideological and social structures, they revealed to onlookers their complicity in maintaining them, then enlisted viewers in processes of re-patterning to transform subjugating habits of mind and behavior. Explicitly challenging assumptions that underwrote normative social relations and ideologies, both performances aimed to reform society individual by individual, one action at a time. Moreover, both contributed to the radicalizing body politic circa 1960 in events that eventually spilled onto the streets.

"Simply Doing": Ann Halprin's Choreographic Methodology, 1955–1962

I think of the late 1950s and up to the mid-1960s as being a very crucial time in the arts for dealing with one of the most prevalent issues of the time which was antiestablishment, and which led to the hippie movement. During that period we were often referred to as avant-garde. Though we were doing things that were new or against the common values, we were really attempting to search out what was authentic, what was real, as opposed to accepting what was the conformity of the time.

(Halprin 1995, 5)

In 1955, Halprin traveled to New York City from her home in San Francisco to perform in an American National Theater Academy (ANTA)—sponsored dance festival performance. As I discussed in chapter 1, ANTA was the governing body of the Dance Panel, the committee formed of members of the modern dance establishment responsible for making recommendations for government sponsorship of international tours. At the festival, Halprin performed her work *The Prophetess*, a character-centered piece depicting Diana, a prophetess, as she led her people into battle. Halprin was well received on all counts by the modern dance establishment. *New York Times* critic John Martin's comment is an example, "[The solo] showed [Halprin] to be a dancer of genuine authority who knows how to make a dance as well as how to dance it. We shall be seeing more of her" (May 9, 1955, 26).

Whereas Martin and other critics' commendations might have clinched her entrée into the establishment circle, to Halprin the weeks she spent at the dance festival meant something else entirely: "For two weeks I watched modern dancers performing. Something inside me started going dead. Something disturbed me. I noticed that everybody in Martha Graham's company all looked like imitations of Martha Graham, everybody in Doris Humphrey's company all looked like imitations of Doris Humphrey, all the dancers looked like imitations of the leading choreographer. I wasn't able to connect. I felt depressed, discouraged, distrustful, and I knew that my career as a modern dancer had just died" (1981).

Halprin's statement speaks to the degree to which, by 1955, normativity had been inscribed upon modern dancing bodies through particular methods of training and the exertion of world views. What others had accomplished through radical aesthetic departures, Halprin accomplished through physical departure, leaving New York City and returning to California where she had lived since 1945 with her husband, landscape architect Lawrence Halprin. Shortly after, she asserted her newfound commitment to developing her own work and working methods by resigning from her position at the Halprin-Lathrop school for modern dance in San Francisco, an institution she had cofounded in 1946 with Welland Lathrop, a Bay Area dancer and choreographer. At its founding, the school, which housed both a studio for classes and a performing company, had served as the only western outpost for the New York modern dance establishment (Highwater 1978, 201). In breaking ranks with Lathrop, therefore, Halprin distanced herself further from the modern dance establishment.

At first, Halprin worked in virtual seclusion at her home in Kentfield, where her husband, along with architect Arch Lauterer, designed and built her an outdoor dance "deck."[8] There, surrounded by the natural beauty of the seaside woodlands, she became conscious of her priorities as a choreographer. She shed the expectation that her dance should *interpret* the meaning of human experience writ large and instead concentrated on making dances based on ordinary occurrences.

One day that she spent outdoors proved particularly illuminating in this respect. As she remembered in an interview,

It happened that I was looking at the sunlight on a tree. For no reason at all and with no apparent preparation I became intensely aware of a foghorn in the bay, a red berry at my side and passing birds overhead. I saw each thing first as a separate element and then as independent elements related in unpredictable ways. The multiplicity of implications stimulated exciting dimensions of a new kind of meaningfulness— certainly not in any literal sense, but implications arising from my own humanness in response to the object, the sound, the light, the space, the time. (quoted in Palludan, n.d.)

What Halprin found "meaningful" about this experience was not that it symbolized anything in particular, but that it made her mindful of how it felt to be alive. She became aware of her "humanness" both in relation to the stimuli outside her body which triggered her senses (like the sound of the foghorn, the sights of the sunlight and a berry, and the sense of the birds moving) and in terms of her subjective personal response to these stimuli, registered in emotions, physical sensations, and ideas. In one sense, Halprin's response invokes the universalism of the postwar modern dance establishment both in its earnest attempt to identify the fundamental elements of the human experience and in its determined elision of human difference. In another, however, Halprin's observations led to another place altogether, identifying a condition of existence—that of individual perception, self, and surrounding world—that could convey universality in terms of action.

Turning to two of her earliest influences, children and the human body, she advanced this notion of action springing from the ordinary experience of being in the world. Looking to children to recapture a more intuitive approach to movement, she involved herself with the Marin County Dance Co-operatives, an organization she founded in 1947, dedicated to "giving Bay Area children and adults an experience in creative dance and an awareness of the potential of rhythm and movement as they manifest in daily life."[9] She wanted to "see how their bodies moved" and to get a sense of "what they danced about," so that she could understand "how their feelings connected to their movements." These observations led her to conclude that "their movement was natural and they danced about real things in their lives" (Halprin 1981, 15).

For information about the body/mind connection, she looked to the work of Margaret H'Doubler, with whom she had studied as an undergraduate at the University of Wisconsin-Madison, and Mabel Elsworth

Todd, a professor at Columbia University's Teacher's College, two academic kinesiologists who studied the intrinsic expressivity of the human body. Both were more fascinated by the reciprocal and dynamic relationship between the body and mind than they were with traditionalist concerns such as form and codified dance technique (Banes 1995, 3).[10]

Todd's *The Thinking Body* (1937), one of the seminal early twentieth-century texts for the academic study of dance, illustrates this approach to movement studies. Here, pictures of idealized dancers were nowhere to be found. Instead, detailed drawings of the body's anatomical structures, similar to those one might find in a medical textbook, assisted Todd in her thorough discussion of the body's function. She considered such topics as the muscular action involved in standing, or the responsibilities of the "thigh-joints . . . which are 'the hub of the universe' for our personal world. They must have every muscle fiber of their arcs free to respond to the multiple responsibilities thrown upon them from all directions as lines of force converge toward the hub from the many possible angles of impact" (M. Todd 1937, 207). Todd's analyses of the function of and interrelationships among anatomical structures backed up her idea that "living, the whole body carries its meaning, and tells its own story" (295). This thesis relied upon three assumptions: (1) "the individual is a totality and cannot be segregated as to intellect, motor and social factors"; (2) the body registers the individual's thoughts and emotions, or in other words, "for every thought supported by feeling, there is a muscle change"; (3) and there is a reciprocal relationship between an individual's state of physical well-being and balance and his or her state of mental health.

Drawing on Todd's research, as well as on her experience studying with H'Doubler, Halprin arrived at her version of the "natural body." This constituted the action of simply being, which involved movement even if only at the level of breathing. This discovery led to a philosophy of dance based on the following principles: (1) Not the imparting of a codified technique, teaching people to dance is a matter of helping them become aware of what they already possess as physical beings; (2) the choreographer should act as "a guide who works to evoke the art within us all" (Halprin 1968, 164), not the evolutionary source or subject of the work created; and (3) the significance of choreography is vested in its ability to render meaning intrinsic to common experience, not simply if it met externally imposed formal or stylistic requirements.

While blinded to what human difference might bring to bear on these principles, Halprin's core beliefs had relevant social implications. For instance, the potency of a person was something she or he already possessed, in the movement of being alive, and this potency, when discovered and cultivated, could instigate individual and collective agency through the work of upsetting normative ideological and behavioral hierarchies.

Repudiating Habit, Part II

In workshops she held on her dance deck in Kentfield throughout the late 1950s, Halprin began to translate her aesthetic philosophy into her work with a loosely formed company of dancers, some of whom had studied with her at the Halprin-Lathrop school. As she recalled, "They simply wanted to have the opportunity to stay in contact with the activities I was interested in. They also wanted to explore and work together. I wanted to explore in a particular way, breaking down any preconceived notions I had about what dance, or movement, or composition was" (Halprin 1995, 77).[11] She chose improvisation as a grounding for these experiments. Yet the dancers' self-expression was not her goal. Rather, she used improvisation as Cunningham had used chance operations, to generate the unexpected. In her words, "I was trying to get at subconscious areas, so things would happen in an unpredictable way. *I was trying to eliminate stereotyped ways of reacting*" (Halprin 1995, 77; emphasis mine).

Based on her knowledge of anatomy and kinesiology, improvisational structures led dancers to perform simple physical tasks, such as rotating or flexing particular body parts. There was always the possibility that moving in a certain way would provoke an emotional response for a dancer. Yet the tasks themselves were devoid of any intrinsic emotional content. Rather than contemplate the greater significance of what they were doing, Halprin and the dancers asked themselves scientifically minded questions: Is it possible to "articulate this part of the body, and isolate it from another part of the body. What is the efficient way to do that movement? Do we really need this or is it just habit?" (1995, 77). Occasionally, when the dancers were improvising, "breathing became sound, or some heightened feeling stimulated certain associative responses . . . a word came, or a sound, or a shout" (79). Eventually, Halprin built in structures that prompted verbal free association so that the dancers could talk as they were performing tasks. In this, Halprin sought to help her students discover a responsive place from which to move. Task-oriented improvisatory structures aimed to rid dancers of their tendencies to imitate (an ingrained habit formed over years of studying conventional modern dance), while also prompting them to explore their bodies as forms of mobilization. As she put it, "Doing a task created an attitude that would bring the movement quality into another kind of reality. It was devoid of a certain kind of introspection *In doing these tasks we were not playing roles or creating moods, we simply did something*" (D. Turner 1989, 103; emphasis mine). Efficacy occurred in fulfillment of simple tasks, which in their doing could provoke transitions from one state of mind to another.

After four years of holding relatively informal workshops, in 1959 Halprin assembled a core group of performers with whom to work, including artists schooled in media other than dance such as theater, visual art, music, architecture, and poetry. With this interdisciplinary group she called the San Francisco Dancers' Workshop (SFDW), Halprin solidified her sense of "total theater," performance that combined elements of music, sound, lights, vocalizations, and architectural elements. A "theater where everything was experienced for the first time," total theater further broke down the boundaries between life and art, thus revealing the symbiosis between them (Halprin 1968, 164).[12]

Defamiliarization characterized her approach to the instruction of company members, thus turning on its head her earlier notion of the "natural" body. Introducing the performers to the anatomical complexity of their bodies, so that they would not take them or their movement for granted, she asked them to see movement not as "natural" but as the result of complex physiochemical mechanics. Structuring the group's improvisations around tasklike behavior, and incorporating this material into her pieces, she pushed the performers to consider how any movement, whether considered "dance" or not, was a form of dancing. Directing performers to respond spontaneously to circumstances that arose in their improvisations or in performance, she asked them to imagine ways that their identities in life merged with those performed on stage (Maletic 1967, 13). Defamiliarization, applied in these ways, drove her creative process over the next four years in works that increasingly cultivated the condition of unpredictability. This resulted in *Trunk Dance* (1959), *Four Square* (1959), *The Flowerburger* (1959), *Rites of Women* (1959), *Birds of*

FIG. 7.2 Anna Halprin's *Trunk Dance* (1957). Photo by Chester Kessler. Courtesy of the Office of Anna Halprin.

America or Gardens Without Walls (1960), *Automobile Event* (1962), *Four-Legged Stool* (1962), and *Five-Legged Stool* (1962).

In an interview, Halprin addressed what she saw as the problem of predictability. Over the course of time she had been holding her workshops, she realized that the group's improvisations had become overly complicated and strangely reliable. The performers had become so accustomed to the music the musicians played, and the musicians so familiar with the movement tendencies of the dancers, that each group knew how to prompt the other to invoke a particular response. What was more, the company used "objects, props, and space in a deterministic way" (Halprin 1995, 79). Halprin became concerned that the group's improvisatory work, meant to be investigative, had become too anchored in cause and effect.

As an antidote, she modified how the company was working by "isolating" compositional materials, hoping, thereby, to eliminate any possibility that causality would creep into the creative process. She took the musicians out of the compositional equation until the score had been set.

Then she designed an elaborate charting system on which to record options for movement. The charting system led to movement experimentation as follows:

> I took every possible anatomical combination of movements, put them all on sheets of paper and gave them numbers. One sheet had to do with flexion and different joints; another sheet had to do with extension. I would pick some elements and make a pattern. I tried to do them and I got into the wildest combinations of movements, things I never could have conceived myself. All of the sudden, my body began to experience new ways of moving. We applied this in bigger compositional ways. We would experiment with all the elements we worked with, even combinations of people. (Halprin 1995, 81)

She enhanced this method through the use of scores, which supplied externally determined guidelines for any given piece. "A very rigid structure," the score "[was] carefully predetermined and schedules both the sequence of events and the stage materials with which these are involved" (Halprin quoted in Kostelanetz 1970b, 13). Like the charting system, scores regularized the act of performing, while at the same time allowing for spontaneous problem solving and decision making.

With the purpose of *repudiating habit*, a goal not unlike those of Cunningham and Taylor, Halprin explored how she could use imposed structures to promote freedom. Structural devices that offered opportunities for choice, Halprin's charts and scores were similar to Cunningham's rules governing the use of chance operations for any given work, or Taylor's postural vocabulary. Each functioned to establish guidelines for expressions of creative autonomy in which performers could think and act on the spot. In Halprin's case, structures distanced the dancers from their working process, objectifying the work of combining movement elements into longer phrases, and thus disrupting their unstudied impulses with imposed tasks. While they disoriented the dancers, they also released them from their own preferences and habits. Disrupting the process of impetus and response in the physical chain, Halprin instead underlined the contingencies involved in mobilization.

Halprin's efforts to defamilarize the ordinary coincided with other artists in Cunningham's and Taylor's artistic milieu, who emulated Marcel Duchamp's undertaking of making art out of quotidian materials. As I have discussed in chapter 5, alongside artistic compatriots such as John Cage, Robert Rauschenberg, and Jasper Johns, Cunningham and Taylor experimented with the ways in which they could translate Duchamp's "ready-made" into choreographic terms. They saw an application of Duchamp's vision in the creation of dances that incorporated movement common in daily life. Accordingly, they composed works that took "found" movement, such as gestures, postures, and actions like walking, running, jumping, sitting, and standing, out of their mundane contexts and put them into the context of choreography. They found freedom in taking ordinary things (including movements) out of context.

Nevertheless, in these cases, it took significant effort to ensure that "ready-made" material would retain its "naturalness," especially given Cunningham's and Taylor's aesthetic priorities—to make visually challenging work that also obscured the very fact of their queer male bodies in action. Accomplishing these goals required compositional techniques proper to dance choreography—like synchronization, stylization, setting to counts—in general, modifying "non-dance" material so that it would both unstudied and artful. As Taylor related in his discussion of the process leading up to *Epic*, the dancers labored for hours during rehearsal to master a "neutral" countenance and spontaneous physical quality so as to look unaffected in performance.

Halprin was far less enamored with the prospects of the "ready-made" for movement innovation. In fact, in a 1963 interview she stated, "The ready-made holds no interest for me. It's the *unfolding* which involves me" (Renouf 1963, 345, emphasis in original). Like her contemporaries, Halprin exploited the quotidian for choreography; yet she mined it more for its potential for spontaneity and ongoingness and less for "objects" or staged effects. Where the others maintained elements of stylization that demanded technical dance training, Halprin steered away from training methods that she believed got in the way of a performer's kinesthetic intuition. Where the others choreographed movement to "counts" or rhythmic phrases, Halprin asked performers to execute tasklike movement as it would occur in the speed of real time. Where the others used improvisation only rarely during the creative process, Halprin used this technique exclusively prior to setting a performance score. Where the others coached dancers on the maintenance of an unaffected performance presence, she directed performers to express themselves in a manner demanded by the moment. She utilized methods of free-association to encourage the performers to respond intuitively to any rehearsal or performance situation.

In all of these ways, Halprin's work was more unsettlingly ordinary than that of the others. Although both Cunningham and Taylor labored to create the quality of the everyday in their work, in no way did their dances look or evoke the feeling of the mundane. To the contrary, their use of compositional techniques and structures, which modified both movement material and its performance by performers, served to maintain a distance between art and life in its very conservation of their differences. If her contemporaries' utilization of the tools of choreographic artifice, therefore, kept up the imaginary fourth wall separating the performance from the spectators, Halprin's techniques were meant to demolish this wall, further blurring distinctions between art and life, and cultivating the permeability necessary to allow a flow from one realm to another.

The Politics of "Seeing the Ordinary Anew": *Five-Legged Stool* (1962)

Halprin sought to enlarge her and her dancers' possibilities for action in the world in *Five-Legged Stool*, which premiered in 1962 and effectively culminated her experimentation to that end to date. Here, Halprin deployed similar techniques of defamiliarization to challenge conventional notions about what was and what should be. Exemplifying a new phase in Halprin's artistic development, the work functioned as a kind of "total theater," in which performers and viewers became commonly implicated and, therefore, involved in the creation of reality. Deliberately not catering to audience members' expectations, Halprin instead forced viewers to question their assumptions about what was "ordinary" or "natural" in the first place. In these ways, Halprin's dance cultivated viewers' critical judgment and interpretive faculties, positioning them as equal (albeit unwitting) partners in the work of meaning making.

Five-Legged Stool marked the renewal of Halprin's interest in the cross-fertilization of the arts. Compared with *Trunk Dance, Four Square, The Flowerburger*, and *Rites of Women* (all choreographed in 1959) for which Halprin had maintained a separation between the artists in collaboration, the concept behind *Five-Legged Stool* encouraged an interplay among the various artists with whom she was working. The piece combined movement, sound, objects, the spoken word, and visual design.[13] According to

FIG. 7.3 Anna Halprin's *Four Legged Stool* (1962). Photo © Warner Jepson. Courtesy of the Office of Anna Halprin.

critic Robert J. Pierce's 1975 account of a performance,[14] "It was designed as a sensory experience without continuity or meaning—what the audience saw was what that dance was about. The performers used the stage, the aisles, the basement, the ceiling, and even the sidewalk outside to perform on. They poured water, changed clothes, threw colorful objects up in the air, fell down, handed empty wine bottles up to a disembodied hand dangling from the ceiling. At the end, feathers wafted down onto an empty stage for a full five minutes."

In a typical theater setting, the viewer, who has ostensibly paid money to see a show, assumes the role of consumer, and the performer, who will ostensibly be paid for his or her performance, assumes the role of spectacle or entertainment. In this relationship, the spectator possesses the privilege of the gaze, while the performer is the object of this gaze, his or her body intended for the viewer's delectation and pleasure. *Five-Legged Stool*, however, made little distinction between these roles. As Halprin explained, "Up until then, we had been content with using the space we had (a traditional proscenium theater). But I got discouraged with having to be up there in that relationship to an audience. I began to look at the lobby, the aisles, the ceilings, the floor. Suddenly I thought, 'Who says we have to stay on that stage? This is a whole building'" (1995, 85).

As a solution, Halprin situated the audience at the center of the theater, and staged the performance "all around them, above them and below them and in front of them, and outside, sometimes they would hear things from the street" (Halprin 1995, 85).

The performers' feeling, that they were entitled to use the entire space of the theater, clashed with the audiences' expectation that they were entitled to inhabit this space unmolested by the performers. Performers' behavior during the performance further communicated their lack of concern for the spectators' entertainment. Dancers performed tasks in real time and with task-appropriate exertion. One of Halprin's tasks, for example, involved bringing forty wine bottles onto the stage and placing them near a stool. The object was to hand each bottle to a dancer positioned near a trapdoor in the ceiling. Every time she handed a bottle to this dancer, she had to pick it up, balance on the stool, and reach over her head. "Sufficiently compelling in itself," the task demanded her "full attention. It took [her] forty minutes." Meanwhile, performer John Graham executed this task: "[He] had a plank that was on a diagonal resting on a ceiling beam and the floor. He crawled up to the ceiling and his task was to slide down that beam head first" (Halprin 1995, 84). According to Halprin,

> We were doing things that were very unexpected. Breaking rules without letting them in on it. Going into their territory. I mean I buy a ticket and I sit in my seat, somehow or other I'm buying my space. And what are you doing in my space? What are the boundaries now? You're getting me all stirred up; does this give me permission to react any way I want? So I began to realize that we were breaking tradition, that we were involving other people who weren't in on the process. (1995, 8)

Halprin's comments touch on the significance of performers' occupation of their designated performance space *as if* it needed to be taken over.

Other strategies to destabilize viewer expectation involved juxtaposition. The score for *Five-Legged Stool*, for example, specified that performers vary the order of their execution of tasks from one performance to another. This meant that each time the piece was performed, the progression of events would be different and thus in an unpredictable order. The arbitrary mixture of task-oriented scenarios broke up any narrative through-line, thus making her work both incongruous and inscrutable. In her words, "There was an attempt to really break down cause and effect. I wanted everything to have such a sensory impact that an audience would not question why. I didn't want anything to look like it had meaning or continuity" (Halprin 1995, 84–85). Halprin's costuming decision, to exchange leotards and tights for secondhand street clothes (including shoes), revealed a similar intention not to cater to viewers. Dressed in ordinary clothes, not "costumes," performers were conceivably indistinguishable from spectators. Whereas in traditional modern dance their costumes would have functioned as a marker of their status as objects of spectacle, in this case their clothing served to camouflage their status and function as "performers." Wearing street clothes as costumes had a significant impact on the way performers saw themselves as well. According to Halprin, "We danced with shoes on. I felt like a naughty little girl that first day, because a modern dancer used bare feet, and I was wearing high-heels. A. A. Leath was wearing tennis shoes. This was a really important breakthrough for us. . . . It was the last time we ever really thought of ourselves as dancers" (Halprin 1995, 85).

Defamiliarization of the conventional rules of engagement in the theater promoted conditions of instability that gave dancers an advantage over disoriented audience members. Unlike in a typical theatrical situation, when an audience is asked to "willfully suspend their disbelief," Halprin's theater functioned as an extension of daily life. Its events occurred in real time in a setting that had been transformed from a theater to a protest site. Audience reaction confirms this reading. Rather than sit quietly and politely, audiences "talked noisily, walked out, or threw things at the stage." According to Halprin, "Five Legged Stool was given 16 performances, and each time the reaction was violent" (Pierce 1975, 93). Halprin interpreted the meaning of the audience response to the premier of *Five-Legged Stool* in these terms:

> *Something happened in that performance that we never experienced before, and which began to establish a next step.* We got a violent audience reaction. That's when people started throwing things at us. People would whisper to each other, they would talk so that everyone could hear. . . . They talked during the performance; they talked to the person next to them as if that person were ten miles away, as if everything they said to each other was a public announcement. *There was a definite kind of involvement we had never experienced before, nor did we know what to do with it, or why it was there.* (Halprin 1995, 85; emphasis mine)

As she recalled, the experiences of performing *Five-Legged Stool* in California in 1962, and around Europe in 1963, made her aware that she had the "kind of power to stir people up" (Halprin 1995, 93). "For the first time," she reflected, "I realized there was a real *encounter* going on between audience and performers. . . . *We learned . . . that we and the audience had power*" (1995, 93, 95; emphasis mine).

Newly recognizing her work as an "encounter" between dancers and audience members that ultimately incited both groups to do something, Halprin's "next step" was to find other ways of redesignating roles for performers and viewers so as to prompt both groups constantly to renegotiate the terms of their engagement. To the performers, for example, she begged questions such as "Why did we have to be in a proscenium arch?" and "Who said we couldn't speak, sing, build environments?" (Halprin 1995, 6). In their probing performers recognized that, in their involuntary efforts to bow to convention, they had been complicit in maintaining restrictions they had come to see as limiting.

Assuming a similar mode of critical thinking, viewers also became active members of Halprin's total theater asking questions such as "What does it mean to be a viewer?" "Why are we are supposed to sit in these seats and be quiet while the performance is going on?" and "Who said we can't speak, or throw things at the performers?"[15] While some viewers obviously felt threatened by Halprin's vision—why else would they have thrown shoes at or talked back to the performers?—others must have seen an opportunity in it. As dancer and choreographer Nancy Stark Smith observed in a published conversation with Halprin, "It sounds like you started out with the kind of mood of the times, of challenging the assumptions that were in your field, and in the process you realized that you were cutting across more than artistic boundaries but also social taboos" (Stark Smith quoted in Halprin 1995, 8).

The Mobilization of Social Action

Sit-ins at Woolworth's staged similar kinds of encounters, this time with the goal of challenging the rules of social engagement dictated by Jim Crow laws. Whereas Halprin's dances took on the power relations inherent in the proscenium theater, direct action protests attacked the ones that had been institutionalized in segregated public spaces such as lunch counters, buses, swimming pools, public libraries, churches, art galleries, beaches, and drinking fountains. Clearly, the stakes as well as their risks differed significantly for each group. While Halprin and her dancers sought to expand the range of their personal artistic expression, the sit-in protesters sought to claim the status of full citizenship for themselves. While artists deployed defamiliarization to free themselves from the conventions of modern dance and the theater (extensions of normative social life), protesters used it to combat segregation and demand the same treatment given to whites.

In spite of these important differences, the sit-ins were analogous to Halprin's artistic practices in two crucial respects: their mode of operation (to occupy and agitate) and their provocation of viewers to respond. Deploying comparable tactics of defamiliarization to foster the unexpected, both groups aimed to destabilize power relations by making it difficult for participants (doers and viewers) to resort to ingrained patterns of thinking and behavior. Focusing on three phases of the sit-ins, including the mobilization of participants, the development of a protest technique, and the protest event itself, this section concentrates on how protesters used theatrical strategies to make the ordinary strange. In the larger scheme of this book, this is to show how tactics of action that were being cultivated in the field of modern dance were similarly operative in other social and political arenas. In this light, Halprin's choreographic practices offer an illuminating counterpoint that both casts the protesters' tactics as those of occupation and agitation and helps to highlight the drama and impact of the protest events themselves.

The first phase of a protest occurred much before the actual event, during a process of mobilization in which "ordinary people" were transformed into protesters. In the context of the American civil rights movement, this process involved getting African Americans, particularly those living in the South under Jim Crow, to think beyond the ideology that contained them. There were many roadblocks in the way of black agency. In *Stride Toward Freedom*, King enumerated some of them:

> Some of the passivity of the uneducated could, like that of the educated, be attributed to the fear of economic reprisals. Dependent on the white community, they dared not protest against unjust racial conditions for fear of losing their jobs. But perhaps an even more basic force at work was their corroding sense of inferiority, which often expressed itself in a lack of self-respect. Many unconsciously wondered whether they actually deserved any better conditions. *Their minds and souls were so conditioned to the system of segregation that they submissively adjusted themselves to things as they were.* (King 1958, 37; emphasis mine)

If African Americans had been socially "conditioned" both to accept their unequal status and to adjust to the cultural system that perpetuated it, then, in preparation for protest, they needed to cultivate what Jane Mansbridge has called an "oppositional consciousness," "an empowering mental state that prepares members of an oppressed group to act to undermine, reform, or overthrow a system of human domination" (2001, 5). Thus, protesters had to learn not only to question the system of racial segregation under Jim Crow, but also to re-imagine themselves as having equal status to whites.

One of the most difficult tasks of political mobilization was getting individuals to break the mental and physical habits that reinforced their feelings of inferiority and passivity. This challenge was not unlike the ones Halprin faced when she began holding her dance workshops in the late 1950s, when she assembled a group of dancers who shared a common interest in "breaking down preconceived notions" about dancing. Before her dancers could move with agency, or what she called "authenticity," they needed to unlearn many of the habits they had picked up over years of studying conventional modern dance technique. By heightening dancers' experiences of their bodies through improvisatory exercises meant to objectify their experience of moving, Halprin prodded them to question experiences of corporeality that they had previously taken for granted. As the dancers became more aware of the forces that exerted influence on them as they moved, they also become conscious of the choices that they could make either to regard or to disregard these forces. In this way, performers learned to see themselves as the "authors" of their own actions.

Similarly, the leaders of the civil rights movement developed strategies to encourage people to interrogate what they had come to accept as "normal" or "ordinary." The point was to help people learn to disregard thoughts and cultural evidence that reinforced their feelings of inferiority and passivity, and instead to begin thinking of themselves as agents of their own lives. King, for example, asked people to focus on what he called "agape," which in Greek meant "love in action," "a willingness to sacrifice in the interest of mutuality," and "a willingness to go to any length to restore community" (King 1958, 105). Similarly, Gregg urged protesters to direct their action toward the pursuit of "human unity," which he defined as "a power that can overcome all differences of race, nationality, ideology or culture" (Gregg 1959, 10). According to Braden, many have misinterpreted these directives due to their Christian connotations, taking them as endorsements to "love thy enemy." But she explained, "[Love] is not, affection for the individual one is fighting. Rather, it is an attempt to understand his corruption and the source of it and to see the evil as something that has made him a victim too. Even more basically, it was a way of looking at one's opponent which holds out the possibility of ultimate reconciliation—not, it should be emphasized, through compromise but through transformation" (Braden 1989, 135).

The focus on love transformed people in two ways: it underlined their status as vital and equal members of a community, and it clarified their perception of their antagonists, viewing them not as enemies but as equal victims of an oppressive social system.

Like the first phase of the protests, the second one took place prior to the actual event. Here techniques of transforming thought through focus on love were converted into directives for action. In developing their methods, leaders of the movement drew on precedents of nonviolent direct action, as portrayed in instructive texts and as previously enacted. They sought to mobilize participants in order to foster their sense of agency. Yet they also saw the need to contain participants' potentially explosive energy so as to sufficiently compel and win the sympathy of witnesses while simultaneously disarming adversaries. Seeking methods that could achieve these diverse ends, organizers labored to construct social situations whose unpredictability favored the protesters. Halprin's movement practices aimed too at just this sort of unpredictability. In particular, Halprin organized improvisations around tasks that directed the dancers' intention and movement while providing opportunities for spontaneous deviation as any situation unfolded. The tasks provided structures while also allowing for individual problem solving and decision making. They could be arranged freely, and could theoretically yield a different outcome every time. And they permitted dancers to "simply do something;" mundane actions with, therefore, no intrinsic emotional or symbolic significance—movement provided performers with an honest way of remaining neutral while performing.

To "compose" the elements of direct action protest, organizers drew on the precedents of King and Gregg, both of whom had adapted Mohandas Gandhi's method of "passive resistance" to the cause of black civil rights in the United States. Recognizing the possibility that Gandhi's approach would be misinterpreted by activists on the ground as more of the same in its passivity, King repackaged it thus:

> The phrase "passive resistance" often gives the false impression that this is a sort of a "do-nothing method" in which the resister quietly and passively accepts evil. But nothing is further from the truth. *For while the nonviolent resister is passive in the sense that he is not physically aggressive toward his opponent, his mind and emotions are always active, constantly seeking to persuade his opponent that he is wrong. The method is passive physically, but strongly active spiritually. It is not passive non-resistance to evil, it is active nonviolent resistance to evil.* (1958, 102; emphasis mine)

Not a "do-nothing method," passive resistance was the opposite, an "active" means of "persuasion" through the activity of maintaining one's physical and emotional control. Thus, passive resistance cultivated a state of oppositional consciousness, enlisting the will and heart of the protester both to endure violence and to believe so strongly in a cause as to resist the impulse to fight back. In this way, protesters sought to override their instinctive movement responses to what they perceived as danger in ways not unlike Halprin's dancers' use of charts and scores to accomplish the same in the face of audience hostility.

King's adaptation of passive resistance not only spoke to protesters' states of mind, it also enumerated the following directives for their tolerant response to racist adversaries:

(1) [The passive resister] does not seek to defeat or humiliate the opponent, but to win his friendship and understanding.

(2) The attack is directed against forces of evil rather than against persons who happen to be doing the evil. It is evil that the nonviolent resister seeks to defeat, not the persons victimized by evil.

(3) [Passive resistance implies] a willingness to accept suffering without retaliation, to accept blows from the opponent without striking back.

(4) [Passive resistance] avoids not only external violence but also internal violence of spirit. The nonviolent resister not only refuses to shoot his opponent but he also refuses to hate him. (1958, 102,103)

Scoring the interaction between protester and adversary, these directives provided the means for protesters to express their oppositional consciousness through meaningful, if nonviolent, actions.

Likewise, Gregg's techniques centered on a state of being that he called "moral jiu-jitsu," a form of "superior wisdom" that could direct protesters' decision making in the moment-to-moment experience of conducting a protest. As he put it,

Nonviolent resistance acts as a sort of moral jiu-jitsu. The nonviolence and good will of the victim act in the same way that the lack of physical opposition by the user of physical jiu-jitsu, does, causing the attacker to lose his moral balance. The user of nonviolent resistance, knows what he is doing and having a more creative purpose, keeps his moral balance. He uses the leverage of a superior wisdom to subdue the rough and direct force of his opponent. (Gregg 1959, 44)

Like the aesthetic philosophy behind Halprin's tasks, moral jujitsu allowed protesters—"users of physical jiu-jitsu"—to resist compromising social conditions while simultaneously maintaining the moral high ground and avoiding violent confrontation. Emphasizing self-control, both mental and physical, it valued mental agility over violence and depended on protesters' ability to neutralize their emotion and depersonalize their interaction with adversaries. Drawn from the model of passive resistance, such techniques led to situations of measured unpredictability that favored protesters because such techniques threw their adversaries off mental and moral balance.

Organizers of the sit-ins of the early 1960s adapted King's and Gregg's principles into specific rules of engagement for a given situation. Below is a list of rules enumerated by the organizers of lunch-counter sit-ins in Knoxville, Tennessee, for example,

(1) Demonstrators must face the counter at all times. Reading is permissible, but sit-inner should look up when waitress is near, as though to say, "I am ready to order now." Use care in selection of reading matter.

(2) Demonstrators must not eat or drink at the counter unless the food or drink is served them by employees of that establishment. If a sympathizer places food in front of you which he has ordered, thank him, explain your rule, ask him to remove it, but if he does not, gently push it to one side and to rear of counter.

(3) Do not hide your face with your hands.

(4) If you chew gum, do it so people hardly notice it.

(5) Demonstrators should always be neatly dressed in clean clothing, and should be careful to avoid "B.O." (Proudfoot [1961] 1990, xli)

Like Halprin's performance scores, these rules delineated a plan for action. Methodically, they directed protesters through a situation, serving to defuse and to depersonalize it. Seeking privileges given to whites under Jim Crow, protester organizers set forth rules for audience engagement by protesters that would strengthen their demands for equal treatment. Their rules dictated specific kinds of nonviolent responses over more provocative ones, and established an optimal mindset for responding to onlooker hostility. In this case, protesters needed *to be and to appear to be* principled and disciplined. Attending to protesters' spatial orientation, demeanor, clothing, reading material, and absence of body odor, the Knoxville directives, for example, illustrate how organizers saw their challenges in theatrical and even choreographic terms. Halprin similarly used externally imposed directives, like tasks or on charts, to subvert her and her dancers' habits of thought and behavior with the goal of enlarging their possibilities for being in the world.

It is important to point out, however, that comparison between each group's utilization of these strategies, in order to meet dramaturgical demands placed on them by audiences, breaks down at this point in racial terms. The demand of consistency placed on the protesters in Greensboro begins to suggest how these situations differed. Writings by King and Gregg as well as the Knoxville directives convey the extent to which civil rights organizers expected protesters to maintain the consistency of their self-presentation and comportment. They also suggest the degree to which the visionaries and organizers of the movement anticipated consistency as a standard to which protesters would be held in the court of public opinion. Those overseeing the protests expected protesters to not only "look the part" in their proper clothing, but also to "act the part" by remaining calm and "loving" even in the face of hostility and violence. By acting as though they belonged there, protesters provoked bystanders, regardless of their position on racial matters, to question their assumptions about conventions dictated by Jim Crow. Accordingly, King and Gregg believed that protesters' "demonstration [of their] sincerity and deep conviction" through "voluntary suffering" would bring skeptical onlookers to their side (Gregg 1959, 47). In Gregg's words, "The sight and realization of this is profoundly impressive and moving" (ibid.).

By contrast, owing to their white privilege and social status as artists, Halprin and her company were given the option of seeking consistency in their self-presentation. Ultimately, they rejected this in favor of using arbitrary juxtaposition of task-oriented scenarios in order to thwart viewers' attempts to find coherence in what they were doing. Halprin's decision to costume her dancers in secondhand street clothes instead of attire that would mark them as "dancers" reveals a similar privilege in the prerogative not to cater to viewers.

A culmination of the previous phases of the protest, the third—the event itself—brought the dramatic elements of everyday life to the fore by presenting ordinary life as theater. Diverging from earlier precedents, the sit-ins of the early 1960s did more than stage a massive refusal to tolerate racism as had previous marches, work stoppages, and boycotts. Rather, the action of sitting actualized the changes protesters sought, staging an occupation of public spaces from which they had been prohibited and a demonstration of protesters' prerogative to sit where they pleased. In other words, by sitting, protesters acted *as if* they were entitled to such rights, both signaling their refusal to accept the status quo and constituting an alternative reality.

Gregg realized the extent to which doing something like this possessed what he called "the subtle power of genuine drama," when the protest "works upon the mind and heart of the opponent." As he explained, "In this drama the movement and confronting of ideas and forces cause in both the opponent and the spectator a clearer and profounder realization of human relations, a reconciliation of impulses and an illumination, enlargement and enrichment of consciousness" (1959, 57). In this case, "drama" did not cheapen or undermine the significance of sitting in. Quite the opposite, it communicated the protesters' demands in such a way as to move participants and bystanders to subsequent action, expressed not only in their words and deeds, but in their hearts and minds as an "enlargement and enrichment of consciousness."

Gregg's articulation of the situation in these terms is amplified by sociologist Erving Goffman's contemporaneous discussion of the moral imperative that accompanied such performances of reality *as if*. As Goffman explained in his 1959 book *The Presentation of Self in Everyday Life*, "When an individual projects a definition of the situation and thereby makes an implicit or explicit claim to be a person of a particular kind, he automatically exerts a moral demand upon the others, obliging them to value and treat him in the manner that persons of his kind have a right to expect." In other words, Goffman believed that doing something not only actualized an individual's desire to "be a person of a particular kind," but demanded an accompanying response from those watching—a moral demand that exerted an obligation to respond in kind. In Goffman's words, "the others find, then, that the individual has informed them as to what is and as to what they *ought* to see as the 'is'" (13; emphasis in original). As

FIG. 7.4 Day 1 of the Woolworth's Sit-In, February 1960. Original four, left to right: David Richmond, Franklin McCain, Ezell Blair, and Joseph McNeil. Courtesy of *Greensboro News and Record.*

both Gregg and Goffman suggest, in the context of direct-action protests the application of theatrical techniques to cast ordinary situations as performances demonstrated the power of action to transform what "ought" to be into tangible reality.

The constitution of an alternative reality circa 1960 was no small task, however. Just as audiences had reacted to Halprin's work with distain and hostility, so onlookers met the sit-in protests by calling the protesters names, waving Confederate flags, and threatening more violence including bomb scares (Kowal 2004, 136).

Yet the cause and tactics of action were undeniably contagious. Public response to both events extended beyond the confines of the immediate situations. Just as Halprin's artistic tactics became precedents for a generation of revolutionary artists in their drive to overthrow existing practices of dance modernism, Greensboro became a template for direct-action protesters across the nation. In ways not unlike improvisatory artists, protesters deployed the directions for sitting-in as scores, recognizing that they could be adapted and repeated in numerous ways, in any place, by diverse groups of people, yet all with the intention of provoking the same reaction. As field organizer for the Student Nonviolent Coordinating Committee (SNCC) (and later a U.S. congressman), John Lewis later recalled, "seeing people sitting in the Carolinas on television every night. It gave us a sense of kinship, a bond. We said, 'If they can do it in Montgomery and Greensboro, we can do it in some of these smaller cities'" ("Greensboro Blacks Supported Sit-Ins," 1980, A-6+).

Conclusion

In this book I have attempted to shed light on the modern dancers, dance makers, and audiences who contributed to a cultural sea change that occurred during the postwar years. In the modern dance field, this involved a redefinition of the dancing body as a moving body, stressing function over expression as an ultimate goal. In the broader cultural arena, it pertained to changes in the ways ordinary Americans came to view and to use movement as a metaphor and a catalyst for social and political reform. What remained consistent across the board was a growing understanding of the body's inherent power to counteract forces of normalization and inertia that tapped individual and collective potency to stand for change.

Like many other Americans, members of the modern dance community found themselves negotiating these forces. Occupying marginal positions within society, choreographers mapped their identities as artists onto other culturally precarious gender, sexual, racial, and/or ethnic identities. In deploying action to constitute their experiences of difference, choreographers figured "conditions of possibility" (Jameson 1984, 183) that resonated with movements in the larger body politic.

How To Do Things with Dances illustrates how choreography that posed questions to dominant cultural assumptions or standards by way of metaphor, as in Limón's *The Moor's Pavane*, Graham's *Night Journey*, or Sokolow's *Rooms*, for example, yielded to increasingly actualized modes of deploying movement to do something in the world. Pearl Primus' writings home from Africa are central to this shift in their articulation of a theory and practice of choreographic "effectiveness." And Primus' contention that movement was constitutive resonates throughout the rest of the book. For Merce Cunningham and Paul Taylor, for example, it became operative as a means of registering artistic and social dissent through embodied subject formation. In different but corresponding ways, for Talley Beatty, Katherine Dunham, Donald McKayle, and Anna Halprin, action aided in breaking down the fourth wall separating performers from audience members. Performing something *as if* it were true constituted a step along the way to *making* it true; in other words, the doing of an action made that action plausible even if it appeared to be improbable.

These choreographic efforts were not coordinated by any means, nor did they begin to cohere in meaningful ways prior to the early 1960s, artistically or socially. Marginalized and separated by reductive definitions of their "human" purview, choreographers sought to redefine (and ultimately to reclaim) measures of "humanity" through the lenses of their individualized worldviews. Artists whose work had been subject to criticism for its limited "human" significance (too "Negro," as in the case of Pearl Primus or Katherine Dunham, or not "Negro" enough in the case of Talley Beatty) or for its "dehumanization" of dancers (Sokolow, Cunningham, Taylor), and others not covered in this book whose work had met similar objections, struck out on their own. Each invented new forms and approaches to dancing and dance making in ways that emphasized the body's intrinsic movement capacity.

This account of the field offers an alternative assessment of the legacy of postwar modern dance, suggesting that its hallmark is not the formation or ascendance of an objectivist aesthetic, nor the methods of indeterminacy it generated. In contrast, I believe that its legacy is the very struggle to define what dance modernism was as well as the outcome of that struggle—a tacit consensus, or resignation in some cases, that the goal of modern dance artists was not to arrive at a common artistic ideology or a shared set of methods to achieve it. Put another way, in their labor to reach aesthetic and ideological consensus, postwar dance practitioners, as a collective and yet diverse community of artists, reaffirmed the disciplinary valuation of diversity over homogeneity, invention over standardization, and heterogeneity over unanimity—their labors providing a foundation for the innovations in dance practice attributed to the 1960s and running alongside nascent social and political movements.

Nowhere was the potency of action in the real world more apparent than in the example of Greensboro, subsequent "sit-ins," and the actions they spawned into the 1960s. Activists took the potential of action to a new level in its application for the transformation of everyday life. Using similar tools and techniques as those being pioneered in postwar modern dance, they formulated new approaches to attaining social justice and cultivated mental and physical capacities to exert their oppositional consciousness. Strategies of defamiliarization, for instance, helped protesters combat feelings of inferiority and passivity by providing productive avenues by which people could interrogate what they had come to accept as "normal" or "ordinary"; these strategies also provided structures to reinforce tactics of passive resistance to gain an advantage over hostile onlookers, or ideas about how to highlight the arbitrariness of social conventions under Jim Crow.

Yet, as this book has attempted to show, there were other Americans besides these dancers and civil rights protesters whose actions during the postwar period helped to usher in a radicalized body politic by the early 1960s. Consider, for example, women and men who rejected normative definitions of their identities and made alternative life choices within or outside of marriage; social scientists and public intellectuals who publicly challenged reigning social conventions surrounding individual responsibility and collectivism for their hindrance of individual subject formation; African-American intellectuals and activists who petitioned the United Nations both to raise public consciousness about the legacy of racial injustice in the United States and to weigh in on its bearing, not only on black Americans, but also on the country's standing in the world; and biological scientists, whose studies redefined measures of identity so as to value individual choice and circumstances over mutable morphological characteristics. While the senses of action and the contexts in which it occurred may differ in each of these examples, my argument is that each effort aided in laying the groundwork for a more popular understanding of the body's constitutive power.

In his 1960 inaugural address, President John F. Kennedy crystallized these meanings for many Americans when he intoned, "And so my fellow Americans: ask not what your country can do for you—ask what you can do for your country" ("Text of Kennedy's Inaugural," 1961). In historical literature, but perhaps even more in the popular imagination, Kennedy's address has become iconic for its articulation of the "can-do" politics that characterized the 1960s. As historian Terry Anderson contends, "JFK resurrected 'can do' politics that had been sidetracked during the cold war and McCarthyism, and with his flash and dash he stirred America out of its slumber" (1995, 59).

People look to leaders to provide accounts of "reality" that ring true, as well as to direct them to concerted action in response. Yet, for words to have results, to move people to action, they must express what people already know and ask them to do things they are already prepared to do. In many ways, Kennedy owed his rhetorical and political success to those whose collective work had paved the way to this interpretation of his speech. He owed it to the precedent of Dr. Martin Luther King Jr., who saw in the mobilization of bodies the capacity to "transform" democracy "from thin paper to thick action" (King 1955),[16] and he owed to the other men and women I have summoned in this book, whose actions provided a foundation for change in the decade before.

Notes

Introduction

1. For an extended aesthetic and cultural analysis of Ailey's *Revelations* see DeFrantz 2004b.
2. I have composed this narrative of the sit-ins based on both primary and secondary sources. It is therefore not meant to be a definitive account, but rather a means of establishing a sequence of events.
3. In Huizinga's words: "The rite produces the effect which is then not so much *shown figuratively* as *actually reproduced* in the action. The function of the rite, therefore, is far from being merely imitative; it causes the worshippers to participate in the sacred happening itself" (1950, 14–15; emphasis in original).
4. Austin was responding to logical positivists, like Rudolph Carnap and A. J. Ayer, who developed a criterion of empirical verifiability to distinguish meaningful scientific claims from meaningless metaphysical claims to which they referred simply as "nonsense." Thanks go to David Bullwinkle for pointing this out.
5. Other examples included the naming of a ship, "as uttered when smashing the bottle against the stem"; the bequeathing of a possession to someone else, "as occurring in a will"; and the act of making a bet ([1962] 1972, 5).
6. Examples of the first case are: Graff 1997; Foulkes 2002; Manning 2004. Examples of the second case are Banes 1983, 1989, 1993, and 2003. For a notable exception with respect to political theater see Cohen-Cruz 2001, 96–97.
7. Sally Banes, has claimed, for example that "the late 1940s and early 50s were not creative years in modern dance" (Banes 1987, 5), and Lynn Garafola has argued, "by the late 1950s modern dance and ballet had joined the Establishment" (Garafola 1988, 177).
8. For more on the composition and functions of the Dance Panel see chapter 1 as well as Prevots 1998, 37–52.
9. As I discuss in chapter 1, dance critics Walter Terry and John Martin both spoke about dance in these terms in the years just following World War II.
10. Thanks to Anthea Kraut for helping me articulate this connection.
11. Primus' thought on these matters comes to fruition in an essay she published on her return in *Theatre Arts* magazine in December 1950. Entitled "Earth Theatre," the essay constructs a new theater in which modern dance and dramatic artists might reinvest their efforts: "And so the earth becomes the stage: the curve of endless skies the backdrop. The setting is the jungle itself with its giant trees and twisting vines; the bald tops of mountains, with their rocky fingers jutting out, form the wings. The props are made from the bones and hair of the earth. And the actors are merely men and women!" (41).
12. After much deliberation, I have decided not to include a chapter on Alwin Nikolais in this book due to thematic restraints. Please see my article on Nikolais published elsewhere (Kowal 2007).
13. For example see Banes 1987, 1989, and 1993; Morris 2006.
14. For example, see Copeland 2004, 8.
15. This is a reference to Susan Sontag's influential essay "Against Interpretation," which served as a rallying cry for experimental choreographers in the early 1960s. As Sally Banes

has argued, Sontag's essay "called for an erotics of art that would replace hermeneutics" along with formalist-driven critical approaches (1993, 246).

16. The idea that movement constitutes a kind of efficacious speech, for instance, is investigated in several recently published books and essays: Román 1998; Foster 2002b; Gere 2004; DeFrantz 2004; and Goldman 2007.

17. For another example of scholarly work in art history on transnational avant-gardes see Mercer 2005.

18. I use "world-making" in the sense investigated in Buckland 2002, as an act of "reimagining creatively" (6).

Chapter 1. Setting the Stage

1. Long a promoter of dance as a medium of communication, Terry, whose career as a dance critic had been interrupted by Army service during the war, spent time teaching modern dance to Egyptian students in Cairo while he was stationed in Africa. He also gave lectures on American dance to Allied forces there (Kowal 1998, 785). On his return to civilian life, he dedicated himself to increasing the public's knowledge of all forms of dance. He knew firsthand that dance could bring people together, bridging cultures and worldviews through the medium of the human body, adding the role of cultural ambassador to his occupation as a dance critic.

2. Guilbaut 1983 makes a similar set of arguments about Abstract Expressionism during the cold war. As he puts it: "It is not my intention to impute to the artists of the avant-garde any precise political motive or to suggest that their actions were the product of some sort of conspiracy. What I argue is this: that from compromise to compromise, refusal to refusal, adjustment to adjustment, the rebellion of artists born of frustrations within the left, gradually changed its significance until ultimately it came to represent the values of the majority, but in a way (continuing with the modernist tradition) that only a minority was capable of understanding" (3).

3. Graham and Hawkins separated in 1950. For more see de Mille 1991.

4. A survey conducted by Hadley Cantril, director of the Office of Public Opinion Research at Princeton University, demonstrated empirically this heightened internationalist consciousness. Published in the *New York Times* in April of 1945, the poll found that "ever since our entry into the war . . . the great bulk of us believe that even before the fighting ceases we must do our part in devising some machinery to secure the peace. . . . More than 90 percent of us . . . want the United States to join an international organization. More than 80 percent of us believe . . . that we, along with other nations should make part of our armed forces available when necessary to stop aggression." These figures marked a reversal in public opinion eight years before, when, according to Cantril, a Gallup poll found that "less than 10 per cent of the population thought our Government should pursue a foreign policy which did everything possible to prevent wars even if it meant fighting countries that start wars; more than 90 per cent said we should have a foreign policy which did everything possible to keep us out of foreign wars." Noting that "[s]uch a stand represented a pretty radical reversal of the position held before Pearl Harbor," Cantril concluded, "[e]vents thus seem to have shaped our point of view. . . . Events have taught us that power brings both privilege and responsibility."

5. As Truman put it in a press conference, "UNO must be trusted to work out international

problems as they arise; the way to build trust between nations is for all nations to get behind UNO and make it work" (Cantril 1945).

6. Commenting on this sense of "preeminence" among business and government leaders, Melvyn Leffler notes, "Given their country's overwhelming power, they now expected to refashion the world in America's image and create the American century. They intended to promote world peace and foster international stability at the same time that they safeguarded national security, perpetuated American power, and further augmented American prosperity" (1992, 3).

7. Support for such an organization was tepid before the United States' entry into the war, one of the main reasons why Woodrow Wilson never committed to the League of Nations. Planning for a United Nations, or a world governing body whose membership would be composed of any nation fighting against Germany and Japan, solidified after the United States entered the war (Gaddis 1972, 24–31).

8. Some historians contend that U.S. belief that it was the sole possessor of nuclear technology played into the hand of Truman in the formulation of "a tough policy aimed at forcing Soviet acquiescence to American plans for Eastern and Central Europe" (Alperovitz 1965, 13). In the words of Secretary of War [Henry Stimson], the bomb was a "master card" of diplomacy (Stimson quoted in Alperovitz 1985, 1). Yet others assert "atomic diplomacy was not a poker game." The strategy of withholding information cut both ways. "Both Roosevelt and Truman had kept the Manhattan Project a secret from their Russian ally and the American policymakers initially assumed that their atomic monopoly would give them, in Secretary of War Stimson's words, 'all of the cards' in negotiating with the Russians." Secrecy on the part of all sides, made "the bomb and the issue of its international control . . . additional source[s] of contention in the intensifying Cold War" (Schrecker 1998, 156–157).

9. As Boyer argues: "Clearly . . . the weeks and months following August 6, 1945, were a time of cultural crisis when the American people confronted a new and threatening reality of almost unfathomable proportions. Equally clearly, the dominant immediate response was confusion and disorientation" (1994, 25).

10. Such a view was expressed by *Newsweek* columnist Raymond Motley in August 20, 1945, who wrote: "The use of atomic power in warfare together with the prospect of peace makes it imperative that Americans prepare their minds, their government, and their manner of life for something new in our experience" ("How to Behave Like a World Power," 92).

11. Foster continues: "Thus the dancers, while they clearly felt the emotions about which they were dancing, also became abstract embodiments of the emotions themselves. Dancers did not represent people, or even mythical or stereotypical versions of people, but rather the essential characteristics of a range of human feelings" (1986, 150).

12. As Martin put it: "This essential unity makes what might seem to be a complex subject actually a very simple one." "The most sacred ritual dance of a primitive people, the French court ballet and the Lindy hop, are all simply different aspects, different stages of development, of exactly the same thing; at their roots, if we trace them back, we will find them to be quite indistinguishable from each other" (1946, 6–7).

13. In the context of 1930s radicalism, for example, universalism in dance expressed class solidarity that ran across national borders. The individual body stood for the collective—culturally diverse bodies aligned along common socioeconomic concerns. By the

late 1930s, developments within modern dance echoed those of the Popular Front, whose politics became increasingly international as members turned their attention to antitotalitarian movements abroad. As Michael Denning asserts, "Popular Front public culture was the politics of international solidarity" (1997, 11). Having followed the anti-fascist, antitotalitarian struggles in places like the Spanish Republic (against Franco), China (against imperial Japan), Ethiopia (against Mussolini), and the expanding Third Reich, leftists concentrated on the Hitler's invasion of the Soviet Union and the Japanese attack on Pearl Harbor, both in 1941. Denning explains, "[These events] inaugurated an official anti-fascist alliance between the U.S. and the USSR, and the anti-fascist politics of the Popular Front merged with the politics of war mobilization, the struggles to define the aims and objectives of the war" (11).

14. Lippincott quotes Huxley from the *New York Herald-Tribune*, September, 2, 1948.

15. Mark Franko has questioned the dichotomy suggested by this comparison by arguing that art and politics are not mutually exclusive. Just because art has a political function does not mean that it does not have "lasting artistic values" (Franko 2002, 39). According to Franko, in accomplishing what he calls "social reduction" these groups enriched the modernist project. In his words, "Modern dance of the 1930s frequently showed existence reduced to its material base as an emotional body. It resembles the modernist aesthetic reduction to essentials without the purity of modernism's grasp of essence. The transmission of feelings in and to bodies was an act fostering social depth with both subjective and ideological ramifications" (41).

16. Critics Walter Terry and John Martin were fond of the rhetoric of dance as a "human common denominator." For instance, see Martin 1933; Terry 1946.

17. The Truman Doctrine, which introduced the strategy of containment, came to define U.S. foreign policy for years to come. As Schrecker explains, "Over the next few years, the Cold War escalated as both the United States and the Soviet Union took ostensibly defensive actions that looked ever more threatening to the other side. . . . Moreover, as the antagonism intensified, containment took on an increasingly military cast—and an increasingly global one" (1998, 158).

18. Universalism depended upon the assumption that all people shared a common experience of humanness, which included a desire for "freedom." The rationale was that if people could agree on the aspects of life they shared with one another, they could reach consensus on the "important" matters and move past what were assumed to be superficial cultural differences (including race, ethnicity, religion, nationality). If countries had a grievance against one another, they would appeal to a third party representing the international community, such as the UN General Assembly, or Security Council, in order reach a peaceful resolution. Given these outlets and routes of mediation, countries would not be driven to unilateral action to achieve their foreign policy or geopolitical objectives. Realism, on the other hand, was "skeptical of any scheme for compressing international affairs into legalist concepts. It held that the content was more important than the form, and would force its way through any formal structure placed upon it. It maintained that the thirst for power was still dominant among so many peoples that it could not be assuaged or controlled by anything but counterforce" (Kennan quoted in Gaddis 2005b, 26–27). Not wholly opposed to forming international alliances based upon common security interests, realism was, nonetheless, more pragmatic than universalism in focusing on what were determined to be five geopolitical strong points (the

United States, Great Britain, Germany and central Europe, the Soviet Union and Japan) and in requiring that alliances be based "upon a real community of interest and outlook, which was to be found only among limited groups of governments, and not upon the abstract formalism of universal international law or international organization" (Gaddis, 27). Moreover, realism eschewed the universalist goal of "restructuring" the world order; this was a goal thought impossible, and if pursued would pose an obstacle to unilateral military action if ever warranted (Gaddis, 28).

19. Truman himself was prone to universalist thinking, "carrying in his wallet a copy of the portion of Tennyson's poem 'Locksley Hall' that predicted a 'Parliament of Man, the Federation of the world.'" To the journalist John Hersey, Truman acknowledged his wishes of this nature. "We're going to have that someday. . . . I guess that's what I've really been working for ever since I first put that poetry in my pocket" (Hersey quoted in Gaddis 2005b, 49–50; Gaddis quotes John Hersey, "Mr. President," *New Yorker*, XXVII, April 7, 1951).

20. Gaddis points out that NSC-68 "was not intended as a repudiation of Kennan. He was consulted at several stages in the drafting process of the final document . . . The objective rather was to systematize containment, and to find the means to make it work. But the very act of reducing the strategy to writing exposed the differences that had begun to develop between Kennan and the administration" (2005b, 88).

21. Gaddis compares it to the United States Constitution in that it "was a document more sweeping in content and implications than its originators intended" (2005b, 88). Klein argues: "In the end, the members of the NSC did rely on anticommunism to sell Truman's agenda: NSC 68 is one of the core expressions of the global imaginary of containment. But the internal debate also marked a recognition that fear and the negative logic of anticommunism could not by themselves serve as unifying concepts that the global expansion of American power demanded" (2003, 39).

22. Gaddis 2005b notes that Truman's speech explicitly counterposed "two ways of life," democracy and totalitarianism, not communism and capitalism (64). In Truman's words: "At the present moment in world history nearly every nation must choose between alternative ways of life. The choice is too often not a free one. One way of life is based upon the will of the majority, and is distinguished by free institutions, representative government, free elections, guarantees of individual liberty, freedom of speech and religion, and freedom from political oppression. The second way of life is based upon the will of a minority forcibly imposed upon the majority. It relies upon terror and oppression, a controlled press and radio, fixed elections, and the suppression of personal freedoms. I believe that it must be the policy of the United States to support free people who are resisting attempted subjugation by armed minorities or by outside pressures" (Truman quoted in Gaddis 1972, 351). For more on the international political ramifications of the speech see Gaddis 1972, 351–52; Leffler 1992, 141–43; Schrecker 1998, 157. For more on the domestic political context see Leffler 1992, 145; Gaddis 1972, 345; Larson 1985.

23. Walter Hixson points out that the American Society of Newspaper Editors had formerly been opposed to any cultural propaganda program (1997, 14).

24. Truman called for funds of almost $80 million, up from the almost $32 million allocated in 1948 with the Smith-Mundt Act, which outlined the terms by which the United States should and would conduct public diplomacy. For more see Hixson 1997, 11.

25. Hixson 1997 quotes the *Foreign Relations Series of the United States, 1952–1954 II*, 137.

26. Membership of the 1955 Dance Panel included: Doris Humphrey, choreographer; Walter Terry, dance critic for the *New York Herald Tribune*; Martha Hill, director of the Dance Department at the Juilliard School and codirector of the American Dance Festival at Connecticut College; Lucia Chase, director of the Ballet Theater Foundation; Emily Coleman, music and dance editor for *Newsweek* and a member of the Music Critics Circle of New York; Hyman Faine, Executive Secretary, American Guild of Musical Artists; Lincoln Kirstein, general director of the New York City Ballet; Agnes de Mille, choreographer; and Bethsabée de Rothschild, head of the Rothschild Foundation, benefactress of ANTA, a patroness of the Martha Graham Dance Company, and sponsor of several modern dance festivals. Four regional dance critics joined in 1956: Margaret Lloyd from the *Christian Science Monitor*; George Beiswanger from *Theater Arts*, *Dance News*, *Dance Observer*, and *Dance Magazine*; Alfred Frankenstein from the *San Francisco Chronicle*; and John Rosenfield from the *Dallas Morning News*. See Prevots 1998, 42. In my citations, I will refer to these minutes by their date. See the references list for more information.

27. Limón and his company were sent abroad again in 1957 to tour Europe including Poland and Czechoslovakia, then under soviet control. See Garafola 1999, 121–22.

28. See also Dance Advisory Panel minutes December 22, 1955.

29. For more on the history of racism in early twentieth-century modern dance see, for example: Gottschild 1998; Foulkes 2002; Manning 2004; Kraut 2006 and 2008; and Shea Murphy 2007.

30. According to Ewald (1986), McCarthy gave his speech on communist subversion in the State Department by chance. Having arrived in Wheeling with two speeches, McCarthy asked those who had invited him which speech they would like to hear, one on housing or another on communists in government. His hosts chose the latter (7).

31. It had also been discovered that Dr. Klaus Fuchs, one of the architects of the atomic bomb, "was a Soviet spy" (Ewald 1986, 7). For more on the cultural significance of the Hiss trial and conviction see Whitfield [1991] 1996.

32. Janet Collins was also discussed and rejected by the panel (Prevots 1998, 101).

33. Especially in modern dance, but even in ballet, there were performers who crossed the color line (Prevots 1998, 94; Graff 1997; Foulkes 2002; Manning 2004). These performers included most notably Arthur Mitchell, Donald McKayle, and Katherine Dunham.

34. The Symphony of Chile commissioned the work (Hill 2002, 293); I will analyze the cultural and political implications of this work in the context of the early civil rights movement in chapter 7.

35. Chapter 4 examines Primus' performances in U.S. venues such as the Café Society in light of her yearlong trip to Africa in 1949.

36. According to Prevots (1998, 65), it was not until 1962, during the administration of President John F. Kennedy, that the Dance Panel became "more receptive to choreographers outside of the mainstream . . . both the changing times and the addition of new members helped alter the perspectives of the Panel; what had seemed radical only five years earlier now began to seem acceptable."

37. Quoting Michel Foucault: "[W]hat makes the domination of a group, a caste, or a class, together with the resistance and revolts that domination comes up against, a central phenomenon in the history of societies is that they manifest in a massive and global form, at the level of the whole social body, the locking-together of power relations with relations of strategy and the results proceeding from their interaction (1994, 348).

Chapter 2. Precursors to Action: Graham & Limón

1. For a list of the works Limón presented on his 1955 tour, see Martin, November 14, 1954. For a discussion of some of the works Graham presented on her tour, including *Appalachian Spring* and *Night Journey*, see *Dance Observer* February and March 1956.

2. For accounts of the transformation in family life during the postwar years, especially as it affected women, see Chafe 1991; Gluck 1987; Rupp 1978; and Campbell 1984.

3. For example, images used in postwar advertising were meant to seduce women out of the workplace and back to the home. For a visual account of peacetime propaganda, see this exhibition catalogue: Lupton 1993. For a study of gender in 1950s television culture, see Spigel 1992.

4. William Whyte and David Riesman recognized the shortcomings of such a philosophy of individualism, especially if it led to an individual's loss of autonomy in his or her efforts to belong, and yet in these seminal works neither support outright anticonventionalism.

5. Hoover directed the FBI from 1924 to 1972. During the cold war years, he became notorious for his long-running and concentrated anticommunist crusade and for the "secret FBI files" that he kept for use as blackmail, against both targets and informants. For more, see Schrecker 1998 and F. Saunders 2000.

6. These numbers include all babies born in the United States, not broken down by race or ethnicity. The number of births decreased until 1948 and stayed fairly constant until 1951 when it began to meet and even surpass the surge of 1947 (Carter, et al., "Table Ab11–30"). In 1957, the rate peaked at 4,300,000. This rate steadily increased until 1961, when it began slowly to taper off.

7. This quotation appears in Breines 2002, 167.

8. According to Lloyd, all that remained from this alliance was the New Dance Group, "a non-profit corporation, maintaining a professional company and school and charging nominal rates for tuition. Most of its classes were held after 5 p.m., because most of its clients were working girls and boys" (1949, 174).

9. de Mille ([1956] 1991) also details Graham's romantic relationship with composer Louis Horst, whom she met at Denishawn.

10. For a fascinating analysis of the contradictory forces of normalization within Graham's *Appalachian Spring*, in this case with respect to an absent Native American "Indian girl" who "continues to haunt the stage," see Shea Murphy 2007, 148–68.

11. According to Hartmann 1982, "between 1940 and 1945, the female labor force grew by more than 50 percent, as the number of women at work outside the home jumped from 11,970,000 (with an additional 2.19 million unemployed) in 1940 to 18,610,000 (420,000 unemployed) in 1945. The proportion of all women who were employed increased from 27.6 to 37 percent, and by 1945 they formed 36.1 percent of the civilian labor force. Three-fourths of the new female workers were married; by the end of the war, one of every four wives was employed" (21).

12. According to Honey 1984, women employed in the production of durable goods rose from 8 percent in 1939 to 25 percent in 1944. These jobs paid an average of 40 percent more to women than those typically held by women did.

13. Hartmann 1982 provides the following information about postwar female employment: "By 1946 the female labor force had declined from its wartime peak of 19,170,000 to

16,896,000. Women's share of the civilian labor force decreased from 35.4 percent in 1944 to 28.6 percent in 1947; and the proportion of all women in the job market fell from 36.5 percent to 30.8 percent." However, by the end of the decade, the number (not the proportion) of women working outside of the home surpassed that at the war's peak (24).

14. See for example, Young 1945 and 1946; "Priestess Speaks," 1947; "Purely Symbolic: *Appalachian Spring*," 1945; "She Is the Priestess of the Intellectual Ballet," 1947; Gibbs 1947; "Portrait," 1947; Smith, "Dance: Artistic Calvinist," 1948.

15. Siegel notes a stark difference between the independent and assertive protagonist of *Frontier* (1935), who expresses her autonomy in her confident approach to space, and the Bride, whose identity is defined through her relationships with other characters (1979, 144–45). Sally Banes agrees, contending that "by her postwar years, Graham seems to have fallen in step with the 'feminine mystique' that celebrated men's return from the war and promised to send women home from the labor force" (Banes 1995, 166; see also Goldberg 1986, 17).

16. Banes observes that Graham's "personal situation must especially have shaped her interpretation of the Oedipus myth in *Night Journey*. She created the role of the tortured, remorseful Jocasta for herself and that of Oedipus, Jocasta's husband-son, for Hawkins, her own husband-to-be" (1995, 157).

17. My description of the piece follows the 1958 filmed version in *Martha Graham in Performance* (198–).

18. Rounding out the cast, Paul Taylor played Tiresias, and female members of her company, the Chorus.

19. Graham's choreographic citation of gender-identified signs is hyperbolic—heterosexuality is "an endless repetition of itself." And Graham's characters "naturalized heterosexuality" through "compulsive and compulsory repetition" (Butler 1991, 21).

20. The articles that I examine demonstrate the extent to which dominant cultural expectations about gender coincided with other dominant assumptions having to do with race, class, and sexual orientation. Although none of the authors whose work I looked at expressed these assumptions literally, their works make plain that the men and women they had in mind were white, affluent, and heterosexual. The articles that I surveyed were selected from the *Reader's Guide to Periodicals,* volumes from 1947 to 1960. I culled articles using the subject headings "men," "women," "masculinity," "femininity," and "homosexuality."

21. For more examples of such writings, see Lawton, 1948; "Men Are Weaker Sex," 1950; "Mind Your Wife and Live Longer," 1951; and "I'd Hate to Be a Man," 1955.

22. Thanks to Yvonne Hardt for pointing this out to me.

23. Similarly with characters such as the Husbandman and Oedipus, Graham broke the masculine mode. As Ramsay Burt argues: "Graham subverted the norms of gender representation by reappropriating images of men for her own pleasure and that of other women" (Burt 1995, 115).

24. In Elin Diamond's words, theatrical "realism is more than an interpretation of reality passing as reality." "It *produces* 'reality' by positioning its spectator to recognize and verify its truths" (Diamond 1993, 336).

25. These included Othello and Iago in *The Moor's Pavane* (1949), Creon in *Antígona* or *Antigone* (1951), The Man and The Stranger in *The Visitation* (1952), Don Juan and Don Gonzalo in *Don Juan Fantasia* (1953), Judas and Christ in *The Traitor* (1954), and The Emperor Jones and The White Man in *The Emperor Jones* (1956).

26. Quotations in the two paragraphs above appear in Atwood 1958. For an example of articles that typified efforts to explain men's physical decline, see "How to Keep Your Husband Alive," 1958; "Today's Jobs: The Killing Pace," 1956; "Mind Your Wife and Live Longer," 1951; and "Our Men Are Killing Themselves," 1956.

27. *The Moor's Pavane* pairs Othello with Desdemona and Iago with Emilia; *Antigone* matches Creon with Antigone; in *The Visitation*, The Man partners His Wife; and in *Don Juan Fantasia* Don Juan circulates among the Ladies.

28. According to Marcia Siegel, Doris Humphrey played a significant role in the choreographic process for *The Moor's Pavane*. She selected the music and choreographed the ending. For more, see Siegel 1987, 246–47.

29. My description of the dance follows the March 5, 1955, version, telecast by the Canadian Broadcasting Company on *José Limón: Three Modern Dance Classics* 1999.

30. For a compelling discussion about Limón's "relation to his Indigenous identity" in the context of the U.S. cold war agenda, see Shea Murphy 2007, 169–94.

31. Julia Foulkes makes this point about the work of Ted Shawn (2002, 85–88).

32. I believe that the same argument cannot be made about the relationship between Desdemona and Emilia, as it falls along the lines of traditional representations of female friendship. When they are together the women are set apart from the men, often at center stage; they appear to occupy a domestic space, like a bedroom chamber. Nevertheless, even in this intimate setting, their interaction is markedly less physical and less emotionally fraught. They are depicted as would a lady and her chambermaid; Emilia appears to be helping Desdemona do her hair, or teasing her gently with the handkerchief. In miming these domestic activities, the women establish more concretely the terms of their relation. Emilia seems obviously to be attempting to win Desdemona's confidence so as to get the handkerchief from her. Clearly, none of these situations come close in intensity to the simmering interaction between Othello and Iago. For more on issues of lesbian visibility see Jane Desmond's and Susan Manning's essays in (Desmond 2001).

33. As Diana Fuss points out, "the language and law that regulates the establishment of heterosexuality as both an identity and an institution, both a practice and a system, is the language and law of defense and protection: heterosexuality secures its self identity and shores up its ontological boundaries by protecting itself from what it sees as the continual predatory encroachment of its contaminated other, homosexuality" (1991, 3).

Chapter 3. Action Is Ordinary: Sokolow

1. Now known as the New School for Social Research, the institution, founded in 1919, has long been known for its support of progressive thought and academic freedom. In 1933 it created the University of Exile, an intellectual home for German scholars fleeing Hitler's mistreatment.

2. For more on the correlation between the Revolutionary dance and socialist political movements, see Graff 1997, 11–13.

3. John Martin praised the young Sokolow in another review, singling her out from her peers Mehlman and Maslow. "The Dance: Young Talent," *New York Times*, December 2, 1934. "Anna Sokolow, Lily Mehlman and Sophie Maslow have had the benefit of several years in Martha Graham's concert group. Miss Sokolow, especially, appears now an artist of great gifts. Her dancing covers an unusually wide range and is characterized through-

out by fine integrity and imagination. Her wit is devastating and in her current solos she turns it full blast upon certain romantic insincerities. Of all the young dancers in the field there is none who seems more completely ready to come forth on her own or more likely to make a great career when she finally does."

4. I am using the term "socialist realism" to describe the aesthetic of the Workers Dance League following Graff (2001, 318).

5. John Martin wrote of the same concert in "Dance Debut Here by Anna Sokolow" (November 15, 1937), "If the cheering began perhaps partly as a gesture of friendliness, it soon became quite obviously more than that as the young dancer's simplicity of manner and fine integrity took hold." "Both as a dancer and as a composer Miss Sokolow bids fair to take a high place in the American field. She has learned the mechanics of her craft to the point where they seldom if ever arise as obstacles in her path . . . But what is infinitely more to the point, she has a wide and true emotional range, which can sound the depths of feeling and dash off straight way to the most delicate spoofing."

6. *Slaughter of the Innocents* later called *Madrid* (1937) drew from Herbert Kline's documentary *Heart of Spain,* which included "footage of the bombing of Spanish civilians." According to Warren: "In this compelling solo, Anna turned continuously, a full skirt swirling about her, arms and body expressing the anguish of loss" (1991, 71).

7. "Her aim [in Mexico] was not to impose a credo but to enable the Mexican dancers to realize themselves." Little groups of dancers she taught called themselves "Las Sokolovas" (Hering June 1955b, 37). As Sokolow recalled in an interview she did for ADF in 1991, "they called me one of their own" (*Anna Sokolow Interviewed at ADF*).

8. While undeniably patronizing, Denby's review was nevertheless the most instructive in its prescriptions for Sokolow's further artistic development. As he put it, Sokolow needed to find a way of channeling her physical "energy" into "muscular actions that would give the torso plastic variation" (1986, 181).

9. For more thorough accounts of these works, see N. Jackson 2000, Morris 2006; and Rossen 2006.

10. Sokolow's *The Bride* (1946), which depicted a Jewish wedding, drew a parallel to Graham's *Appalachian Spring.*

11. The reviewer for *Dance Magazine* commented: Sokolow's dances "impress" with "their warmth and honesty." Her work "adds appreciably to the effectiveness of the show with its feeling for urban sensuality and jazz movement." Also noted was Sokolow's skill in "express[ing] the mood and tempo of the big city" (Goodman 1947, 14).

12. *The End of Ideology* was published in 1960. I am reading it as a fifties text, following Bell's assessment of its periodization in his introduction: "These essays, in the main, deal with the social changes in the American of the fifties" (13).

13. For more on the culture of consensus, see Brinkley 2001.

14. For more on the conditions for black workers see, for example, Patterson 1996, 19.

15. "Between 1940 and 1960, the proportion of working wives doubled, and of all persons who entered the labor market in the decade after 1949, three-fifths were married women. By 1960, some 40 percent of American women were employed, fully or part-time" (Leuchtenberg 1983, 74).

16. According to Leuchtenburg (1983, 73), when *McCall's* magazine first used the word "togetherness" in 1954, many readers thought the concept so aptly described their times that they credited the magazine's editors with its coinage. In response, the magazine crowed:

"From a little cloud, like a woman's hand, it has risen to blanket the consciousness of an entire nation, popping up everywhere from Macy's to the halls of Congress."

17. For more on the history of "welfare capitalism" see, for example, Ewen 1976.
18. For more on wartime building acts and strategies see Plunz 1990, 247–48.
19. For more on Sokolow's choreographic method, see Sabin 1953.
20. My description is drawn from two sources. First is the performance of *Rooms* by the Dayton Contemporary Dance Company, ADF, June 27, 1986. Video obtained from the ADF Archives, Duke University, Lilly Library. Second is a series of performances at the University of Minnesota, Twin Cities campus, by University Dance Theater, October 27, 28, 29, 2006, at the Southern Theater, which I saw live.
21. For more on the involvement of the insurance industry in New York City housing construction see Plunz 1990, 253.
22. Initiative to build the East River Houses came in part from French architect Le Corbusier's visit to New York City in 1935; he remarked that city "skyscrapers were too small." Whereas prior thinking about domestic housing stipulated that it should be relatively low to the ground, Le Corbusier's "city in a park" model prompted rethinking of these assumptions (Plunz 1990, 240–42). In this case, "six of the twenty-eight buildings were high-rise" (245). As Plunz points out, "With the completion of the East River Houses, the decades-old prejudice that the poor should not live in towers was reversed by the realities of housing cost" (245).
23. On p. 272, Plunz cites a study by Oscar Newman, *Defensible Space: Crime Prevention Through Urban Design* (New York: Macmillan, 1972), that compares the Brownsville Houses with the Van Dyck Houses, both projects in Brooklyn. The Van Dyck Houses, fourteen-story high-rises, had 50 percent more crime in a typical year and needed 39 percent more upkeep, "even though the two projects were adjacent to each other." "Newman argued that the difference in design approach accounted for much of the difference in statistics. For example, the scale of towers prevented normal exercise of family territoriality. The removal of large numbers of units from visual contact with open space prevented proper public surveillance."
24. According to Plunz, "nearly 30 percent of the area of East Harlem is covered with postwar subsidized housing" (1990, 245).
25. Soon after, Governor Dewey and O'Dwyer began acting on this information, allocating funding for the purchase of 1,345 huts and beginning the process of reconverting military barracks and bungalows at the Fox Hills Army Terminal on Staten Island and the Manhattan Beach Coast Guard Station for habitation by returning GIs and their families ("5,000 Quonset Huts," 1945; "1,345 Huts," 1946).
26. According to Plunz, "Between 1945 and 1950 nine state-financed and twelve city-financed public housing projects were completed in New York City, against considerable financial odds" (1990, 261). Robert Caro documents the activity of Robert Moses, a man who he calls the "greatest builder in the history of America, perhaps in the history of the world" (January 5, 1998, 43). In his various official capacities, Moses supervised the construction of 627 miles of roadway including all seven bridges that connect the five boroughs to one another, fifteen expressways that cut across the city, and sixteen parkways that join the city to neighboring counties (Long Island and Westchester). Additionally he constructed or contributed to the reconstruction of every city park (adding 20,000 acres to existing designated park space) and playground (658 in all). Finally, he "controlled—controlled

absolutely—the New York City Housing Authority," which, during his tenure, "built 1,082 apartment houses, containing 148,000 apartments which housed 555,000 people, more," points out Caro, "than, at the time, lived in Minneapolis" (43). For more on Moses see also: Caro (1974) and Plunz (1990), especially p. 281.

27. As Plunz observes, with respect to Stuyvesant Town: "A combination of brick walls and low commercial and parking structures surrounds the perimeter of the development; pedestrian and vehicular access was limited to eight entry points. The Manhattan grid-iron was completely obliterated and the internal open spaces heavily landscaped. In the central lawn the roads form the 'Stuyvesant Oval,' which framed the patrol booth for police at its center. The panoptic placement of the housing blocks allowed most of the ground area to be surveyed from a single point. The 'tower in the park' was advantageous in terms of control, from the 'inside out' as well as the 'outside in'" (1990, 255).

28. According to Caro, "to build his expressways, [Moses] evicted from their homes two hundred and fifty thousand persons, in the process ripping out the centers of a score of neighborhoods, many of them friendly, vibrant communities that had made the city a home to its people. To build his non-highway public works, he evicted perhaps two hundred and fifty thousand more; a 1954 City Planning Commission study of just seven years of Robert Moses' eviction policy was to call it 'an enforced population displace-ment' completely unlike any previous population movement in the City's history. And, since the people he evicted were overwhelmingly black, Hispanic, and poor, the most defenseless of the city's people, and since he refused, despite the policy of the city's elected officials, to make adequate provision . . . for their relocation, the policies he fol-lowed created new slums almost as fast as he was eliminating old ones, and tragically, were to be a major factor in solidifying an already existing ghettoization of New York-the dividing up of its residents by color and income" (1998, 43).

29. "The suburban house in Westchester was well removed from the problematic towers of East Harlem. All possibility of contact had been eliminated, except for the slight visual discomfort experienced from the windows of a commuter train passing along upper Park Avenue or an automobile passing along Harlem River Drive. . . . 'Urbanism as a way of life' was eclipsed by the suburbs" (Plunz 1990, 274).

Chapter 4. Action Is Effective: Primus

1. This list includes: Primus 1949, 1950a, 1950b, 1951; Martin June 28, 1949; Terry May 20, 1949; and Hering 1950. Why are these writings important? Neither the significance of Primus' artistic and ethnographic work, nor the impact of her legacy on modern dance and modern dancers, can be disputed. Yet Primus is still a relatively unknown and mis-understood figure in the field of dance history. Whereas her near contemporary, Kather-ine Dunham, receives wide acknowledgment for helping to pioneer what was called at midcentury "Negro dance" (Manning 2004), Primus is typically relegated to a marginal position. Unlike Dunham, who founded a dance company that toured extensively both internationally and across the United States, Primus usually performed solo or with a small pickup ensemble that she maintained as a company, if at all, only for brief periods. According to Primus biographer Peggy Schwartz, Primus' initial trip to Africa played a pivotal role in her life. When she returned, she typically framed her dancing in "ethno-logic" terms, performing lecture-demonstrations in places like New York City's Ameri-

can Museum of Natural History, or in entertainment-oriented venues like the Café Society nightclub in Greenwich Village, favored by African-American jazz singers and musicians. Frequent trips abroad and involvement in humanitarian projects especially in Liberia, disrupted her subsequent performing career, as did Primus' growing sense that her mission in life was more educational than it was artistic.

Like Dunham, who traveled to Haiti in the late 1930s, Primus used her trip to position herself as an authority on the issue of Africanist performance practices. However, unlike Dunham, who published numerous articles and several books on the subject, Primus who wrote in fits and starts, published few of her writings, and, when she did, sought out more popular outlets like weekly magazines. As Schwartz puts it, Primus was so consumed with "living her anthropology," and, likewise, so engrossed with her role as educator, that she neglected to establish the kinds of institutions or to seek public acknowledgment of her work in ways that would ensure a legacy (Schwartz 2006). Primus' vast archival materials were held privately; until only recently they sat, uncatalogued, in boxes at the American Dance Festival archive. For all of these reasons, any historical account of Primus is itself fragmented and frustratingly incomplete. Acknowledging the patchwork of sources from which to construct an account of Primus during the postwar period, this chapter uses writings about Primus' trip as a basis for understanding the meanings of diaspora both for the artist and for readers. While diverse in genre (letters, essays, articles, profiles) and addressing various audiences, they provide insight into the ways in which Primus mined her experiences for new ideas so as to more effectively and imaginatively engage in the discourse that surrounded her.

2. I have adopted Susan Manning's term "Negro" dance as a way of marking the complex situation of modern dancers of African descent at midcentury. In part, this consisted of "developing . . . technique[s] that will be as important to the white man as to the Negro"; "dignifying" material drawn from the "culture and history of Africans in the New World" (Dunham quoted in Manning 2004, xiv, and Manning 2004, xiv, respectively); and treating subject matter from the point of view of peoples of color, as writer Leonore Cox put it in 1936: "to dance [themes] not as other groups have danced them, nor as other groups might dance them, but the way we, Negroes, respond to them" (Cox quoted in Manning 2004, xiv).

3. Here I am indebted to Susan Manning's pioneering scholarship teasing out the "mutually constitutive" relationships among midcentury dance practices. As she argues: "Negro dance and modern dance were mutually constitutive categories, and their interdependent representations of blackness and whiteness shifted in tandem over time" (2004, xv).

4. The program also included *Rock Daniel* and *Hard Time Blues*.

5. For more on how Jewish American dancers negotiated this terrain, see Foulkes 2000 and Rossen 2006.

6. It is interesting to note, however, that even within these limited parameters, Primus felt it possible to embody a white subject position in *Strange Fruit*.

7. This section's heading comes from M. Carter 1944, 5.

8. For more on Primus' early life and career, see Green 2002, 110.

9. The quotation is taken from Melville J. Herskovits, "The Negro's Americanism," in Alain Locke (ed.), *The New Negro* [1925] (New York: Atheneum, 1968) 353. Note that, as Ramsey shows, Herskovits changed his position in light of his own and Dunham's fieldwork in the Caribbean (2000).

10. For more on Dunham's postwar activity, see Hill 2002.
11. Put another way, "The inability of the United States to declare a resolute position with regard to Democratic ideals and contrasts made between Jim Crow and Hitlerism weakened its position as defender of equality and freedom and damaged its credibility" (L. Baker 1999, 193).
12. According to Plummer 1996, 85 percent of NNC members were also members of the Communist Party (171–74).
13. The *Time* magazine reporter spoke to Primus following an appearance at Café Society, the famed and racially integrated jazz club in Greenwich Village. For more on Café Society and its significance in the postwar years, see Scott and Rutkoff 1999, 266.
14. Susan Manning generously furnished the document from the Claude Barnett Collection at the Chicago Historical Museum.
15. At the time of this writing, my efforts to ascertain more information about Primus' government records via State Department file have proved inconclusive. While correspondence with R. Ross, December 11, 2006, confirmed that Primus was never called to testify before HUAC, correspondence with J. Vernon, December 14, 2006, could not confirm or deny that Primus' passport was ever revoked.

    Primus' FBI file, furnished to Victoria Phillips Geduld on November 9, 2007 (U.S. Department of Justice, Federal Bureau of Investigation, "Primus, Pearl," FOIPA No.1080919–000/190–), and graciously shared with me, does confirm that Primus had been under investigation by the FBI since September 1944 (file 100–61887) and that a "Security Division, Dept. of State agent" "picked-up" her passport "about April 12, 1952" while Primus was in Los Angeles, "appearing at Philharmonic Auditorium" (document signed "Hood").

    Subsequently, on October 2, 1952, Primus voluntarily went to the FBI office in New York City "to advise the FBI of her past connection with the Communist Party, as suggested to her by [an agent at] the Passport Division, U.S. State Department and Mr. [Herbert Monte] Levy [Staff Counsel] of the Civil Liberties Union" ("Office Memorandum, United States Government," November 3, 1952).

    Following this meeting, and advice by Levy, Primus submitted a signed affidavit detailing her involvement with organized labor, "sympathies with" the Communist Party, contact with party members, and periodic disillusionment with the party and its aims. As Primus put it: "My reason for joining the Communist Party, if in fact I did so, was that I believed that the lot of the Negro in the United States would be best served by the Communist Party" ("New York City, October 16, 1952," 3). However, as Primus related, several times between 1944 and 1947, she had "doubts as to the efficiency of [the party's] manner in improving the lot of the Negro." She went on, "I still believed that they were sincerely interested in improving the Negro's life but felt that their methods were not the best" (4).

    Following her admissions and further investigation Primus' passport was reissued in June 1953 ("Office Memorandum, United States Government," June 18, 1953).
16. Current research on the history of ethnography underlines the significance of ethnographers who themselves identify with marginalized groups. Knowledge gained when "the marginalized analyze their own situation" complicates the process of information gathering and analysis shedding light on the subject position of the ethnographer as well as the practices of the studied group (Harrison and Harrison 1999, 1–4).

17. Primus' reflexivity situates her work within a "women's tradition" in American anthropology that included Ruth Benedict, Katherine Dunham, Margaret Mead, and Zora Neale Hurston (Harrison and Harrison 1999, 19). Awareness of positionality played a significant role in the ethnography of Dunham and Hurston who used their research also as a source for their own choreographic production. VèVè Clark documents this turn as a transition from *milieux* (research) to *lieux* (performance), or an embodiment of cultural memory—"performing the memory of difference" (Clark 1994, 189). Conversely, their use of techniques including genre blurring, use of the first person (autobiographical anthropology), and self-consciousness about the ways in which they situated themselves relative to their informants provoked questions within anthropology about issues of "objectivity and authority" (Harrison and Harrison 1999, 19).

18. In her essay "Need for Study of Dances of Primitive Peoples" (undated), Katherine Dunham laid the groundwork for Primus' idea that tribal dance practice could serve as an aesthetic resource for dance modernism writing in 1941: "In art, it is likely that a study of dances of various groups of primitive would lead to the discovery of those principles of technique which are fundamental and universal in character, and to their incorporation into a basic dance form which has not yet been developed by the modernists" (Clark and Johnson 2005, 520).

19. Such deployments valued predictable hierarchies such as "center" over "periphery," "intellectual" over "emotional," "objective" over "subjective," "technological" over "manual," "conscious" over "unconscious," and "individual" over "communal" (Sims 2005, 87). In other words, in "marking the appropriation of the ancestral arts of black artists to the purposes of modern art," an artist's deployment of a primitivist discourse to communicate their experiences inverts the assignment of what Sims calls "primogeniture and recognition." Those acting as "agents of industrialization, urbanization, secularization and commodification and technological innovation" (Westerners) assume more value than those subjected under colonialism (Non-Westerners).

20. I thank Nadine George for conversing with me on this point at the SDHS Annual Conference, Alberta, Canada, June 2006.

21. I examine this subject again in chapters 7 and 8.

Chapter 5. Action Is Finding Subjectivity

1. In comments about Cunningham's 1945 solo concert at the Hunter College, Edwin Denby wrote: "With his physical elegance and originality of gesture Mr. Cunningham combines a rare good sense in what a man dancing alone on the stage may with some dignity be seen to be occupied in doing. *A man alone* can suggest he is looking for something invisible, that he is trying out a trick, that he is having a bad time or that he is just fooling. Cunningham's dances express these lyric possibilities with real imagination and subtlety. . . . He does not create onstage different objective characters, but rather lyric variations of his own character" (emphasis mine, Denby quoted in Vaughan 1997, 36–37).

2. G. Morris (2006), for example, pairs Cunningham and Nikolais in her chapter entitled "Objectivism's Consonance" (166–204).

3. Besides collaborating with Cage, Cunningham sometimes worked with composers David Tudor, Christian Wolff, and Earle Brown, who was married to Cunningham

dancer Carolyn Brown. While acknowledging Cunningham's alliances with these composers, this chapter will concentrate on his collaboration with Cage and Rauschenberg.

4. Seigel writes that "[i]t was in New York that irony first became a defining feature of [Duchamp's] relation to the public, drawn to him precisely in response to the uncertainty of his intentions" (1995, 132).

5. Original quotation comes from: *Revue anarchiste*, 1893.

6. Jonathan Katz has documented the ways in which in the late 1940s Cage turned to Zen Buddhism "to solve both his personal and his artistic problems" (Katz 1999b, 234).

7. For an illuminating discussion of the personal and cultural significance of Cage's fascination with Zen Buddhism, see Katz (1999b) and Jones 1993. See also: G. Morris 2006, 175–81.

8. Wolff, Cage, and Cunningham were fond of the Bollingen edition of the *I Ching* or *Book of Changes*, trans. Richard Wilhelm, foreword by C. G. Jung (Princeton, NJ: Princeton University Press, 1950).

9. Cage employed these methods in *Music of Changes*, his first chance-determined piece, premiered in 1952 at the Cherry Lane Theater in New York, in which he used chance operations to facilitate controlled accidents. For more on this piece see Tomkins 1976, 111.

10. This section's heading comes from Remy Charlip quoted in Vaughan 1997, 62.

11. At that time, Cage was married to Xenia Kashevaroff Cage, from whom he separated in the mid-1940s. See Retallack 1996, xlv, n. 23.

12. Martha Graham recruited Cunningham for her company during the 1939 session of the Bennington School of Dance, held that year at Mills College in Oakland, California. At the time, he was enrolled at the Cornish School, in Seattle, Washington, where he studied dance and theater. Declining graduation from Cornish, he followed Graham to New York City and became a member of her dance company. As Mercier Cunningham, he debuted as the Acrobat in *Every Soul Is a Circus* (1939), appearing with Graham and Erick Hawkins. Cunningham remained with the Graham company until 1944, after having originated roles such as March in *Letter to the World* (1940), Christ in *El Penitente* (1940), Yankee in *Land Be Bright* (1942), and the Revivalist Preacher in *Appalachian Spring* (1944).

13. Cage's comments about the experience of collaborating with Cunningham on this piece echo those of Cunningham. David Vaughan has quoted Cage as saying, "We were able to work independently, and we were getting free of this business of fitting one thing to another. I had long had that idea of letting the two arts collaborate without following each other, but it was with *Root of an Unfocus* that we really made some kind of progress" (1997, 31).

14. Fittingly, the year of *Root*'s performance, Cunningham left Graham's company. As she remembered, "He stayed as long as he validly could." Graham is quoted in Vaughan 1997, 35. The quotation originally comes from Commanday 1974.

15. Cunningham's participation in the summer workshops offered at Black Mountain College were crucial to this early development. During those years most afflicted by antiinnovationist, anticonformist anxiety, Cunningham found ways of translating his unconventional ideas into art works without inhibition. He gained most during the summers of 1952 and 1953, during which he honed his ideas about choreography in the presence of others, like David Tudor and Robert Rauschenberg, and presented his work to the community. Having been ostracized by the modern dance traditionalists, Cunningham felt

that Black Mountain College "was the *only* place at that time . . . where he could have been both welcomed and let alone to the extent that he was" (for more, see Duberman 1993, 383).

16. In spite of his rejection by the modern dance establishment Cunningham managed to receive two big commissions during this period: In 1946, Lincoln Kirstein commissioned him and John Cage to collaborate on their most ambitious work to date, a ballet called *The Seasons* for the Ballet Society. Founded by Kirstein, Ballet Society "provided George Balanchine with a situation in which he could make ballets without concern for commercial considerations" (Vaughan 1997, 39). Also, as discussed, in 1952 Leonard Bernstein commissioned *Symphonie* and *Les Noches*, for Brandeis University. However, Bernstein did not write the music, which was composed by Pierre Schaeffer in collaboration with Pierre Henry. For more on Cunningham's early commissions see Vaughan 1997, 39–43, 63–64.

17. This was one of several seminal essays Cunningham wrote in the early 1950s including "The Function of a Technique for Dance" (1951), "Space, Time and Dance" (1952), and "The Impermanent Art" (1952). In all, Cunningham argued for the viability of alternative motivations for choreographic invention (all essays are published in Vaughan 1997).

18. Cage used the *I Ching* to compose *Music of Changes* (for the piano) and *Imaginary Landscape No. 4* (for twelve radios).

19. The original passage appears in Charlip, "Composing by Chance," *Dance Magazine* January 1954, 17,19.

20. The original quote appears in "A Collaborative Process between Music and Dance," 175–76 (source not included in Vaughan 1997, 280, n. 4).

21. For more on Taylor, see Cohen 1965, 91–102; Mazo 1977, 257–70; P. Taylor 1987. In addition to the entries in the above-cited texts, I have found many articles and reviews that together chronicle Taylor's career including: Jowitt 1978; Croce 1978, 1980, and 1983; Coe 1981; Tobias 1980; Moss 1984; and Reardon 1997, respectively.

22. James Waring and David Vaughan cofounded Dance Associates in 1951 or 1952, a choreographers' collective that included Paul Taylor. From a number of sources I have gleaned an incomplete list of other participants including: Toby Armour, Karen Butt, Remy Charlip, Anita Dencks, Richard Englund, David Gordon, Marvin Gordon, Benjamin Harkarvy, Alec Rubin, Paul Sansasardo, Marian Sarach, Lee Theodore, composer John Herbert McDowell, and dancer and costume designer Ruth Sabodka. For more on Dance Associates see P. Taylor 1987, 53–54; Vaughan 1975–76; Wroble 1998, 809–11. Additionally, I discussed the activities of the Dance Associates in an interview with David Vaughan on November 6, 2007.

23. In my interview with Taylor, he discussed how, unlike it had been for Cunningham, ballet was not a resource for movement invention. He said that Balanchine had offered him a place in his company, but he had refused, "because I couldn't see myself as a ballet dancer" (Kowal November 7, 2008).

24. In my interview with Taylor on November 7, 2007, he confirmed his close association with Rauschenberg and Johns. He described New York as a "hotbed" with many approaches to art "rubbing off on each other." He also discussed his interest during this period in the work of other visual artists like Elsworth Kelly and Cy Twombly. Cunningham worked with Rauschenberg too, having been introduced to him by Cage. Cage had met the artist in the spring of 1951 at the Betty Parsons Gallery and purchased one of his

collages. That fall, Cage and Rauschenberg collaborated on a "twenty-two-foot-long Rauschenberg 'print' created by automation." Cunningham first collaborated with Rauschenberg in 1954, on *Minutiae*. For the piece, he built a three dimensional object which combined "paint, fabric, and paper (mostly from comic strips), as well as a mirror hanging on a string, revolving in a hole in the front panel." As Vaughan notes, the assemblage "relates both to the 'Red Paintings' that he [had recently] exhibited at the Charles Egan Gallery, New York . . . and the 'Combines' he was beginning to make, such as *Charlene*," from the same year (Cunningham quoted in Vaughan 1997, 84).

25. For more on Jasper Johns, see Tomkins 1980; Johnston 1996; Silver 1993; Katz 1999a; Perloff 2001.

26. Rauschenberg and Johns were also known for continually painting over their paintings, or adding to or subtracting from "finished" works. For more, see Kotz 1990. Whereas Rauschenberg, Kaprow, and Cage collected actual material from the city to use in their work, Jasper Johns's materialism was expressed in his view that every painting was itself an object. For more on Johns, see Kotz 1990, 89.

27. This section's heading comes from Cunningham's "Space, Time and Dance" (1952), in Vaughan 1997, 67.

28. Judith Butler's reinterpretation of Foucault's statement that the "soul is the prison of the body" enriches the discussion of the significance of Cunningham's acts. Arguing against a determinist reading of the passage, Butler interprets it in light of Foucault's dynamic conception of power relations and her idea that a person's identity is not fixed but "reiterated or rearticulated" through successive, performative declarations. Thus, the subject that "is brought into being through the performative effect of the interpolating demand is much *more* than a 'subject' . . . it becomes the occasion for a further making." The act of performance, "thus, becomes the non-place of subversion, the possibility of a reembodying of the subjectivating norm which is at once a redirecting of the normativity of the norm" (Butler 1995, 241–42; emphasis original).

29. Comparing this aspect of Cunningham's work to Bertolt's Brecht's critique of "the natural" or what he calls "intentional disunity," Roger Copeland maintains that "no one, and that includes Brecht himself, has carried this principle of separation farther than Merce Cunningham" (Copeland 1994, 194).

30. Merce Cunningham premiered *Antic Meet*, accompanied by John Cage's *Concert for Piano and Orchestra*, with set and costume designs by Robert Rauschenberg, at the American Dance Festival (ADF) in the summer of 1958. It was billed as a humorous dance, while its companion piece *Summerspace* was billed as a "lyric dance." Although I cite Vaughan's account, my impressions of the piece are drawn from multiple viewings and/or sources: a film of a 1964 performance in Finland; the description in Vaughn's book, which is of the original performance; and an "Event for Television," broadcast on WNET New York in 1976. At the time of my research, the Finnish film of the performance was the only visual record of the originally performed work. This film however lacks footage of scenes 1 and 2. In the "Event for Television," "room for two" and "bacchus and cohorts" are performed as part of a choreographic collage composed of many scenes from other pieces as well. Thanks to D. Vaughan for making this film available to me.

31. Other reviewers' responses to the piece were mixed. And, while the audience seemed to respond favorably to its comedy, "certain faculty members [at the ADF] were clearly not in sympathy with his aesthetic" (Vaughan 1997, 103). Cunningham remembers that *Antic*

Meet was "well received" on its premier because it was funny, and, according to Vaughan, "as if in confirmation of this observation, *Antic Meet* usually got the best reviews in a mixed bill" (1997, 109).

32. *3 Epitaphs* is the official title of Paul Taylor's dance, although it was called "Three Epitaphs" in many reviews written during the period in question. To address any confusion at the outset, I have left the review titles as they appeared in their original publication. My descriptions of *3 Epitaphs*, *Fibers* and *Insects and Heroes* are based on my viewings of the following films: *3 Epitaphs* appearing on *Paul Taylor: Three Modern Classics* 1981; *Insects and Heroes* 1961; and *Fibers* 1961.

33. Taylor quoted in Diamond 1999.

34. Writing about a performance of the work one year later, Lawrence Witchel expressed similar amusement: "Taylor, by virtue of his youth, is capable of making fun of the art form he expresses. In his dance 'Three Epitaphs' he makes hilarious fun of himself and his colleagues. Since 'Three Epitaphs' appears at the end of the show, one can't help feeling that perhaps his entire concert was not to be taken seriously" (Witchel 1957).

35. Merce Cunningham's *Nocturnes* (1956) set a precedent for the oddity displayed in Taylor's *Fibers*. Rauschenberg designed the set and costumes for *Nocturnes*. Men and women were costumed differently, but in ways that complicated stereotypical gender presentation. All of the dancers wore white garments. The men were distinguished by face paint—red on one side and white on the other—while the women were marked by headpieces. In one section of the dance, a woman wore what looked like tiny white horns, in another section, each of the women wore a different kind of white veil. For photographs and a description of the dance, see Vaughan 1997, 92–97.

36. Taylor premiered *Insects and Heroes* at the American Dance Festival at Connecticut College in the summer of 1961, marking the formation of the Paul Taylor Dance Company. My description of the dance follows this original performance and is based on a film of it at the Paul Taylor Archives. In *The Complete Guide to Modern Dance*, Don McDonagh notes that after its premier, Taylor noticeably revised the piece (for more see 1976, 316–17). While Doris Hering reviewed the original performance, Lennon and Alhen reviewed the revised version when Taylor was touring Western Europe in 1962.

37. Thanks to Amy Jacobus for helping me clarify this idea.

38. Somerville 2000 also notes work by Nancy Stepan, Londra Schiebinger, and Sander Gilman.

39. Outlaw demonstrates the connection between early science and mimetic theory commenting: "The concept of ['race'] provided a form of 'typological thinking,' a mode of conceptualization that was the center of the agenda of emerging praxis at the time [eighteenth century], that served well in the classification of human groups. Plato and Aristotle, of course, were precursors of such thinking: the former with his theory of Forms; the latter through his classification of things in terms of their 'nature'" (1990, 63). Elin Diamond's theory of mimesis is also apt in this context: "Mimesis, from its earliest and varied enunciations, posits a *truthful* relation between the world and word, model and copy, nature and image, or, in semiotic terms, referent and sign, in which potential difference is subsumed by sameness" (1993, 363; italics in original).

40. Outlaw 1990 quotes Banton 1975, 13. For a discussion of the impact of Charles Darwin's findings on the science of "race" see Outlaw 1990, 64.

41. Outlaw 1990, 65.

42. Framing Louis Horst's blank review in the November 1957 issue of *Dance Observer* was the heading: "Paul Taylor and Dance Company, Y.M.-Y.W.C.A., October 20, 1957."

43. The critic for *Dance News* shared Terry's insight, writing that Taylor's "effort to find the 'still point' in his approach to movement" had resulted in "an excursion into non-dance" ("Seven New Dances by Paul Taylor," 1957).

44. On this point, John D'Emilio in *Sexual Politics, Sexual Communities* concurs, remarking that Kinsey's "information served not to ameliorate hostility toward gay men and women, but to magnify suddenly the proportions of the danger they allegedly posed." He notes however that "in the long run the information provided by Kinsey would become an important element in the rationale for law reform" (1983, 37).

45. Quoting Foucault, "[What] makes the domination of a group, a caste, or a class, together with the resistance and revolts that domination comes up against, a central phenomenon in the history of societies is that they manifest in a massive and global form, at the level of the whole social body, the locking-together of power relations with relations of strategy and the results proceeding from their interaction" (1994, 348).

Chapter 6. Uses of Action 1: Beatty, Dunham, & McKayle

1. Quotation is from a program note for a performance before a segregated audience in Louisville, Tennessee, Memorial Auditorium October 19, 1944 (Clark and Wilkerson, 1978, 88).

2. Thanks to Priya Srinivasan to helping me formulate this point as well as for her comments on this chapter.

3. In his autobiography, McKayle gives a detailed account of the experience preparing and performing on television, including his memory of a moment in which he realized his work would be seen by millions of viewers across the country: "On the way to the stage, I passed a room where a sixteen-millimeter film camera was set up in front of a monitor to record the direct shoot that was to be beamed out live to all CBS hookups across the country. This kinescope would be the remaining record of the performance" (McKayle 2002, 118).

4. In the postwar period, the most notable instance of the use of nonviolent direct action prior to the sit-ins in Greensboro was the bus boycott in Montgomery, Alabama, organized by Martin Luther King Jr., in December 1955. In Montgomery, protesters staged a boycott of public transportation in their challenge of Jim Crow laws that forced them to sit at the back of city buses. For more see King 1958.

5. According to Stephan and Abigail Thernstrom, "King became a convinced advocate of nonviolence only after experiencing violence directed against his wife and infant daughter." After a stick of dynamite blew up on King's front porch on January 30, 1956, the day the Montgomery Improvement Association voted to pursue legal action against the city, an angry crowd of African Americans surrounded the house. They were met by police, with whom they exchanged threats of violence (1997, 111). Acknowledging the futility of the situation (as the police possessed an overwhelming capacity of force), King "calmed the angry crowd . . . by warning that 'he who lives by the sword, dies by the sword'; 'love your enemies,' 'meet hate with love,' he urged" (King 1958, 136).

6. In *Civilities and Civil Rights*, William H. Chafe asserts that "[i]n the long view of history, the Greensboro sit-ins will justifiably be seen as the catalyst that triggered a decade of

revolt—one of the greatest movements in history toward self-determination and human dignity. America would never be the same again once students discovered the power of direct-action protest and others followed their example" (1980, 137). According to Jack Bloom, "By the end of February, thirty-two cities in North Carolina, South Carolina, Virginia, Tennessee, Florida, Maryland, Kentucky, and Alabama had experienced sit-ins and other demonstrations protesting racial restrictions. By the end of March another forty-one cities had been subject to these demonstrations, and Georgia, Texas, Louisiana, and Arkansas were added to the list of states struck. In April even Mississippi joined" (1987, 157).

7. In Kowal 2004, I offer a detailed analysis of the Greensboro sit-ins as "choreography."

8. In the next chapter, I will examine the ways in which choreography of Anna Halprin in the late 1950s and early 1960s deployed tactics of defamiliarization similarly to disrupt normative conventions of thinking and behaving.

9. CORE's membership included former members of the MOWM.

10. Sending a message to black leaders did not always happen peacefully or in an organized fashion. Singh details how, in the early 1940s, "incidents of racial violence, often involving servicemen, police, and war production workers," increased in cities across the country (105). In Detroit, for example, a conflict erupted between black and white residents that lasted for over forty hours, killing thirty-four and wounding hundreds of others. And, in 1943 and 1944, racial conflicts in New York City and Philadelphia caused President Roosevelt to activate over 13,000 members of the national guard (2004, 105–6).

11. Gandhi had used passive resistance in leading Indians in their drive for independence from Great Britain, finally acquired in 1947 after twenty-six years of struggle. For more on Gandhi's method of "passive resistance," see Gregg 1959, 24–29.

12. "CORE Rules for Action," published by the Congress of Racial Equality, New York in Laue [1965] (1989, 7).

13. By the mid-1960s, even the "new tactics" suggested by Lomax, such as nonviolent direct action protest, seemed too little, too late. As David Chalmers argues, "[B]y 1966 the mood and phase had changed. Street marches were no longer an effective instrument" (1991, 31). The Black Power movement partly filled the void. For more on black nationalism, see Carmichael and Hamilton 1967 and Grier and Cobbs 1968.

14. In the next chapter, I will detail the "training" process for protesters which involved, in effect, giving people an improvisatory "score" or structure for performing the act of sitting-in. It involved both the preparation for the event as well as contingency plans that would govern how protesters would respond to onlookers in a variety of situations.

15. Conditions in the South contributed to the perception that "older techniques of legal and legislative action had proved themselves limited instruments" (Meier and Rudwick 1970, 7). The Supreme Court's 1954 *Brown v. Board of Education* ruling outlawing the segregation of public schools had encountered "massive resistance" and incited violence throughout the South (Bartley 1969). In spite of NAACP and community-based efforts to register black voters, which had raised the total number of those eligible from 250,000 to 1.25 million and a quarter, "black people were still disfranchised in most of the South" (Meier and Rudwick 1970, 7). Court rulings ordering the desegregation of public accommodations "were largely ignored" (ibid.). Hooligan incidents of violence and intimidation of blacks were on the rise and membership in the Ku Klux Klan "expanded considerably," its tactics of cross burnings, house torchings, and lynchings increasing as

well. In fact, of the eleven lynchings of blacks during the 1950s, eight occurred during 1955 (Patterson 1996, 396–97).

Furthermore, legislators and politicians failed to uphold the law due to their own racist beliefs. On the congressional level, in 1956, nineteen of the South's twenty-two senators and eighty-two of its 106 representatives combined forces to pen the "Southern Manifesto," a document declaring their opposition to school desegregation (Patterson 1996, 398). On the state level, governors such as James Byrnes of South Carolina and Herman Talmadge of Georgia expressed blatant hostility toward the Supreme Court as well as their intention to defy its ruling. Talmadge, for example, commented, "I do not believe in Negroes and whites associating with each other socially or in our school systems, and as long as I am governor, it won't happen" (quoted in Patterson 1996, 392). Neither could ordinary citizens be counted on to follow the dictates of the courts. Citizens' council groups, composed of "respectable people, including bankers, lawyers, and businessmen" (Patterson 1996, 397), sprouted up in cities and towns across the South. According to James Patterson, however, these groups "publicly deplored violence but condoned a great deal of it and did not act to bring perpetrators to justice. They stood four-square for the perpetration of Jim Crow, including racial segregation in the schools. They repeatedly denounced the Supreme Court, liberals, and northerners in general" (ibid.).

Conditions perpetuating racism were not limited to the South: in spite of court orders upholding the equal rights of blacks, discrimination in employment, housing, and healthcare was widespread throughout the United States. Patterson points out, in fact, that "discrimination in housing solidified an already widespread de facto segregation in northern schools." This, he observes, "prevented black children from attending much-better-financed white schools. In short, African-American children were denied the basic right of equal opportunity" (1996, 384). What is more, "poverty afflicted 50 percent or more of blacks even in the economically good years of the mid-1950s." And, starting in 1954, the rate of unemployment among blacks began to rise (Meier and Rudwick 1970, 7).

16. My description of the solo is taken from the performances of the piece featured in *Free to Dance*, vol. II. These include portions of the piece performed by Beatty, and other portions performed by Jerome Stigler from Dayton Contemporary Dance Ensemble.

17. This essay was originally published in the *Antioch Review*, Summer 1945, 60–101.

18. This essay, "Blues People," was originally published the *New York Review*, February 6, 1964.

19. See also Wright 1957, 109.

20. Richard Powell marks a trend among black visual artists in the postwar period of "expressions of universal goodwill or the circumventions of politics" (114). But he also examines the work of others who "adopted a humanitarian stance in their work and, reminiscent of the activist politics of artists in the 1930s, directed their efforts toward an art of social engagement and protest" (114). This group included Elizabeth Catlett, Charles White, Philip Evergood, Robert Gwathmey, and Jacob Lawrence. As Powell details, "These artists, frustrated rather than heartened by race relations in the post-war years, joined organizations like the NAACP and the National Negro and Civil Rights Congresses; they exhibited in galleries and art venues that—in this period of abstraction and thematic disengagement in the arts—promoted figurative or social realist work; and they aligned themselves with like-minded, civil rights activists, both in the U.S. and abroad, risking from right-wing factions the dreaded 'Communist' label" (1997, 114, 116). Moreover, they associated themselves with the larger milieu of activist artists primarily living in

New York City. These included playwright Lorraine Hansberry (*Raisin in the Sun*, 1959), who wrote the essay for White's 1961 exhibition catalogue at the ACA Gallery in New York City. Powell contends that "seen alongside" events like the 1955 Montgomery Bus Boycott, works by these artists "raised the specter of inequality in a so-called American democracy, drew attention to the frightening truths about white-on-black violence, and focused on examples of endurance and moral tenacity in the face of these obstacles" (118).

21. This quotation comes from an interview of Ralph Ellison conducted by Richard G. Stern, originally published in *December*, Winter 1961.

22. Similarly, in an essay examining the poetry of Sterling Brown, Beverly Skinner argues, "Adherents of a black and blues ontology couch their critique of an oppressive, racist system in an intentionally ambiguous language and in an ambiguous expressivity, both of which celebrate a culture whose autonomous existence has paradoxically thrived, fed by its own special view of the system. The culture can exist separately from the dominant culture because of its ability to flourish in spite of systemic abuse" (1998, 1000).

23. My account is based on McKayle's reconstruction of the dance at the University of Iowa in fall 2006.

24. The Symphony of Chile commissioned *Southland*. It was premiered in Santiago in January 1951, although Dunham had conducted rehearsals in Buenos Aires (Hill 2002, 293).

25. My synthesis of the piece is taken from the detailed description offered by Hill (2002, 293–310).

26. Dunham came before the Dance Advisory Panel several times for decisions about state-sponsored touring. During a meeting on August 28, 1958, for example, Dunham was discussed by members. The minutes summarize the discussion as follows:

> In a *Variety* article last summer Miss Dunham talked about the unsatisfactory treatment she felt she had received from this Program. We have since received [a] letter from her Congressman, forwarding her account of interviews she has had with this office. We have not heard from Miss Dunham directly, but should she present herself again, we wish to know what action should be taken. The Panel some time ago felt she had fallen off in her presentations, but more recently had said that they would consider a specific project if it came up. . . . Miss Dunham is a great artist and a great showman, and should be given the fullest consideration. (Dance Advisory Panel Meeting 1958; see also Prevots 1998, 102–5 for more information)

27. The Montgomery bus boycott began on December 1, 1955, in Montgomery, Alabama. It was prompted by the action of Mrs. Rosa Parks, a middle-aged seamstress, part-time department-store clerk, and administrator at the local National Association for the Advancement of Colored People (NAACP), who did not move to the back of a bus as directed by the white driver. Interestingly, Parks' action bears the hallmarks of Skinner's "black and blues ontology," in that she expressed outrage not through a direct confrontation with the driver, but by deliberately ignoring the racist protocol of Jim Crow. Describing Parks' act, Reverend Martin Luther King Jr. commented, "eventually the cup of endurance runs over, and the human personality cries out, 'I can take it no longer.' Mrs. Parks' refusal to move back was her intrepid affirmation that she had had enough. It was an individual expression of a timeless longing for human dignity and freedom" (Martin Luther King Jr. 1958, 44). Parks' noncompliance may have landed her in jail, but this did

not quell the resolve of Montgomery blacks, who carried out a community-wide boycott of the city's buses that lasted for almost a year. Eventually, in November 1956, the U.S. Supreme Court upheld a U.S. District Court decision that Alabama's laws requiring the segregation of public buses were unconstitutional. The court ruling validated the efforts of the NAACP, whose lawyers had argued the case. They took the result as an endorsement of their belief that the best route to racial equality was through the courts and local and federal legislatures. Nevertheless, the success of the boycott illustrated the power of nonviolent direct action as a form of mass protest. Accordingly, in 1957, King founded the Southern Christian Leadership Conference (SCLC), an organization dedicated to the coordination of direct-action activities across the South (Meier and Rudwick 1970, 6). Indeed, while the resolution of the Montgomery bus boycott did not weaken the argument that it was best to pursue civil rights through legal means, it suggested that waiting on courts was certainly not the swiftest way of effecting change.

28. For more on the Greensboro Four see Proudfoot [1962] 1990; Chafe 1980; Kowal 2004.

29. As I have shown in earlier chapters, establishment critics and practitioners of modern dance sought the demonstration of "humanity" in works of choreography regardless of who choreographed them. They favored the work of artists who drew on lived experience for their subject matter, while they also expected that choreographers would pursue the universal implications of these subject experiences, thus enlarging the "human" implications of their choreography. As I discussed in chapter 4 with respect to Pearl Primus, whereas choreographers of Anglo or even Latin descent (e.g., José Limón) had more flexibility when it came to adopting subject matter outside of their particular personal experience, African-American choreographers were criticized when they strayed too far from what was assumed to be "Negro" subject matter. For more on this see Manning 2004.

30. For more on the aesthetic expectations for the representation of black masculinity in midcentury modern dance, see DeFrantz 1996 and 2004b.

31. For example, in review of Alvin Ailey's 1959 season at the 92nd YM-YWHA, P. W. Manchester commented, "After so many modern dance performances in which dancers drift about with blank faces and a general neutralization that denies the existence of sex even in the midst of the most complex entwinings, how refreshing to enter the stage world created by Alvin Ailey in which the men are men and the women are frankly delighted about it."

32. My description is taken from the 1960 television broadcast performed by the original cast including McKayle, Mary Hinkson, and Alfred Desio as soloists, Leon Bibb as the singing soloist, and set to music arranged by Robert Corman and Milton Okun.

33. These lyrics were confirmed through e-mail correspondence with McKayle on April 20, 2007.

34. These lyrics were confirmed through e-mail correspondence with McKayle on April 20, 2007.

35. For example, see DeFrantz 2004a and Morris 2006.

Chapter 7. Uses of Action 2: Halprin

1. Ann Halprin changed her name to "Anna" in 1972. Since she is known as Anna today, in this chapter I will refer to her as "Anna." In subsequent footnotes, I will cite her name as it is written on any given publication.

2. Halprin founded her company, the San Francisco Dancers' Workshop, in 1959.

3. In my correspondence with Halprin (her letter dated July 28, 1999) I learned that she and her family had been involved in the civil rights movement. In answer to my question about the extent of her involvement she answered: "I was part of it and my family was jailed." While her answer gives insight into her political consciousness at the time of the civil rights movement, I have so far been unable to reach Halprin to learn the details of her activity and her jailing. For a fuller account of *Ceremony of Us*, including an interview with Halprin, a score of "instructions to performers," and a review, see Halprin 1995, 152–68.

4. For more, see Banes 1983, 1989, and 1993; and Burt 2006.

5. On July 13, 1957, Merce Cunningham gave a lecture-demonstration at Halprin's home in Kentfield, California. On her "dance-deck," he performed excerpts from *Suite for Five* (1956), *Dime a Dance* (1953), and *Untitled Solo* (1954). For excerpts of his lecture, see Vaughan 1997, 100–101.

6. In this interview, Halprin characterized her approach to choreography in the following way: "Labels are just what I wish to avoid in my compositions. I'm searching for diversity and spontaneity that defy categories because they're never in the same place in quite the same way twice. There's a Sanskrit term which argues my orientation to dance: *See an ordinary object for the first time* (emphasis in original)."

7. As Fredric Jameson has pointed out, "The purpose of the Brechtian estrangement-effect is . . . a political one in the most thoroughgoing sense of the word; it is, as Brecht insisted over and over, to make you aware that the objects and institutions you thought to be natural were really only historical: the result of change, they themselves henceforth become in their turn changeable" (Jameson 1972, 58). For more on Bertolt Brecht's Epic theater, see Willett [1957] 1964.

8. For more on the chronology of Halprin's early career, see Diane Turner 1989 and Ross 2006.

9. From a collection of Halprin's writings between 1949 and 1957, see "The Marin County Dance Co-operatives: Teaching Dance to Children" in Halprin 1995, 25.

10. For more on Halprin's work with H'Doubler, see J. Ross 2000.

11. The interview with Rainer was originally published in the *Tulane Drama Review*, vol. 10, no. 5, Winter 1965.

12. In her discussion of Halprin's early work, Janice Ross traces the choreographer's ideas to the work of Marcel Duchamp and John Cage. According to Ross, the three shared the notion that "if one shifted the context around mundane sounds, objects or actions, if one reframed the unnoticed, then this focusing of our perception could render the familiar strange, and the strange was art" (73). See Ross in Halprin 1995, 72–74.

13. Halprin speaks about the great degree to which she collaborated with artists on *Five-Legged Stool*, especially painter Jo Landor (Halprin 1995, 84).

14. A film of this piece is not available, so I must rely upon Pierce's account.

15. I have imagined these questions based on the ones the performers asked.

16. This quotation comes from King's address to the members of the First Montgomery Improvement Association (MIA) in December 1955. The full passage from which it is taken follows: "We are here this evening for serious business. [Audience:] (*Yes*) We are here in a general sense because first and foremost we are American citizens (*That's right*), and we are determined to apply our citizenship to the fullness of its meaning. (*Yeah. That's right*) We are here also because of our love for democracy (*Yes*), because of our deep-seated belief that democracy transformed from thin paper to thick action (*Yes*) is the greatest form of government on earth. (*That's right*)" (King 1955).

REFERENCES

"1,345 Huts to Ease Housing Need Here." *New York Times*, January 6, 1946, 34.

"5,000 Quonset Huts Urged on City Housing Crisis." *New York Times*, December 17, 1945, 1.

"Aaron and Martha." *Newsweek*, May 28, 1945, 106–107.

Ailey, Alvin. *Revelations: The Autobiography of Alvin Ailey*. Secaucus, N.J.: Carol Publishing Group, 1995.

Albright, Ann Cooper. *Choreographing Difference: The Body and Identity in Contemporary Dance*. Hanover, N.H.: Wesleyan University Press / University Press of New England, 1997.

Alhen, Robert. "U.S. Dance Troupe Wins Applause with Modernist Program in Paris." *New York Times International Edition*, April 14, 1962.

Alperovitz, Gar. *Atomic Diplomacy: Hiroshima and Potsdam, the Use of the Atomic Bomb and the American Confrontation with Soviet Power*. New York: Simon and Schuster, 1965.

———. *Atomic Diplomacy: The Use of the Atomic Bomb and the American Confrontation with Soviet Power*. [1965] New York: Viking Penguin Inc. Reprint, 1985.

"'American Dance' Season in Its Final Week." *New York Times*, May 15, 1955, X8.

Anawalt, Sasha. "For Donald McKayle, the Dance Goes On." *New York Times*, December 15, 1991, H25.

Anderson, Jack. "Ann Halprin Believes the Potency of Avant-Garde Theatre and Dance Increases When Artists Learn Each Other's Arts." *Dance Magazine*, November 1966.

———. "Dancers and Architects Build Kinetic Environments." *Dance Magazine*, 1966.

———. "The Paradoxes of James Waring." *Dance Magazine*, November 1968, 64–67, 90–91.

———. "San Francisco." *Ballet Today*, March 1961, 18.

Anderson, Terry. "The Struggle." In *The Movement & the Sixties*, 43–86. Oxford: Oxford University Press, 1995.

"Anna Sokolow." *Dance Magazine*, January 1944, 9.

"Anna Sokolow Dance Company." *Dance Magazine*, April 1958, 26–27.

"Anna Sokolow Dance Company." *Dance Magazine*, February 1959, 28.

Anna Sokolow Interviewed at ADF. VHS. Durham: American Dance Festival, Duke University, Lilly Library, 1991.

Appadurai, Arjun. "Disjuncture and Difference in the Global Cultural Economy." In *The Phantom Public Sphere*, edited by Bruce Robbins, 269–95. Minneapolis: University of Minnesota Press, 1993.

Appy, Christian G., ed. *Cold War Constructions: The Political Culture of United States Imperialism, 1945–1966*. Amherst: The University of Massachusetts Press, 2000.

Aronowitz, Stanley. *False Promises: The Shaping of American Working Class Consciousness*. New York: McGraw-Hill, 1973.

Aschenbrenner, Joyce. *Katherine Dunham: Dancing a Life*. Urbana and Chicago: University of Illinois Press, 2002.

Ashton, Dore. *About Rothko*. New York: Oxford University Press, 1983.

———. "The City and the Visual Arts." In *New York: Culture Capital of the World*, edited by Leonard Wallock, 123–155. New York: Rizzoli, 1988.

————. *The New York School: A Cultural Reckoning*. Berkeley: University of California Press, 1972.

Atwood, William. "Why Does He Work So Hard?" *Look*, March 4, 1958, 71–74.

Ausfeld, Margaret Lynn. "Circus Girl Arrested: A History of the Advancing American Art Collection, 1946–48." In *Advancing American Art: Politics and Aesthetics in the State Department Exhibition, 1946–48*, 11–34. Montgomery, Ala.: Museum of Fine Arts, 1984.

Auslander, Philip, and Carrie Sandahl, ed. *Bodies in Commotion: Disability & Performance*. Ann Arbor: The University of Michigan Press, 2005.

Austin, J. L. *How to Do Things with Words*. Cambridge: Harvard University Press. Reprint, 1972.

Badiou, Alain. *Deleuze: The Clamor of Being*. Translated by Louise Burchill. Edited by Michael Hardt, Sandra Buckley, and Brain Massumi. Vol. 16, *Theory Out of Bounds*. Minneapolis: University of Minnesota Press, 2000.

Bagli, Charles V., and Janny Scott. "110 Building Site in N.Y. Is Put up for Sale." *New York Times*, August 30, 2006.

Baker, Houston A., Jr. *Blues, Ideology, and Afro-American Literature: A Vernacular Theory*. Chicago: University of Chicago Press, 1984.

————. "Critical Memory and the Black Public Sphere." In *The Black Public Sphere*, edited by The Black Public Sphere Collective, 5–38. Chicago: University of Chicago Press, 1995.

Baker, Lee D. *From Savage to Negro: Anthropology and the Construction of Race, 1896–1954*. Berkeley: University of California Press, 1999.

Bakhtin, Mikhail M. *The Dialogic Imagination*. Translated by Caryl Emerson and Michael Holquist. Edited by Michael Holquist. Austin: University of Texas Press, 1981.

Balcom, Lois. "Anna Sokolow." *Dance Observer*, January 1944, 9.

————. "The Negro Dances Himself." *Dance Observer*, December 1944, 122–24.

————. "What Chance Has the Negro Dancer?" *Dance Observer*, November 1944, 110.

Baldwin, Hanson W. "A Two-Bloc World?" *New York Times*, October 26, 1945, 4.

Banes, Sally. *Dancing Women: Female Bodies on Stage*. New York: Routledge, 1995.

————. *Democracy's Body: Judson Dance Theater 1962–1964*. Ann Arbor: University of Michigan Research Press, 1983.

————. *Greenwich Village 1963: Avant-Garde, Performance, and the Effervescent Body*. Durham: Duke University Press, 1993.

————. "Gulliver's Hamburger: Defamiliarization and the Ordinary in the 1960s." In *Reinventing Dance in the 1960s: Everything Was Possible*, edited by Sally Banes, 3–23. Madison: University of Wisconsin Press, 2003.

————. "Introduction." In *Anna Halprin, Moving toward Life*. Hanover, N.H.: Wesleyan University Press / University Press of New England, 1995.

————. *Reinventing Dance in the 1960s: Everything Was Possible*. Madison: University of Wisconsin Press, 2003.

————. *Terpsichore in Sneakers: Post-Modern Dance*. Middletown, Conn.: Wesleyan University Press, 1987.

Baraka, Amiri Imanu. *Blues People*. New York: William Morrow, 1963.

Barr, Alfred H., Jr. "Is Modern Art Communistic?" *New York Times Magazine*, December 14, 1952, 22–23.

Barry, Joseph A. "At Last the 'Radiant City.'" *New York Times Magazine* (June 4, 1950): 22+.

Bartlett, K. S. "Talley Beatty Company in Vivid Performance at John Hancock Hall." *Boston Globe*, January 15, 1952.

Bartley, Numan. *The Rise of Massive Resistance: Race and Politics in the South During the 1950s*. Baton Rouge: Louisiana State University Press, 1969.

Battey, Jean. "Booing Doesn't Faze Way-out Dancer." *The Washington Post and Times Herald*, April 11, 1959, 10.

Beckford, Ruth. *Katherine Dunham: A Biography*. New York: Marcel Dekker, 1979.

Beiswanger, George. "New London: Residues and Reflections." *Dance Observer*, February 1957, 21–23.

Belgrad, Daniel. *Culture of Spontaneity: Improvisation and the Arts in Postwar America*. Chicago: The University of Chicago Press, 1998.

Bell, Daniel. *The End of Ideology: On the Exhaustion of Political Ideas in the Fifties*. [1960] New York: The Free Press. Reprint, 1962.

Bennett, Susan. *Theater Audiences: A Theory of Production and Reception*. London: Routledge, 1990.

Benston, Kimberly. "I Yam What I Yam: The Topos of (Un)Naming in Afro-American Literature." In *Black Literature and Literary Theory*, edited by Henry Louis Gates Jr., 151–74. New York: Routledge. Reprint, 1990.

Bernstein, Harry. "Sophie Maslow and Company, Daniel Nagrin and Anna Sokolow and Company." *Dance Observer*, June–July 1959, 94.

Berube, Michael. *Coming Out under Fire: The History of Gay Men and Women and World War II*. New York: Free Press, 1990.

Bhabha, Homi. "Of Mimicry and Man: The Ambivalence of Colonial Discourse." *October* 28 (Spring 1984): 125–133.

Blake, Peter. "Le Corbusier." *New York Times Magazine*, June 25, 1950, 4.

Bloom, Jack. *Class, Race, and the Civil Rights Movement*. Bloomington: Indiana University Press, 1987.

Blyth, R. H., ed. *Japanese Life and Character in Senryu*. Tokyo: Hokuseido Press, 1960.

Borstelmann, Thomas. *The Cold War and the Color Line: American Race Relations in the Global Arena*. Cambridge, Mass.: Harvard University Press, 2001.

Boyer, Paul. *By the Bomb's Early Light: American Thought and Culture at the Dawn of the Atomic Age*. Chapel Hill: The University of North Carolina Press, 1994.

Braden, Anne. "The Southern Freedom Movement in Perspective." In *We Shall Overcome: The Civil Rights Movement in the United States in the 1950s and 1960s*, vol. 1, edited by David J. Garrow, 55–150. Brooklyn: Carlson, 1989.

Brands, H. W. *The Devil We Know: Americans and the Cold War*. New York: Oxford University Press, 1993.

Brecht, Bertolt. *Brecht on Theatre: The Development of an Aesthetic*. Translated by John Willett. Edited by John Willett. New York: Hill and Wang, 1964.

Breines, Wini. "The Other Fifties: Beats, Bad Girls, and Rock and Roll." In *Young, White, and Miserable: Growing up Female in the Fifties*, 127–166. Boston: Beacon, 1992.

Brinkley, Alan. "The Illusion of Unity in Cold War Culture." In *Rethinking Cold War Culture*, edited by Peter J. Kuznick and James Gilbert. Washington, D.C.: Smithsonian Institution Press, 2001.

Brockway, Merrill. "Merce Cunningham and Dance Company," *Dance in America*. VHS. New York: WNET/Thirteen, 1977.

Brooks, Daphne. *Bodies in Dissent: Spectacular Performances of Race and Freedom, 1850–1910*. Durham: Duke University Press, 2006.

Brown, Earle, Remy Charlip, Marianne Simon, and David Vaughan. "The Forming of an Aesthetic: Merce Cunningham and John Cage." *Ballet Review* 13, no. 3 (1985): 23–40.

Browning, Barbara. "Breast Milk Is Sweet and Salty (a Choreography of Healing)." In *Of the Presence of the Body: Essays on Dance and Performance Theory*, edited by André Lepecki, 97–112. Middletown, Conn.: Wesleyan University Press, 2004.

Buckland, Fiona. *Impossible Dance: Club Culture and Queer World-Making*. Middletown, Conn.: Wesleyan University Press, 2002.

Burns, Stewart. "We Shall All Be Free." In *Social Movements of the 1960s: Searching for Democracy*, 1–52. Boston: Twayne, 1990.

Burt, Ramsay. "Dance, Gender and Psychoanalysis: Martha Graham's *Night Journey*." *Dance Research Journal* 30, no. 1 (1998): 34–53.

———. "Dissolving in Pleasure: The Threat of the Queer Male Dancing Body." In *Dancing Desires: Choreographing Sexualities On & Off the Stage*, edited by Jane Desmond, 209–242. Madison: University of Wisconsin Press, 2001.

———. *Judson Dance Theater: Performative Traces*. London: Routledge, 2006.

———. *The Male Dancer: Bodies, Spectacles, Sexualities*. London: Routledge, 1995.

Butler, Judith. *Bodies That Matter: On the Discursive Limits of "Sex."* New York: Routledge, 1993.

———. *Gender Trouble: Feminism and the Subversion of Identity*. New York: Routledge, 1990a.

———. "Imitation and Gender Insubordination." In *Inside/Out: Lesbian Theories, Gay Theories*, edited by Diana Fuss, 13–29. New York: Routledge, 1991.

———. "Performative Acts and Gender Constitution: An Essay in Phenomenology and Feminist Theory." In *Performing Feminisms: Feminist Theory and Theatre*, edited by Sue Ellen Case, 270–282. Baltimore: Johns Hopkins University Press, 1990b.

Cage/Cunningham. VHS. Directed by Elliot Caplan. West Branch, N.J.: Kultur, 1991.

Cage, John. *Empty Words*. Middletown, Conn.: Wesleyan University Press, 1979.

———. "In This Day . . . " *Dance Observer*, January 1957, 10.

———. *Silence: Lectures and Writings*. Middletown, Conn.: Wesleyan University Press, 1961.

Campbell, D'Ann. *Women at War with America: Private Lives in a Patriotic Era*. Cambridge: Harvard University Press, 1984.

Cantril, Hadley. "How Real Is America's 'Internationalism'?" *New York Times*, April 29, 1945, SM5.

Caplan, Elliot, and Merce Cunningham. "Points in Space." BBC TV in association with Cunningham Dance Foundation, 1987.

Carmichael, Stokely, and Charles V. Hamilton. *Black Power: The Politics of Liberation in America*. New York: Vintage, 1967.

Caro, Robert. "The City-Shaper." *The New Yorker*, January 5, 1998, 38–50.

———. *The Power Broker: Robert Moses and the Fall of New York*. New York: Knopf, 1974.

Carter, Alexandra, ed. *Rethinking Dance History: A Reader*. London: Routledge, Taylor and Francis Group, 2004.

Carter, Michael. "Pearl Primus Dances Out Social Problems." *Afro-American*, July 22, 1944, 5.

Carter, Susan B. et al. "Table Ab11–30 Live births, deaths, infant deaths, marriages, and divorces, by race: 1909–1998." In *Historical Statistics of the United States Millennial Edition On Line*. http://hsus.cambridge.org/HSUSWeb/HSUSEntryServlet (accessed January 9, 2009).

Case, Sue-Ellen, ed. *Performing Feminisms: Feminist Critical Theory and Theatre*. Baltimore: The Johns Hopkins University Press, 1990.

Case, Sue-Ellen, Philip Brett, and Susan Leigh Foster, ed. *Cruising the Performative: Interventions into the Representation of Ethnicity, Nationality, and Sexuality.* Bloomington: Indiana University Press, 1995.

"Ceremony of Us." *The Drama Review* 13, no. 4 (1969): 132–43.

Cerf, Walter. "Book Review: J. L. Austin's *How to Do Things with Words.*" *Mind* 75, no. 298 (1966): 262–85.

Chafe, William. *Civilities and Civil Rights: Greensboro, North Carolina, and the Black Struggle for Equality.* New York: Oxford University Press, 1980.

———. *The Paradox of Change: American Women in the Twentieth Century.* New York: Oxford University Press, 1991.

Chalmers, David. *And the Crooked Places Made Straight: The Struggle for Social Change in the 1960s.* Baltimore: Johns Hopkins University Press, 1991.

Chambers, Ross. *Room for Maneuver: Reading (the) Oppositional (in) Narrative.* Chicago: University of Chicago Press, 1991.

"Chaos, Damn It!" *Time*, November 20, 1950.

Charlip, Remy. "Composing by Chance." *Dance Magazine,* January 1954, 17, 19.

Chatterjea, Ananya. *Butting Out: Reading Resistive Choreographies through Works by Jawole Willa Jo Zollar and Chandralekha.* Middletown, Conn.: Wesleyan University Press, 2004.

Chauncey, George. *Gay New York: Gender, Urban Culture, and the Making of the Gay Male World, 1890–1940.* New York: Basic, 1994.

———. "Offering the Cream of a Half-Century of Name-Brand Gay Life and Gossip." *New York Times*, December 30, 1997, E12.

Chujoy, Anatole. "Paul Taylor and Dance Company, Hunter Playhouse, N.Y., Feb. 13." *Dance News*, March 1960.

———. "Paul Taylor and Dance Company, Hunter Playhouse, N.Y., Jan. 12." *Dance News*, February 1961.

Church, Marjorie. "Anna Sokolow." *Dance Observer*, March 1948, 32.

———. "Anna Sokolow and Dance Unit." *Dance Observer*, March 1937, 41.

———. "Anna Sokolow and Dance Unit." *Dance Observer*, April 1937, 41.

———. "'The Dance in the Social Scene.'" *Dance Observer*, December 1937, 27, 30.

———. "Talley Beatty and Company Performance at the Central High School of Needle Trades, New York." *Dance Observer*, January 1948, 7.

Clark, Clifford E., Jr. "Ranch House Suburbia: Ideals and Realities." In *Recasting America*, edited by Lary May, 171–194. Chicago: University of Chicago Press, 1989.

Clark, Keith. "Re-(W)Righting Black Male Subjectivity: The Communal Poetics of Ernest Gaines's 'a Gathering of Old Men.'" *Callaloo* 22, no. 1 (1999): 195–207.

Clark, VèVè A. "Performing the Memory of Difference in Afro-Caribbean Dance: Katherine Dunham's Choreography, 1938–87." In *History and Memory in African-American Culture*, edited by Geneviève Fabre and Robert O'Meally, 188–204. New York and Oxford: Oxford University Press, 1994.

Clark, VèVè A., and Sara E. Johnson, ed. *Kaiso! Writings by and About Katherine Dunham.* Madison, Wis.: The University of Wisconsin Press, 2005.

Clark, VèVè A., and Margaret Wilkerson, ed. *Kaiso! Katherine Dunham: An Anthology of Writings.* Berkeley: University of California Press, 1978.

Claude Barnett Collection. "Pearl Primus Surrenders Passport to State Department." Box 291, Folder 7: Associated Negro Press, Chicago History Museum, n.d.

Clayton, Jay. *The Pleasures of Babel: Contemporary American Literature and Theory*. New York: Oxford University Press, 1993.

Clifford, James. "Histories of Tribal and Modern." In *Discourses: Conversations in Postmodern Art and Culture*, edited by Russell Ferguson et al., 408–24: New Museum of Century Art and M.I.T. Press, 1990.

———. *Routes: Travel and Translation in the Late Twentieth Century*. Cambridge: Harvard University Press, 1997.

———. *Writing Culture: The Poetics and Politics of Ethnography*. Berkeley: University of California Press, 1986.

Cockcroft, Eva. "Abstract Expressionism: Weapon of the Cold War." *Artforum* June (1974): 39–41.

Coe, Robert. "A Master of Modern Dance." *New York Times Magazine*, April 5, 1981.

Cohen-Cruz, Jan. "Motion of the Ocean: The Shifting Face of U.S. Theater for Social Change since the 1960s." *Theater* 2001 31(3): 95–107.

Cohen, Selma Jeanne. "Dance as a Form of Pure Movement." *Christian Science Monitor*, January 28, 1961a.

———. "Donald McKayle, Kevin Carlisle and Cos. 92nd Street 'Y'" May 10, 1959." *Dance Magazine*, July 1959, 17+.

———. *The Modern Dance: Seven Statements of Belief*. Middletown, Conn.: Wesleyan University Press, 1965.

———. "Paul Taylor and Dance Company, Hunter Playhouse, January 14, 1961." *Dance Magazine*, March 1961b, 23.

Coleman, Martha. "On the Teaching of Choreography." *Dance Observer* December (1950): 148–50.

"Community Recreation Film Available to Civic Groups." *The American City*, July 1950, 7.

Cooper, Lee E. "Housing Shortage Held Due to Stay for 2 More Years." *New York Times*, September 21, 1947, R1.

———. "Housing Shortage Most Keenly Felt in Largest Cities." *New York Times*, October 26, 1947, R1.

———. "Many Factors Involved in the Housing Crisis." *New York Times*, May 25, 1947, E7.

Copeland, Roger. "Beyond Expression: Merce Cunningham's Critique of 'the Natural.'" In *Dance History: An Introduction*, edited by Janet Adshead-Lansdale and June Layson. London: Routledge, 1994.

———. *Merce Cunningham: The Modernizing of Modern Dance*. New York: Routledge, 2004.

Croce, Arlene. *Afterimages*. New York: Knopf. Reprint, 1977.

———. "Dancing: 'La Sacre' without Ceremony." *The New Yorker*, May 19, 1980.

———. "Dancing: Lechery in Nuns." *The New Yorker*, June 19, 1978, 82–84.

"Cunningham and His Dancers," *Ballet Review* 15:3, Fall 1987, 19–40.

Cunningham, Merce. "The Function of a Technique for Dance." In *Merce Cunningham: Fifty Years*, edited by Melissa Harris. New York: Aperture, 1951, 60–61.

———. "The Impermanent Art." In *Merce Cunningham: Fifty Years*, edited by Melissa Harris. New York: Aperture, 1952, 86–87.

———. "Space, Time and Dance." In *Merce Cunningham: Fifty Years*, edited by Melissa Harris. New York: Aperture, 1952, 66–67.

———. "Summerspace Story: How a Dance Came to Be." *Dance Magazine*, June 1966, 52–54.

"Dance Advisory Panel, International Cultural Exchange Program Minutes." Edited by The American National Academy and Theater and the U.S. Information Agency: Special Collections Division, Mullins Library, University of Arkansas, Fayetteville, March 10, 1955, April 7, 1955, May 5, 1955, September 15, 1955, October 13, 1955, November 17, 1955, December 22, 1955, January 19, 1956, March 20, 1958.

"Dance: Artistic Calvinist." *New Republic*, March 15, 1948, 30.

"Dance Magazine's 1961 Awards: Three Women in American Dance." *Dance Magazine*, March 1962, 32, 34, 52.

"Dancers to Tour in South America." *New York Times*, November 12, 1954, 15.

D'Emilio, John. "The Homosexual Menace: The Politics of Sexuality in Cold War America." In *Passion and Power: Sexuality in History*, edited by Kathy Peiss. Philadelphia: Temple University Press, 1989.

———. *Sexual Politics, Sexual Commodities: The Making of a Homosexual Minority in the United States, 1940–1970*. Chicago: University of Chicago Press, 1983.

D'Emilio, John, and Estelle B. Freedman. *Intimate Matters: A History of Sexuality in America*. Chicago: University of Chicago Press, 1997.

"Debunking State Department Art." *New York Journal American,* November 26, 1946, 17.

DeFrantz, Thomas. "The Black Beat Made Visible: Hip Hop Dance and Body Power." In *Of the Presence of the Body: Essays on Dance and Performance Theory*, edited by Andre Lepecki, 64–81. Middletown, Conn.: Wesleyan University Press, 2004a.

———. *Dancing Revelations: Alvin Ailey's Embodiment of African American Culture*. New York: Oxford University Press, 2004b.

———. "Simmering Passivity: The Black Male Body in Concert Dance." In *Moving Words: Re-Writing Dance*, edited by Gay Morris, 107–120. London: Routledge, 1996.

"A Defense of Modern Art." *New York Times*, March 28, 1950, 30.

De Hart-Mathews, Jane. "Art and Politics in Cold War America." *American Historical Review* 81 (1976): 762–87.

de Mille, Agnes. *Martha: The Life and Work of Martha Graham*. New York: Random House, 1991.

Denby, Edwin. "Cunningham Solo." *New York Herald Tribune*, January 10, 1945.

———. "Dancers, Buildings and People in the Streets." *Dance Magazine*, June 1966, 55–60.

Denning, Michael. *The Cultural Front: The Laboring of American Culture in the Twentieth Century*. New York: Verso, 1997.

Desmond, Jane. "Dancing Out the Difference: Cultural Imperialism and Ruth St. Denis's 'Radha' of 1906." *Writings on Dance 9*, (Autumn 1993): 40–54.

Desmond, Jane C. "Making the Invisible Visible: Staging Sexualities through Dance." In *Dancing Desires: Choreographing Sexualities On and Off the Stage*, edited by Jane C. Desmond, 3–32. Madison: University of Wisconsin Press, 2001.

Desmond, William. *Art, Origins, Otherness*. Albany: State University of New York Press, 2003.

Devree, Howard. "Modernism under Fire." *New York Times*, September 11, 1949.

"Dewey Drives First Fox Hills Nail to Start Housing Relief Program." *New York Times*, December 28, 1945, 11.

Diamond, Elin. "Mimesis, Mimicry, and the 'True-Real.'" In *Acting Out: Feminist Performances*, edited by Lynda Hart and Peggy Phelan. Ann Arbor: University of Michigan Press, 1993.

———. *Unmaking Mimesis: Essays on Feminism and Theater*. London: Routledge, 1997.

Dionne, E. J., Jr., and Kayla Meltzer Drogosz. "The Promise of National Service: A [Very] Brief History of an Idea." *National Civic Review* Winter (2003): 21–26.

"Display Ad." *New York Times*, April 17, 1955, X2.

Dixon, Melvin. "The Black Writer's Use of Memory." In *History and Memory in African-American Culture*, edited by Geneviève Fabre and Robert O'Meally, 18–27. New York: Oxford University Press, 1994.

"Donald McKayle and Co. . . . 92nd Street 'Y' March 23, 1958." *Dance Magazine*, May 1958, 65–65.

"Donald McKayle and Company Hunter Playhouse November 24 and 25, 1956." *Dance Magazine*, January 1957, 79–80.

"Dondero on the Left." *Newsweek*, June 20, 1949.

"Doom Eager Dance." *Newsweek*, January 10, 1944, 85.

Doss, Erika. *Benton, Pollack, and the Politics of Modernism: From Regionalism to Abstract Expressionism*. Chicago: University of Chicago Press, 1991.

Duberman, Martin. *Black Mountain: An Exploration in Community*. New York: Norton, 1993.

"Dudley-Maslow-Bales Trio and New Dance Group." *Dance Observer*, March 1949, 38.

Dudziak, Mary L. *Cold War Civil Rights: Race and the Image of American Democracy*. Princeton: Princeton University Press, 2000.

Dunbar, June. *José Limón*. New York: Routledge, 2000.

Duncan, Isadora. "The Dance of the Future." In *Dance as a Theatre Art: Source Readings in Dance History from 1581 to the Present*, edited by Selma Jean Cohen, 123–129. Princeton: Princeton Book Company, 1974.

Duncan, Kathy. "Nikolais . . . " *Village Voice*, February 28, 1977, 60.

Duncan, Ronald, ed. *Selected Writings of Mahatma Gandhi*. Boston: Beacon Press, 1951.

Dunham, Katherine. "Need for Study of Dances of Primitive Peoples." In *Kaiso!: Writings by and About Katherine Dunham*, edited by VèVè Clark and Sara E. Johnson, 520–521. Madison: University of Wisconsin Press, 2005.

———. "The Negro Dance." In *Kaiso!: Writings by and About Katherine Dunham*, edited by VèVè Clark and Sara E. Johnson, 217–226. Madison: University of Wisconsin Press, 2005.

———. *A Touch of Innocence*. New York: Harcourt, Brace & World, 1959.

Dunn, Elizabeth. "What Is a Man?" *Newsweek*, June 1948, 64–65.

———. "Pearl Primus Is Dead at 74; a Pioneer of Modern Dance." *New York Times*, October 31, 1994, B8.

"The Dybbuk, a Dance Play by Anna Sokolow." *Dance Magazine*, May 1951.

"Editorial Comment around the Nation on President Kennedy's Inauguration." *New York Times*, January 21, 1961, 10.

Ehrenreich, Barbara. *The Hearts of Men: American Dreams and the Flight from Commitment*. Garden City, N.Y.: Anchor Press/Doubleday, 1983.

Elam, Harry J., Jr., and Kennell Jackson, ed. *Black Cultural Traffic: Crossroads in Global Performance and Popular Culture*. Ann Arbor, Mich.: University of Michigan Press, 2005.

Elder, Robert E. *The Information Machine: The United States Information Agency and American Foreign Policy*. Syracuse: Syracuse University Press, 1968.

Ellison, Ralph. *Shadow and Act*. New York: Random House. Reprint, 1964.

Ellison, Teren Damato. "Tally Beatty." In *The International Dictionary of Modern Dance*, edited by Taryn Benbow-Pfalzgraf, 46–49. Detroit, Mich.: St. James Press, 1998.

Emery, Lynne Fauley. *Black Dance: From 1619 to Today.* 2nd ed. Princeton, N.J.: Dance Horizons, 1988.

Engerman, David C., Nils Gilman, Mark H. Haefele, and Michael E. Latham, ed. *Staging Growth: Modernization, Development, and the Global Cold War.* In *Culture, Politics and Cold War,* series editor, Christian G. Appy. Amherst: University of Massachusetts Press, 2003.

Epstein, Barbara. *Political Protest and Cultural Revolution: Nonviolent Direct Action in the 1970s and 1980s.* Berkeley: University of California Press, 1991.

Ewen, Stuart. *The Captains of Consciousness: Advertising and the Social Roots of the Consumer Culture.* New York: McGraw, 1976.

Fabre, Genevieve, and Robert O'Meally, ed. *History and Memory in African-American Culture.* New York: Oxford University Press, 1994.

Fanon, Frantz. *Black Skin White Masks.* Translated by Charles Lam Markmann. New York: Grove Weidenfeld, 1967.

Farrell, Thomas F. "Object Lesson in Race Relations." *New York Times,* February 12, 1950, 16, 36.

Farrell, William M. "City to Spend $200,000,000 for Housing 17,000 Families." *New York Times,* March 13, 1948, 1.

Faubion, James D., ed. *Michel Foucault: Power.* Vol. 3 in *Essential Works of Foucault, 1954–1984.* Edited by Paul Rabinow. New York: The New Press, 1994.

Fensham, Rachel. "Deterritorializing Dance: Tension and the Wire." *Discourses in Dance* 1, no. 2 (2002): 5–28.

Fer, Briony, David Batchelor, and Paul Wood. *Realism, Rationalism, Surrealism: Art between the Wars.* New Haven: The Open University, 1993.

Ferguson, Russell, William Olander, Marcia Tucker, and Karen Fiss, ed. *Discourses: Conversations in Postmodern Art and Culture.* Edited by Marcia Tucker. 3 vols. Vol. 3, *The New Museum of Contemporary Art, New York: Documentary Sources in Contemporary Art.* Cambridge, Mass.: The MIT Press, 1990.

Fibers. VHS. Chor. Paul Taylor. Perf. Paul Taylor Dance Company. Hunter College, New York, N.Y., 1961.

Fischer-Hornung, Dorothea, and Alison D. Goeller, ed. *Embodying Liberation: The Black Body in American Dance.* Piscataway, N.J.: Transaction Publishers, 2001.

Fishman, Robert. *Bourgeois Utopias: The Rise and Fall of Suburbia.* New York: Basic Books, 1987.

Folgarait, Leonard. *So Far from Heaven: David Alfaro Siqueiros' the March of Humanity and Mexican Revolutionary Politics.* Cambridge: Cambridge University Press, 1987.

Foreman, Joel, ed. *The Other Fifties: Interrogating Mid-century American Icons.* Urbana: University of Illinois Press, 1997.

Foster, Susan Leigh. "Choreographies of Protest." *Theatre Journal* 55 (2003): 395–412.

———. *Choreography and Narrative: Ballet's Staging of Story and Desire.* Bloomington: University of Indiana Press, 1996.

———. "Closets Full of Dances." In *Dancing Desires: Choreographing Sexualities On and Off the Stage,* edited by Jane Desmond, 147–208. Madison: University of Wisconsin Press, 2001.

———. *Dances That Describe Themselves: The Improvised Choreography of Richard Bull.* Middletown, Conn.: Wesleyan University Press, 2002a.

———. *Reading Dancing: Bodies and Subjects in Contemporary American Dance.* Berkeley: University of California Press, 1986.

————. "Walking and Other Choreographic Tactics: Danced Inventions of Theatricality and Performativity." *SubStance* 31, no. 98/99 (2002b): 125–46.

Foucault, Michel. *Discipline and Punish: The Birth of the Prison*. New York: Random House, 1979.

————. "The Ethics of the Concern for Self as a Practice of Freedom." In *Michel Foucault: Ethics. Essential Works of Foucault, 1958–1984*, edited by Paul Rabinow, 281–301. New York: Free, 1997.

————. *The History of Sexuality, Volume I: An Introduction*. Translated by Robert Hurley. New York: Vintage Books, 1990.

————. "The Subject and Power." In *Michel Foucault: Power*, edited by James D. Faubion, 326–48. New York: The New Press, 1994.

————. *The Uses of Pleasure*. New York: Random House, 1985.

Foulkes, Julia. "Angels 'Rewolt!': Jewish Women in Modern Dance in the 1930s." *American Jewish History* 88, no. 2 (2000): 233–52.

————. *Modern Bodies: Dance and American Modernism from Martha Graham to Alvin Ailey*. Chapel Hill: University of North Carolina Press, 2002.

Franklin, Paul B. *Men in the Making: Case Studies in the Work and Personae of Vaslav Nijinsky, Charlie Chaplin, and Marcel Duchamp, 1909–1929*. Ann Arbor, Mich.: UMI Dissertation Services, 1999.

Franko, Mark. *Dancing Modernism/Performing Politics*. Bloomington: Indiana University Press, 1995.

————. *Excursion for Miracles: Paul Sanasardo, Donya Feuer, and Studio for Dance, 1955–1964*. Middletown, Conn.: Wesleyan University Press, 2005.

————. "Given Movement: Dance and the Event." In *Of the Presence of the Body: Essays on Dance and Performance Theory*, edited by André Lepecki. Middletown, Conn.: Wesleyan University Press, 2004.

————. "History/Theory—Criticism/Practice." In *Corporealities: Dancing Knowledge, Culture, and Power*, edited by Susan Leigh Foster, 25–52. New York: Routledge, 1996.

————. *The Work of Dance: Labor, Movement, and Identity in the 1930s*. Middletown, Conn.: Wesleyan University Press, 2002.

Frascina, Francis, ed. *Pollock and After: The Critical Debate*. New York: Harper & Row, 1985.

Frascina, Francis, and Jonathan Harris, ed. *Art in Modern Culture: An Anthology of Critical Texts*. London: Phaidon Press in association with the Open University, 1992.

Freeland, Richard M. *The Truman Doctrine and the Origins of McCarthyism: Foreign Policy, Domestic Politics, and Internal Security 1946–1948*. New York: Alfred A. Knopf, 1972.

Fried, Richard M. *Nightmare in Red: The McCarthy Era in Perspective*. New York: Oxford University Press, 1990.

Friedan, Betty. *The Feminine Mystique*. New York: Norton, 1983.

Friedman, Michael. *Reconsidering Logical Positivism*. Cambridge: Cambridge University Press, 1999.

"From 9 to 5 They Work for Their Living . . . From 5 to 9 They Live in One Room (and Like It)." *House and Garden*, December 1949, 139.

Fuss, Diana. *Inside/Out: Lesbian Theories, Gay Theories*. New York: Routledge, 1991.

Gaddis, John Lewis. *The Cold War: A New History*. New York: The Penguin Press, 2005a.

————. *Strategies of Containment: A Critical Appraisal of American National Security Policy During the Cold War*. Oxford: Oxford University Press, 2005b.

———. *The United States and the Origins of the Cold War 1941–1947*. New York: Columbia University Press, 1972.

———. *We Now Know: Rethinking Cold War History*. Oxford: Clarendon Press, 1997.

Gaines, Kevin K. *Uplifting the Race: Black Leadership, Politics, and Culture in the Twentieth Century*. Chapel Hill: University of North Carolina Press, 1996.

Galbraith, John Kenneth. *The Affluent Society*. Boston: Houghton, 1958.

Garafola, Lynn. "Toward an American Dance: Dance in the City." In *New York: Culture Capital of the World, 1940–1965*, edited by Leonard Wallock, 157–88. New York: Rizzoli International Publications, 1988.

———, ed. *José Limón: An Unfinished Memoir*. Hanover, N.H.: Wesleyan University Press / University Press of New England, 1999.

Garber, Marjorie, and Rebecca L. Walkowitz, ed. *Secret Agents*. New York: Routledge, 1995.

Gardner, Lloyd C. *A Covenant with Power: America and World Order from Wilson to Reagan*. New York: Oxford University Press, 1984.

Gates, Henry Louis, Jr. *Figures in Black: Words, Signs, and the 'Racial' Self*. New York: Oxford University Press, 1987.

Genauer, Emily. "Still Life with Red Herring." *Harper's Magazine* (September 1949): 88.

"Genuine Africa." *Time*, May 21, 1951, 98–102.

Gere, David. *How to Make Dances in an Epidemic: Tracking Choreography in the Age of Aids*. Madison: University of Wisconsin Press, 2004.

Gibbs, Angelica. "The Absolute Frontier." *The New Yorker* (1947): 28–37.

Gilfond, Henry. "Anna Sokolow and Dance Unit." *Dance Observer*, May 1936, 54.

———. "Workers' Dance League." *Dance Observer*, December 1934, 89–90.

Gilroy, Paul. "Exer(or)Cising Power: Black Bodies in the Black Public Sphere." In *Dance in the City*, edited by Helen Thomas, 21–34. New York: St. Martin's Press, 1997.

"Give Me Land, Lots of Land." *Life*, June 15, 1953, 48.

Gluck, Sherna Berg. *Rosie the Riveter Revisited: Women, the War and Social Change*. Boston: Twayne, 1987.

Goffman, Erving. *The Presentation of Self in Everyday Life*. New York: Anchor, 1959.

Goldberg, David Theo, ed. *Anatomy of Racism*. Minneapolis: University of Minnesota Press, 1990.

Goldman, Danielle. "Bodies on the Line: Contact Improvisation and Techniques of Nonviolent Protest." *Dance Research Journal* 39, no. 1 (Summer 2007): 60–74.

Goldwater, Barry. *The Conscience of a Conservative*. Shepherdsville, Ky.: Victor, 1960.

Goodkin, Richard. *The Tragic Middle: Racine, Aristotle, Euripides*. Madison: University of Wisconsin Press, 1991.

Goodman, Ezra. "Broadway Choreographers." *Dance Magazine*, March 1947, 13–15.

Goodman, Saul. "Paul Taylor." *Dance Magazine*, June 1959, 48.

Gordon, Eugene. "An African Dance Festival." *Daily Worker*, December 16, 1943, 5.

Gottschild, Brenda Dixon. *Digging: The Africanist Presence in American Performance, Dance and Other Contexts*. [1996] Westport, Conn.: Praeger. Reprint, 1998.

Graebner, William. *Age of Doubt: American Thought and Culture in the 1940s*. Boston: Twayne, 1991.

Graff, Ellen. "The Dance Is a Weapon." In *Moving History/Dancing Cultures: A Dance History Reader*, edited by Ann Dils and Cooper Albright, 315–22. Middletown, Conn.: Wesleyan University Press, 2001.

————. *Stepping Left: Dance and Politics in New York City, 1928–1942.* Durham: Duke University Press, 1997.

Graham, Martha. *Blood Memory.* New York: Doubleday, 1991.

Greenberg, Clement. *The Collected Essays and Criticism.* Edited by John O'Brian. 4 vols. Chicago: University of Chicago, 1988.

————. "Toward a Newer Laocoon." *Partisan Review* 7 (1940): 307–8.

"Greensboro Blacks Supported Sit-Ins." *Greensboro Daily News*, January 27, 1980.

Gregg, Richard B. *The Power of Nonviolence.* Nyack, N.Y.: Fellowship, 1959.

Grier, William H., and Price M. Cobbs. *Black Rage.* New York: Basic Books, 1968.

Griffith, Robert. *The Politics of Fear: Joseph McCarthy and the Senate.* Amherst: University of Massachusetts Press, 1987.

Grimm, Thomas. "Errand into the Maze." In *Dance in America.* WNET/Thirteen, New York: PBS, 1989.

Gruen, John. "With 'Raisin' He Rises to the Top." *New York Times*, November 4, 1973.

Guilbaut, Serge. *How New York Stole the Idea of Modern Art: Abstract Expressionism, Freedom, and the Cold War.* Translated by Arthur Goldhammer. Chicago: University of Chicago Press, 1983.

————. "The New Adventures of the Avant-Garde in America." *October* 15, (Winter 1980): 61–78.

Guthman, Louise. "Donald McKayle and Company Hunter Playhouse November 24 and 25, 1956." *Dance Observer*, January 1957, 11.

————. "Pearl Primus." *Dance Observer*, August–September 1954, 106.

————. "Sophie Maslow and Company." *Dance Observer*, December 1956, 152–53.

Hall, Bob, and Thrasher, Sue. "Julian Bond: The Movement, Then and Now." *Southern Exposure* 3, no. 4 Winter (1976): 5–16.

Hall, Stuart. "What Is This 'Black' in Black Popular Culture." In *Stuart Hall: Critical Dialogues in Cultural Studies*, edited by David Morley and Kuan-Hsing Chen, 465–75. London: Routledge, 1996.

Halprin, Anna. "Discovering Dance." *Lomi School Bulletin* (1981): 14–18.

————. *Moving toward Life: Five Decades of Transformational Dance.* Edited by Rachel Kaplan. Hanover, N.H.: Wesleyan University Press / University Press of New England, 1995.

————. "Mutual Creation." *TDR*, October 1968, 163–175.

Halprin, Lawrence. "A Discussion of the Five-Legged Stool." *San Francisco Sunday Chronicle*, April 29, 1962.

Harding, James M., and John Rouse, ed. *Not the Other Avant-Garde: The Transnational Foundations of Avant-Garde Performance.* Ann Arbor: University of Michigan Press, 2006.

Harris, Jonathan. *Federal Art and National Culture: The Politics of Identity in New Deal America.* Cambridge: Cambridge University Press, 1995.

————. "Modernism and Culture in the USA, 1930–1960." In *Modernism in Dispute: Art since the Forties*, edited by Francis Frascina, Paul Wood, Jonathan Harris, and Charles Harrison, 3–74. New Haven: Yale University Press / Open University, 1993.

Harrison, Ira E., and Faye V. Harrison. "Introduction: Anthropology, African Americans and the Emancipation of a Subjugated Knowledge." In *African-American Pioneers in Anthropology*, edited by Ira E. Harrison and Faye V. Harrison, 1–26. Urbana and Chicago: University of Illinois Press, 1999.

Hartley, Russell. "Parades and Changes, Scandal and Delight: Ann Halprin's Dancers Workshop Takes Two Controversial Works on a European Tour." *Dance Magazine*, October 1965, 50, 74.

Hartmann, Susan. *The Home Front and Beyond: American Women in the 1940s*. Boston: Twayne Publishers, 1982.

Hauptman, William. "The Suppression of Art in the McCarthy Decade." *Art News*, October 1973, 48–52.

Hawes, Elizabeth. *New York, New York: How the Apartment House Transformed the Life of the City (1869–1930)*. New York: Alfred A. Knopf, 1993.

Hayden, Dolores. *Building Suburbia*. New York: Pantheon Books, 2003.

Heard, Frances. "How to Get Individuality in a Small Standard Apartment." *House Beautiful*, September 1954, 128–130.

Henriksen, Margot A. *Dr. Strangelove's America: Society and Culture in the Atomic Age*. Berkeley: University of California Press, 1997.

Herbert, James. *The Political Origins of Abstract-Expressionist Art Criticism*. Stanford, Calif.: Humanities Honor Program, 1985.

Hering, Doris. "American Dance Festival #11." *Dance Magazine*, October 10, 1958, 33–34.

———. "Annabelle Gold and Orpheus Trio." *Dance Magazine*, May 1955, 68, 78.

———. "Anna Sokolow Dance Company." *Dance Magazine*, April 1958, 26–27.

———. "Anna Sokolow Dance Company." *Dance Magazine*, February 1959, 28.

———. "Dance Associates, Master Theater, December 4 and 4, 1956." *Dance Magazine*, February 1957, 12–13+.

———. "Dance Associates." *Dance Magazine*, August 1955.

———. "Donald McKayle and Company 92nd Street 'Y' April 22, 1962." *Dance Magazine*, June 1962, 64.

———. "Donald McKayle and Company Hunter Playhouse November 10–11, 1962." *Dance Magazine*, January 1963, 30.

———. "Donald McKayle and Co. with Mary Hinkson July 25–29, 1961." *Dance Magazine*, September 1961, 26, 28.

———. "Fourteenth American Dance Festival, Connecticut College, August 17–20, 1961." *Dance Magazine*, October 1961, 21–22, 26–27, 45–46, 60–61.

———. "Jacob's Pillow: Fourth and Fifth Week Performances." *Dance Observer*, September 1961, 26.

———. "Julliard Dance Theatre; Katherine Litz; Sophie Maslow Company." *Dance Magazine*, April 1958, 24–26.

———. "Little Fast Feet." *Dance Magazine*, July 1950, 21–23.

———. "Merce Cunningham and Dance Company, December 29 through January 3, 1954, Theatre De Lys." *Dance Magazine*, February 1954.

———. "My Roots Are Here." *Dance Magazine*, June 1955, 36–39; 59.

———. "The Paul Taylor Dance Company, Hunter Playhouse, November 8 and 9, 1962." *Dance Magazine*, January 1963, 28.

———. "Review of Nikolais' Totem." *Dance*, March 1960, 69+.

———. "Reviews: Pearl Primus and Her Company." *Dance Magazine*, March 1956, 13, 75–76.

———. "Reviews: Reflections on the Ninth Annual American Dance Festival—August 16–19—Connecticut College." *Dance Magazine*, October 1956, 10–11.

———. "Seven New Dances by Paul Taylor, 92nd Street 'Y,' October 20, 1957," *Dance Magazine*, December 1957, 83–84.

———. "Sophie Maslow and Company." *Dance Magazine*, January 1960, 27, 80.

———. "Sophie Maslow and Company; Anna Sokolow's Theatre Dance Co." *Dance Magazine*, June 1956, 67, 75.

———. "While There Is Youth." *Dance Magazine*, January 1945, 10–11, 22.

Hewitt, Andrew. *Social Choreography: Ideology as Performance in Dance and Everyday Movement*. Durham: Duke University Press, 2005.

Highwater, Jamake. *Dance: Rituals of Experience*. New York: A&W, 1978.

Hill, Constance Valis. "Katherine Dunham's *Southland*: Protest in the Face of Repression." In *Dancing Many Drums: Excavations in African American Dance*, edited by Thomas De-Frantz, 289–316. Madison: University of Wisconsin Press, 2002.

"Historical Statistics of the United States." Cambridge University Press.

Hixson, Walter L. *Parting the Curtain: Propaganda, Culture, and the Cold War, 1945–1961*. New York: St. Martin's Press, 1997.

Hobbs, Stuart D. *The End of the American Avant Garde*. New York: New York University Press, 1997.

Hodgson, Godfrey. *America in Our Time*. New York: Vintage, 1976.

Holloway, Joseph E., ed. *Africanisms in American Culture*. Bloomington: Indiana University Press, 2005.

Honey, Maureen. *Creating Rosie the Riveter: Class, Gender and Propaganda During World War II*. Amherst: University of Massachusetts Press, 1984.

Horan, Robert. "The Recent Theater of Martha Graham." *Dance Index*, January 1947, 4–23.

Hornbeck, James S., ed. *Apartments and Dormitories: An Architectural Record Book*. New York: McGraw-Hill, 1958.

Horst, Louis. "11th American Dance Festival." *Dance Observer*, August–September 1958, 101–2.

———. "12th American Dance Festival." *Dance Observer*, August–September 1959, 101–2.

———. "13th American Dance Festival." *Dance Observer*, August–September 1960, 103–4.

———. "Anna Sokolow and Company." *Dance Observer*, April 1955, 51.

———. "Anna Sokolow and Company." *Dance Observer*, April 1958, 55.

———. "Anna Sokolow Theatre Dance Company." *Dance Observer*, April 1956, 57.

———. "December 31, 1953, January 1, 1954." *Dance Observer*, February 1954.

———. "Merce Cunningham Dance Company, Brooklyn Academy of Music, January 12, 1957." *Dance Observer*, February 1957, 24–5.

———. "Merce Cunningham Dance Company." *Dance Observer*, February 1954, 26.

———. *Modern Dance Forms in Relation to the Other Modern Arts*. Princeton: Dance Horizons, 1961.

———. "Modern Music, Drama and Dance." *Dance Observer*, February 1955, 25.

———. "New Dance Group." *Dance Observer*, May 1954, 73–74.

———. "Paul Taylor and Dance Company, Y.M.-Y.W.C.A., October 20, 1957." *Dance Observer*, November 1957, 139.

———. "Sophie Maslow, Anna Sokolow and Companies." *Dance Observer*, August–September 1956, 103.

———. "Sophie Maslow and Company." *Dance Observer*, January 1960, 7.

"Housing: The Boom Is over and So Is the Shortage." *Newsweek*, September 10, 1951, 80.

"Housing Shortage at 'Crisis' Stage Indicated by Nation-Wide Survey." *New York Times*, December 9, 1945, 127.

"Housing Shortage Easing, Moses Says." *New York Times*, August 12, 1947, 25.

"Housing Shortage Easing, Moses Says." *New York Times*, December 24, 1947, 34.

"Housing Shortage Held Far from End." *New York Times*, January 31, 1949, 9.

"Housing: Up from the Potato Fields." *Newsweek*, July 3, 1950, 67–72.

Howe, Irving. *Decline of the New*. New York: Harcourt, Brace and World, 1970.

"How to Keep Your Husband Alive." *Look* (August 17, 1958): 35–36.

"How Long Can Boom in Housing Go On?" *U.S. News*, February 4, 1955, 76–78.

Hughes, Allen. "Paul Taylor: Dance or Dada?" *Dance62*, January 1963, 30.

Huizinga, Johan. *Homo Ludens: A Study of the Play-Element in Culture*. [1950] New York: Beacon Press. Reprint, 1955.

Humphrey, Doris. *The Art of Making Dances*. Edited by Barbara Pollack. New York: Rinehart, 1959.

Hunt, Michael H. *Ideology and U.S. Foreign Policy*. New Haven: Yale University Press, 1987.

Huyssen, Andreas. *After the Great Divide: Modernism, Mass Culture, Postmodernism*. Bloomington: Indiana University Press, 1986.

I Ching or Book of Changes. Translated by Richard Wilhelm. Princeton, N.J.: Princeton University Press, 1950.

"'Inbal' from Israel." *New York Times*, December 15, 1957, 246.

Insects and Heroes. VHS. Palmer Auditorium, Connecticut College, New London, Conn., 1961.

Isaacs, Harold R. *Two-Thirds of the World: Problems of a New Approach to the Peoples of Asia, Africa, and Latin America, Bold New Programs*. Washington, D.C.: The Public Affairs Institute, 1950.

Jack, Homer, ed. *The Gandhi Reader*. New York: AMS Press, 1956.

Jackson, Kenneth. *Crabgrass Frontier: The Suburbanization of the U.S.* New York: Oxford University Press, 1985.

Jackson, Naomi M. *Converging Movements: Modern Dance and Jewish Culture at the 92nd Street Y*. Middletown, Conn.: Wesleyan University Press, 2000.

Jackson, Shannon. *Lines of Activity: Performance, Historiography, Hull-House Domesticity*. Ann Arbor: University of Michigan Press, 2000.

Jaffe, Natalie. "Merce Cunningham Dances Performed." *New York Times*, August 14, 1963, 27.

Jameson, Fredric. "Periodizing the 60s." In *The 60s without Apology*, edited by Sohnya Sayres et al., 178–209. Minneapolis: University of Minnesota Press in cooperation with *Social Text*, 1984.

———. *The Prison-House of Language*. Princeton: Princeton University Press, 1972.

———. *Postmodernism, or, the Cultural Logic of Late Capitalism*. Durham: Duke University Press, 1995.

———. *Signatures of the Visible*. New York: Routledge, 1990.

"Jam Session." *Life*, October 11, 1943, 117–24.

Jarman, Rufus. "The Curious Ways of Manhattan Cliff Dwellers." *Saturday Evening Post*, April 19, 1952, 38–39, 104+.

Johnson, David K. *The Lavender Scare: Cold War Persecution of Gays and Lesbians in the Federal Government*. Chicago: University of Chicago Press, 2004.

Johnson, Harriet. "Tally Beatty and Company at the Y.M. & Y.W.H.A." *Dance Observer*, November 1948, 122.

Johnston, Jill. "Cunningham, Limón." *The Village Voice*, September 5, 1963, 10, 15+.

———. *Jasper Johns: Privileged Information*. New York: Thames and Hudson, 1996.

———. "The New American Modern Dance." In *The New American Arts*, edited by Richard Kostelanetz, 162–93. New York: Horizon Press, 1965.

———. "Paul Taylor & Co." *The Village Voice*, February 17, 1960.

Jones, Carolyn. "Finishing School: John Cage and the Abstract Expressionist Ego." *Critical Inquiry* 19 (Summer 1993): 628–65.

José Limón: Three Modern Dance Classics. Canada: CBC Home Video, 1955/1957.

Jowitt, Deborah. "Dance: Memorials." *The Village Voice*, June 27, 1968.

———. *Jerome Robbins: His Life, His Theater, His Dance.* New York: Simon and Schuster, 2004.

———. "Man, the Marvelous Mechanism." *Village Voice* (October 19, 1982): 83.

———. *Time and the Dancing Image.* New York: Morrow, 1988.

Kaiser, Charles. *The Gay Metropolis 1940–1996.* Boston: Houghton Mifflin, 1997.

"Kaleidoscope." Palmer Auditorium, Connecticut College, New London, Conn., 1956.

Kaplan, E. Ann, ed. *Postmodernism and Its Discontents: Theories, Practices.* London: Verso, 1988.

Kaprow, Allan. "The Legacy of Jackson Pollock." *Art News* 70, no. 4 (1958): 24–26, 55+.

Katz, Jonathan. "Dismembership: Jasper Johns and the Body Politic." In *Performing the Body: Performing the Text*, edited by Amelia Jones and Andrew Stephenson, 170–185. New York: Routledge, 1999a.

———. *Gay American History: Lesbians and Gay Men in the U.S.A.* New York: Crowell, 1976.

———. "John Cage's Queer Silence: Or, How to Avoid Making Matters Worse." *GLQ* 5, no. 2 (1999b): 231–52.

Katz, Jonathan D., and Moira Roth. *Difference/Indifference: Musings on Postmodernism, Marcel Duchamp and John Cage.* In *Critical Voices in Art, Theory and Culture* series, edited by Saul Ostrow. The Netherlands: G and B International, 1998.

Kealiinohomoku, Joanne. "An Anthropologist Looks at Ballet as a Form of Ethnic Dance." In *Moving History/Dancing Cultures: A Dance History Reader*, edited by Ann Dils and Ann Cooper Albright, 33–43. Middletown, Conn.: Wesleyan University Press. Reprint, 2001.

Kessler-Harris, Alice. *Out to Work: A History of Wage-Earning Women in the United States.* New York: Oxford University Press, 1982.

King, Dr. Martin Luther, Jr. 1955. Address to First Montgomery Improvement Association (MIA) Mass Meeting at Holt Street Baptist Church. In *A Call to Conscience: The Landmark Speeches of Martin Luther King, Jr.*, Stanford University, http://www.stanford.edu/group/King/publications/speeches/MIA_mass_meeting_at_holt_street.html (accessed January 10, 2008).

———. *Stride toward Freedom: The Montgomery Story.* New York: Harper, 1958.

Kinsey, Alfred, Wardell B. Pomeroy, and Clyde E. Martin. *Sexual Behavior in the Human Male.* Philadelphia: Saunders, 1948.

Kisselgoff, Anna. "Pearl Primus Rejoices in the Black Tradition." *New York Times*, June 19, 1988, 17–18, 29.

Klein, Christina. *Cold War Orientalism: Asia in the Middlebrow Imagination, 1945–1961.* Berkeley: University of California Press, 2003.

Knight, Peter, ed. *Conspiracy Nation: The Politics of Paranoia in Postwar America.* New York: New York University Press, 2002.

Koritz, Amy. "Re/Moving Boundaries: From Dance History to Cultural Studies." In *Moving Words: Re-Writing Dance*, edited by Gay Morris, 88–106. New York: Routledge, 1996.

Kostelanetz, Richard. *John Cage.* New York: Praeger, 1970a.

———. *John Cage (Ex)Plain(Ed).* New York: Schirmer Books, 1996.

——. *Master Minds: Portraits of Contemporary American Artists and Intellectuals.* New York: MacMillan, 1967.

——. "Metamorphosis in Modern Dance." *Dance Scope* 5, no. 1 (1970b): 6–21.

Kotz, Mary Lynn. *Rauschenberg: Art and Life.* New York: Harry N. Abrams, 1990.

Kowal, Rebekah J. "Alwin Nikolais' Queer Objectivity." In *The Returns of Alwin Nikolais: Bodies, Boundaries and the Dance Canon,* edited by Randy Martin and Claudia Gitelman, 82–106. Middletown, Conn.: Wesleyan University Press, 2007.

——. "Dance Travels: 'Walking with Pearl.'" *Performance Research* 12, no. 2 (2007), 85–94.

——. "Interview with David Vaughan." New York, November 6, 2007.

——. "Interview with Donald McKayle." Iowa City, September 22, 2006.

——. "Interview with Paul Taylor." New York, November 7, 2007.

——. "Modern Dance and American Culture in the Early Cold War Years." Ph.D. dissertation. New York University, 1999.

——. "Staging the Greensboro Sit-Ins." *TDR: The Drama Review* 48, no. 4 (2004): 135–44.

——. "Visible Difference: Modern Dance and the Representation of Gender in the Early Cold War Years." In *Dance Selected Research,* vol. VI, edited by Lynette Young Overby and Billie Lepczyk, 93–124. New York: A.M.S. Press, 2007.

——. "Walter Terry." In *The Scribner Encyclopedia of American Lives,* edited by Timothy J. DeWerff, 784–86. New York: Charles Scribner's Sons, 1998.

Kozloff, Max. "American Painting During the Cold War." *Artforum* xi, no. 9 (1973): 43–54.

Kramer, Hilton. "Jackson Pollock & the New York School, II." *The New Criterion* (February 1999), 14–19.

Kraut, Anthea. "Between Primitivism and Diaspora: The Dance Performances of Josephine Baker, Zora Neale Hurston, and Katherine Dunham." *Theatre Journal* (2003): 433–50.

——. *Choreographing the Folk: The Dance Stagings of Zora Neale Hurston.* Minneapolis, Minn.: University of Minnesota Press, 2008.

——. "Recovering Hurston, Reconsidering the Choreographer." *Women and Performance: A Journal of Feminist Theory* 16, no. 1 (2006): 71–90.

Krevitsky, Nik. "Anna Sokolow and Company." *Dance Observer,* May 1951, 71.

——. "Dudley-Maslow-Bales and Company." *Dance Observer,* March 1950, 44.

——. "Jane Dudley, Sophie Maslow, William Bales and Company." *Dance Observer,* March 1951, 42–43.

——. "Merce Cunningham and Company, Hunter Playhouse, January 21, 1951." *Dance Observer,* March 1951, 41–42.

Krock, Arthur. "Inaugural Contrast: Kennedy Dramatizes the Change but the Basic Aspirations Remain." *New York Times,* January 22, 1961, 1.

Kuznick, Peter J., and James Gilbert, ed. *Rethinking Cold War Culture.* Washington: Smithsonian Institution Press, 2001.

Lacy, Madison Davis. "Steps of the Gods." In *Free to Dance.* U.S.A.: National Black Programming Consortium, 2000.

Larson, Deborah Welch. *Origins of Containment: A Psychological Explanation.* Princeton, N.J.: Princeton University Press, 1985.

Laue, James H. *Direct Action and Desegregation, 1960–1962.* Brooklyn: Carlson. Reprint, 1989.

Lawton, George. "Proof That She Is the Stronger Sex." *New York Times Magazine,* December 12, 1948, 7+.

Leffler, Melvyn P. *A Preponderance of Power: National Security, the Truman Administration, and the Cold War*. Stanford, Calif.: Stanford University Press, 1992.

Leja, Michael. "The Mythmakers and the Primitive: Gottlieb, Newman, Rothko, and Still." In *Reframing Abstract Expressionism*. New Haven: Yale University Press, 1993.

———. *Reframing Abstract Expressionism: Subjectivity and Painting in the 1940s*. New Haven: Yale University Press, 1993.

Lennon, Peter. "Every Man a Hero." *The Manchester Guardian*, April 18, 1962.

Leonard, George B. "The American Male: Why Is He Afraid to Be Different?" *Look* (February 18, 1958): 95–104.

Lesschaeve, Jacqueline, ed. *The Dancer and the Dance: Merce Cunningham in Conversation with Jacqueline Lesschaeve*. New York: Marion Boyers, 1985.

Leuchtenburg, William. *A Troubled Feast: American Society since 1945*. Boston: Little, 1983.

Lewis, Robert. *Manufacturing Suburbs: Building Work and Home on the Metropolitan Fringe*. Philadelphia, Penn.: Temple University Press, 2004.

Lhamon, W. T. *Deliberate Speed: The Origins of a Cultural Style in the American 1950s*. Washington: Smithsonian Institution, 1990.

"Limón Ends Polish Trip." *New York Times*, October 23, 1957, 38.

Limón, José. "The Virile Dance." *Dance Magazine* (December 1948), 20–21.

Lippincott, Gertrude. "Freedom in the Arts." *Dance Observer*, April 1948a, 44–45.

———. "No Compromise." *Dance Observer*, November 1948b, 117–19.

"Little Primitive." *Time*, August 25, 1947, 42–44.

Lloyd, Margaret. *The Borzoi Book of Modern Dance*. New York: Alfred A. Knopf, 1949.

———. "Changing Fashions in Dance: Paul Taylor, Ultramodernist of Mystery." *Christian Science Monitor* (February 20, 1960).

Logan, Rayford. "The Negro Wants First-Class Citizenship." In *What the Negro Wants*, edited by Rayford Logan, 1–30. Chapel Hill: The University of North Carolina Press, 1944.

———, ed. *What the Negro Wants*. Chapel Hill: University of North Carolina Press, 1944.

Lomax, Louis E. *The Negro Revolt*. New York: Harper and Row, 1962.

Louchheim, Aline B. "Six Abstractionists Defend Their Art." *New York Times Magazine*, January 21, 1951, 151.

Louis, Murray. "The Contemporary Dance Theater of Alwin Nikolais." *Dance Observer*, January 1960, 6.

Ludington, Townsend, ed. *A Modern Mosaic: Art and Modernism in the United States*. Chapel Hill: University of North Carolina Press, 2000.

Lundberg, Ferdinand, and Marynia F. Farnham. *Modern Woman: The Lost Sex*. New York: Harper, 1947.

Lupton, Ellen. *Mechanical Brides: Women and Machines from Home to Office*. New York: Princeton Architectural Press, 1993.

Lynes, Russell. "Is There a Lady in the House?" *Look* (July 22, 1958): 19–21.

Maletic, Vera. "The Process Is the Purpose: An Interview by Vera Malatic." *Dance-Scope* 4, no. 1 (1967): 11–18.

Malone, Jacqui. *Steppin' On the Blues: The Visible Rhythms of African American Dance*. Urbana and Chicago: University of Illinois Press, 1996.

Manchester, P. W. "The Season in Review." *New York Times*, July 6, 1959.

Manning, Susan. "Black Voices, White Bodies: The Performance of Race and Gender in *How Long Brethren*." *American Quarterly* 50, no. 1 (1998): 24–46.

———. *Ecstasy and the Demon: Feminism and Nationalism in the Dances of Mary Wigman.* Berkeley: University of California Press, 1993.

———. "Looking from a Different Place: Gay Spectatorship of American Modern Dance." In *Dancing Desires: Choreographing Sexualities On and Off the Stage*, edited by Jane Desmond, 403–414. Madison: University of Wisconsin Press, 2001.

———. *Modern Dance, Negro Dance: Race in Motion.* Minneapolis: University of Minnesota Press, 2004.

Mansbridge, Jane. "Complicating Oppositional Consciousness." In *Oppositional Consciousness*, edited by Jane Mansbridge and Aldon Morris, 238–64. Chicago: University of Chicago Press, 2001.

———. "The Making of Oppositional Consciousness." In *Oppositional Consciousness*, edited by Jane Mansbridge and Aldon Morris, 1–19. Chicago and London: University of Chicago Press, 2001.

Marks, Marcia. "The Subject Is People." *Dance Magazine*, February 1963, 30–34.

Marquis, Alice Goldfarb. *Art Lessons: Learning from the Rise and Fall of Public Arts Funding.* New York: Basic Books, 1995.

Martha Graham in Performance. VHS. West Long Branch: Kultur, 198–.

Martin, John. "Brilliant Dancing by Pearl Primus." *New York Times*, October 5, 1944a, 18.

———. "The Dance: A Backward Look at 1950." *New York Times*, December 31, 1950, X1.

———. "The Dance: Advices." *New York Times*, June 28, 1949.

———. "Dance: An Artist." *New York Times*, February 26, 1961.

———. "The Dance: Bright Augury." *New York Times*, February 26, 1956.

———. "Dance Debut Here by Anna Sokolow." *New York Times*, November 15, 1937, 14.

———. "The Dance: Diplomacy." *New York Times*, January 23, 1955, X11.

———. "The Dance: The Far East." *New York Times*, October 15, 1933, X7.

———. "The Dance: Festival." *New York Times*, April 9, 1950, X7.

———. "The Dance: Five Artists." *New York Times*, February 21, 1943, X5.

———. "The Dance: In 1955." *New York Times*, January 1, 1956, X6.

———. "The Dance: To the N.D.L." *New York Times*, June 16, 1935, X4.

———. "The Dance: New Life." *New York Times*, February 19, 1956, X9.

———. "The Dance: Radical Art." *New York Times*, January 21, 1934, X8.

———. "The Dance: Rovings." *New York Times*, October 21, 1951, 106.

———. "Dance: Smorgasbord, Many Works, Soloists Fill ANTA Stage." *New York Times*, May 9, 1955, 26.

———. *The Dance: The Story of the Dance Told in Pictures and Text.* New York: Tudor Publishing Company, 1946.

———. "Dance: A Study in Despair." *New York Times*, May 16, 1955, 26.

———. "The Dance: Survey." *New York Times*, June 19, 1955, X3.

———. "The Dance: A Tour." *New York Times*, November 14, 1954, X13.

———. "The Dance: With Words." *New York Times*, June 30, 1935, X4.

———. "The Dance: Young Talent." *New York Times*, December 2, 1934, X8.

———. "Doris Humphrey Forms New Julliard Group." *New York Times*, April 10, 1955, X7.

———. *Introduction to the Dance.* New York: W. W. Norton & Company, 1939.

———. *The Modern Dance.* New York: A. S. Barnes, 1933.

———. "Something to Talk About: Dance." *Mademoiselle*, November 1943, 139, 201, 203.

———. "Success Scored by Dance League." *New York Times*, November 26, 1934, 12.

———. "Upbeat for Modern Dance." *New York Times Magazine*, May 1, 1955, 28–29.

———. "Victory for the Grahamites." *New York Times Magazine* (May 7, 1944a): 20–22.

———. "Worker's League in Group Dances." *New York Times*, December 24, 1934, 16.

Martin, Randy. *Critical Moves: Dance Studies in Theory and Politics*. Durham: Duke University Press, 1998.

———. "Modern Dance in the American Century." In *A Modern Mosaic: Art and Modernism in the U.S.*, edited by Townsend Luddington, 203–26. Chapel Hill: University of North Carolina Press, 2000.

———. *Performance as a Political Act: The Embodied Self*. New York: Bergin and Garvey, 1990.

———. "Toward a Kinesthetics of Protest." *Social Identities* 12, no. 6 (2006): 791–801.

Martin, Randy, and Claudia Gitelman, ed. *The Returns of Alwin Nikolais: Bodies, Boundaries and the Dance Canon*. Middletown, Conn.: Wesleyan University Press, 2007.

Marymor, Rod. "An Interview with Anna Halprin." *City Arts*, January 1980, 29.

Mason, Joseph B. *History of Housing in the U.S. 1930–1980*. Houston: Gulf Publishing Company Book Division, 1982.

May, Elaine Tyler. *Homeward Bound: American Families in the Cold War Era*. New York: Basic, 1988.

May, Lary, ed. *Recasting America: Culture and Politics in the Age of Cold War*. Chicago: The University of Chicago Press, 1989.

Mayer, Michael S. "Introduction." In *Diary of a Sit-In* by Merril Proudfoot, ix–xxxvi. Chicago: University of Illinois Press. Reprint, 1990.

Mazo, Joseph. *Prime Movers: The Makers of Modern Dance in America*. Princeton, N.J.: Princeton Book Company, 1977.

McDonagh, Don. "Anna Sokolow 1910–2000." *Dance Magazine*, July 2000, 50–51.

———. *The Complete Guide to Modern Dance*. Garden City, N.Y.: Doubleday, 1976.

———. *The Rise and Fall and Rise of Modern Dance*. Pennington, N.J.: A Capella Books, 1990.

McKayle, Donald. "Black New Deal? Interview. About the Problems Facing the Negro Dancer." *Dance and Dancers*, June 1967, 19–21, 40.

———. *Transcending Boundaries: My Dancing Life*. London: Routledge, 2002.

McNay, Lois. *Foucault: A Critical Introduction*. New York: Continuum, 1994.

Mecklenberg, Virginia. "Advancing American Art: A Question of Style." In *Advancing American Art: Politics and Aesthetics in the State Department Exhibition, 1946–48*, edited by Virginia Mecklenberg, 34–66. Montgomery, Ala.: Museum of Fine Arts, 1984.

Meier, August, and Elliott Rudwick. *Black Protest in the Sixties*. Chicago: Quadrangle, 1970.

Melley, Timothy. *Empire of Conspiracy: The Culture of Paranoia in Postwar America*. Ithaca: Cornell University Press, 2000.

Mercer, Kobena, ed. *Cosmopolitan Modernisms*. London: Institute of International Visual Arts (inIVA) and The MIT Press, 2005.

Messer, Robert L. *The End of an Alliance: James F. Byrnes, Roosevelt, Truman, and the Origins of the Cold War*. Chapel Hill: The University of North Carolina Press, 1982.

Meyerowitz, Joanne. *Not June Cleaver: Women and Gender in Postwar America*. Philadelphia: Temple University Press, 1994.

Miller, Frieda S. "What's Become of Rosie the Riveter?" *New York Times Magazine* (May 5, 1946): 21+.

"Mind Your Wife and Live Longer." *Better Homes and Gardens*, November 1951, 122+.

"'Mister Johnson': Choreography by Pearl Primus." *Dance Observer*, June–July 1956, 91.

Montagu, Ashley. *Man's Most Dangerous Myth: The Fallacy of Race*. Cleveland: The World Publishing Company. Reprint, 1964.

Moore, Lillian. "Bravos and Boos for Avant-Garde Dance." *New York Herald Tribune*, August 14, 1963.

Moore, Sally F., and Barbara G. Meyerhoff. "Introduction: Secular Ritual: Forms and Meanings." In *Secular Ritual*, edited by Sally F. Moore and Barbara G. Meyerhoff, 3–24. Amsterdam: Van Gorcum, 1977.

"More News Items from the Martha Graham 'ANTA' Tour." *Dance Observer*, March 1956, 41.

Morris, Gay. *A Game for Dancers: Performing Modernism in the Postwar Years, 1945–1960*. Middletown: Wesleyan University Press, 2006.

Morris, John D. "House Unit to Hear Dulles on Hiss Tie." *New York Times*, December 24, 1952, 7.

Morrison, Toni. "Romancing the Shadow." In *Playing in the Dark: Whiteness and the Literary Imagination*. New York: Vintage Books, 1992.

———. "The Site of Memory." In *Inventing the Truth: The Art and Craft of Memoir*, edited by William Zinsser, 183–200. Boston: Mariner Books, 1998.

Moskin, J. Robert. "The American Male: Why Do Women Dominate Him?" *Look*, February 4, 1958, 77–80.

Moss, Howard. "Real Guys." *The New York Review*, May 31, 1984, 31–33.

Motherwell, Robert. "The Modern Painter's World." *Dyn*, no. 6 (1944): 9–14.

Motherwell, Robert, and Ad Reinhardt, ed. *Modern Artists in America: First Series*. New York: Wittenborn Schultz, 1950.

Motley, Raymond. "How to Behave Like a World Power." *Newsweek*, August 20, 1945, 92.

"Mr. Cunningham." *New York Herald Tribune*, February 21, 1960.

Murphy, Ann. "Lucas Hoving and José Limón: Radical Dancers." In *José Limón*, edited by Jane Dunbar, 59–70. New York: Routledge, 2002.

Murphy, Margaret. "Anna Sokolow: Choreographer." U.S.A.: Dance Horizons Video, [1980] 1990.

Murray, Albert. *Stomping the Blues*. New York: McGraw-Hill, 1976.

"Museum Demands Freedom for Arts." *New York Times*, March 28, 1950, 33–34.

"Must We Change Our Sex Standards?" *Reader's Digest* (June 1948): 6.

Myrdal, Gunnar. *An American Dilemma: The Negro Problem and Modern Democracy*. New York: Harper and Row. Reprint, 1962.

Nadel, Alan. *Containment Culture: American Narratives, Postmodernism, and the Atomic Age*. Durham: Duke University Press, 1995.

"Negro Women Give Honors." *New York Times*, June 11, 1950, 41.

"Negroes Fail to Obtain Service." *Greensboro Daily News*, February 10, 1960.

Nelson, Angela M. S., ed. *"This Is How We Flow": Rhythm in Black Cultures*. Charleston: University of South Carolina Press, 1999.

"New Mortgage Money Flows—and Homebuilding Shoots Up." *Newsweek*, May 3, 1954, 67, 71.

"New York Needs Housing." *New York Times*, February 27, 1947, 20.

"News Items from the Martha Graham 'ANTA' Tour." *Dance Observer*, February 1956, 24–25.

Nikolais, Alwin. "The New Dimension of Dance." *Impulse* 1959, 43.

Ninkovich, Frank A. *The Diplomacy of Ideas: U.S. Foreign Policy and Cultural Relations, 1938–1950*. Cambridge: Cambridge University Press, 1981.

Nitze, Paul H. "NSC-68: Forging the Strategy of Containment." National Defense University Press, 1950. Reprint, 1996.

Novack, Cynthia J. "The Body's Endeavors as Cultural Practices." In *Choreographing History*, edited by Susan L. Foster, 177–84. Bloomington: Indiana University Press, 1995.

———. *Sharing the Dance: Contact Improvisation and American Culture*. Madison: University of Wisconsin, 1990.

O'Connor, Francis. *Jackson Pollack*. New York: Museum of Modern Art, 1967.

O'Donnell, Mary. "Anna Sokolow." *Dance Observer*, April 1940, 55.

O'Hara, Frank. *Jackson Pollack*. New York: Braziller, 1959.

Oppenheimer, Martin. *The Sit-in Movement of 1960*. Brooklyn: Carlson, 1989.

"Our Men Are Killing Themselves." *Saturday Evening Post* (1956): 25.

"Our World Role." *New York Times*, December 2, 1945, E1.

Outlaw, Lucius T., Jr. "Toward a Critical Theory of 'Race.'" In *Anatomy of Racism* edited by David Theo Goldberg, 117–124. Minneapolis: University of Minnesota Press, 1990.

Owen, Norton. "Afterword." In *José Limón: An Unfinished Memoir*, edited by Lynn Garafola, 117–124. Hanover, N.H.: Wesleyan University Press / University Press of New England, 1999.

Patterson, James T. *Grand Expectations: The United States, 1945–74*. Oxford: Oxford University Press, 1996.

"Paul Taylor and Dance Company, Y.M.-Y.W.C.A., October 20, 1957." *Dance Observer*, November 1957, 128.

Paul Taylor: Dance Maker. VHS. Directed by Matthew Diamond. U.S.A.: The Four Oaks Foundation, 1999.

Paul Taylor: Three Modern Classics. VHS. Choreographed by Paul Taylor, produced by Judy Kinberg for WNET/Thirteen. Performed at the American Dance Festival, Durham, N. C., summer 1981 by the Dance in America series, telecast on WNET/13 New York on January 11, 1982.

"Pearl Primus." *Dance Observer*, February 1946, 24.

"Pearl Primus." *Dance Observer*, June 1946, 76–77.

"Pearl Primus: Foremost Dancer to Unveil New, Exciting Work Based on Year-Long Study of African Peoples." *Ebony* January 1951, 54–58.

"Pearl Primus Surrenders Passport to State Department." Anonymous, undated press release, Associated Negro Press. Claude Barnett Collection, box 291, folder 7, Chicago History Museum.

Peiss, Kathy, and Christina Simmons with Robert A. Padgug, ed. *Passion and Power: Sexuality in History*. Philadelphia: Temple University Press, 1989.

Pennsylvania, State Museum of. In http://server1.fandm.edu/levittown/default/html (accessed February 2007).

"People Are Talking About . . . " *Vogue*, August 1, 1943, 48.

Pepis, Betty. "Condensed Living." *New York Times Magazine,* April 20, 1952, 46–47.

———. "Making the Most of Little." *The New York Times Magazine*, January 8, 1950, 36–37.

Perloff, Marjorie. "Watchman, Spy, and Dead Man: Jasper Johns, Frank O'Hara, John Cage and the 'Aesthetic of Indifference.'" *Modernism/Modernity* 8, no. 2 (2001): 197–223.

Perloff, Marjorie, and Charles Junkerman, ed. *John Cage: Composed in America*. Chicago: University of Chicago Press, 1994.

Perpener, John O., III. *African-American Concert Dance: The Harlem Renaissance and Beyond*. Bloomington, Ill.: University of Illinois Press, 2001.

Phelan, Peggy. "Trisha Brown's *Orfeo*: Two Takes on Double Endings." In *Of the Presence of the*

Body: Essays on Dance and Performance Theory, edited by André Lepecki, 13–28. Middletown, Conn.: Wesleyan University Press, 2004.

———. *Unmarked: The Politics of Performance*. New York: Routledge, 1993.

Pierce, Robert J. "The Anna Halprin Story: Dancing in the Streets, in Prisons, in Hallways." *Village Voice* (March 10, 1975): 93.

Plummer, Brenda Gayle. *Rising Wind: Black Americans and U.S. Foreign Affairs, 1935–1960*. Chapel Hill: University of North Carolina Press, 1996.

Plunz, Richard. *A History of Housing in New York City: Dwelling Type and Social Change in the American Metropolis*. New York: Columbia University Press, 1990.

Polcari, Stephen. *Abstract Expressionism and the Modern Experience*. Cambridge: Cambridge University Press, 1991.

"Portrait." *Life*, December 22, 1947, 70.

Potter, Michelle. "'A License to Do Anything': Robert Rauschenberg and the Merce Cunningham Dance Company." *Dance Chronicle* 16, no. 1 (1993): 1–43.

Powell, Richard J. *Black Art and Culture in the 20th Century*. New York: Thames and Hudson, 1997.

Preger, Marianne. "Paul Taylor and James Waring at the Henry Street Playhouse, May 6, 1956." *The Village Voice*, May [exact date unknown] 1956.

Preston, Stuart. "Modernism under Fire: Newest Attack Is Full of Contradictions." *New York Times*, September 11, 1949, X6.

Prevots, Naima. *Dance for Export: Cultural Diplomacy and the Cold War*. In *Studies in Dance History: A Publication of the Society of Dance History Scholars* series, edited by Lynn Garafola. Hanover, N.H.: Wesleyan University Press / University Press of New England, 1998.

Prickett, Stacey. "Primus." In *International Dictionary of Modern Dance*, edited by Taryn Benbow-Pfalzgraf, 644–47. Detroit: St. James Press, 1998.

"Priestess Speaks." *Time*, March 10, 1947, 80.

Priestly, J. B. "Priestly Appraises New York." *New York Times Magazine*, January 4, 1948, SM2.

Primus, Pearl. "Africa." *Dance Magazine*, March 1958, 43–48.

———. "Africa Dances." *Dance Observer*, December 1949, 147.

———. "Earth Theatre." *Theatre Arts*, December 1950b, 41–43.

———. "In Africa." *Vogue*, October 15, 1950a, 98–99, 145+.

"Proof That She Is the Stronger Sex." *New York Times Magazine* (December 12, 1948): 7+.

Proudfoot, Merril S. *Diary of a Sit-In*. Chicago: University of Illinois Press. Reprint, 1990.

"Purely Symbolic: Appalachian Spring." *Time* (May 28, 1945): 60.

"Queen to See 2 U.S. Stars." *New York Times*, October 13, 1951, 23.

Rajchman, John. *Michel Foucault: The Freedom of Philosophy*. New York: Columbia University Press, 1985.

Ramsey, Kate. "Melville Herskovits, Katherine Dunham, and the Politics of African Diasporic Dance Anthropology." In *Dancing Bodies, Living Histories: New Writings About Dance and Culture*, edited by Lisa Doolittle and Anne Flynn, 196–217. Banff, Alberta: Banff Centre Press, 2000.

Rauschenberg, Robert. "Artist's Statement." In *Sixteen Americans*, edited by Dorothy C. Miller, 56. New York: Museum of Modern Art, 1959.

Reardon, Christopher. "A Star System That Leaves No One in a Shadow." *New York Times*, February 23, 1997, 10.

Reinhart, Charles. *Donald McKayle Interviewed by Charles Reinhart at the American Dance Festival, 27 June*. VHS. Durham, N.C.: American Dance Festival, 1990.

Renouf, Renee. "It Could Be This or It Could Be That: An Interview with Ann Halprin." *Genesis West* 4 (1963): 343–348.

Reston, James. "President Kennedy's Inaugural—Speech or Policy?" *New York Times*, January 22, 1961, 10.

Retallack, Joan, ed. *Musicage: Cage Muses on Words, Art, Music*. Hanover, N.H.: University Press of New England / Wesleyan University Press, 1996.

"Retired American Art." *Newsweek*, July 5, 1948, 68.

"Review of Paul Taylor's Three Epitaphs." *Dance Magazine*, April or May 1956.

Revill, David. *The Roaring Silence: John Cage, a Life*. New York: Arcade Publishing, 1992.

Riesman, David, with Nathan Glazer and Reul Denney. *The Lonely Crowd: A Study of the Ongoing American Character*. [1950] New Haven: Yale University Press. Reprint, 1977.

Robin, Ron. *The Making of the Cold War Enemy: Culture and Politics in the Military Industrial Complex*. Princeton and Oxford: Princeton University Press, 2001.

Rodman, Selden. *Conversations with Artists*. New York: Devin-Adair, 1957.

Rogosin, Elinor. "Keeping Up with Merce Cunningham." In *The Dance Makers: Conversations with American Choreographers*, 61–72. New York: Walker and Company, 1980.

Román, David. *Acts of Intervention: Performance, Gay Culture, and Aids*. Bloomington: Indiana University Press, 1998.

Roose-Evans, James. "Pity the Poor Public!" *Dance Observer*, January 1957.

Rose, Barbara. *An Interview with Robert Rauschenberg*. New York: Vintage Books, 1987.

Rosenberg, Harold. "The American Action Painters." In *The Tradition of the New*, 23–39. [1952] New York: Da Capo Press. Reprint, 1994.

Ross, Janice. *Anna Halprin: Experience as Dance*. Berkeley: University of California Press, 2006.

———. "Anna Halprin and the 1960s: Acting in the Gap between the Personal, the Public, and the Political." In *Reinventing Dance in the 1960s: Everything Was Possible*, edited by Sally Banes, 24–50. Madison: University of Wisconsin Press, 2003.

———. *Moving Lessons: Margaret H'Doubler and the Beginning of Dance in American Education*. Madison: University of Wisconsin Press, 2000.

Ross, Rodney A. E-mail, December 11, 2006.

Rossen, Rebecca Leigh. "Dancing Jewish: Jewish Identity in American Modern and Postmodern Dance." Ph.D. dissertation. Northwestern University, 2006.

Roth, Moira. "The Aesthetic of Indifference." In *Difference and Indifference: Musings on Postmodernism, Marcel Duchamp and John Cage*, edited by Moira and Jonathan D. Katz Roth. Australia: G+B Arts International, 1998.

Rubin, Joan Shelley. *The Making of Middlebrow Culture*. Chapel Hill: University of North Carolina Press, 1992.

Rupp, Leila J. *Mobilizing Women for War: German and American Propaganda, 1939–1945*. Princeton: Princeton University Press, 1978.

Ruyter, Nancy Lee Chalfa. *Reformers and Visionaries: The Americanization of the Art of Dance*. New York: Dance Horizons, 1979.

Sabin, Robert. "Choreography Class at a Ballet School." *Dance Magazine*, June 1953, 36–37.

Sandler, Irving. *American Art of the 1960s*. New York: Harper and Row, 1988.

Saull, Richard. *Rethinking Theory and History in the Cold War: The State, Military Power and Social Revolution*. London: Frank Cass Publishers, 2001.

Saunders, Frances Stonor. *The Cultural Cold War: The CIA and the World of Arts and Letters*. New York: New Press, 2000.

Saunders, Garry. "Pearl Turns to Africa." *Picture Post*, November 1951.

Sayres, Sohnya, Anders Stephanson, Stanley Aronowitz, and Frederic Jameson, ed. *The 60s without Apology*. Minneapolis: University of Minnesota Press in cooperation with *Social Text*, 1984.

Schechner, Richard. "From Ritual to Theater and Back: The Efficacy Entertainment Braid." In *Richard Schechner: Performance Theory*, 112–69. New York: Routledge, 2003.

Schlesinger, Arthur, Jr. *The Vital Center: The Politics of Freedom*. Brunswick, N.J.: Transaction Publishers. Reprint, 1998.

Schlossberg, Linda. "Rites of Passing." In *Passing: Identity and Interpretation in Sexuality, Race and Religion*, edited by Linda Schlossberg and Maria Carla Sanchez, 1–12. New York: New York University Press, 2001.

Schrecker, Ellen. *The Age of McCarthyism: A Brief History with Documents*. Edited by Natalie Zemon Davis and Ernest R. May, *The Bedford Series in History and Culture*. Boston, New York: Bedford Books of St. Martin's Press, 1994.

———. *Many Are the Crimes: McCarthyism in America*. Princeton, N.J.: Princeton University Press, 1998.

Schwartz, Peggy. Conversation, December 8, 2006.

Scott, William B., and Peter M. Rutkoff. *New York Modern: The Arts and the City*. Baltimore: John Hopkins University Press, 1999.

Sedgwick, Eve Kosofsky. *Epistemology of the Closet*. Berkeley: University of California Press, 1990.

Segal, Edith. "Pearl Primus Thrills Broadway." *Daily Worker*, October 7, 1944, 11.

Sell, Mike. *Avant-Garde Performance & the Limits of Criticism: Approaching the Living Theatre, Happenings/Fluxus, and the Black Arts Movement*. Ann Arbor: University of Michigan Press, 2005.

———. "The Black Arts Movement: Performance, Neo-Orality, and the Destruction of the 'White Thing.'" In *African American Performance and Theater History: A Critical Reader*, edited by Harry J. Elam and David Krasner. New York: Oxford University Press, 2001.

Serlin, David H. *Replaceable You: Engineering the Body in Postwar America*. Chicago: University of Chicago Press, 2004.

Shapiro, David, and Cecile Shapiro. "Abstract Expressionism: The Politics of Apolitical Painting." In *Pollack and After: The Critical Debate*, edited by Francis Francina. New York: Harper and Row, 1985.

Sharrer, Honore. "Pearl Primus Back from South Discusses New Dance Themes." *Daily Worker*, September 28, 1944, 11.

"She Is Priestess of the Intellectual Ballet." *Life*, March 17, 1947, 101–4.

Shea Murphy, Jacqueline. *The People Have Never Stopped Dancing: Native American Modern Dance Histories*. Minneapolis: University of Minnesota Press, 2007.

Shetley, Vernon. "Merce Cunningham." *Raritan* 8, no. 1 (1989): 72–3.

Siegel, Marcia B. *Days on Earth: The Dance of Doris Humphrey*. New Haven: Yale University Press, 1987.

———. *The Shapes of Change: Images of American Dance*. Boston: Houghton Mifflin, 1979.

Silver, Kenneth A. "Modes of Disclosure: The Construction of Gay Identity and the Rise of Pop Art." In *Hand-Painted Pop: American Art in Transition 1955–62*, edited by Russell Ferguson, 179–203. The Museum of Contemporary Art, Los Angeles, 1993.

Sims, Lowery Stokes. "The Post-Modernism of Wilfredo Lam." In *Cosmopolitan Modernisms* edited by Kobena Mercer. London: Institute of International Visual Arts (inIVA) and MIT Press, 2005.

Singh, Nikhil Pal. *Black Is a Country: Race and the Unfinished Struggle for Democracy*. Cambridge: Harvard University Press, 2004.

Skinner, Beverly. "Sterling Brown's Poetic Ethnography: A Black and Blues Ontology." *Callaloo* 21, no. 4 (1998): 998–1011.

Smith, Cecil. "Dance: Artistic Calvinist." *New Republic* (March 15, 1948): 30.

Somerville, Siobhan B. *Queering the Color Line: Race and the Invention of Homosexuality in American Culture*. Durham: Duke University Press, 2000.

Sontag, Susan. "Against Interpretation." In *Against Interpretation and Other Essays*. New York: Farrar, Straus & Giroux, 1966.

"Sophie Maslow and Company." *Dance Observer*, March 1954, 42.

Sorell, Walter. "Conversation with Pearl Primus." *Dance Magazine*, October 1959, 14–15, 17.

———. *The Dance Has Many Faces*. New York: Columbia University Press, 1966.

———. "Exciting Theater Dances." *Providence Sunday Journal*, November 25, 1962.

Speckman, Maybelle. "Broadway Applauds Marin Dancer." *Independent Journal*, June 4, 1955, M6.

Spigel, Lynn. *Make Room for TV: Television and the Family Ideal in Postwar America*. Chicago: University of Chicago Press, 1992.

Steinhorn, Leonard. *The Greater Generation: In Defense of the Baby Boom Legacy*. New York: Thomas Dunne Books, 2006.

Stepan, Nancy Leys. "Race and Gender: The Role of Analogy in Science." In *The Anatomy of Racism*, edited by David Theo Goldberg, 38–57. Minneapolis: University of Minnesota Press, 1990.

Stich, Sidra. *Made in U.S.A.: An Americanization in Modern Art, the 50s & 60s*. Berkeley: University of California Press, 1987.

Stilgoe, John. *Borderland: Origins of the American Suburb, 1820–1939*. New Haven: Yale University Press, 1988.

Stowe, Leland. "What's Wrong with American Women?" *Reader's Digest* (1949): 49–51.

Streibert, Theodore. "Testimony before the Senate Committee on Foreign Affairs." edited by Senate Committee on Foreign Affairs, 1956.

"Summerspace: Excerpts." Palmer Auditorium, Connecticut College, New London, Conn., 1958.

Swain, Martica. *Surrealism in Exile and the Beginning of the New York School*. Cambridge: MIT Press, 1995.

Sykes, Taylor D., and Maltby Littleton. *Advancing American Art: Painting, Politics, and Cultural Confrontation at Mid-Century*. 2nd ed. Tuscaloosa: The University of Alabama Press, 1999.

"Talley Beatty, Nina Fonaroff, Yuriko." *Dance Observer*, January 1947, 7.

Tanai, Sara Levi. "A Letter to Dance Magazine about Inbal and Anna Sokolow." *Dance Magazine*, June 1955, 39.

Taylor, Diana. *The Archive and the Repertoire: Performing Cultural Memory in the Americas*. Durham: Duke University Press, 2003.

Taylor, Paul. *Private Domain*. New York: Knopf, 1987.

Tcherny, Kolya. "Paul Taylor: Last Sunday at the YM-YWHA." *The Village Voice*, October 20, 1957.

Telberg, Lelia K. "Valerie Bettis, Anna Sokolow, Louis Johnson and Companies." *Dance Observer*, January 1958, 12–13.

Temko, Allan. "The Flowering of San Francisco." *Horizon*, January 1959.

Terry, Walter. "American Dance Festival." *New York Herald Tribune*, August 20, 1961.

———. "Avant-Garde Dance." *New York Herald Tribune*, December 21, 1963.

———. *The Dance in America*. New York: Harper & Brothers, 1956a.

———. "Dance: Donald McKayle." *New York Herald Tribune*, April 23, 1962.

———. "Dance: New Dance Group." *New York Herald Tribune*, January 15, 1962.

———. "Dance: Old and New Guards." *New York Herald Tribune*, September 10, 1961.

———. "Experiment? Joke? Or War of Nerves?" *New York Herald Tribune*, October 27, 1957.

———. "The Fearsome Ethnologic Dance." *New York Herald Tribune*, July 3, 1949.

———. "Mr. Taylor." *New York Herald Tribune*, February 21, 1960.

———. "Paul Taylor." *New York Herald Tribune*, January 16, 1961.

———. "Paul Taylor's Dancers—Not So 'Avant.'" *New York Herald Tribune*, May 23, 1962.

———. "Report from Two Dancers Abroad; Primus in Africa, Mabry in France." *New York Herald Tribune*, May 20, 1949.

———. "San Francisco Workshop Does 'Parades and Changes' in Nude." *World Journal Tribune* (April 24, 1967).

———. "Value of Dance to Unesco's Cultural Program Discussed." *New York Herald Tribune*, December 8, 1946.

"Text of Kennedy's Inaugural Outlining Policies on World Peace and Freedom." *New York Times*, January 21, 1961, 8.

Thernstrom, Stephan, and Abigail Thernstrom. *American in Black and White: One Nation Indivisible*. New York: Simon and Schuster, 1997.

Thomas, Helen. *Dance, Modernity and Culture: Explorations in the Sociology of Dance*. London and New York: Routledge, 1995.

Tobias, Tobi. "Taylor's Domain." *Dance Magazine*, August 1980, 60–61.

"Today's Jobs: The Killing Pace." *Newsweek* (1956): 81–84.

Todd, Arthur. "'Copper and Brass' Choreography by Anna Sokolow." *Dance Observer*, January 1958, 13.

———. "Mexico Responds to Modern Dance." *Dance Observer*, March 1951, 39–40.

Todd, Mabel Elsworth. *The Thinking Body: A Study of the Balancing Forces of Dynamic Man*. Brooklyn: Dance Horizons, 1937.

Tomkins, Calvin. *The Bride and the Bachelors: Five Masters of the Avant-Garde*. New York: Penguin, 1976.

———. *Duchamp*. New York: Henry Holt, 1997.

———. *Off the Wall: Robert Rauschenberg and the Art World of Our Time*. Garden City, N.Y.: Doubleday, 1980.

Tomko, Linda J. *Dancing Class: Gender, Ethnicity, and Social Divides in American Dance, 1890–1920*. Bloomington: Indiana University Press, 1999.

Townsend, Julie. "Alchemic Visions and Technological Advances: Sexual Morphology in Loie Fuller's Dance." In *Dancing Desires: Choreographing Sexualities On & Off the Stage*, edited by Jane Desmond, 73–96. Madison: University of Wisconsin Press, 2001.

Turner, Diane M. "Anna Halprin: An Artist and an Influence." In *Dance: Current Selected Research*, edited by Lynette Young Overby. New York: A.M.S. Press, 1989, 97–113.

"Two Works by Anna Sokolow Performed by Her Theatre Dance Company." *Dance Magazine*, April 1956, 60–61.

"Up from the Potato Fields." *Time*, July 3, 1950, 67–72.

"Urban Redevelopment Progress in the National Emergency." *The American City*, March 1951, 121.

U.S. Department of Justice, Federal Bureau of Investigation, "Primus, Pearl," FOIPA No. 1080919–000/190.

U.S. House of Representatives, ed. "Congressional Record." 2317–8, 1949.

———. "Congressional Record." 3233–35, 1949.

———. "Congressional Record." 6372–75, 1949.

———. "Congressional Record." 11750, 1949.

———. "Congressional Record." 11584–87, 1949.

———. "Congressional Record." 12099–100, 1949.

U.S. Senate. Committee on Expenditures in Executive. *Employment of Homosexuals and Other Sex Perverts in Our Government*. Washington: GPO, 1950.

Vachon, Ann. "José Limón." In *The International Dictionary of Modern Dance*, edited by Taryn Benbow-Pfalzgraf. New York: St. James Press, 1998.

"Valerie Bettis & Co., Louis Johnson & Co., the Anna Sokolow Dance Co." *Dance Magazine*, January 1958, 72, 82.

Vaughan, David. "Cunningham and His Dancers." *Ballet Review* 15, no. 3 (1987): 19–40.

———. *Merce Cunningham: Fifty Years. Chronicle and Commentary*. Edited by Melissa Harris. New York: Aperture, 1997.

———. "More Dancers and Their Work." *Dance and Dancers*, July 1956, 22–3.

———. "Non-Objective Choreographers." *Dance Magazine*, November 1957, 20–23.

———. "Remembering James Waring." *Ballet Review* 5, no. 4 (1975–76), 102–107.

Vernon, John. E-mail, December 14, 2006.

Von Eschen, Penny M. *Race against Empire: Black Americans and Anticolonialism 1937–1957*. Ithaca: Cornell University Press, 1997.

———. *Satchmo Blows up the World: Jazz Ambassadors Play the Cold War*. Cambridge Mass.: Harvard University Press, 2004.

Wallace, Michelle. "Modernism, Post-Modernism, and the Problems of the Visual in Afro-American Culture." In *Out There: Marginalization and Contemporary Culture*, edited by Russell et al. Ferguson. Cambridge and New York: MIT Press / New Museum of Contemporary Art, 1990.

Wallock, Leonard, ed. *New York: Culture Capital of the World, 1940–1965*. New York: Rizzoli International Publications, 1988.

Warren, Larry. *Anna Sokolow: The Rebellious Spirit*. Princeton, N.J.: Princeton Book Company, 1991.

Waskow, Arthur I. *From Race Riot to Sit-In: 1919 and 1960, a Study in the Connections between Conflict and Violence*. Garden City, N.Y.: Doubleday, 1966.

Weinstein, Marybeth. "Woman's Case for Women's Superiority." *New York Times Magazine* (1955): 26–27.

Weiss, Jessica. *To Have and to Hold: Marriage, the Baby Boom, and Social Change*. Chicago: University of Chicago Press, 2000.

"What Fools We Mortals Be." *Greensboro Daily News*, February 10, 1960.

"What the President Proposes for Home Owners and Slum Clearance." *Newsweek*, February 1, 1954, 20.

White, E. B. *Here Is New York*. New York: Harper & Brothers, 1949.

White, Walter. *A Rising Wind*. New York: Doubleday, Doran and Company, 1945.

Whitfield, Stephen J. *The Culture of the Cold War*. 2nd ed. Baltimore The Johns Hopkins University Press, [1991] 1996. .

Whyte, William H. *The Organization of Man*. New York: Simon and Schuster, 1956.

Wiegman, Robyn. *American Anatomies: Theorizing Race and Gender*. Durham: Duke University Press, 1995.

Wiese, Andrew. *Places of Their Own: African American Suburbanization in the Twentieth Century*. Chicago: University of Chicago Press, 2004.

Wightman, Richard, and T. J. Jackson Lears Fox, ed. *The Culture of Consumption: Critical Essays on American History, 1880–1980*. New York: Pantheon, 1983.

Williams, Raymond. *Marxism and Literature*. Oxford: Oxford University Press, 1977.

Witchell, Lawrence. "Dance Associates." *East*, December 13, 1956.

———. "Paul Taylor." *East*, 14 February 14, 1957.

———. "Paul Taylor. Concert of 7 New Works at the Kaufman Auditorium, Sunday, Oct. 20, 1957." *East*, October 1957.

Wood, Robert. *Suburbia: Its People and Their Politics*. Boston: Houghton Mifflin, 1958.

Woodford, Barbara Pollack, and Charles Humphrey. *Dance Is a Moment: A Portrait of José Limón in Words and Pictures*. Pennington, N.J.: A Dance Horizons Book: Princeton Book Company, 199.

"Workers' Dance League." *Dance Observer*, May 1934, 43–44.

Wright, Richard. *Black Boy: A Record of Childhood and Youth*. New York: Harper & Row, 1945.

———. *Native Son*. New York and London: Harper & Brothers, 1940.

———. *White Man Listen!* New York: Doubleday, 1957.

Wroble, Lisa. "James Waring." In *The International Dictionary of Modern Dance*, edited by Taryn Benbow Pfalzgraf, 809–11. New York: St. James Press, 1998.

Young, S. "Martha Graham." *New Republic* (June 4, 1945): 790.

———. "Martha Graham and Dance Company." *New Republic* (February 4, 1946): 158.

Zellmer, David. "Anna Sokolow." *Dance Observer*, June–July 1946, 75–76.

———. "New Dance Group Festival Series." *Dance Observer*, February 1946, 20–21.

INDEX

Coomaraswamy, Ananda, 156
Cooper, Lee, 113
Copeland, Roger, 173, 274n29
Copland, Aaron, 22, 57
CORE. *See* Congress of Racial Equity
Cornish School of the Arts, 158, 272n12
Council on African Affairs (CAA), 132–33, 201
Cronkite, Walter, 196
Cullen, Countee, 131
cultural diplomacy, 32–42, 259n8, 261n24
culture of consensus, 11, 97–100, 103, 254, 260n18, 266n13
Cunningham, Merce: use of chance methods, 158–74, 234, 237–39; collaborators of, 271n12, 272n8, 272n13, 273n24; critical opinion of, 44, 48–49, 183–84, 271n1, 273n16, 274nn30–31; dance career of, 272n12, 272nn14–15, 275n35, 281n5; and foundness, 17, 194, 227–28; and mutability, 185–92, 271n2, 274nn27–29; and the purpose of art, 11–12, 273n17; and the "ready-made self," 151–58, 210, 254
Cunningham, Merce, works of: *Antic Meet*, 173–75, 190, 274n30–31; *Changeling*, 168–70; *Dime a Dance*, 164, 281n5; "The Function of a Technique for Dance," 161, 273n17; *Lavish Escapade*, 168–71; *Nocturnes*, 275n35; *Root of an Unfocus*, 158, 185, 272n13; *Sixteen Dances for Soloist and Company of Three*, 162, 164, 190; *Solo Trilogy*, 167; "Space, Time and Dance," 161, 273n17; *Suite by Chance*, 153; *Summerspace*, 172, 175, 274n30; *Symphonie Pour Un Homme Seul*, 161; *Untitled Solo*, 167–70, 173, 281n5
Currier, Ruth, 183

dadaism, 154, 191
Dafora, Asadata, 120, 128
Daily Worker, 125, 133
Dance Advisory Panel, 35, 37, 47–49, 279n26
Dance Associates, 164, 190–92, 273n22
Dance Magazine, 12, 174, 178, 191, 223–24, 262n26, 266n11, 273n19
Dance Observer, 12, 28, 37–40, 126–27, 139, 190, 208, 223, 262n26, 263n1, 276n42
Dance of Beauty (Primus), 127
Dancers' Workshop, 226, 235, 280n2
Davis, Benjamin, 137
Deep Song (Graham), 122
defamiliarization, as artistic technique: in direct

action protest, 197, 230; in Cunningham and Taylor's choreography, 152, 175, 185; in Halprin's creative process, 234–55, 277n8; and Pearl Primus, 119, 149; in Sokolow's *Rooms*, 92, 116
Defense Department, U.S., 132
de Mille, Agnes. *See* Mille, Agnes de
democracy, 256, 261n22; as "freedom" for artists, 29, 40, 50, 53, 189; and normalcy, 85; and race, 45, 129, 132–34, 137, 270n11, 279n20, 281n16; in universalism, 10, 34–35
Denby, Edwin, 95, 124–25, 266n8, 271n1
Denishawn, 89, 263n9
Depression era, impact on dance, 21, 38, 50, 86, 91, 100, 200
diaspora, African, 16, 117–125, 130–33, 140, 143–44, 148–49, 202–204, 207, 269n1
Dickerson, Earl B., 136
Dime a Dance (Cunningham), 164, 281n5
"Dink's Blues," 219
direct action protest: bus boycotts as, 276n4, 280n27; in dance or theatrical context, 17, 252; and Gandhi, 277n11; Halprin's work as, 227–28; sit-ins as, 196–204, 215, 244, 255, 277n6; technique of, 247–49, 277n13. *See also* nonviolent direct action
Dixon, Melvin, 142–44, 205
Dixon Gottschild, Brenda, 14, 262n29
domestic containment. *See* containment, domestic
Du Bois, W. E. B., 130–32, 135, 202
Duchamp, Marcel, 154–56, 165, 237–38, 272n4, 281n12
Duncan, Isadora, 89
Dunham, Katherine, 17, 125, 140, 194–95, 224, 229, 254, 262n33, 268n1; choreographing diaspora, 121, 123; critical reception of, 208, 279n24; and the Dance Panel, 44, 46–48, 279n26; reaction to racism, 210–16
Dunham, Katherine, works of: *Southland*, 46, 199, 210–25, 279n24; *Tropics and Le Jazz Hot*, 208
Dunn, Elizabeth, 70

"Earth Theatre" (Primus), 142, 257n11
East magazine, 191
East River Houses, 111, 113, 267n22
Ebony, 145
effeminacy, 83

Great Society, 200

Green, Richard, 127

Greensboro Four, 5, 215, 280n28

Greensboro sit-ins: aligned with artistic practice, 17, 244, 277n7; description of, 4–6, 211, 215, 252, 255, 276n4, 276n6; as nonviolent direct action, 196–97

Gregg, Richard B., 246–52

Gwathmey, Robert, 209, 278n20

Halprin, Anna, 17, 226–30, 254, 280nn1–2, 281nn8–10, 281nn12–13; choreographic methodology of, 230–34; dance deck of, 234, 281n5; and defamiliarization, 239–44, 277n8; and repudiating habit, 234–39; and social action, 244–53, 281n3

Halprin, Anna, works of: *Automobile Event*, 236; *Birds of America or Gardens Without Walls*, 236; *Ceremony of Us*, 226–28, 281n3; *Five-Legged Stool*, 239, 241, 281n13; *The Flowerburger*, 235, 239; *Four-Legged Stool*, 236; *Four Square*, 235, 239; *The Prophetess*, 230; *Rites of Women*, 235, 239; *Trunk Dance*, 235–36, 239

Halprin-Lathrop school for modern dance, 231, 234

Halprin, Lawrence, 231

Hansberry, Lorraine, 209, 225, 279n20

Harding, James M., 14

Hard Times Blues (Primus), 120, 125

Harlem riots, 200

Harwood, Jonathan, 188

Hawkins, Erick, 22–23, 57, 60, 66, 68, 71, 258n3, 264n16, 272n12

H'Doubler, Margaret, 232–33, 281n10

Henry, Jules, 73

Henry Street Settlement House, 89–90

Hering, Doris, 88, 94, 174, 183–84, 190, 218, 223, 266n7, 268n1, 275n36

Her Name Was Harriet (McKayle), 196–97, 229

Herskovits, Melville, 131, 140, 269n9

heterosexuality, 53, 69, 72, 75, 172, 216, 219, 264nn19–20, 265n33

"he-woman," 73–74

high-rise housing project, 111, 267nn22–23

Hill, Martha, 46–48, 261n16

Hinduism, 156

Hinkson, Mary, 219–20, 280n32

Hiroshima, atomic bombing of, 23, 26, 97

Hiss, Alger, 43, 262n31

Hodes, Stuart, 46

Holocaust, 95

Homo Ludens (Huizinga), 7

homosexuality, 57, 80, 83, 108, 155, 188, 190, 192, 264n20, 265n33; equated with communist subversion, 55–56; invisibility of, 55, 188; as a psychological symptom, 186

Hoover, J. Edgar, 54, 263n5

Hopkins, Kenyon, 86, 106, 110

Horst, Louis, 89–90, 171, 190, 263n9, 276n42

housing, societal impact of, 100–4, 110–15. *See also* tenement housing

House Un-American Activities Committee (HUAC), 43, 116, 270n15

Hoving, Lucas, 72, 75, 77, 79, 81

Howard University, 133

HUAC. *See* House Un-American Activities Committee

Hughes, Langston, 131, 225

Huizinga, Johan, 7, 257n3

humanism, 28–32, 81, 122, 136, 185, 254, 280n29

Humphrey, Doris, 27, 36, 48, 57, 145, 231, 262n26, 265n28

Humphrey, Doris, works of: *Day on Earth*, 36; *Night Spell*, 36; *New Dance*, 36; *Ritmo Jondo*, 36; *Ruins and Visions*, 36; *Story of Mankind*, 36

Hunton, Alphaeus, 132

Hurston, Zora Neale, 121, 125, 271n17

Huxley, Julian, 229, 260n14

ICAA. *See* Council on African Affairs

I-Ching, 156, 162, 271n8, 273n18

Immediate Tragedy (Graham), 122

improvisation, in dance, 105, 227, 235–38, 246–47, 253, 277n14

Inbal, 96–97

indeterminacy. *See* chance

Inness-Brown, H. Alwyn, 35

Insects and Heroes (Taylor), 177, 180, 182–84, 275n32, 275n36

integration, global imaginary of, 29, 34–35, 40, 42, 52, 122, 157

International Artistic Exchanges, Circle of, 19

International Committee on African Affairs (ICAA). *See* Council on African Affairs

International Festival of Music, Theater, and Dance, 19

Martin, John, 13, 72, 137, 139; on Dunham, 208; on Graham, 24; on Halprin, 230–31; on Limón, 37; on modern dance, 27–28, 30–31, 85, 92, 257n9, 260n16; on Primus, 123–25; on Sokolow, 87, 96, 265n3, 266n5

Marx, Karl, 29, 97, 99

masculinity, 53, 55, 69–72, 83, 169, 171, 174, 262n20, 280n30

Maslow, Sophie, 90, 96, 265n3

matrimony. *See* marriage

Mbadiwe, Kingsley Ozuomba, 120

McCain, Franklin, 4, 252

McCarthyism, 42, 50, 116, 256

McCarthy, Joseph, 43, 191, 262n30

McGiffert, Jack, 196

McKayle, Donald: civil disobedience of, 216–25, 229, 254; and the Dance Panel, 44, life of, 46, 111; television broadcasts of; 194–97, 276n3; use of the black body, 17, 122, 209, 262n33

McKayle, Donald, works of: *Games*, 195, 199, 210–16, 212–13, 221, 223–25, 279n23; *Her Name Was Harriet*, 196–97, 229; *Rainbow 'Round My Shoulder*, 194–95, 211, 216–23, 229, 280nn32–34; *They Called Her Moses*, 196

McKenzie, Aza Bard, 105

McNeil, Joseph, 4, 252

memory, sites of, 142–47

Mercer, Kobena, 145, 268n17

Mérida, Carlos, 93

method acting, 214

Metropolitan Life (insurance company), 111, 113

Mille, Agnes de, 258n3, 262n26, 263n9

minstrelsy, 122

modern dance: "basicness" of, 27; bodies as agents of change, 6, 148; Cunningham's indictment of, 162; efficacy in movement, 7–8, 11–12, 17, 30, 119, 141–42, 149, 195, 197, 226–29, 235; founding of dance schools, 9, 32, 89, 231–32, 273n16, 273n22, 280n2; legibility of, 84–85, 154; originality in, 123–29, 149, 271n1; patronage with colleges and universities, 9, 32; policing boundaries of, 51, 85; power to conduct progressive social change, 1, 8, 10, 14, 20, 150, 152, 192, 222, 228, 243–44, 253; question for cultural legitimacy, 9, 50; role of costuming in, 39, 68–69, 75–76, 89, 138, 170–71, 176–79, 182, 242, 250, 273n22, 274n30, 275n35; universalism,

44, 122; use of narrative constructs, 16, 53, 85, 122

Modern Dance/Negro Dance (Manning), 45, 119, 122–23, 130, 145, 208, 268n1, 269nn2–3

Montagu, Ashley, 134

Montgomery Bus Boycott, 215, 279n20, 279n27

Moore, Jack, 183

Moor's Pavane, The (Limón), 15, 30, 36, 52, 75–85, 189, 253, 264n25, 265nn27–28

Morrison, Toni, 187, 214–15

Moses, Robert, 112–14, 267n26, 268n28

Moskin, Robert, 74

Motherless Child (Primus), 129

Mourner's Bench (Beatty), 199, 204–10, 212, 215, 216–17, 224–25

MOWM. *See* March on Washington Movement

Murphy, Ann, 72, 78, 106

Music Advisory Panel, 48

Myrdal, Gunnar, 134

"mythic abstraction." *See* modern dance universalism

NAACP, 134–35, 201, 277n15, 278n20, 279n27

Nagasaki, atomic bombing of, 23, 26, 97

National Association for the Advancement of Colored People. *See* NAACP

nationalism, 94

National Lawyers Guild, 135

National Negro Congress (NNC), 135, 200–1, 270n12, 278n20

National Security Report of April 1950 (NSC-68), 33–34

natural body, 227–35

"Negro" dance, 45, 119–25, 130, 145, 208, 268n1, 269nn2–3

Negro Revolt, The (Lomax), 202

Negro Spirituals (Tamiris), 122

New Dance Group, 119, 263n8

New Dance League, 72

New Deal, 97, 200

New Negro, The (Locke), 131, 269n9

New School, 91, 265n1

Newsweek, 22, 70, 102, 259n10, 262n26

New York City, 143–44, 158, 200, 230–31, 270n15, 277n10; cosmopolitan nature of, 12, 16, 24–25, 103, 115, 273n24, 279n20; housing in, 6, 86–89, 104, 112, 114, 267nn21–22, 267n26, 268n28; dance performances, 22–23, 57, 93–95, 195–96, 272n9

New York Herald Tribune, 12, 19, 29, 95, 137,
    260n14, 262n26
New York Post, 134
New York Times, 11, 24–25, 87, 92, 102, 123, 137,
    190, 230, 258n4, 265n3
New York Times Magazine, 70
New World Africanism, 131
Night Journey (Graham), 15, 37, 40, 52, 65–71,
    77, 85, 189, 253, 263n1, 264n16
Nikolais, Alwin, 12, 44, 48–49, 153–54, 164, 176,
    257n12, 271n2
92nd Street Y, 1, 195, 280n31
Nitze, Paul F., 33
NNC. See National Negro Congress
nonviolent direct action, 196–204, 215, 247–49,
    253, 276n4, 277n13, 280n27
Nora, Pierre, 142
normalization: choreographic approach to the
    idea of, 14–22, 166, 170, 184–93, 229, 274n28;
    and the civil rights movement, 246, 253, 255;
    in Dance Panel deliberations, 44, 184–93;
    and the domestic culture of containment,
    53–58, 125, 152; pertaining to gender con-
    struction, 14, 64–69, 75, 81, 84–85, 263n10
North Carolina Agricultural and Technical
    College (A&T), 4
NSC-68. See National Security Report of April
    1950
nuclear family, 54, 57–58, 103, 189

objectivism, 8, 12–14, 153–54, 254, 271n17, 271n2
Ocko, Edna, 116
O'Donnell, Mary, 94–95
O'Dwyer, Mayor William, 112, 267n25
Omnibus, 195
Organization Man (Whyte), 53
Othello (Shakespeare), 30, 75–82, 264n25,
    265n27, 265n32

Parkchester, 111
Parks, Rosa, 215, 279n27
Parsons, Talcott, 73
"passing," 84
passive resistance. See direct action protest
Pearl Harbor, 22, 25, 93, 258n4, 260n13
performative effectiveness. See efficacy
Peter Cooper Village, 113–14
Pierce, Robert J., 241, 281n14
Poitier, Sidney, 225

Pollock, Jackson, 151
Popular Front, 10, 93, 119, 201–2, 260n13
postwar internationalism, 10, 26, 31, 122
Preger, Marianne, 191
Presentation of Self in Everyday Life, The (Goff-
    man), 251
President's Emergency Fund for International
    Affairs. See Emergency Fund for Interna-
    tional Affairs
Priestly, J. B., 103–105, 111
Primus, Pearl, 254, 262n35, 270n13, 270n15;
    aligns work with civil rights, 130–37; and
    authenticity, 125–30; and the Dance Panel,
    44–48; and the African diaspora, 16–17,
    117–25, 204, 268n1; and the effectiveness of
    dance, 11–12, 147–50, 154; and "negro" sub-
    ject matter, 269n6, 271n17, 280n29; writing
    of, 137–47, 202, 257n11
Primus, Pearl, works of: African Ceremonial, 119,
    125–26; Dance of Beauty, 127; "Earth Theatre,"
    142, 257n11; Hard Times Blues, 120, 125;
    Motherless Child, 129; Rock Daniel, 119, 125,
    269n3; Slave Market!, 129; Strange Fruit, 120,
    126, 269n6
propaganda, art and, 29, 31, 50, 92, 133, 261n23
Prophetess, The (Halprin), 230
protests, and social action. See Big Three Unity
    Rally; boycotts, as social action; direct
    action protest; Freedom Rides; Greensboro
    sit-ins; Harlem riots; Jim Crow: defiance
    against; March on Washington Movement
    (MOWM); Montgomery Bus Boycott;
    Satyagraha; sit-ins
protest dance, 199, 208
Purcell, Henry, 76, 78

queerness. See homosexuality

race, as biological category, 130–31, 152, 188, 255
race riots, 226
racial prejudice, 46, 132–34, 152, 187, 194–97,
    203, 211, 267n22; double standard, 45, 48;
    and its relationship to Hitlerism/Nazi
    regime, 129, 133–34, 270n11. See also Jim
    Crow; protests, and social action; segrega-
    tionism
racial uplift, 136, 202
Rainbow 'Round My Shoulder (McKayle), 194–
    95, 211, 216–23, 229

ABOUT THE AUTHOR

Rebekah J. Kowal is an associate professor of dance at the University of Iowa. She has published articles in TDR and a chapter in *The Returns of Alwin Nikolais: Bodies, Boundaries and the Dance Canon* (Wesleyan, 2007). Kowal won the 2008 Gertrude Lippincott Award from the Society of Dance History Scholars for her article on Pearl Primus, a version of which appears in *How To Do Things with Dance*.